Advances in Spatial Science

The Regional Science Series

This series contains scientific studies focusing on spatial phenomena, utilising theoretical frameworks, analytical methods, and empirical procedures specifically designed for spatial analysis. Advances in Spatial Science brings together innovative spatial research utilising concepts, perspectives, and methods relevant to both basic science and policy making. The aim is to present advances in spatial science to an informed readership in universities, research organisations, and policy-making institutions throughout the world.

The type of material considered for publication in the series includes: Monographs of theoretical and applied research in spatial science; state-of-the-art volumes in areas of basic research; reports of innovative theories and methods in spatial science; tightly edited reports from specially organised research seminars. The series and the volumes published in it are indexed by Scopus.

More information about this series at http://www.springer.com/series/3302

Michael Beenstock • Daniel Felsenstein

The Econometric Analysis of Non-Stationary Spatial Panel Data

Springer

Michael Beenstock
Department of Economics
Hebrew University of Jerusalem
Jerusalem, Israel

Daniel Felsenstein
Department of Geography
Hebrew University of Jerusalem
Jerusalem, Israel

ISSN 1430-9602 ISSN 2197-9375 (electronic)
Advances in Spatial Science
The Regional Science Series
ISBN 978-3-030-03613-3 ISBN 978-3-030-03614-0 (eBook)
https://doi.org/10.1007/978-3-030-03614-0

Library of Congress Control Number: 2018964414

This Springer imprint is published by the registered company Springer Nature Switzerland AG
The registered company address is: Gewerbestrasse 11, 6330 Cham, Switzerland

Acknowledgements

The genesis of this book is a research collaboration that started in 2006 and has subsequently spawned 15 journal papers and book chapters. Over this period, we have fused our respective backgrounds in time series analysis and spatial data analysis. This volume summarizes our work on integrating spatial econometrics with the econometric analysis of nonstationary time series.

We owe a debt of thanks to a group of research assistants who have helped along the way since 2006. Some of them have also appeared as coauthors of earlier published papers on which the chapters of this book are based.

In chronological order, we would like to thank Olga Kazanina, Shalva Zonenshvili, Assaf Romm, Nadav ben Zeev, Dan Feldman, Ziv Rubin, and Dai Xieer. Their contributions created and upgraded the spatial data series on which the empirics of this book are based. In addition, they provided assistance in programming and executing the various Stata, Eviews and Matlab routines that underpin many of the estimation procedures presented here. We are also indebted to three anonymous reviewers whose critical and multiple readings of this text have sharpened many of our ideas.

Contents

Chapter 1
Space and Time are Inextricably Interwoven

1.1 Introduction

Our chief purpose in writing this book is to fill what we think is an important lacuna in the econometric analysis of spatial panel data. The standard assumption in the econometric analysis of spatial panel data is that the data are covariance stationary, i.e. the means, variances and covariances of the data do not depend on when and where they are measured (Baltagi 2013; Elhorst 2014; Pesaran 2015). However, there are many examples of nonstationary panel data such as wages, gross regional product, and employment, which because they tend to increase over time, cannot be stationary by definition. Their sample moments depend on when they are measured, and they may also depend on where they are measured. Also, if their data generating processes are random walks, their variances and covariances must increase over time. The application to nonstationary data of spatial panel data econometrics intended for stationary panel data runs the risk of estimating spurious and nonsense regression coefficients as originally mooted by Yule (1897, 1926) for time series data, and more recently by Phillips and Moon (1999) for nonstationary panel data.

To resolve this methodological dilemma we draw on the principles of panel cointegration, developed since 1999 for nonstationary panel data, and extend them to nonstationary spatial panel data. To these ends, we provide the methodological background to the unit root revolution, which transformed the econometric analysis of nonstationary time series in the 1980s, and the econometric analysis of nonstationary panel data in the 2000s.

Although our main purpose is to connect spatial panel data econometrics to unit root econometrics, a secondary purpose is to connect unit root econometrics to spatial econometrics. The econometric analysis of nonstationary panel data rests on the awkward assumption that the panel units are independent. This assumption is reasonable when the panel data refer to randomly sampled individuals or firms since they are unrelated. Matters are, however, different in the case of spatial data since

M. Beenstock, D. Felsenstein, *The Econometric Analysis of Non-Stationary Spatial Panel Data*, Advances in Spatial Science,
https://doi.org/10.1007/978-3-030-03614-0_1

Table 1.1 Taxonomy of spatial econometric theory

	$T = 1 \quad N \to \infty$	T fixed $\quad N \to \infty$	N fixed $\quad T \to \infty$
Stationary data	Case 1a	Case 2a	Case 3a
Nonstationary data	Case 1b	Case 2b	Case 3b

neighboring spatial units are unlikely to be independent. There are many examples in the literature where this assumption is violated, especially when the data refer to countries or regions, but also to data on firms, local authorities and courts.

Pesaran (2006) relaxed this assumption by assuming for stationary panel data that the dependence between panel units is induced by common factors (as we explain in Chap. 10) so that panel units depend to a greater or lesser degree on the same common factors. Subsequently, Kapitanios et al. (2011) extended cross-section dependence induced by common factors to the case of nonstationary panel data. We fulfill our secondary purpose by suggesting as an alternative to common factors that the dependence between panel units is spatial. Specifically, we "spatialize" the econometric analysis of nonstationary panel data. In doing so, we recognize that what appears to be spatial dependence may not be spatial at all, but induced by common factors. As we illustrate in Chap. 10, spatial econometricians may be mistaken in taking for granted that the dependence between panel units is spatial.

The 3×2 matrix in Table 1.1 may be useful in placing our central contribution in its scientific and historical contexts, where T denotes the number of time periods and N denotes the number of spatial units. The largest literature by far in spatial econometric theory is concerned with case 1a in which T is fixed at 1 and refers to spatial cross-section data. The asymptotic properties with respect to N of maximum likelihood (ML), instrumental variables (IV) and generalized method of moments (GMM) estimators have been studied extensively (Anselin 1988; LeSage and Pace 2009; Baltagi 2013; Elhorst 2014; Pesaran 2015). Indeed, chronologically, case 1a was the first to be investigated.

There is a modest literature on case 1b, initiated by Fingleton (1999), which we discuss in Chap. 5. This case is pertinent because it sets the scene for our chief purpose (case 3b). Even if $T = 1$ or is fixed, spatial cross-section data are nonstationary in the presence of spatial unit roots because the sample moments of the data depend on where they are measured as mooted by Granger (1969). Cases 2 and 3 refer to spatial panel data. As mentioned in our opening paragraph, the literature on cases 2a and 3a, which developed during the 2000s has been extensively reviewed by Baltagi (2013), Elhorst (2014) and Pesaran (2015). In this literature the panel data are stationary and either T is fixed and $N \to \infty$ (case 2a), N is fixed and $T \to \infty$, or both N and T tend to infinity.

Finally, the literature on nonstationary spatial panel data (cases 2b and 3b) is sparse. We review this literature in Chap. 7 where we extend it in two main ways. First, we develop the asymptotic theory for spatiotemporal unit root tests for spatial panel data in which cross-section dependence is spatial when N is fixed and $T \to \infty$ (case 3b). We also compute critical values to test the null hypothesis of the presence of a spatiotemporal unit root. Second, we develop the asymptotic theory for residual-based cointegration tests when the data contain spatiotemporal unit roots. Here too N is fixed and $T \to \infty$. We compute critical values for spatial panel cointegration tests for models, which include spatial lagged variables. The former are an alternative to the test proposed by Pesaran (2007), who assumed that cross-section dependence is induced by common factors, and the latter is an alternative to the critical values calculated by Banerjee and Carrion-I-Silvestre (2017), who also assume that cross-section dependence is induced by common factors. We do not consider case 2b because in spatial panel data N is typically fixed, so the natural way to carry out the asymptotic analysis is with respect to $T \to \infty$.

In trying to bridge the gap between unit root and spatial econometrics, we have written our book with two audiences in mind. The first comprises spatial economists who may be unfamiliar with unit root econometrics. The second comprises economists who may be familiar with unit root econometrics but are unfamiliar with spatial econometrics. These audiences may include other disciplines too, such as meteorologists, climate scientists, environmental scientists, geophysicists and astronomers who use spatial time series that may be nonstationary.

1.2 Spatial Econometrics

The language of spatial econometrics draws on concepts from the econometric analysis of time series. A possible reason for this might be that spatial econometricians hoped that time series econometricians would find spatial econometrics more accessible. For example, the term "spatial lag" refers to spillovers from neighboring spatial units in cross-section data. However, this lag does not depend on time but on space. It is assumed to apply instantaneously across space since cross-section data are observed at the same point of time. This means by default that exogenous shocks are assumed to transmit themselves instantaneously across space, to neighbors and to neighbors' neighbors. If the unit of observation is sufficiently long, e.g. the cross-section data are annual, it might be reasonable to assume that spatial spillovers occur within a year. If, on the other hand, spatial diffusion is slow a year might be insufficiently long. The shorter the temporal unit of observation and the slower the spatial diffusion, the less reasonable the timelessness of the spatial lag effect.

This problem is sharper if the data refer to instantaneous phenomena that exist at each point in time, such as house prices, rather than flow phenomena, such as gross regional product, that are measured over time. A spatial lag in cross-section data for house prices implies that it takes the same time for house prices to propagate over space regardless of the distance between spatial units. For example, a shock in the most north-westerly spatial unit of NUTS2 transmits itself to the most south-easterly unit, over a thousand kilometers away, just as rapidly as if the shock had occurred in the neighboring unit. The timelessness of the spatial lag effect also becomes less reasonable the greater the geographical coverage of spatial data.

Another term that spatial econometricians have borrowed from time series is "spatial autocorrelation", which occurs when error terms of neighboring spatial units are correlated. The timelessness of spatial autocorrelation is less problematic than the timelessness of spatial lags. The error terms of neighbors might be correlated simply because there happen to be unobserved contemporaneous factors, such as the weather, that are common to neighbors. On the other hand, spatial autocorrelation might in fact express temporal autocorrelation. This will happen if error terms are temporally correlated between neighbors. For example, if the error terms in unit A depend on the lagged error terms in neighboring unit B, the error terms of units A and B will appear to be spatially autocorrelated in cross-section data. Therefore, to determine whether error terms are truly spatially autocorrelated it is necessary to use spatiotemporal data, where variables are observed over time as well as across space.

Textbooks on spatial econometrics (Anselin 1988; LeSage and Pace 2009) have traditionally focused on spatial cross-section data. However, they usually include a chapter on spatial panel data. Because panel data are also observed over time these chapters inevitably involve basic concepts from time series. Typically, the data are assumed to be stationary (in the temporal sense) and the models are static (in the temporal sense) but involve spatial dynamics. This asymmetry is awkward since it is not obvious why spatial dynamics should be acknowledged, but temporal dynamics be ignored.

LeSage and Pace (2009) too include a chapter on spatiotemporal data in their textbook. They seem to resolve this awkward asymmetry by specifying temporal as well as spatial dynamics in their analysis of spatial cross-section data. This looks promising, as their purpose is to demonstrate, "How spatiotemporal data generating processes are related to many of the cross sectional models popular in spatial econometrics." (p. 189) Specifically, they specify a model in which a dependent variable (y), observed in N spatial units over T time periods, is hypothesized to depend on x, the spatial lag of x, the temporal lag of y and the temporal lag of the spatial lag of y:

$$y_t = \alpha + \beta x_t + \delta W x_t + \pi y_{t-1} + \phi W y_{t-1} + \varepsilon_t \tag{1.1}$$

where t labels time periods, y_t is a column vector of length N, α is a vector of N spatial specific effects, W is an $N \times N$ spatial connectivity matrix, δ is the spatial Durbin lag coefficient on x, π is the temporal lag or autoregressive coefficient, ϕ is the temporal–spatial lag coefficient, and ε_t is a vector of N iid disturbances. LeSage and Pace claim that the parameters of Eq. (1.1) may be estimated using spatial cross-section data. They base this assertion on a Monte Carlo simulation exercise in which $N = 50{,}000$, $T = 250$ and the cross-section regression is carried out in the last time period (T), i.e. Eq. (1.1) is estimated with data for y_T, x_T and y_{T-1}, and the parameter estimates turn out to be close to their true values. They conclude (p. 200), "Results from this experiment should be viewed as a demonstration that it is reasonable to rely on cross-sectional spatial regression models to analyse sample data generated by spatiotemporal processes." LeSage and Pace seem to argue that the timelessness of spatial cross section data is not a drawback for estimating long-run spatial relationships.

There are several problems with this claim. First, matters would have been different had T been smaller, as it invariably is in practice. By the 250th time period the effects of initial conditions have had time to dissipate, and all the observations have had time to settle down into their long-run equilibria. Initial conditions naturally matter more the smaller is T. A more suitable value of T might have been 10 or 20 rather than 250. Indeed, had the cross-section model been estimated for e.g. $T = 10$ rather than $T = 250$, the cross-section parameter estimates might have been different to their true values in the Monte Carlo analysis.

Secondly, because N is so large the cross-section is dominant; the ratio of N/T is 200, which greatly exceeds its typical value in actual panel data. Matters might have been different had N/T been in double figures or less, which would have provided a greater role for the time series to influence the parameter estimates. For these reasons it is not advisable to rely on cross-section data to estimate spatiotemporal dynamics. The interpretation of cross-section parameter estimates as a snap-shot in time in which the variables have reached their long-run equilibria is excessively strong, especially in spatially dependent data.

Our view is that it is preferable to include temporal phenomena in estimating spatial models, and to recognize that although distance matters, so does time. It generally takes longer for occurrences to spillover the further the location in which the occurrence occurred. Indeed, time and space are inextricably interwoven. Cross-section data provide at best a snap-shot of what is happening. If economic or physical behavior are inherently dynamic, a snap-shot taken in period t is likely to be different than one taken in period $t - 1$. To complete the picture one needs a continuum of snapshots, to distinguish between short-term and long-term behavior. Compare, for example, the snapshot taken after the first second of the 100 meters final in the Olympic Games with the snap shot in the final second. Usain Bolt starts slow but finishes fast.

In principle, the relation between spatial panel data to spatial cross-section data is no different to the relation between panel data and cross-section data in general. The advantages of panel data over cross-section data are well known and do not need to be repeated here. These advantages do not of course undermine the enormous methodological importance of the econometric analysis of cross-section data, which is the traditional starting point in econometric textbooks. Nor do they undermine the enormous methodological importance of the spatial econometric analysis of cross-section data. Nevertheless, spatial econometricians need to be more aware of the econometric analysis of time series. Our purpose is therefore to take stock of key developments over the last 25 years, especially regarding the econometric analysis of nonstationary time series, and relate them to the research agendas of spatial econometrics.

1.3 Time and Space

Whereas spatial econometrics is insufficiently integrated with time series econometrics, time series econometrics is completely unintegrated with spatial econometrics. For example, macroeconomists typically ignore spatial phenomena in the study of international growth convergence (Barro and Sala-I-Martin 1991). Trade economists typically ignore spatial phenomena in gravity models (Patuelli and Arbia 2016). Labor economists typically ignore spatial phenomena even in the study of local labor markets. Economists may make sure that their standard errors are clustered appropriately and are robust with respect to heteroscedasticity and even to autocorrelation, but they seem to be unaware of the fact that spatial autocorrelation affects standard errors too (Driscoll and Kraay 1998). This oversight is particularly unfortunate since the behavior of economic phenomena over time and space are not necessary analogous.

In time series, what happened in the past affects the future. Time is uni-dimensional and uni-directional and sequential since it only moves forward; $t - 1$ occurs before time t. Moreover, it moves forward linearly because the difference between t and $t - 1$ is the same as the difference between $t - 1$ and $t - 2$. Hence, the data generating process (DGP) involves statistical relations with t on the left hand-side and $t - 1$ on the right-hand side:

$$y_t = \pi y_{t-1} + \varepsilon_t \tag{1.2}$$

y_t depends on y_{t-1} through the AR coefficient π but not vice versa. If y is stationary π must be less than 1 in absolute value, and is typically positive in economic data. In contrast, space is multi-dimensional and multi-directional with north-south and east-west dimensions. There is no natural sequencing in space as there is in time. Moreover, the distances between spatial observations, unlike the differences between temporal observations, are not usually identical. Or in the words of Whittle (1954, p. 434), "At any instant in a time series we have the natural distinction of past and future, and the value of the observation at that instant depends only on past values. That is, the dependence extends only in one direction: backwards...(In) the more general two dimensional case of (say) a field, a dab of fertilizer at any one point in the field will ultimately affect soil fertility in *all* directions." If for simplicity space is bilateral, e.g. east-west with coordinates labelled by s, the first-order counterpart to Eq. (1.2) for spatial data would be:

$$y_s = \lambda\left(y_{s+1} + y_{s-1}\right) + \varepsilon_s \tag{1.3}$$

where $s + 1$ refers to neighboring spatial units to the west of s and $s - 1$ refers to the neighboring spatial units to the east.

In this case the dependence between y_s and y_{s-1} and y_{s+1} is bi-directional because y_{s+1} and y_{s-1} depend on y_s. Space is directionless because $s + 1$, s and $s - 1$ are mutual neighbors. This is the 'I am my neighbor's neighbor' phenomenon, which means that spatial influences do not necessarily decay over distance unless λ is less than a half (Chap. 5). It was thought that uni-directional time series would generate stronger covariation than multi-directional spatial series, which dilutes covariation (Griffith and Paelinck 2007). The implications of this are non-trivial. Tobler's First Law of Geography famously states the 'everything is related to everything else but near things are more related than distant things' (Tobler 1970, p. 236). This has motivated nearly all spatial analysis from gravity modeling through transportation models and to spatial demand analysis. However, this only holds if spatial processes are stationary, so that the effect of social or economic shocks will decay over distance and consequently distance matters.

In Chap. 5 we show that in spatial cross-section data spatial impulse responses do not decay with distance when $\lambda = ½$ in Eq. (1.3), in which case these data are spatially nonstationary; they have a spatial unit root. Shocks that occur in remote spatial units have the same impulse response as shocks that occur in proximate spatial units, i.e. the attenuating effect of distance does not exist. More generally, a spatial unit root is induced when the SAR coefficient equals 1/n where n is the number of neighbors. Since $n = 2$ in Eq. (1.3) a spatial unit root is induced when $\lambda = ½$. By contrast, temporal unit roots arise when $\pi = 1$ in Eq. (1.2), in which case impulse responses do not decay with time, and the data are nonstationary. Shocks that occurred in the distance past have the same effect today as do contemporaneous shocks. Because spatial unit roots depend on the number of neighbors, and there is no such counterpart for temporal unit roots, space and time are inherently different.

Finally, time has a natural beginning because it is sequential while space, which is not sequential, does not. The "unconnected spatial unit" discussed in Chap. 5, is a contrivance introduced into spatial econometrics to provide space with an artificial beginning, since unconnected units affect other units, but are not affected in return, i.e. they transmit impulses but do not receive them. Because time has a beginning, initial value problems may arise in dynamic time series models, since the initial observations are used as lagged dependent variables, and therefore do not have residuals. However, because space does not have a beginning, initial value problems do not arise in spatial econometrics.

Instead, boundary effects may arise because the observations on the boundary of the data are spatially related to the observations beyond the boundary (Anselin 1988, Sect. 11.2), which are not included in the data. Boundary effects arise when the data are a subset of a larger spatial population. In this case, boundary effects may induce bias in the parameter estimates. However, in most cases spatial datasets are not subsets of larger spatial populations that they are intended to represent. They usually comprise the spatial population, such as all the states of the US.

In cases 3a and 3b in Table 1.1, N is assumed to be fixed but T tends to infinity. Hence, the asymptotics are with respect to T alone. This reverses the practice of fixing T and letting N tend to infinity as in case 2a. Whereas T may tend to infinity (unless the world comes to an end) the idea that N tends to infinity is more nuanced in cross-section data in general and in spatial cross-section data in particular. Regarding cross-section data in general Davidson and MacKinnon (2009, p. 92) have this to say. "At first sight, this may seem like a very odd notion. After all, any given data set contains a fixed number of observations.... In the case of a model with cross-section data we can pretend that the original sample is taken from a population of infinite size, and we can imagine drawing more and more observations from that population." The consistency properties of estimators are based on a pretense or heurism, which should be judged by their methodological usefulness.

In the case of spatial data matters are more complex regarding N tending to infinity. Cressie (1993, p. 480) originally distinguished between two asymptotic concepts for spatial data: "increasing-domain asymptotics" and "infill asymptotics". In the former, the sample is drawn from a subset of space that is potentially infinite; the frontier of space has no end. In the latter, space is fixed and finite and subdivided into an infinite number of locations. Anselin (2007, pp. 921–922) draws attention to these concepts as follows. "A pure increasing-domain structure is obtained when the minimum distance between neighboring locations remains bounded away from zero as the sample size grows. One can conceive of this situation as a sampling structure where new data points are added at the edge such that the observation 'region' becomes unbounded. In contrast, infill asymptotics are obtained when the sample region is bounded, but the number of data points increases. This yields a denser and denser sampling surface with the minimum distance between sample locations approaches zero as $N \rightarrow \infty$." Increasing domain asymptotics means that space is unbounded. Infill asymptotics means that space does not matter because distances tend to zero. The time-series counterpart to infill asymptotics would be to fix T in terms of calendar time, and to divide T into an infinite number of milliseconds. Infill asymptotics are not used in time series because calendar time is important for testing hypotheses about temporal dynamic processes. Physical space is the counterpart to calendar time, which is necessary for testing hypotheses about spatial dynamics. It is for these reasons that in cases 2a and 2b we fix N and let T tend to infinity.

Regarding the percentage of observations on the edge of space when under increasing-domains, Cressie (p. 478) adds, "As the spatial dimension d increases, edge effects become more important.... For $d \geq 1$, this percentage goes to zero like $N^{-1/d}$ as the sample size tends to infinity. Hence for $d \geq 2$, it does not go to zero fast enough to annihilate the $N^{-1/2}$ terms that arise from central limit theory." For example, in a chessboard lattice ($d = 2$), 36 observations are on the edge if $N = 100$ and 396 when $N = 10{,}000$. The square roots of N are 10 and 100. The edge observations increase by a factor of 39.6 whereas the square root of N increases by only tenfold. Since, in practice d is at least 2 (north-south, east-west) increasing-domain asymptotics are conceptually problematic even if space is infinite according to Cressie.

Elhorst (2014, p. 55) also expresses concern about increasing-domain asymptotics. "Furthermore, when data on all spatial units within a study area are collected it is questionable whether they are still representative of a larger population. For a given set of regions, such as counties in a state or all regions in a country, the population may be said to be sampled exhaustively and the individual spatial units have characteristics that set them apart from a larger population." This concern suggests, for example, that Mexico and Canada cannot be regarded as belonging to the increasing-domain for the US, or Jordan and Syria for Israel.

We distinguish between edge effects, which are "immovable" and edge effects induced by sampling. In the case of regions within a country, Marin county in California is situated on an immovable edge of the US, the Pacific Ocean. Fairfax county in Virginia is not. Suppose, however, that Fairfax county happens to be on the edge of the data for reasons of sampling. There are counties beyond Fairfax, which have not been included in the data. Parameters estimated from spatial cross-section data are generally biased by such edge effects (Anselin 1988, Sect. 11.2) in a similar way to which the initial value problem may induce bias in dynamic time series models when the error terms are autocorrelated. Whereas in time series the number of initial values is small (it equals 1 in first order dynamics), the number of edges in space is much larger. Therefore, the spatial edge problem is more severe than is the initial value problem in time series. We are mainly concerned with immovable edge effects.

The space-time analogy is examined in greater depth in this book. At this juncture it should be noted that the indifference of time series econometrics to spatial analysis has led to analytical blind spots with respect to the nature of spatial data, the importance of spatial scale, and the issue of spatial topology or shape. These issues are dealt with in the chapters ahead.

1.4 Methodological Solipsism

Econometrics is compulsory in BA, MA and PhD programs in economics. Typically, students are taught the econometrics of cross-section data first. Subsequently, they are taught the rudiments of time series econometrics, including some exposure to unit root econometrics. Electives include courses on panel data, limited dependent variables, duration analysis, and even nonparametric econometrics. By contrast, they are never taught spatial econometrics, not even as an elective. Indeed, even in departments specializing in economic geography and spatial economics, courses on spatial econometrics are typically not offered.

General textbooks on econometrics (as opposed to specialized texts on panel data) do not mention spatial econometric theory. By contrast, they all include the econometric analysis of stationary time series, and since 2000 they include the econometric analysis of nonstationary time series. A rare but telling exception is the inclusion of five pages on spatial econometrics in the seventh edition of William Greene's *Econometric Analysis* (2012). Wooldridge (2010) consciously excludes spatial econometrics from his textbook because he thinks, "…the asymptotic theory needs to be altered." (p. 6). In reference to empirical studies using data on US states or countries, he says, "…it makes little sense to fix the time series dimension and let the cross-section dimension grow." (p. 7). It can't grow because the number of US states and the number of countries is naturally bounded. This point is similar to the one raised by Cressie and Elhorst.

Since Anselin (1988, Chap. 10), textbooks on spatial econometrics have included a chapter on spatiotemporal data, which has involved the econometric analysis of time series data. Specialist textbooks on the econometric analysis of time series (Hamilton 1994; Enders 2004) have avoided the issue of special econometrics completely. Hopefully, this book will narrow the gap between time series and spatial econometrics.

Although we hope that time series econometricians will find interest in the integration of spatial econometrics and time series econometrics, we have written this book mainly for spatial econometricians. We have assumed, therefore, that the reader understands basic spatial econometrics especially for spatial cross-section data, but does not necessarily understand the econometric analysis of time-series beyond such standard topics as serial correlation and the basics of dynamic econometrics. We assume, for example, that the reader is not sufficiently familiar with unit root econometrics, which has transformed and even revolutionized the econometric analysis of time series, especially since the discovery of cointegration theory by Engle and Granger (1987). We believe that the growing interest in spatial panel data econometrics (Elhorst 2014) necessitates a deeper knowledge of time series econometrics in general, and of nonstationary panel data econometrics in particular. We also believe that just as spatial lags and spatial autocorrelation have, as mentioned, their antecedents in the econometric analysis of time series, so may ideas from unit root econometrics serve as antecedents for theoretical developments in spatial econometrics. These include, for example, concepts such as spatial nonstationarity and spatial cointegration (Fingleton 1999).

1.5 The Chapters Ahead

The main methodological theme in this book is concerned with the econometric analysis of nonstationary spatial panel data. This theme is not mentioned by Baltagi (2013) and Pesaran (2015) despite the fact that they include chapters on nonstationary panel data that are not spatial. Typically, the $N \times N$ matrix $I_N - \lambda W$ is assumed to be invertible, where N is the number of spatial units, λ denotes the SAR coefficient and W is an $N \times N$ spatial connectivity matrix. Since invertibility implies stationarity, the issue of nonstationarity is side-stepped. This theme is important because many spatial panel datasets in economics are nonstationary. In Chap. 2 we present key concepts and developments in the econometric analysis of nonstationary time series and panel data. These concepts and developments include unit root tests to determine whether time series data are stationary or not, and cointegration theory and tests to determine whether parameters estimated with nonstationary time series are spurious or genuine. We also introduce concepts that only apply to time series data such as error correction, super-consistency, weak exogeneity, Granger causality, vector autoregressions and autoregressive conditional heteroscedasticity. It is therefore timely to place unit root econometrics on the methodological agenda of spatial econometrics.

We also hope that time series econometricians will be interested in what we have to say. Therefore, in Chap. 3 we present the basic principles of spatial econometrics, including spatial lag models, spatial autocorrelation, spatial heterogeneity, and MAUP (modifiable areal unit problem). The latter refers to the role of spatial scale and topology in hypothesis testing. Spatial econometricians may want to skip Chap. 3 just as time series econometricians might want to skip Chap. 2.

Whereas Chaps. 2 and 3 are simply intended to be informative, the remaining chapters are based on material that we have published during the last 10 years. Since its inception in 1973, spatial econometricians have taken the spatial connectivity matrix (W) to be exogenous. We begin in Chap. 4 by suggesting nested and non-nested tests for discriminating between alternative definitions of W and alternative concepts of connectivity. We note that whereas in cross-section data there is no alternative to fixing W, matters are different in spatial panel data, and especially long panels where T > N. In this case it may be feasible to estimate W instead of fixing it exogenously (Beenstock and Felsenstein 2012). We discuss different identifying restrictions for W and provide an empirical illustration in which W is estimated from nonstationary spatial panel data.

Spatial panel data may be nonstationary for either or both of two reasons. First, because they are temporally nonstationary. However, they may be temporally stationary, but spatially nonstationary. Indeed, as already noted, spatial cross-section data may be spatially nonstationary (case 1b in Table 1.1). The differences between these two types of nonstationarity are the focus of Chap. 5, which is based on Beenstock et al. (2012), where we explain that whereas spatial panel data in economics are typically nonstationary in the temporal sense, they are typically stationary in the spatial sense. If they happen to be spatially nonstationary, and the data are spatially cointegrated as defined in Chap. 5, the super-consistency property of the parameter estimates is stronger in spatial data than it is in time series data. We suggest that this phenomenon is induced by the fact that whereas time series data are sequential, spatial data are not. Therefore, one learns more rapidly from nonstationary spatial data than from nonstationary time series data. In Chap. 5 we also report critical values for spatial unit roots and cointegration tests in spatial cross-section data, obtained by Monte Carlo simulation assuming a spatial unit root and no cointegration under the null hypotheses.

Chapters 6–10 focus on nonstationary spatial panel data. There are several interwoven themes including the tension between single equation contexts where there is only one outcome of interest, and multivariate contexts where there are several outcomes of interest. The most important theme is the tension between what we call "local cointegration", "spatial cointegration", and "global cointegration". In the former, spatial variables are excluded from cointegrating vectors. In the second only spatial variables are included, and in the latter spatial and non-spatial variables are included in cointegrating vectors. A third tension is between tests for cointegration and tests for error correction, which may be local, spatial and global. A fourth tension is between weak (spatial) and strong cross-section dependence, induced by common factors.

We begin in Chap. 6 with spatial vector autoregressions (SpVAR), which are "spatialized" vector autoregressions in which there are several variables that are dynamically related in space and time. Although SpVARs are becoming increasingly popular (Beenstock and Felsenstein 2007), we express major methodological reservations about them. The main problem is that because the structural parameters in VAR models are not identified, hypothesis testing is not feasible. This methodological criticism carries over to SpVAR models. Nevertheless, SpVARs may serve as useful data descriptions, which may be helpful in gaining familiarity with the data.

We argue in Chap. 7 that the response to the methodological criticisms of SpVARs is the estimation of spatial vector error correction models (SpVECM). SpVECMs involve testing for spatial panel cointegration between spatial and non-spatial variables, and estimating error correction models, which characterize the temporal and spatial dynamics between the state variables that are cointegrated. Although critical values for unit root tests and cointegration tests have been calculated for strong cross-section or spatial dependence (Pesaran 2007 for unit roots, and Banerjee and Carrion-I-Silvestre 2017 for cointegration), critical values have not been calculated for weak or spatial cross-section dependence. We therefore use Monte Carlo simulation methods to calculate critical values for unit roots in which the DGP has spatial and temporal features. We also use Monte Carlo simulation to calculate critical values for cointegration involving spatial variables. Note that whereas the Monte Carlo simulation exercise in Chap. 5 refers to cross-section data, the present exercise refers to nonstationary spatial panel data. In the latter, unit roots may be induced by both temporally autoregressive and spatially autoregressive parameters of the DGP.

Chapter 7 also demonstrates that OLS estimates of spatial cointegrating vectors are super-consistent. This means conveniently that spatial lagged dependent variables in nonstationary spatial panel data are weakly exogenous for SAR and other coefficients, so that these parameters may be estimated without recourse to ML, IV or GMM. We show that whereas consistency and identification are inextricably interwoven in stationary panel data, because causality and identification are synonymous, matters are different if the data are nonstationary. We show that when the data are nonstationary super-consistent parameter estimates do not generally imply that the variables concerned are causally related. Indeed, much of economic theory is concerned with long-term relationships between variables irrespective of the direction of causality. Nevertheless, in models involving more than one outcome of interest, the principles of identification for nonstationary data are the same as for stationary data.

Cointegrated variables are dynamically related through error correction. Directions of causality between these variables are determined through the error correction models though which they are dynamically related. If these variables are difference stationary, their first differences are stationary. Since error correction models are specified in first differences, their parameter estimates are merely root T consistent instead of super-consistent. Consequently, conventional econometric principles apply to the estimation of error correction models. We conclude Chap. 7 by considering spatial error correction in which error correction models include spatial lags of variables. We introduce spatial error correction models (SpECM) which refer to single equations. Subsequently, we introduce spatial vector error models (SpVECM) which refer to multiple equations.

Whereas Chap. 7 is entirely methodological and analytical, Chaps. 8 and 9 report empirical illustrations of the concepts featured in Chap. 7. Chapter 8, which is based on Beenstock and Felsenstein (2010) and Beenstock et al. (2018) is concerned with spatial cointegration in single equation contexts, in which there is only one outcome of interest, and in multiple equation contexts in which there is more than one outcome of interest. Specifically, we focus on two such variables, house prices and housing construction in Israel.

Chapter 9 is concerned with spatial error correction in single and multiple equation contexts. Apart from technical issues involved in the transition from single equation contexts to multiple equation contexts, Chap. 9 also deals with conceptual issues in the identification and estimation of causal effects in cointegrated systems. Indeed, conditions for identification in cointegrated spatial panel data models are conceptually different from those in models estimated using stationary spatial panel data. Our empirical illustration continues with the example of housing starts and house prices for which spatial unit root tests were presented in Chap. 7, and spatial cointegration tests were presented in Chap. 8.

In Chaps. 6–9 it is taken for granted that cross-section dependence between panel units is spatial or weak. If instead the cross-section dependence is strong, spatial econometrics would not be appropriate. There is an existential question, therefore, whether spatial econometrics is methodologically irrelevant. If the cross-section dependence is strong, the dependence is induced exogenously by observed or unobserved common factors rather than by spatial endogeneity. The tension between weak and strong cross-section dependence is the focus of Chap. 10, which is based on Beenstock (2017), and Beenstock et al. (2017).

We begin Chap. 10 by defining weak and strong cross-section dependence and discuss tests to distinguish empirically between these types of cross-section dependence. We introduce the common correlated effects (CCE) estimator proposed by Pesaran (2006), which is appropriate if cross-section dependence happens to be strong. The spatial view of cross-section dependence is based on the idea that there are causal spillover effects between spatial units. Strong cross-section dependence is based on the idea that cross-section dependence is induced by a common cause or factor, which affects the panel units differentially.

If cross-section dependence is weak or spatial, spatial units are causally related; what happens when one region has causal effects on other regions and vice-versa. If, instead, cross-section dependence is strong, spatial units are not causally related. In terms of the classifications of the reflection problem proposed by Manski (1995), weak cross-section dependence induces "endogenous effects" whereas strong cross-section dependence induces "correlated effects". An epidemiological example serves to illustrate the difference between weak and strong cross-section dependence. The spread of contagious diseases such as ebola is causal and spatial because ebola is infectious. Therefore, quarantine will inhibit the spread of the disease. Eventually, the spread of the disease weakens and the epidemic runs its course. Spatial units remote from the outbreak are unlikely to be affected. By contrast, bilharzia is a disease caused by a common factor (river snails) which affects people who enter infected rivers bare-foot. The spread of the disease appears to have a spatial dimension simply because people who live closer to infected rivers are more likely to develop bilharzia. Due to heterogeneity, individuals have different degrees of susceptibility to, or immunity from, the disease. However, patients with bilharzia cannot infect others because bilharzia is not infectious. Also, as long as rivers remain infected, bilharzia will persist; the disease does not run its course. Nor will quarantine help. Only treating the rivers and advising people to wear shoes will make a difference. Ebola induces weak cross-section dependence, whereas bilharzia induces strong cross-section dependence.

Spatial economists traditionally assume that cross-section dependence is weak and spatial either by default or because they are unaware of the alternatives. For example, cross-section dependence in house prices may be weak because it is induced by spatial spillovers, or it may be strong because it is induced by macroeconomic factors that affect regional house prices differentially. In cross-section data it is impossible to distinguish between weak and strong cross-section dependence. Matters are different in panel data. Indeed, one of the advantages of spatial panel data over spatial cross-section data is that they enable to the distinction between different types of cross-section dependence.

The empirical illustration of weak and strong cross-section dependence presented in Chap. 10 concerns the effect of regional investment grants and foreign direct investment on regional investment in Israel. We argue that strong and weak cross-section dependence may coexist. Perhaps not for ebola and bilharzia, but there are most probably many other contexts in which regional outcomes are affected by common factors, as well as by spatial spillover or interactions. Indeed the epidemiology of zika is both weak and strong. It is strong insofar as the presence of zika carrying mosquitos constitute a common factor to those exposed to the zika virus. It is weak insofar as zika may transmitted between humans.

Chapter 10 also includes tests for weak and strong cross-section dependence in the cointegrating vectors for housing starts and house prices that featured in Chap. 8, and in the SpECMs and SpVECMs for these variables featured in Chap. 9. In the event of evidence of strong cross-section dependence, we estimate the models concerned using the common correlated effects (CCE) estimator, which is supposed to eliminate or at least mitigate the presence of strong cross-section dependence. We also check whether this supposition is empirically valid.

Transparent Spatial Econometric Theory

Spatial econometric theory tends to be opaque and inaccessible because it requires extensive knowledge of linear algebra. For example, the matrix $A = I_N - \lambda W$ is typically assumed to be invertible. A condition for this is that $\omega_{\min}^{-1} < \lambda < \omega_{\max}^{-1}$ where $\omega_{\min}$ is A's smallest eigenvalue and $\omega_{\max}$ is its largest. Another condition is due to the Levy–Desplanques theorem according to which A is invertible if $|a_{ii}| > \sum_{j \neq i}^{N} |a_{ij}|$ (Aquaro et al. 2015), ensuring that A is strictly diagonal dominant. Since $a_{ii} = 1$ and $a_{ij} = \lambda w_{ij}$ this condition applies if λ is a fraction and W is row-summed to 1.

In the interest of transparency and accessibility we frequently simplify by assuming that there only two spatial units ($N = 2$). The number of eigenvalues in spatiotemporal dynamic models equals NMP, where M refers to the number of variables and P refers to the order of temporal dynamics. If the temporal dynamics are first order, there is only one variable ($M = 1$) and $N = 2$ there are only two eigenvalues, which is convenient for analytical purposes. This is especially helpful in the context of spatiotemporal models where the interaction between space and time is difficult to see when N is large. However, it is also helpful in spatial cross-section contexts.

Indeed, we show in Chap. 4 that when N = 2 the A matrix does not have to be diagonally dominant for invertibility. The forest is sometimes easier to see for the trees when there are fewer trees. Matters are naturally more complex when N is larger than 2. However, the general principles tend to be similar.

This simplification in the interest of transparency does not always work. The minimal combination of NMP in spatial vector error correction model has N = M = 2 and P = 1, in which case there are four eigenvalues, which unfortunately are too many for analytical purposes and transparency.

1.6 Overview

Figure 1.1 provides an overview and summary of the interconnected themes in this book. It also clarifies the nature of our contribution to the study of the econometric analysis of spatial panel data. At node 0 a dataset is obtained consisting of spatial panel data. The first step is to classify these data into stationary and nonstationary variables (nodes 1 and 2) as discussed in Chap. 2. This classification depends on cross-section dependence in the data. If there is no cross-section dependence standard panel unit root tests, such as Im et al. (2003), may be used to classify the data (Chap. 2). If the data are stationary (node 1.1), standard panel data econometrics may be used to test hypotheses. The appropriate model may be static (node 1.1S) or dynamic (node 1.1D). The econometric theory for nodes 1.1S and 1.1D is the focus of textbooks on panel data econometrics (Baltagi 2013; Pesaran 2015) because in this case it makes no difference whether the panel data are spatial or not.

If instead the data are nonstationary the relevant node is 2.1 in which case the data may be trend stationary (node 2.1TS) or difference stationary (node 2.1DS) as discussed in Chap. 2. In the former case, deviations from deterministic time trends are stationary. In the latter case, first differences are stationary. There is, of course no guarantee that the data must be trend or difference stationary. If they are not, they may be trend stationary or difference stationary in second differences (Chap. 2). However, such cases are rare in economics. Unit root tests for independent spatial panel data are discussed in Chap. 2.

At node 2.1 hypotheses must be tested using the standard methodologies of panel cointegration (Baltagi 2013). At node 2.1TS deterministic time trends are specified in the cointegrating vectors because the data generating processes include deterministic time trends. At node 2.1DS deterministic time trends are not specified in cointegrating vectors. Hypotheses about cointegrating vectors are tested at nodes 2.1TSS and 2.1DSS. Since by definition cointegrating vectors exclude temporal dynamics, these nodes are static. Their dynamic counterparts are represented by error correction models (nodes 2.1TSD and 2.1DSD). Panel cointegration tests for independent spatial panel data and error correction are discussed in Chap. 2. This completes the taxonomy of cases in which there is no cross-section dependence between the panel units. Since these cases are standard in the literature (Baltagi 2013; Pesaran 2015), we have nothing to add beyond their summaries in Chap. 2.

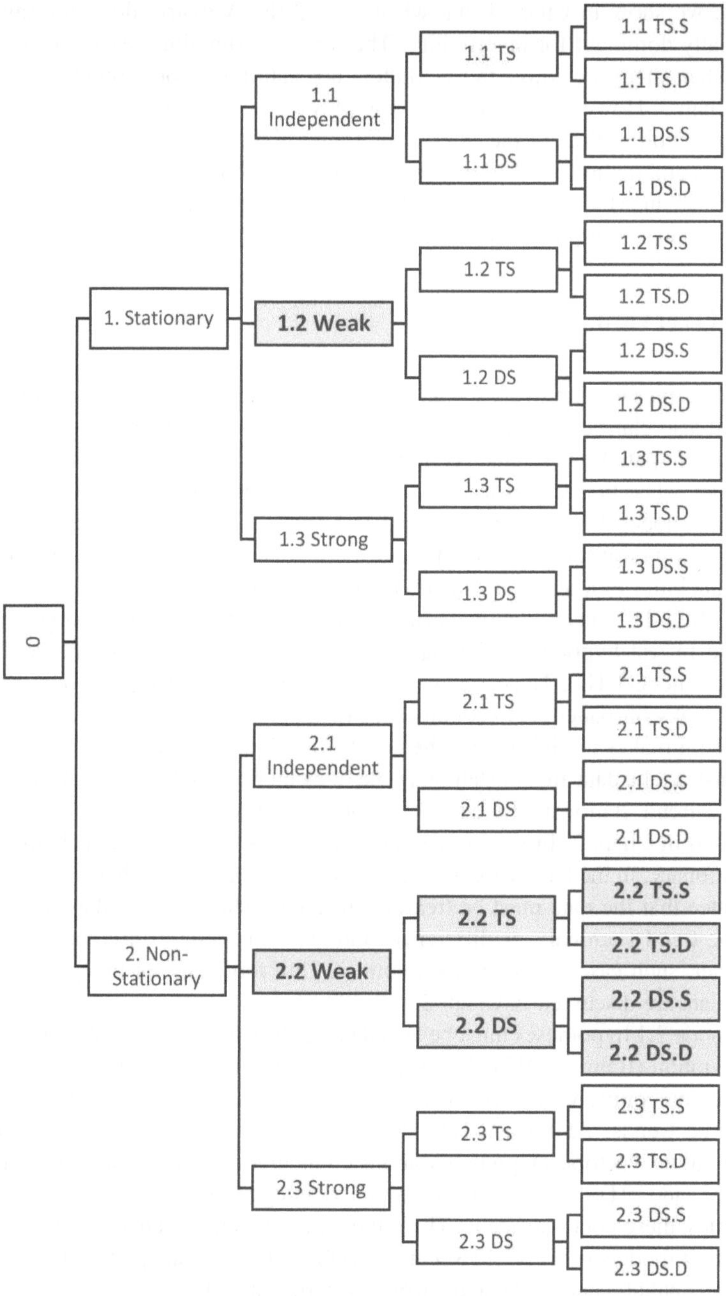

Fig. 1.1 Taxonomy of panel data models. *TS* trend, *S* stationary, *DS* difference stationary, *S* static, *D* dynamic

Matters are very different when there is cross-section dependence between panel units. Two types of dependence have been highlighted in the literature (Chudik et al. 2011). Dependence is strong when it is induced by common factors, and it is weak when it is spatial (see above). As explained in Chap. 10, Pesaran proposed a statistical test in which the null hypothesis is weak (spatial) dependence. He also proposed a panel unit root test (Pesaran 2007) in which the null hypothesis is that the data are nonstationary when spatial dependence is strong. Therefore, statistical methods are available for determining nodes 1.3 and 2.3. In the event of node 1.3, Pesaran (2006) proposed the common correlated effects (CCE) estimator, which is introduced in Chap. 2. In the event of node 2.3, panel cointegration methodology and critical values for hypothesis testing have been developed by Kapitanios et al. (2011) and Banerjee and Carrion-I-Silvestre (2017) as discussed in Chap. 2 and in detail in Chap. 10. Therefore, econometric methods are available for nodes such as 1.3S, 1.3D, 2.3DSS and 2.3DSD. Since this literature is more recent than it is for independent panel data, it is inevitably less familiar.

If cross-section dependence is weak (spatial), the methodological situation is less developed than for strong dependence because unit root tests for spatial panel data are not currently available. Therefore, it is not possible to determine nodes 1.2 and 2.2. Elhorst (2014) has provided an excellent methodological review for the case of spatially dependent panel data that are stationary (node 1.2). If instead the relevant node is 2.2, there is currently a methodological vacuum because cointegration theory and critical values for hypothesis testing have not yet been developed. Consequently, methodologies for all nodes stemming from node 2.2 are not available. In Chap. 7 we extend initial attempts (Beenstock and Felsenstein 2015) to fill these lacunae by developing panel unit root tests and panel cointegration tests for spatially dependent panel data. This makes it feasible to evaluate whether nodes 1.2 or 2.2 are empirically relevant. If node 2.2 is relevant, it also makes it feasible to implement nodes such 2.2DSS and 2.2DSD. In Chaps. 7–9 we provide empirical illustrations of spatial unit root tests and spatial panel cointegration tests based on material that we have published.

In summary, Fig. 1.1 highlights methodological lacunae regarding the econometric analysis of nonstationary panel data in the presence of spatial cross-section dependence. Our main purpose is to fill these lacunae, which are indicated in bold in Fig. 1.1.

These lacunae are also featured in Table 1.2, which distinguishes between six types of panel data econometrics, according to whether or not the panel data are stationary and whether or not the panel units are independent. Element A in Table 1.2 refers to the textbook case, developed in the 1960s and 1970s, in which the panel data are stationary and the panel units are independent. Element B refers to

Table 1.2 Taxonomy of panel data econometrics

	Independent	Weak dependence	Strong dependence
Stationary data	A: 1960s, 1970s	B: 2003–2008	C: 2006
Nonstationary data	D: 1999–2003	E: lacuna	F: 2007–2011

the econometric analysis of spatially dependent panel data in which the data are stationary. Elhorst (2003) discusses the case in which there are spatial dynamics but no temporal dynamics, and Yu et al. (2008) discuss the case in which there are temporal as well as spatial dynamics. Element C refers to the common correlated effects estimator of Pesaran (2006) in which the panel units are strongly dependent and the data are stationary.

The econometric analysis of nonstationary panel data in which the panel units are independent developed intensively (element D) at the turn of the milleneum, Unit root tests were published by Im et al. (2003) and others, cointegration tests by Pedroni (1999) and others, and spurious regression theory by Phillips and Moon (1999) for independent panel data. Element F refers to the unit root test for strongly dependent panel data (Pesaran 2007) and a cointegration test (Banerjee and Carrion-I-Silvestre 2017).

Element E in Table 1.2 is empty because there is no literature on the case of nonstationary panel data that happen to be weakly or spatially dependent. This is the lacuna referred to in Fig. 1.1, which is the main focus of our present efforts.

We conclude this chapter by providing a list of symbols that we use throughout the book.

α	Spatial fixed effect or intercept
β	Coefficient vector for exogenous covariates
δ	Spatial Durbin lag coefficient
ε	Identically and independently distributed random variable (iid)
ϕ	Temporally lagged SAR coefficient
γ	Coefficient vector for endogenous covariates
η	Factor loading
λ	Spatial autoregression coefficient (SAR)
π	Temporal autoregression coefficient (AR)
θ	Drift
σ	Standard deviation
ρ	Spatial autocorrelation coefficient (SAC)
τ	Residual autocorrelation coefficient
ω	Eigenvalue or root
ξ	Error correction coefficient
ζ	Spatial error correction coefficient
d	Order of differencing
$i = 1,2,\ldots,N$	Spatial panel unit i
$p = 1,2,\ldots,P$	Temporal lag order AR(P)
r	Correlation coefficient
$t = 1,2,\ldots,T$	Time period t
u	Regression error
w_{ij}	Element of W
B	Wiener process (continuous Brownian motion)
S	Spatial lag operator

W	Spatial connectivity matrix with elements w_{ij}
~	Spatial lag ($\tilde{y}_i = \sum_{j \neq i}^{N} w_{ij} y_j = S y_i$)
^	Estimate of parameter ($\widehat{\beta}$)
-	Cross-section average ($\bar{y}$)
Δ	Temporal difference operator
$\tilde{\Delta}$	Spatial difference operator
$O_p(\ )$	Asymptotic order of magnitude in probability
⇒	Weak convergence in probability
~	Distributed as

References

Anselin L (1988) Spatial econometrics: methods and models. Kluwer Academic, Dordrecht

Anselin L (2007) Chapter 26: Spatial econometrics. In: Mills TC, Patterson K (eds) Palgrave handbook of econometrics. Econometric theory, vol 1. Palgrave Macmillan, Basingstoke

Aquaro M, Bailey N, Pesaran MH (2015) Quasi maximum likelihood estimation of spatial models with heterogeneous coefficients. Mimeo, University of Warwick

Baltagi BH (2013) Econometric analysis of panel data, 5th edn. Wiley, Chichester

Banerjee A, Carrion-I-Silvestre JL (2017) Testing for panel cointegration using common correlated effects estimators. J Time Ser Anal 38:610–636

Barro R, Sala-I-Martin X (1991) Convergence across states and regions. Brook Pap Econ Act 1:107–182

Beenstock M (2017) How internally mobile is capital? Lett Spat Resour Sci 10(3):361–374

Beenstock M, Felsenstein D (2007) Spatial vector autoregressions. Spat Econ Anal 2(2):167–196

Beenstock M, Felsenstein D (2010) Spatial error correction and cointegration in nonstationary panel data: regional house prices in Israel. J Geogr Syst 12(2):189–206

Beenstock M, Felsenstein D (2012) Nonparametric estimation of the spatial connectivity matrix by the method of moments using spatial panel data. Geogr Anal 44:386–397

Beenstock M, Felsenstein D (2015) Spatial spillover in housing construction. J Hous Econ 28:42–58

Beenstock M, Feldman D, Felsenstein D (2012) Testing for unit roots and cointegration in spatial cross-section data. Spat Econ Anal 7(2):203–222

Beenstock M, Felsenstein D, Rubin Z (2017) Does foreign direct investment polarize regional earnings? Lett Spat Resour Sci 10(3):385–409

Beenstock M, Felsenstein D, Xieer D (2018) Spatial econometric analysis of spatial general equilibrium. Spat Econ Anal 13(3):356–378

Chudik C, Pesaran MH, Tosetti E (2011) Weak and strong cross-section dependence and estimation of large panels. Econ J 14(1):C45–C90

Cressie NAC (1993) Statistics for spatial data. Wiley, New York

Davidson R, MacKinnon JG (2009) Econometric theory and methods. Oxford University Press, New York

Driscoll JC, Kraay AC (1998) Consistent covariance matrix estimation with spatially dependent panel data. Rev Econ Stat 80:549–560

Elhorst JP (2003) Specification and estimation of spatial panel data models. Int Reg Sci Rev 26(3):244–268

Elhorst JP (2014) From spatial cross-section data to spatial panel data. Springer, Berlin

Enders W (2004) Applied time series analysis, 2nd edn. John Wiley, New York

Engle R, Granger CWJ (1987) Co-integration and error correction: representation, estimation and testing. Econometrica 35:251–276
Fingleton B (1999) Spurious spatial regression: some Monte Carlo results with spatial unit roots and spatial cointegration. J Reg Sci 39:1–19
Granger CWJ (1969) Spatial data and time series analysis. In: Scott A (ed) Studies in regional science, London papers in regional science. Pion, London, pp 1–24
Greene WH (2012) Econometric analysis. Prentice Hall, Upper Saddle River, NJ
Griffith DA, Paelinck JP (2007) An equation by any other name is still the same: on spatial econometrics and spatial statistics. Ann Reg Sci 41:209–227
Hamilton J (1994) Time series analysis. Princeton University Press, Princeton, NJ
Im K, Pesaran MH, Shin Y (2003) Testing for unit roots in heterogeneous panels. J Econ 115:53–74
Kapitanios G, Pesaran MH, Yamagata T (2011) Panels with nonstationary multifactor error structures. J Econ 160:326–348
LeSage JP, Pace RK (2009) Introduction to spatial econometrics. CRC, Boca Raton, FL
Manski CF (1995) Identification problems in the social sciences. Harvard University Press, Cambridge
Patuelli R, Arbia G (2016) Spatial econometric interaction modelling. Springer, Cham
Pedroni P (1999) Critical values for cointegration tests in heterogeneous panels with multiple regressors. Oxf Bull Econ Stat 61:653–670
Pesaran MH (2006) Estimation and inference in large heterogeneous panels with a multifactor error structure. Econometrica 74:967–1012
Pesaran MH (2007) A simple panel unit root test in the presence of cross section dependence. J Appl Economet 22(2):265–310
Pesaran MH (2015) Time series and panel data econometrics. Oxford University Press, Oxford
Phillips PCB, Moon H (1999) Linear regression limit theory for nonstationary panel data. Econometrica 67:1057–1011
Tobler W (1970) A computer movie simulating urban growth in the Detroit region. Econ Geogr 46 (2):234–240
Whittle P (1954) On stationary processes in the plane. Biometrika 49:434–449
Wooldridge JM (2010) Econometric analysis of cross section and panel data, 2nd edn. MIT Press, Cambridge, MA
Yu J, de Jong R, Lee LF (2008) Quasi-maximum likelihood estimators for spatial dynamic panel data with fixed effects when both n and T are large. J Econ 146(1):118–134
Yule GU (1897) On the theory of correlation. J R Stat Soc 60:812–854
Yule GU (1926) Why do we sometimes get nonsense-correlations between time series? A study in sampling and the nature of time series. J R Stat Soc 89:1–64

Chapter 2
Time Series for Spatial Econometricians

2.1 Introduction: Spurious and Nonsense Regressions

Perhaps the most significant development during the last 50 years in the econometric analysis of time series began in 1976 when David Dickey and Wayne Fuller devised a statistical test for the null hypothesis that the data generating process (DGP) of a time series contains a unit root. In doing so, they solved a methodological problem of longstanding. Standard statistical tests such at t-tests, chi square tests and F-tests are based on the assumption that the data are stationary. A time series is strongly stationary when all its unconditional moments are independent of time; they do not depend on when they are measured. It is weakly stationary, or covariance stationary, when its first two unconditional moments (mean, variance and covariances) are independent of time. If a time series contains a unit root, it cannot be stationary because either its mean and/or its variance and covariances are not independent of time, as they must be if it is stationary. Standard statistical tests cannot be used to test null hypotheses involving unit roots and nonstationarity because they assume that the data are stationary, i.e. the null hypothesis is false. Dickey and Fuller broke new ground by obtaining the distribution of the root of a time series under the null hypothesis that the true root is one. This discovery turned out to be a major game changer.

However, the story really begins much earlier than this, and is almost as old as regression itself. Francis Galton invented regression in 1884 to study mean reversion in the sizes of successive generations of sweat pea seeds. He observed that the progeny of big seeds are smaller than the seeds of their parent seeds, while the progeny of smaller seeds are bigger. In short, Galton discovered regression to the mean, or mean reversion, which a century later was nicknamed as "beta convergence". As we shall see, beta convergent processes generate time series that are stationary. Thirteen years later Yule (1897) discovered "spurious regression". He claimed that if independent time series happen to have time trends, they will be

M. Beenstock, D. Felsenstein, *The Econometric Analysis of Non-Stationary Spatial Panel Data*, Advances in Spatial Science,
https://doi.org/10.1007/978-3-030-03614-0_2

appear to be correlated despite the fact that they are unrelated. Thirty years later Yule (1926) discovered "nonsense regression". He claimed that if independent time series are generated by driftless random walks, they will appear to be correlated despite the fact that they are uncorrelated.

Whereas spurious regression is intuitively obvious, nonsense regression is not. In the former case time trends create the misleading impression that the time series are related. However, in the latter case the data are trendless because the DGPs have no drift. Sixty years later Phillips (1986) showed that nonsense regression is caused by the fact that the variances of time series generated by driftless random walks increase linearly with time. In short, spurious regression is induced by time trends in first moments, whereas nonsense regression is induced by time trends in second moments. The t-statistics of spurious and nonsense regression coefficients increase with the square root of the number of time series observations. Therefore, if spurious and nonsense regressions appear to be statistically insignificant, increasing the sample size will eventually generate t-statistics, which exceed 1.96. However, the results are of course spurious or nonsense.

Yule was unable to suggest a statistical test in which the null hypothesis is that the regression model is spurious or nonsense. This major development did not occur until Engle and Granger (1987) published their seminal work on cointegration, which drew on unit root tests previously developed by Dickey and Fuller. In the meanwhile, for most of the twentieth century statisticians, economists and others either ignored the issue of spurious/nonsense regression, or they de-trended their data by using deviations from trend, or by using first differences. As we shall see, the hypothesis that Y depends on X cannot be tested by using de-trended data for Y and X or by using first differences of Y and X. Since 1987 the econometrics of cointegration has expanded rapidly. Alternative cointegration methodologies have been developed. Importantly for us, cointegration has been extended to test hypotheses using nonstationary panel data. Since many spatial panel datasets are nonstationary, it is obviously crucial for spatial economists to be aware of these methodological developments.

The discovery of cointegration turned out to be a major game changer regarding basic ideas in econometric theory. Perhaps the most important methodological contribution of econometrics concerns hypothesis tests of causality involving the development of the instrumental variables estimator during the 1930s and 1940s, and the generalized method of moments estimator in the 1970s and 1980s. These methodologies are appropriate for cross-section data or stationary time series data. However, the principles of identification and inference are entirely different when time series are nonstationary than when they are stationary. These principles are similar for cross-section data and stationary time series data because identification and causality are inextricably interwoven. Nevertheless, stationary time series data are conceptually different to cross-section data because "weak exogeneity" may arise in the former but not the latter. This means, as we shall see, that it is easier to solve identification problems with stationary time series data than with cross-section data. If, in addition, the time series data happen to be nonstationary but cointegrated, the concepts of causality and identification cease to be inextricably interwoven because the parameter estimates of cointegrating vectors are "super-consistent". Super-consistency radically changes the asymptotic analysis of estimators, especially by undermining such basic concepts as simultaneous equations bias. In summary, the econometric analysis of nonstationary data is entirely different to the econometric analysis of stationary data.

2.2 The Functional Central Limit and Continuous Mapping Theorems

The asymptotic theory of nonstationary time series is based on the functional central limit theorem (FCLT), also known as Donsker's theorem, and the continuous mapping theorem (CMT). FCLT/CMT is for functions of random variables what CLT is for asymptotic distributions of random variables. The intuition behind FCLT is that discrete time series data may be regarded as if they were continuous with the infinite passage of time. The reason for this is that the time span of discrete periods, expressed as a fraction of the time that has passed, tends to zero. For example, if the data are quarterly, a quarter is 2.5% of 10 years, 0.25% of 100 years, and 0% of an infinite number of years. Another way of thinking about this is as follows. Imagine a graph of the Dow Jones index as of 1935. The crash of 1929 appears to be enormous. Look at the graph in 2018. The Great Crash is difficult to detect. Its importance in the great sweep of history has become diluted. The same phenomenon is already happening to the Subprime Crisis of 2007–2008. According to FCLT functions of discrete time series must be normalized by the square root of the time that has passed (T).

According to CMT if the asymptotic distribution of random variable x is X then the asymptotic distribution of f(x) is f(X) provided f( ) is continuously differentiable. In our application of CMT, X is the normal distribution. Hence, if x is normally distributed, so must be functions of x such as f(x). FCLT/CMT enables the derivation of the asymptotic distribution of functions of time series, and forms the basis, for example, of the distribution of the Dickey–Fuller statistic and related cointegration test statistics.

The total passage of calendar time (T) is divided into discrete time periods (t) of length $\Delta t = T/n$. For example, if T is 10 years and $n = 40$ these discrete time periods are quarters. Consider the following Wiener process (B) where ε denotes a standard normal random variable and is identically and independently distributed (iid):

$$B_t = B_{t-1} + \varepsilon_t \sqrt{\Delta t} \tag{2.1a}$$

The expected value of ΔB_t is zero since $E(\varepsilon_t) = 0$ and its variance is $E\left(\varepsilon_t \sqrt{\Delta t}\right)^2 = \Delta t$, i.e. the variance is naturally larger the more discrete the data; more happens during a quarter than during a month. The expected value of B_T equals its initial value, which for convenience is assumed to be zero ($B_0 = 0$), and its variance is $n\Delta t = T$, i.e. the variance increases with the passage of time, as expected.

Let r = t/T index time as a percentage of T. Hence r = 0 when t = 0 and r = 1 when t = T. For example, if T = 100 and t = 77, r = 0.77. Since the data are discrete let r* be the smaller integer for t. For example, when r = 0.778 r* = 0.77 because t = 77.8 is not an integer. Therefore, r* < r except when r refers to integers of t. For example, when t = 78, r = r* = 0.78. As T tends to infinity r* naturally converges on r because all values of r refer to integers of t. This means that as T tends to infinity discrete data appear to behave as if they were continuous.

Let $y_t = y_{t-1} + \varepsilon_t$ (random walk) so that $y_t = \varepsilon_1 + \varepsilon_2 + \ldots + \varepsilon_t$. The expected value of $y_t = 0$ and its variance is t because ε is iiN(0,1). FCLT/CMT states that:

$$\frac{y_t}{\sqrt{T}} \Rightarrow B(r) \sim iiN(0, r) \tag{2.1b}$$

where ⇒ indicates weak convergence, and B is a Wiener process for y. Weak convergence to B(r) comes from FCLT. Its asymptotic distribution comes from CMT. Equation (2.1b) states that if discrete data generated by a random walk are normalized by root T, their limiting distribution is normal with mean zero and variance r, and is independent of T. This may easily be verified. To prevent the variance from increasing without limit with t, it is necessary to divide y_t by the square root of T, so that the variance of $y_t/\sqrt{T} = t/T = r$ as in Eq. (2.1b). The asymptotic order in probability of y_t is defined as the power of T that prevents its first two moments from tending to infinity with the passage of time (T). According to Eq. (2.1b) $y_t \sim O_p(T^{1/2})$, i.e. the power of T is a half. We list several lemmas generated by FCLT/CMT, which shall be used subsequently:

$$\frac{\bar{y}}{\sqrt{T}} \Rightarrow \int_0^1 B(r)dr \sim iiN\left(0, \frac{1}{3}\right) \tag{2.1c}$$

$$\frac{1}{T}\sum_{t=1}^{T} \varepsilon_t y_{t-1} \Rightarrow \int_0^1 B(r)dB(r)dr \sim \frac{1}{2}\left(\chi_1^2 - 1\right) \tag{2.1d}$$

$$\frac{1}{T^2}\sum_{t=1}^{T} y_{t-1}^2 \Rightarrow \int_0^1 [B(r)]^2 dr \sim iiN\left(\frac{1}{2}, \frac{1}{6}\right) \tag{2.1e}$$

$$\frac{1}{T^{\frac{3}{2}}}\sum_{t=1}^{t} t\varepsilon_t \Rightarrow \int_0^1 rdB(r) \sim iiN\left(0, \frac{1}{3}\right) \tag{2.1f}$$

$$\frac{1}{T^{\frac{5}{2}}}\sum_{t=1}^{T} ty_t \Rightarrow \int_0^1 rB(r)dr \sim iiN\left(0, \frac{2}{15}\right) \tag{2.1g}$$

Equation (2.1c) states that the asymptotic order in probability of the sample mean of y is root T, or $O_p(T^{1/2})$, for otherwise the limiting distribution in Eq. (2.1c) would depend on T. Its limiting distribution is normal with mean zero and variance 1/3. Equation (2.1d) states that the asymptotic order in probability of the covariance between y_{t-1} and ε_t is 0. Since the expected value of chi square equals the number of degrees of freedom (df = 1), the expected value of Eq. (2.1d) is zero as expected.

Because the variance of chi square equals 2df, the variance of Eq. (2.1d) is 1. According to Eq. (2.1e) the asymptotic order of the variance of y is 1. Equation (2.1e) states that the covariance between time and ε, or indeed any stationary random variable, has an asymptotic order of ½. Finally, the covariance between y and time has an asymptotic order of 1½ according to Eq. (2.1g). We use Eqs. (2.1a–2.1g) below and in Chap. 7 where the asymptotics depend on T. For further reading see Davidson (1994).

2.3 Univariate Unit Root Tests

The Dickey–Fuller unit root test is based on the following DGP:

$$\Delta y_t = \alpha + (\pi - 1)y_{t-1} + \gamma t + \varepsilon_t \tag{2.2a}$$

where $\varepsilon \sim \text{iid}(0, \sigma^2)$. To begin with suppose that $\gamma = 0$, i.e. there is no deterministic time trend in Eq. (2.2a). If $\pi = 1$, y is a random walk with drift α. The solution for y_t in this case is:

$$y_t = \alpha t + \varepsilon_t + \varepsilon_{t-1} + \ldots + \varepsilon_1 + y_0 \tag{2.2b}$$

Since it is of no consequence, y_0 is initialized at zero. According to Eq. (2.2b) the unconditional expected value and variance of y depend on time. From Eq. (2.2b) the expected value of y_t is αt and the variance of y_t is $E(\varepsilon_t + \varepsilon_{t-1} + \ldots + \varepsilon_1)^2 = t\sigma^2$.; the mean and variance depend linearly on time. Note that because ε is serially independent $E(\varepsilon_t\varepsilon_{t-p}) = 0$, and because ε is homoscedastic $E(\varepsilon^2_{t-p}) = \sigma^2$. The unconditional moments of stationary variables must not depend on time. Therefore, y is not stationary if $\pi = 1$. If $-1 < \pi < 1$ Eq. (2.2b) states that the unconditional expected value of y mean reverts to $\alpha/(1 - \pi)$ while the variance is $\sigma^2/(1 - \pi^2)$. Since both of these population moments do not depend on time y is stationary.

If $\alpha = \gamma = 0$ Eq. (2.2a) is a random walk without drift. The mean of y no longer depends on time, but the variance continues to be linear in t. The OLS estimator for π in this case is:

$$\hat{\pi} = \frac{\sum_{t=1}^{T} y_t y_{t-1}}{\sum_{t=0}^{T-1} y_{t-1}^2} = \pi + \frac{\sum_{t=1}^{T} \varepsilon_t y_{t-1}}{\sum_{t=0}^{T-1} y_{t-1}^2} \tag{2.2c}$$

Under the null hypothesis ($\pi = 1$) and substituting Eqs. (2.1c) and (2.1d) into Eq. (2.2c) we obtain:

$$\text{plim}T(\hat{\pi}-1)=\frac{\int_0^1 B(r)dB(r)dr}{\int_0^1 [B(r)]^2} \tag{2.2d}$$

Because the numerator of Eq. (2.2d) is $O_p(T)$ according to Eq. (2.1d) and the denominator is $O_p(T^2)$ according to Eq. (2.1e), the expression on the right hand side is $O_p(T^{-1})$. Hence, the OLS estimator for π is T-consistent rather than root T-consistent. Henceforth, we shall refer to this property by "super-consistency". Notice also that the numerator is normally distributed according to Eq. (2.1d), and the denominator is normally distributed according to Eq. (2.1e). However, the ratio of random variables that are normally distributed is not normally distributed. Dickey and Fuller used Monte Carlo methods to obtain the numerical distribution of Eq. (2.2d) under the null for three cases: when $\alpha = \gamma = 0$ as in Eq. (2.2d), when $\gamma = 0$ as in Eq. (2.2b), and for Eq. (2.2a).

Suppose we have estimated $\hat{\pi} = 0.8$ from a sample of data observed over T time periods with $\gamma = 0$. We wish to test whether 0.8 is significantly different from 1. A t-test would be inappropriate because according to the Central Limit Theorem distributions derived from the normal distribution are only valid for stationary random variables. Since if $\pi = 1$ the variable is nonstationary, we need the distribution of y under the null hypothesis that it is nonstationary, i.e. that $\pi = 1$. The normal distribution and related distributions can be calculated analytically. By contrast, the distribution of $\hat{\pi}$ under the null hypothesis of $\pi = 1$ cannot be calculated analytically. Critical values may either be expressed in terms of $T(\hat{\pi} - 1)$ or in terms of the $(\hat{\pi} - 1)/\text{sd}(\hat{\pi})$. The latter looks like a t-statistic, but it does not have a t-distribution. Although the two statistics are equivalent, the latter is more popular than the former. If $T = 100$ and size $p = 0.05$ the critical value of $\hat{\pi}$ is 0.89 and the critical value of the Dickey–Fuller "t-statistic" is -2.89. If $\hat{\pi}$ is smaller than 0.89 or if the DF statistic is more negative than -2.89 the null hypothesis: $\pi = 1$ may be rejected. Since $\hat{\pi} = 0.8$ the null hypothesis is rejected and y is assumed to be stationary.

Suppose that the null hypothesis cannot be rejected, i.e. y is nonstationary. To test whether the first difference of y is stationary Eq. (2.2a) is estimated with $\Delta^2 y_t$ as the dependent variable and Δy_{t-1} as the independent variable. If the DF statistic is more negative than -2.89 we may conclude that Δy is stationary, or y is "difference stationary". The order of differencing which transforms y into a stationary variable is denoted by d. In the current example $d = 1$. We write $y \sim I(d)$ as short-hand for saying that y is integrated to order d.

So far it has been assumed that $\gamma = 0$. If this restriction is relaxed and $\hat{\pi}$ is significantly less than 1, y is "trend stationary". y itself is nonstationary because it depends on time, but deviations of y from a deterministic time trend are stationary. The critical value of the DF statistic in this case is -3.45 instead of -2.89 because Eq. (2.2a) involves the use of an additional degree of freedom in the estimation of γ. If, according to Dickey–Fuller statistics y happens to be both difference stationary and trend stationary, Dickey and Fuller (1981) suggest a test to distinguish between the two. Since the difference stationary model is a restricted case of the trend stationary model, with $\gamma = 0$ and $\pi = 1$, this test compares the error sum of squares of the difference stationary model with the error sum of squares of the trend stationary model. This looks like an F-test, however, the critical values of the test statistic do not have an F distribution. In fact when T = 100 and p = 0.95 the critical value is 6.89 instead of 3.1, which is the critical value of $F_{2.97}$.

The critical values are calculated under the assumption that ε in Eq. (2.2a) is iid. Frequently this condition is violated because of serial correlation in the error terms. There are three main solutions to this problem. The first and most popular is the Augmented Dickey Fuller statistic (ADF) in which lags of Δy are specified in Eq. (2.2a). It is well known that serial correlation may be induced by dynamic misspecification. Augmenting Eq. (2.2a) with lags of Δy turns it into a dynamic DF regression, in which the error terms are no longer serially correlated. The ADF statistic is calculated in the same way as the DF statistic and it has the same critical value.

The second solution, suggested by Phillips and Perron (1988), uses the estimated serial correlation in Eq. (2.2a) to calculate robust standard errors for $\hat{\pi}$. The Phillips–Perron statistic is simply a robust DF statistic. Critical values of the Phillips–Perron (PP) statistic are the same as for the DF statistic. Whereas ADF changes both $\hat{\pi}$ and its standard error, PP changes the latter but not the former. A third solution suggested by Elliot et al. (1996) estimates Eq. (2.2a) by GLS rather than OLS. This method estimates $\hat{\pi}$ and the offending parameters of serial correlation in Eq. (2.2a). This DF-GLS statistic has critical values that are slightly stricter than the DF statistic.

Dickey and Fuller's null hypothesis is $\pi = 1$ in which case $y \sim I(1)$. An alternative, suggested by Kwiatowski et al. (1992) is to test the null hypothesis that π is a fraction, in which case $y \sim I(0)$. This test, commonly known as the KPSS test, is based on the following DGP:

$$y_t = \alpha + \gamma t + v_t \tag{2.3a}$$

$$v_t = \beta z_t + \varepsilon_t \tag{2.3b}$$

$$\Delta z_t = e_t \tag{2.3c}$$

$$V_t = \sum_{\tau=1}^{t} v_\tau \tag{2.3d}$$

$$KPSS = \frac{\sum_{t=1}^{T} V_t^2}{T^2 \sigma_v^2} \tag{2.3e}$$

where ε and e are independent iid random variables. Suppose that $\gamma = 0$, i.e. there is no deterministic trend in y. Note that according to Eq. (2.3c) $z \sim I(1)$. Therefore, if β is non-zero y cannot be stationary; it must be I(1) like z. If $\beta = 0$ then $v = \varepsilon$ in which case y must be stationary. The KPSS test statistic in Eq. (2.3e) is a Lagrange multiplier statistic used to test the null hypothesis that $\beta = 0$. If the null hypothesis is true it may be shown that KPSS = ½(1 + 1/T). If it is false, KPSS exceeds this number.

To implement the test, estimates of v are obtained using Eq. (2.3a). If $\gamma = 0$, v is simply the deviation of y from its sample mean. Otherwise it is the deviation from the estimated time trend. If KPSS exceeds its critical value the null hypothesis that y is I(0) is rejected. In this event and if $\gamma = 0$, y is driftless random walk. If KPSS is less than its critical value and γ is non-zero, we cannot reject the null hypothesis that deviations from trend are I(0). In this case y is trend stationary. If y is nonstationary, KPSS may be applied to the first difference of y. This tests the null hypothesis that Δy is I(0). As in the case of the Dickey–Fuller statistic, serial correlation in v complicates matters. The solutions are similar to those already discussed. KPSS in fact use robust estimates of σ_v in Eq. (2.3e).

The DF and KPSS statistics test different hypotheses. The former tests the null hypothesis that d = 1 while the latter tests the null hypothesis that d = 0. The two tests are compatible when the DF statistic is significant and the KPSS statistic is not significant. According to this combination the DF statistic rejects the hypothesis that the time series is nonstationary, while the KPSS statistic does not reject the hypothesis that the time series is I(0) and is therefore stationary. The test statistics are also compatible if the DF statistic is not significant and the KPSS statistic is significant. In this case the DF statistic does not reject the null hypothesis that the time series is nonstationary while the KPSS statistic rejects the null hypothesis of I(0). If both statistics are significant, or both are not significant, then the DF and KPSS statistics are incompatible. In this case there is a dilemma since according to the DF statistic the time series is nonstationary (or stationary), whereas according to the KPSS statistic it is stationary (or nonstationary).

We think that the KPSS test is less informative than its DF counterpart. Suppose the true value of d is 0.4 because the time series has long memory (Maddala and Kim 1999, Chap. 9), but not infinite memory. The KPSS statistic will reject its null hypothesis of d = 0, as it should, because d is greater than zero. However, the DF statistic will reject the null of d = 1, as it should. Therefore, KPSS tests the null of d = 0 when the alternative may be that the time series has long memory, and is in fact stationary.

We recommend Hamilton (1994), Maddala and Kim (1999) and Enders (2004) for further reading on unit root tests and long memory processes.

2.4 Panel Unit Root Test

Panel data combine cross-section and time series data. If the time series are nonstationary the panel data will be nonstationary. Phillips and Moon (1999) have shown that the phenomena of spurious and nonsense regressions also arise in the case of models estimated with nonstationary panel data. Panel unit root tests have been developed during the 2000s. These tests assume that nonstationarity is exclusively induced by temporal nonstationarity. The cross-section dimension is assumed to be stationary. As we discuss in Chap. 5 this assumption may be questionable if the panel data happen to be spatial.

Recent editions of textbooks on the econometric analysis of panel data e.g. Baltagi (2013, Chap. 12) and Pesaran (2015, Chap. 29) include a chapter on unit root tests for panel data. The test that we prefer is the IPS test due to Im et al. (2003). In this test Eq. (2.2a) is estimated for each unit in the panel providing estimates of α_i, π_i and γ_i. We denote by DF_i the Dickey–Fuller statistic estimated for panel unit i. The IPS test is based on the average of these DF statistics, or DFbar, for the N panel units. According to the Central Limit Theorem DFbar tends to be normally distributed. The IPS statistic involves finite sample corrections to DFbar:

$$IPS = \frac{\sqrt{N}[DFbar - E(DFbar)]}{sd(DFbar)} \sim N(0, 1) \tag{2.4}$$

where the expected value and standard deviation for DFbar are provided by Im et al. (2003). If the IPS statistic is more negative than its critical value from the standard normal distribution, i.e. less than -1.64 at $p = 0.05$ (one tail), the null hypothesis of nonstationarity is rejected. Otherwise, the panel data are nonstationary.

We prefer the IPS test because it allows for heterogeneity across the units in the panel in terms of specific effects as well as in terms of unit roots. This means that units in the panel are allowed to have different roots. Like other panel unit root tests, the IPS test assumes that the panel units are independent. Baltagi et al. (2007) have investigated the implications of spatial dependence on panel unit root tests. Specifically, they assume that ε in Eq. (2.2a) is spatially autocorrelated. They find that the size distortions are minor provided the spatial autocorrelation coefficient is less than 0.4. In Chap. 7 we "spatialize" the IPS test by adding a spatial lag to Eq. (2.2a). This treats spatial dependence in panel unit root tests in a more fundamental way.

Pesaran (2007) proposed a panel unit root test (CIPS) in which cross-section dependence is strong because it is induced by a common factor:

$$\Delta y_{it} = \alpha_i + (\pi_i - 1)y_{it-1} + \gamma_i t + \eta_{1i}\Delta y_t + \eta_{2i}y_{t-1} + \varepsilon_{it} \tag{2.5}$$

where y_t refers to the cross-section average of y_{it}, which affects panel i differentially through the factor loadings η_{1i} and η_{2i}. DFbar is calculated as in Eq. (2.4) but the expected value and standard deviation of DFbar are different. As expected, the critical values of IPS become more severe because Eq. (2.5) involves the estimation of 2N factor loadings.

IPS and other panel unit root statistics, like the Dickey–Fuller statistic, test the null hypothesis of a unit root, i.e. the null hypothesis is $d = 1$. Hadri (2000) extended the KPSS statistic to panel data. In this case the null hypothesis is that the panel data are stationary, i.e. $d = 0$. Hadri's test statistic (HLM) is based on the average of the KPSS statistics estimated for individual panel units. According to the Central Limit Theorem HLM has a standard normal distribution. If HLM exceeds its critical value the null hypothesis of stationarity is rejected.

IPS and CIPS refer to panel data that are independent or strongly dependent respectively. As noted in Fig. 1.1, what is missing is a panel unit root test for panel data in which the cross-section dependence is weak (spatial). We fill this methodological gap in Chap. 7 by deriving the distribution of unit roots when cross-section dependence is weak.

2.5 Cointegration (OLS)

Suppose y and x are nonstationary time series but their first-differences are stationary, i.e. $y \sim I(1)$ and $x \sim I(1)$. Suppose the hypothesis to be tested is:

$$y_t = \alpha + \beta x_t + u_t \tag{2.6}$$

Engle and Granger (1987) demonstrated that OLS estimates of β are spurious or nonsense if $u \sim I(1)$ but are genuine if $u \sim I(0)$. In spurious or nonsense regressions the error terms are nonstationary like y and x. In this event t-statistics for $\hat{\beta}$ are $O_p(T^{1/2})$, which means alarmingly that they tend to infinity with T. Therefore, if a spurious or nonsense result is not "statistically significant", simply increase the sample size until it is.

However, in genuine regressions the error terms are stationary. The model for the error terms is:

$$u_t = \tau u_{t-1} + \varepsilon_t \tag{2.7}$$

where ε is assumed to be iid. In spurious and nonsense regressions $\tau = 1$, whereas in genuine regressions $\tau < 1$. In the latter case y and x are "cointegrated" because individually they are I(1) variables, but a linear combination of them is I(0). The intuition is simple. In spurious and nonsense regressions in which $\tau = 1$, error terms are not expected to correct themselves since according to Eq. (2.7), $E_{t-1}(u_t) = u_{t-1}$. By contrast, in genuine regressions $E_t|u_t| < |u_{t-1}|$, i.e. error terms are expected to correct themselves, or mean-revert. This happens because y and x are genuinely related, but it does not happen otherwise. This means that if y and x are cointegrated these variables are dynamically related through "error correction". Cointegration and error correction are mirror images of each other.

Substituting Eq. (2.6) into Eq. (2.7) and rearranging generates the following error correction model (ECM):

$$\Delta y_t = \alpha(1-\tau) + \beta\Delta x_t - (1-\tau)(y_{t-1} - \beta x_{t-1}) + \varepsilon_t \tag{2.8}$$

where $y_{t-1} - \beta x_{t-1}$ is a measure of the disequilibrium between y and x, which is implied by Eq. (2.6). Equation (2.8) states that changes in y vary directly with changes in x and inversely with the disequilibrium of y with respect to x. Notice that estimating Eq. (2.6) in first differences does not test the hypothesis in Eq. (2.6) because Eq. (2.8) also includes the lagged disequilibrium of y with respect to

x. First-differencing may make y and x stationary, but it omits error correction thereby inducing misspecification. This demonstrates the important point that estimating Eq. (2.6) in first differences does not in fact test the hypothesis in Eq. (2.6), which is in levels.

Typically, Eq. (2.8) is estimated using the error terms from Eq. (2.6):

$$\Delta y_t = \phi + \sum_{p=1}^{P} \pi_p \Delta y_{t-p} + \sum_{p=0}^{q} \gamma_p \Delta x_{t-p} + \xi u_{t-1} + e_t \tag{2.9}$$

where e is iid. Since y and x are difference stationary, and u ~ I(0) because y and x are cointegrated, all the variables in Eq. (2.9) are stationary. The lag length parameters P and q may be determined empirically using the general-to-specific methodology (Hendry 1995). The EC coefficient is ξ, which is expected to be negative. Equation (2.9) is a more general ECM than Eq. (2.8) because it allows the dynamic adjustment of y to x to be more flexible. After this adjustment has been completed y tends to y* = constant + βx, which is the long-run value of y given x. Depending on the πs and γs in Eq. (2.9) y may converge upon y* monotonically, or it may overshoot y* temporarily.

If y and x are cointegrated the OLS estimate of β is "superconsistent" (Stock 1987). With stationary data OLS estimates are, of course, root T-consistent, i.e. the rate of asymptotic convergence of $\hat{\beta}$ to β is according to $1/T^{½}$. In the case of nonstationary, cointegrated data the rate of asymptotic convergence is 1/T if the DGP is driftless and $1/T^{1½}$ otherwise. To see this the OLS estimate of β is:

$$\hat{\beta} = \frac{\sum_{t=1}^{T}(x_t - \bar{x})y_t}{\sum_{t=1}^{T}(x_t - \bar{x})^2} = \frac{\sum_{t=1}^{T}(x_t - \bar{x})(\alpha + \beta x_t + u_t)}{\sum_{t=1}^{T}(x_t - \bar{x})^2} = \beta + b$$

$$b = \frac{\sum_{t=1}^{T}(x_t - \bar{x})u_t}{\sum_{t=1}^{T}(x_t - \bar{x})^2} \tag{2.10a}$$

Since x is difference stationary its DGP is $\Delta x_t = \theta + \varepsilon_t$ in which case:

$$\begin{aligned} x_t &= \theta t + E_t \\ E_t &= \varepsilon_t + \varepsilon_{t-1} + \ldots + \varepsilon_1 \end{aligned} \tag{2.10b}$$

If y and x are I(1) but cointegrated, u is I(0) by definition. The numerator of b involves the sum of products of I(1) and I(0) random variables, which has two components according to Eq. (2.10b), ϕtu_t and $E_t u_t$. The numerator of b is:

$$\theta \sum_{t=1}^{T} tu_t + \sum_{t=1}^{T} E_t u_t = O_p\left(T^{3/2}\right) + O_P(T) \tag{2.10c}$$

Therefore the numerator of b increases with $T^{3/2}$ which is the dominant term. The dominant term in the denominator of b is:

$$\theta^2 \sum_{t=1}^{T} t^2 = \theta^2 \frac{T(T+1)(2T+1)}{6} = O_p(T^3) \tag{2.10d}$$

Therefore $b = O_p(T^{3/2})/O_p(T^3) = O_p(T^{-3/2})$ because the denominator grows more rapidly with T than the numerator. When the data are stationary $b = O_p(T^{-1/2})$ in which case $\hat{\beta}$ is root-T consistent. When the data are random walks with drift $\hat{\beta}$ is $T^{3/2}$-consistent, or super consistent. When the data are driftless random walks, i.e. $\theta = 0$, the numerator of b is $O_p(T)$ and the denominator is $O_p(T^2)$ in which case $\hat{\beta}$ is T-consistent. See further Chap. 7.

Asymptotic rates of convergence are therefore more rapid if the data are nonstationary. A related property is that $\text{plim}(\hat{\beta}) = \beta$ even if x and u are not independent because b tends to zero asymptotically. In short, when the data are nonstationary but cointegrated β is identified without recourse to instrumental variables. Matters are, of course, entirely different with stationary data. In finite samples estimates of $\hat{\beta}$ are biased and β is not identified. However, the bias is attenuated (Banerjee and Carrion-I-Silvestre 2017) and varies directly with τ and inversely with the ratio of σ_y/σ_x and of course T. Therefore, in many finite samples β may be identified for all practical purposes, even without recourse to instrumental variables.

Finally, super-consistency implies $\text{plim}(R^2) = 1$ since the error sum of squares grows with T while the total sum of squares grows with T^3. Therefore, $\text{plim}(R^2) = 1$, and R^2 is $O_p(T^{-2})$. This means that asymptotically it makes no difference whether y is regressed on x, as in Eq. (2.6), or whether x is regressed on y. It also means that cointegration tests do not imply causality. If x happens to be a variable determined abroad, β has a causal interpretation. However, if x is determined jointly with y, β has a structural interpretation. It refers to the way in which y and x are related in the long-run according to the theory. Indeed, hypothesis testing and testing for causality are conceptually different. This is very different to the case of stationary data where hypothesis testing and causality are inextricably interwoven through conditions for identification. In this case if β is identified, the hypothesis that y depends on x cannot be rejected, and the estimate of β has a causal interpretation.

To determine whether u is stationary, the Dickey–Fuller statistic is calculated using the estimates of u from Eq. (2.6). The critical values, however, are not the critical values of the DF statistic. They are stricter, i.e. more negative. This is to be expected because the test uses estimates of the error terms rather than the true error terms. MacKinnon (1996) provides critical values for cointegration tests. If the DF regression for the estimates of u has autocorrelated error terms, ADF, PP and DF-GLS statistics may be calculated to correct the cointegration test statistics for autocorrelation, just as in the case of unit root tests for time series data.

Suppose that $z \sim I(1)$ is also specified together with x in Eq. (2.6) and we wish to test whether z is statistically significant. Since the estimates of parameters such as β generally have non-standard distributions, it is not possible to test parameter restrictions using t-tests, F-tests and chi-square tests. Instead, the statistical significance of z may be determined as follows. Estimate Eq. (2.6) with and without z. If y and x are not cointegrated, but y, x and z are cointegrated, this shows that both x and z are relevant for y. If y and x are cointegrated and y, x and z are cointegrated, but z is not cointegrated with either y or x, this shows that z is not relevant since y and x are cointegrated without z. If, however, z is cointegrated with either y or x, and the p-value for cointegration between y, x and z is smaller than the p-value for cointegration between y and x, z should be included in the cointegrating vector.

This issue is related to the problem of calculating confidence intervals for the estimate of β. Since the error terms (u) of Eq. (2.6) generally have nonstandard distributions, estimates of β and other parameters do not have standard distributions. This means that t-statistics, chi square and F statistics are not valid to test hypotheses regarding estimates of β and related parameters. It also means that confidence limits for these parameters cannot be calculated using methods appropriate for stationary data. We have already pointed out that hypothesis testing of estimates of β and other parameters may be carried using cointegration tests, so t-tests etc. are not required and are in any case incorrect. Nevertheless, confidence intervals are of interest in their own right, irrespective of hypothesis testing. Li and Maddala (1997) have proposed a method for bootstrapping confidence intervals by resampling the data for x in Eq. (2.6) using its DGP, and by resampling u in Eq. (2.7) using the empirical distribution function for ε. In Chap. 7 we draw on their idea to bootstrap confidence intervals for cointegrating vectors estimated from nonstationary spatial panel data.

The claim that OLS estimates of β are meaningful despite the fact that there may be reverse causality from x to y, and the error terms (u) are autocorrelated, contradicts standard econometric theory. There is no need for instrumental variables or to handle the problem of autocorrelation. "At first sight, this approach seems to ignore all the precepts of good econometric practice. …Nevertheless, the levels estimator…is not only consistent but **super-consistent** (bold in original)…This result indicates just how different asymptotic theory is when I(1) variables are involved." (Davidson and MacKinnon 2009, p. 627).

The null hypothesis that has been tested thus far is that the variables are not cointegrated. An alternative null hypothesis is that the variables are cointegrated. Shin (1994) has extended the KPSS unit root test to test the null hypothesis of cointegration. Just as we saw that it is possible for the DF and KPSS test statistics to contradict each other, so it is possible that the Engle–Granger cointegration tests contradicts Shin's cointegration test. Just as we suggested that ADF is a superior unit root test to KPSS, so do we suggest that Shin's cointegration test is inferior to its

Engle-Granger counterpart, as well as other methodologies in which the null hypothesis is "no cointegration".

2.6 Cointegration Methodologies

The methodology of cointegration summarized above was originally developed by Granger and Engle. Subsequently several alternative methodologies have been developed. There have been two main aspects to these developments. The first has been concerned with potential finite sample bias in the estimation of Eq. (2.6). These biases arise if the sample is not "asymptotic" so that the estimate of β in Eq. (2.6) does not represent the true long-run relationship between y and x. If the sample starts or ends noisily, the estimate of β might be affected especially if the sample is insufficiently long. For example, if the sample begins at the bottom of a recession and ends at the top of a boom, or vice-versa, the business cycle may distort the secular relationship between y and x. Ideally, Eq. (2.6) should be estimated with cyclically adjusted data since β is independent of the business cycle. However, such data do not exist. Various solutions to this problem have been suggested, which turn Eq. (2.6) from a static regression into a dynamic regression, as discussed shortly.

The second has been concerned with the single equation focus of Eq. (2.6) and recalls the old methodological debate whether hypotheses can be tested one-at-a-time or whether they should be tested jointly. In the latter case, an entire econometric model is required, which jointly determines all the endogenous or state variables. This methodological dichotomy may be summarized succinctly by "FIML v LIML" (full information maximum likelihood v limited information maximum likelihood). In the context of Eq. (2.6) this implies that hypotheses about β cannot be tested without investigating how x is determined. The multi-equation approach to cointegration, developed by Johansen (1988) is based on the view that hypotheses cannot be tested one-by-one. Johansen's method has become the gold standard for cointegration because it deals with the two methodological criticisms of the "asymptotic" approach of Granger and Engle. For example, in the popular time series software, EVIEWS, Johansen's method is the default option for cointegration.

Our view is that each method of cointegration has advantages and disadvantages. We do not think that there is a dominant method. We also think that the first criticism is more important than the second. We are wary of the ambitiousness of multi-equation approaches since they require that the model as a whole be correctly specified. If part of the model is incorrectly specified, specification failure may transmit itself to the parameters of interest since specification failure is contagious. A bad apple can ruin the whole barrel.

Single Equation Methods

Error correction implies cointegration and vice-versa. The Granger–Engle method tests directly for cointegration and subsequently estimates the error correction model as in Eq. (2.9). ECM tests for cointegration work the opposite way round. If there is error correction, there must be cointegration. First, a dynamic regression is estimated using the levels of y and x:

$$y_t = \alpha + \sum_{p=0}^{q} \beta_p x_{t-p} + \sum_{p=1}^{P} \pi_p y_{t-p} + v_t \tag{2.11a}$$

In Eq. (2.11a) q and P are chosen so that the residual error (v) is serially independent since dynamic misspecification typically induces serial correlation. Next, define:

$$y_t^* = \frac{\hat{\alpha}}{1-\hat{\pi}} + \kappa x_t \hat{\pi} = \sum_{p=1}^{q} \hat{\pi}_p \qquad \hat{\beta} = \sum_{p=0}^{P} \hat{\beta}_p \qquad \kappa = \frac{\hat{\beta}}{1-\hat{\pi}} \tag{2.11b}$$

y* is the theoretical value of y that would arise if x remained at its current level. Note that if q = P = 0 Eq. (2.11a) reverts to Eq. (2.6). The dynamics in Eq. (2.11a) are designed to refine the estimate of κ. In an "asymptotic" sample the probability limit of the estimate of β in Eq. (2.6) equals κ. Finally, Eq. (2.9) is estimated with $u = y - y^*$. The EC coefficient ξ is expected to be negative. The ECM cointegration test statistic (Ericsson and MacKinnon 2002) uses the t-statistic for the estimate of ξ. However, this estimate does not have a t-distribution. The critical value is −3.4 when T = 100 and p = 0.05.

Stock and Watson (1993) and Engle and Yoo (1991) among others have suggested different dynamic adjustments to Eq. (2.11a). Stock and Watson's DOLS methodology (dynamic OLS) supplements Eq. (2.6) with leads and lags of Δx. These leads and lags should not matter asymptotically. If the DOLS estimate of β differs from its OLS estimate ($\hat{\beta}$) this is because the sample is not asymptotic. Engle and Yoo's 3 step methodology regresses $\hat{e}_t$ obtained from Eq. (2.9) on x_t. Since e is stationary but x is not, the estimated coefficient $\hat{\varphi}$ is zero asymptotically. If it is not, the sample is not asymptotic and the corrected estimate of β is $\hat{\beta} - \hat{\varphi}/\hat{\xi}$.

Johansen's Method

We illustrate Johansen's method in the simplest possible context involving three I (1) variables, x, y and z, which are hypothesized to be cointegrated in Eq. (2.12a):

$$y_t = \beta_0 + \beta_1 x_t + \beta_2 z_t + u_t \tag{2.12a}$$

The null hypothesis is u ~ I(1). Error correction may apply to all three variables. The ECMs are:

$$\left.\begin{aligned}\Delta y_t &= \xi_1 u_{t-1} + e_{1t}\\ \Delta x_t &= \xi_2 u_{t-1} + e_{2t}\\ \Delta z_t &= \xi_3 u_{t-1} + e_{3t}\end{aligned}\right\} \tag{2.12b}$$

where the ξ's denote error correction coefficients. The ECMs assume for simplicity that the dynamics of all three variables are determined entirely by u. Substituting Eq. (2.12b) into Eq. (2.12a) implies:

$$\Delta y_t = \xi_1\beta_0 - \xi_1\beta_1 x_{t-1} - \xi_1\beta_2 z_{t-1} + \xi_1 y_{t-1} + e_{1t} \tag{2.12c}$$

$$\Delta x_t = \xi_2\beta_0 - \xi_2\beta_1 x_{t-1} - \xi_2\beta_2 z_{t-1} + \xi_2 y_{t-1} + e_{2t} \tag{2.12d}$$

$$\Delta z_t = \xi_3\beta_0 - \xi_3\beta_1 x_{t-1} - \xi_3\beta_2 z_{t-1} + \xi_3 y_{t-1} + e_{3t} \tag{2.12e}$$

Equations (2.12c)–(2.12e) may be vectorized into a vector error correction model (VECM):

$$\Delta Q_t = \Psi_o + \Psi Q_{t-1} + e_t \tag{2.12f}$$

where

$$Q' = (y\;x\;z) \quad e' = (e_1\;e_2\;e_3)$$

$$\Psi = \begin{pmatrix} \xi_1 & -\xi_1\beta_1 & -\xi_1\beta_2 \\ \xi_2 & -\xi_2\beta_1 & -\xi_2\beta_2 \\ \xi_3 & -\xi_3\beta_1 & -\xi_3\beta_2 \end{pmatrix} = \xi\beta' \quad \psi_0 = \beta_0\xi \quad \xi' = (\xi_1\;\xi_2\;\xi_3)$$

$$\beta' = (1\;\; -\beta_1\;\; -\beta_2)$$

Notice that because the matrix Ψ factorizes into two vectors (ξ and β) its rank is 1. If $\xi = 0$ because there is no error correction, the rank of Ψ is zero. Since error correction is the mirror image of cointegration, x, y and z are cointegrated if the null hypothesis that the rank of Ψ is zero can be rejected.

The rank of a matrix is determined by the number of its non-zero eigenvalues. Osterwald–Lenum (1992) computed critical values to test the null hypothesis that all or some of the eigenvalues are zero. If there is only one statistically significant eigenvalue there must be a unique cointegration vector (β), which is the eigenvector associated with this eigenvalue. This eigenvector is in fact u in Eq. (2.12a), which is stationary by definition. If there is more than one eigenvalue that is statistically significant so that the rank of $\hat{\Psi}$ is $r > 1$, there are r cointegrating vectors denoted by $u_1, u_2,..,u_r$, which are stationary. If $r = 0$ the variables are not cointegrated because there is no error correction.

Equations (2.12c)–(2.12e) are unlikely to provide a satisfactory explanation of the dynamics of the state variables, and may be generalized by adding lags of changes in the state variables so that they become:

$$\Delta Q_t = \Psi_0 + \Psi Q_{t-1} + \sum_{p=1}^{P} \Pi_p \Delta Q_{t-p} + e_t \tag{2.12g}$$

where Π_p is a matrix of VAR coefficients. If $P = 0$ Eq. (2.12g) reverts to Eq. (2.12f). If $\Psi = 0$ Eq. (2.12g) becomes a vector autoregression (VAR) rather than a VECM. Therefore, the VECM encompasses the VAR, and the latter is a special case of the former. However, the economic theory to be tested is embodied in Ψ rather than the VAR parameters (Π_p) since if Eq. (2.12a) is corroborated the rank of $\hat{\Psi}$ should be at least 1.

In practice, Eq. (2.12g) is estimated in two stages because the number of VECM parameters is typically large and equals $M + M^2(1 + P)$ where M is the number of variables. In Eq. (2.12a) $M = 3$. Therefore if $P = 4$ the VECM involves no less than 48 parameters to be estimated. Out of these, the parameters of interest include the 9 elements of Ψ while the 39 VAR parameters are "nuisance parameters". Since estimation is by ML, Johansen suggests that the nuisance parameters be "concentrated out" of the likelihood function in the first stage, while in the second stage the parameters of interest (Ψ) are estimated from the concentrated likelihood function. This is rather like seasonally adjusting data in the first stage, and then estimating the parameters of interest using seasonally adjusted data. In the present context the data are "cyclically adjusted" rather than seasonally adjusted.

In our opinion this is the Achilles Heel of Johansen's method. The method assumes that trend and cycle are independent. Although this is a standard assumption in much of macroeconomic theory, it is inconsistent with endogenous growth theory according to which economic development is path dependent. Another disadvantage of Johansen's method is that e in Eq. (2.12g) is assumed to be normally distributed. By contrast, the cointegration method of Granger and Engle does not make strong parametric assumptions about the distribution of the error terms. A third problem is that since Johansen's method is based on FIML, the model must be completely specified. This means that apart from Eq. (2.12a) for y, which is the model of interest, auxiliary hypotheses must be well specified for z and x. In practice researchers rarely do this, in which case FIML estimates for the structural coefficients in Eq. (2.12g) will be inconsistent.

2.7 Panel Cointegration

Just as unit root tests were first developed in a univariate context and subsequently extended to panel data, so cointegration tests were first developed for time series data and subsequently extended to panel data. Phillips and Moon (1999) showed that if panel data happen to be nonstationary, spurious and nonsense regression phenomena might arise in panel data contexts. Panel data parameter estimates are spurious if the error terms are nonstationary. If the error terms are stationary the variables in the model are panel cointegrated and the parameter estimates are genuine.

Panel cointegration tests along the lines of the Granger–Engle cointegration test have been developed by Pedroni (1999, 2004). Pedroni's group t test is the cointegration counterpart to the IPS panel unit root test discussed above. In this test cointegration tests are carried out for each of the N members of the panel, the N test statistics are averaged, and the average is compared to their critical values calculated by Pedroni. Notice that this test does not require that cointegration applies to all members of the panel. Westerlund (2007) has extended the ECM cointegration test to panel data, and Larsson et al. (2001) have extended Johansen's methodology to panel cointegration. Groen and Kleibergen (2003) extend Larrson et al. for cross-section dependence between the panel units. However, whereas Johansen's method is most popular in non-panel data contexts, the opposite is true in panel data contexts, where the most popular method is Pedroni's.

These panel cointegration tests assume that the panel units are independent (Groen and Kleibergen excepted). Banerjee and Carrion-I-Silvestre (2017) have calculated critical values for panel cointegration when the cross-section dependence between the panel units is strong. In this case Eq. (2.12a) would be:

$$y_{it} = \alpha_i + \beta x_{it} + \gamma z_{it} + \eta_{1i} y_t + \eta_{2i} x_t + \eta_{3i} z_t + u_{it} \tag{2.13}$$

where y, x and z are cross-section averages and the ηs are factor loadings. Their null hypothesis is that the error terms in Eq. (2.13) are nonstationary. This test is used in Chap. 10.

There is no counterpart to Eq. (2.13) for weak cross-section dependence. For example, the hypothesis involves spatial lagged variables:

$$y_{it} = \alpha_i + \beta x_{it} + \gamma z_{it} + \lambda y_{it} + \delta_1 \widetilde{x}_{it} + \delta_2 \widetilde{z}_{it} + u_{it} \tag{2.14}$$

where $\sim$ denotes spatial lags. In Chap. 7 we derive spatial panel cointegration tests for the error terms from Eq. (2.14).

2.8 Structural Vector Autoregressions

Vector autoregressions, or VARs for short, were popularized in macroeconomics almost 40 years ago (Sims 1980). This development was largely an expression of dissatisfaction and frustration with structural econometric models that had been the work-horse of macroeconometricians since the Klein–Goldberger model of the US economy was developed in the 1950s and 1960s. Several factors were involved in this methodological revolution. First, structural econometric models had been criticized by Lucas (1976) on the grounds that they ignored the way in which economic agents formed expectations of how macroeconomic policy was set. This criticism, commonly known as "The Lucas Critique", implies that structural economic models will be invalid if policy is changed. For example, models estimated using data for a fixed exchange rate regime will be invalid if, as happened after 1971, exchange rates were floated in the leading industrialized countries. The same applies to changes in the way monetary policy and fiscal policy are conducted e.g. the suspension of New Keynesian monetary policy since 2008. The Lucas Critique means that a model may become obsolescent as soon as it is used to engineer a change in policy. In short, there is a methodological Catch 22. A good model used to determine economic policy ceases to be a good model as soon as it is used by policy makers.

Secondly, macroeconometricians became increasingly aware of the methodological importance of nonstationarity in economic time series, following the seminal paper of Granger and Newbold (1974). The problems of spurious regression and nonsense regression had been discovered a long time ago by Yule (1897, 1926) but had been forgotten or at least overlooked. Macroeconomists began to suspect that their models were spurious, and as of the late 1970s there was no satisfactory methodological solution to this problem.

Third, economic instability and stagflation during the 1970s undermined confidence in models that failed to foresee these developments, or even to explain them ex post facto. This crisis of confidence had two manifestations, theoretical and econometric. The former involved the neoclassical counter-revolution in macroeconomic theory, which undermined the Keynesian foundations of existing econometric models. The latter involved existential skepticism about econometric models irrespective of their theoretical foundations. This skepticism harked back to the Keynes–Tinbergen debate. Keynes believed that econometric forecasting for policy design was not feasible.

For all these reasons macroeconomists such as Sims suggested VARs as a methodological alternative to structural econometric models. Since VARs are usually specified in first differences rather than levels, the problem of nonstationarity does not apply. Also, because VARs are atheoretical they do not pretend to be suitable for policy analysis, and focus instead upon the more modest task of forecasting the future rather than stating how policy might be used to affect the future. VAR modeling became popular very rapidly, largely because it demanded less intellectually of model proprietors. Indeed, it is still popular today.

Subsequently the gap between the structuralists and "VARists" has narrowed. First, as we explained in Chap. 1, structural VAR models (SVAR) offer structural rather than merely statistical interpretations of the economy by imposing untestable restrictions on the VAR parameters. Secondly, Bayesian VAR modelers (BVAR) estimated their VAR models subject to priors about parameters and impulse responses. Third, following the discovery of cointegration, the 1980s witnessed the development of vector error correction models (VECM), which encompass VAR models. Therefore VECMs, which use cointegration to test hypotheses about long term economic structure, use VARs to model their short-term dynamics.

We have already mentioned that the VAR model is a special case of the VECM. What turns Eq. (2.12g) into a VECM is the matrix Ψ. If this matrix is zero, the variables in the model are not cointegrated, and all that remains is the VAR model. It is obvious that because the variables do not cointegrate, the VAR model cannot be used to test hypotheses about the relationship between the variables, because this hypothesis has already been rejected. In short, VAR models are purely statistical and in their own right cannot be used to test hypotheses in economics when the data are nonstationary. Since the vast majority of economic time series data are nonstationary, this is a major limitation.

We introduce SVARs in the simplest context in which y and x are simultaneously related and depend upon mutual first order lags. Also, y and x are assumed to be stationary, since this is a requirement of VAR modeling. The structural model is:

$$y_t = \alpha_1 + \gamma_1 x_t + \pi_{11} y_{t-1} + \pi_{12} x_{t-1} + \varepsilon_t \tag{2.15a}$$

$$x_t = \alpha_2 + \gamma_2 y_t + \pi_{21} y_{t-1} + \pi_{22} x_{t-1} + e_t \tag{2.15b}$$

where for simplicity ε and e are iid and mutually independent. The structural model contains ten structural parameters consisting of two intercepts, six slope coefficients, σ_ε and σ_e. Solving Eqs. (2.15a) and (2.15b) for y_t and x_t gives:

$$y_t = a_{10} + a_{11} y_{t-1} + a_{12} x_{t-1} + v_t \tag{2.15c}$$

$$x_t = a_{20} + a_{21} y_{t-1} + a_{22} x_{t-1} + w_t \tag{2.15d}$$

where:

$$a_{10} = \frac{\alpha_1 + \gamma_1 \alpha_2}{1 - \gamma_1 \gamma_2} \quad a_{11} = \frac{\pi_{11} + \gamma_1 \pi_{21}}{1 - \gamma_1 \gamma_2} \quad a_{12} = \frac{\pi_{12} + \gamma_1 \pi_{22}}{1 - \gamma_1 \gamma_2} \quad v_t = \frac{\varepsilon_t + \gamma_1 e_t}{1 - \gamma_1 \gamma_2}$$

$$a_{20} = \frac{\alpha_2 + \gamma_2 \alpha_{10}}{1 - \gamma_1 \gamma_2} \quad a_{21} = \frac{\gamma_{21} + \gamma_2 \gamma_{11}}{1 - \gamma_1 \gamma_2} \quad a_{22} = \frac{\gamma_{21} + \gamma_2 \gamma_{12}}{1 - \gamma_1 \gamma_2} \quad w_t = \frac{e_t + \gamma_2 \varepsilon_t}{1 - \gamma_1 \gamma_2}$$

Notice that Eqs. (2.15c) and (2.15d) constitute a VAR model in which v_t and w_t covary:

$$\operatorname{cov}(w_t v_t) = \frac{\gamma_1 \sigma_e^2 + \gamma_2 \sigma_\varepsilon^2}{(1 - \gamma_1 \gamma_2)^2} \tag{2.15e}$$

and the variances of the VAR innovations are equal to:

$$\operatorname{var}(v) = \frac{\sigma_\varepsilon^2 + \gamma_1^2 \sigma_e^2}{(1 - \gamma_1 \gamma_2)^2} \tag{2.15f}$$

$$\operatorname{var}(w) = \frac{\sigma_e^2 + \gamma_2^2 \sigma_\varepsilon^2}{(1 - \gamma_1 \gamma_2)^2} \tag{2.15g}$$

The VAR model contains nine parameters comprising the six *a* coefficients in Eqs. (2.15c) and (2.15d), and three elements of its residual variance-covariance matrix in Eqs. (2.15e)–(2.15g). These VAR parameters depend upon the ten structural parameters in Eqs. (2.15a) and (2.15b). Since there are ten structural parameters and only nine VAR parameters, it is impossible to solve the former from the latter. There is an identification deficit of 1. Equations (2.15a) and (2.15b) cannot be estimated consistently by OLS since y_t and x_t are determined simultaneously. Nor can they be estimated by IV because there are insufficient instrumental variables to identify the parameters.

This deficit may be artificially closed by imposing a priori restrictions on the structural parameters. For example, the long term relationship between y and x that is implied by the structural model is:

$$y^* = \frac{\pi_{12} + \gamma_1}{1 - \pi_{11}} x^* = kx^* \tag{2.15h}$$

If k = 1 y is linear homogeneous in x, so that in the long run y increases proportionately with x. For example, if y denotes inflation and x the rate of growth of the supply of money, money neutrality implies that k = 1. Or if k = 0 there is no long-term relationship between y and x. For example, if y denotes inflation and x denotes the rate of unemployment, vertical Phillips Curve theory predicts that $\kappa = 0$. Equation (2.15h) adds a tenth equation to the nine VAR parameters, closes the identification deficit and identifies all the structural parameters. Having thus "identified" the structural parameters it is possible to solve for the structural disturbances or innovations ε_t and e_t.

Other identifying assumptions are based on Choleski factorizations in which variables are related sequentially so that y_n depends contemporaneously on y_{n-1}, y_{n-2} etc., y_{n-1} depends contemporaneously on y_{n-2}, y_{n-3} etc., and so on until y_1 does not depend contemporaneously on other variables in the VAR. In the structural model in Eqs. (2.15a) and (2.15b) y_t and x_t are jointly determined. Choleski factorization would assume in this case that the relationship between y and x is recursive. For example, if $\gamma_1 = 0$, x_t depends upon y_t but y_t does not depend upon x_t. Choleski factorization eliminates the identification deficit by arbitrarily imposing recursivity. If the recursion is reversed so that $\gamma_2 = 0$ instead of γ_1, i.e. y_t depends upon x_t but x_t does not depend upon y_t, the structural parameters that are identified by the VAR model will be different. This means that the estimated structural parameters are as arbitrary as the ordering of the variables in the Choleski decomposition.

There is, however, no way of testing these identifying restrictions. For example, the assumption that k = 0 or 1 cannot be tested. Nor can the ordering of the Choleski factorization be subjected to empirical testing. Typically, such untestable identifying assumptions are of greater scientific interest than the structural parameters, such as γ_{12}, that they "identify". We therefore see SVARs as post-modern constructions that provide theoretical narratives for interpreting the past rather than as a methodology for testing hypotheses that may be used for policy planning regarding the future.

The structural model represented by Eqs. (2.15a) and (2.15b) is intentionally simple. The number of variables (M) is 2 and the order of the VAR (P) is 1. More generally the number of unknown structural parameters is S = M[M(1 + P) + 1] and the number of VAR parameters is V = M[1 + MP + ½(1 + M)]. Subtracting the latter from the former gives the identification deficit as D = S − V = ½ M(M − 1). Notice that the identification deficit does not depend on the VAR order, P, and it increases with the square of the number of variables participating in the VAR. D = 1 when M = 2, as in Eqs. (2.15a) and (2.15b). In a typical VAR model with M = 5, the identification deficit is 10. This means that the SVAR requires its proprietor to impose no less than ten identifying restrictions, none of which can be tested.

In the structural model it was assumed that e and ε are independent. Suppose, however, that these structural shocks are correlated with cov(eε) = ϖ. This increases the number of structural parameters from 10 to 11. The reader may check that Eqs. (2.15e)–(2.15g) consequently depend on ϖ. Since the number of VAR parameters does not change, the identification deficit is 2 instead of 1. If the structural shocks are correlated the identification deficit increases to D = M(M − 1), i.e. it is twice as large than in the previous paragraph. If M = 5 the VAR model proprietor must now make as many as 20 arbitrary restrictions to "identify" the SVAR.

Apart from the identification deficit, a further problem in SVARs is that the data have to be stationary. Since most economic data are nonstationary in the temporal sense, this typically means that the SVAR is estimated using data in first-differences rather than levels. In terms of Eq. (2.12a) this involves Δy and Δx instead of y and x. We have already pointed out that if the hypothesis to be tested is in levels of y and x, it cannot be tested by using data on Δy and Δx.

In summary, SVAR models provide post-modern narratives of history since they rely on non-testable, or immaculate, identifying assumptions.

2.9 Causality, Exogeneity and Predictability

For cross-section data the definition of exogeneity is much simpler than it is for time-series data. Take, for example, the following model in which y and x happen to be stationary:

$$y_t = \alpha + \beta x_t + \pi y_{t-1} + u_t \tag{2.16a}$$

$$x_t = \mu + \theta y_{t-1} + v_t \tag{2.16b}$$

$$u_t = \tau u_{t-1} + \phi v_t + \varepsilon_t \tag{2.16c}$$

where ε and v are assumed to be iid. The parameters of interest are β and π, i.e. we are mainly interested in Eq. (2.16a).

We begin by making the observation that since y_{t-1} depends directly on u_{t-1} and u_t depends on u_{t-1} through τ, it cannot be the case that u_t and y_{t-1} are independent in Eq. (2.16a). This means that OLS estimates of π are biased upwards if τ > 0. The solution to this problem is to estimate the model by GLS rather than OLS.

What about β? x_t cannot be independent of u_t because both x_t and u_t depend on v_t. Furthermore, x_t depends on y_{t-1} via θ. Since we have already established that y_{t-1} and u_t are related, it must be the case that x_t and u_t are related. For both of these reasons x_t and u_t are dependent in which case β is not identified. If, however,

$\phi = \tau = 0$, both x_t and y_{t-1} are independent of u_t in which case x_t and y_{t-1} are "weakly exogenous" for β and π. Why "weakly exogenous"? It is obvious that x depends on y via θ, so x is not exogenous in its usual meaning. What is important is that x_t depends on y_{t-1} rather than y_t. Provided $\phi = \pi = 0$, the parameters of interest are identified despite the dynamic dependence of x upon y. If in addition, $\theta = 0$, x would be "strongly exogenous". However, for purposes of estimation, all we require is weak exogeneity, which in the present context requires the error terms be serially independent ($\pi = 0$) and that the error terms of x and y be independent ($\phi = 0$).

The difference between strong and weak exogeneity does not arise in cross-section data because sequencing or the timing of variables only arises in time series data. Generally speaking the main threat to weak exogeneity is serial correlation. It is therefore particularly important not to treat serial correlation as a nuisance, which may be "dealt with" by GLS or by calculating robust standard errors. In terms of Eq. (2.16a) GLS is consistent if $\beta = 0$, but is not consistent otherwise.

If x_t is weakly exogenous for β there is a causal effect of x_t on y_t. According to Eq. (2.16b) x_t may change for two reasons, either because v_t changed or because y_{t-1} changed. Notice that the latter is also a causal effect. Therefore, u_{t-1} has a causal effect on y_t via x_t.

This kind of causality should not be confused with "Granger Causality", which is about predictability rather than causality. Predictability and causality are different phenomena. Indeed, just because we have found the cause of some phenomenon does not mean that it can be predicted. Also, just because we can predict a phenomenon does not mean that we have discovered its cause. However, in some cases causality implies predictability. For example, the one-step ahead prediction of y in the above model is:

$$E_t(y_{t+1}) = \hat{\alpha} + \hat{\beta}E_t(x_{t+1}) + \hat{\pi}y_t = \hat{\alpha} + \hat{\beta}\hat{\mu} + (\hat{\beta}\hat{\theta} + \hat{\pi})y_t \tag{2.16d}$$

This prediction is informative because there is a causal effect of x_t upon y_t, and x_t depends on y_{t-1}. In this case causality and predictability coincide. Had θ been zero x would be an unpredictable random variable. Therefore, it would not have been possible to use information on x to predict y despite the fact that there is a causal effect of x on y.

Finally, x may predict y without there being a causal effect of x upon y. For example, cooking predicts eating because cooking precedes eating. However, cooking does not cause eating. Hunger is the joint cause of both cooking and eating. Nevertheless, information about cooking is useful for predicting eating. Cooking "Granger-causes" eating. More generally, x Granger-causes y if given past values of y, past values of x predict y. In Eq. (2.15c) x Granger-causes y if a_{12} is statistically significant. In Eq. (2.15d) y Granger-causes x if a_{21} is statistically significant. If both a_{12} and a_{21} are statistically significant there is two-way Granger causality. Equations (2.15c) and (2.15d) test for first order Granger causality because they contain only one lag. More generally, one may test for higher order Granger causality.

If x Granger-causes y this means that, conditional upon lags of y, lags of x predict y. If in Eqs. (2.15c) and (2.15d) the error terms (w and v) happen to be serially independent Granger causality might coincide with causality. For example, if in Eq. (2.15c) x_{t-1} is weakly exogenous, a_{12} has a causal interpretation. Not only does x_{t-1} predict y_t, it also has a causal effect on y_t. More generally, Granger causality is concerned with sequencing rather than causality. Life would be much less predictable in the absence of sequencing.

2.10 Cointegration, Causality and Identification

Suppose y and x in Eq. (2.6) happen to be cointegrated. The fact that x appears on the right hand side of Eq. (2.6) does not mean that β is the causal effect of x on y. Recall, that we have already argued that whether y is regressed on x, or vice-versa, makes no difference asymptotically to the estimate of β. Instead, β expresses the long-run relation between y and x so that y tends to $\alpha + \beta x$, or x tends to $-\alpha/\beta + y/\beta$. Because y and x are cointegrated, the null hypothesis that y and x are unrelated in the long-run is rejected. Consequently, the cointegration test is informative; something has been learnt.

The literature is replete with empirical examples. For example, purchasing power parity (PPP) theory predicts that $\ln P = \alpha + \beta \ln E + \gamma \ln P^* + u$ where P denotes the domestic price level, P* denotes the foreign price level, and E denotes the exchange rate. If lnP, lnP* and lnE are difference stationary PPP predicts that $\beta = \gamma = 1$ and that u is stationary. For small open economies P* is exogenous, but P and E are obviously endogenous and mutually dependent. Consequently there is a causal effect of lnP* on ln(P/E), but although P and E are related in the long-run, their causal nexus is not revealed.

The error correction model, such as Eq. (2.9), is informative about the direction of causality. If the γ coefficients are statistically significance, and e is serially uncorrelated lagged x is weakly exogenous for γ, in which case lagged Δx has a causal effect on current Δy. If the error correction model is specified with Δx on the left hand side of Eq. (2.9) and lagged values of Δy are statistically significant, there would be causal effects of lagged Δy on current Δx. Indeed, these causal effects might run in both directions. The principle of weak exogeneity means that there may be causal effects of x on y and of y on x. It is not a contradiction. In this sense causality in time series is different to causality in cross-section data, because weak exogeneity does not apply to cross-section data. Alternatively, because time series data are sequenced whereas sequencing does not apply to cross-section data, causality may be two-way in time series whereas it can only be one-way in cross-section data.

2.11 Autoregressive Conditional Heteroscedasticity (ARCH)

Suppose in Eq. (2.6) that y and x are stationary and that x is exogenous. It is well-known that if u is heteroscedastic the OLS estimate of β is consistent but the estimate of the variance of β is not consistent. The solution to this problem is WLS (weighted least squares) or the calculation of robust standard errors. This heteroscedasticity is unconditional, which arises in cross-section data.

By contrast in time series data there are two types of heteroscedasticity, unconditional and conditional. The ARCH model, originally proposed by Engle (1982), is the simplest representation of the latter. Denoting the variance of u_t by σ_t^2 the first order ARCH model is:

$$\sigma_t^2 = a + b\sigma_{t-1}^2 \tag{2.17a}$$

where b denotes the ARCH coefficient, which expresses how volatility in period t depends on volatility in the previous period. The conditional volatility at time t equals $a + b\sigma_{t-1}^2$. If volatility mean-reverts $b > 0$ must be less than 1. In this case volatility mean-reverts to its unconditional value:

$$\sigma^2 = \frac{a}{1-b} \tag{2.17b}$$

Whereas conditional volatility depends on time, unconditional volatility does not depend on time. Therefore, unconditional volatility is homoscedastic whereas conditional volatility is heteroscedastic. Because the classical assumptions refer to unconditional homoscedasticity, ARCH does not affect the properties of least squares estimates. In nonlinear models, however, matters are different. Matters would also be different if a and b depended on time. To estimate a and b current and lagged volatility are represented by squares of the current and lagged error terms.

ARCH models imply that the confidence limits of model forecasts depend on time. Confidence intervals will be larger if the errors were larger. Conversely, they are smaller if the model errors were smaller. It is obvious that ARCH models have revolutionized the presentation of model forecasts and projections. The basic ARCH model has been generalized to allow for higher order dynamics (GARCH) and stochastic volatility modelling introduces stochastic effects into Eq. (2.17a). Also various nonlinear ARCH models have been proposed including threshold effects and structural breaks. Finally, VECH models refer to vectors of variables in which volatility depends on the lagged volatility of other variables as well as its own volatility.

The ideas and concepts reported in this chapter will be used extensively in what follows. Needless to say, the contents of this chapter are not intended to be a substitute for study of these topics. We recommend Hamilton (1994) and Hendry (1995) for further reference, and Enders (2004) for a more practical treatment of time series. We recommend Baltagi (2013, Chap. 12) and Pesaran (2015, Chap. 29) for further reference regarding nonstationary panel data.

Having introduced basic ideas in the econometric analysis of time series, in the next chapter we do the same for spatial econometrics.

References

Baltagi BH (2013) Econometric analysis of panel data, 5th edn. Wiley, Chichester
Baltagi BH, Bresson G, Pirotte A (2007) Panel unit root tests and spatial dependence. J Appl Economet 22(2):339–360
Banerjee A, Carrion-I-Silvestre JL (2017) Testing for panel cointegration using common correlated effects estimators. J Time Ser Anal 38:610–636
Davidson JEH (1994) Stochastic limit theory: an introduction for econometricians. Oxford University Press, Oxford
Davidson R, MacKinnon JG (2009) Econometric theory and methods. Oxford University Press, New York
Dickey D, Fuller W (1981) Likelihood ratio tests for autoregressive processes with a unit root. Econometrica 49:1057–1072
Elliot G, Rothenberg T, Stock J (1996) Efficient tests for an autoregressive unit root. Econometrica 64:813–836
Enders W (2004) Applied time series analysis, 2nd edn. John Wiley, New York
Engle R (1982) Autoregressive conditional heteroscedasticity and with estimates of the variance of United Kingdom inflations. Econometrica 50:987–1008
Engle R, Granger CWJ (1987) Co-integration and error correction: representation, estimation and testing. Econometrica 35:251–276
Engle RF, Yoo BS (1991) Cointegrated economic time series: an overview with new results. In: Engle RF, Granger CWJ (eds) Long run economic relationships: readings in cointegration. Oxford University Press, Oxford
Ericsson NR, MacKinnon JG (2002) Distributions for error correction tests for cointegration. Econ J 5:285–318
Granger CWJ, Newbold P (1974) Spurious regressions in econometrics. J Econ 2:111–120
Groen J, Kleibergen F (2003) Likelihood-based cointegration analysis in panels of vector error-correction models. J Bus Econ Stat 21:295–317
Hadri K (2000) Testing for stationarity in heterogeneous panel data. Econ J 3:148–161
Hamilton J (1994) Time series analysis. Princeton University Press, Princeton, NJ
Hendry DF (1995) Dynamic econometrics. Oxford University Press, Oxford
Im K, Pesaran MH, Shin Y (2003) Testing for unit roots in heterogeneous panels. J Econ 115:53–74
Johansen S (1988) Statistical analysis of cointegration vectors. J Econ Dyn Control 12:231–254
Kwiatowski D, Phillips PCB, Schmidt P, Shin Y (1992) Testing the null hypothesis of stationarity against the alternative of a unit root: how sure are we that economic time series have a unit root. J Econ 54:159–178
Larsson R, Lyhagen J, Löthgren M (2001) Likelihood-based cointegration tests in heterogeneous panels. Econ J 4:109–142
Li H, Maddala GS (1997) Bootstrapping cointegrated regressions. J Econ 80:297–318
Lucas RE (1976) Econometric policy evaluation: a critique. Carn-Roch Conf Ser Public Policy 1:19–46
MacKinnon JG (1996) Numerical distribution functions for unit root and cointegration tests. J Appl Economet 11:601–618
Maddala GS, Kim I-M (1999) Unit roots, cointegration and structural change. Cambridge University Press, Cambridge
Osterwald-Lenum M (1992) A note with quantiles of the asymptotic distribution of the maximum likelihood cointegration rank test statistics. Oxf Bull Econ Stat 54:461–471
Pedroni P (1999) Critical values for cointegration tests in heterogeneous panels with multiple regressors. Oxf Bull Econ Stat 61:653–670
Pedroni P (2004) Panel cointegration: asymptotic and finite sample properties of pooled time series tests with an application to the PPP hypothesis. Economet Theor 20:597–625
Pesaran MH (2007) A simple panel unit root test in the presence of cross section dependence. J Appl Economet 22(2):265–310

Pesaran MH (2015) Time series and panel data econometrics. Oxford University Press, Oxford
Phillips PCB (1986) Understanding spurious regressions in econometrics. J Econ 33(3):311–340
Phillips PCB, Moon H (1999) Linear regression limit theory for nonstationary panel data. Econometrica 67:1057–1011
Phillips PCB, Perron P (1988) Testing for a unit root in time series regression. Biometrika 75:335–346
Shin Y (1994) A residual-based test of the null of cointegration against the alternative of no cointegration. Economet Theor 10:91–115
Sims CA (1980) Macroeconomics and reality. Econometrica 58:1–48
Stock J (1987) Asymptotic properties of least squares estimates of cointegrating vectors. Econometrica 55:1035–1056
Stock JH, Watson MW (1993) A simple estimator of cointegrating vectors in higher order integrated systems. Econometrica 61(4):783–820
Westerlund J (2007) Testing for error correction in panel based data. Oxf Bull Econ Stat 69 (6):709–748
Yule GU (1897) On the theory of correlation. J R Stat Soc 60:812–854
Yule GU (1926) Why do we sometimes get nonsense-correlations between time series? A study in sampling and the nature of time series. J R Stat Soc 89:1–64

References

Pesaran MH (2015) Time series and panel data econometrics. Oxford University Press, Oxford
Phillips PCB (1986) Understanding spurious regressions in econometrics. J Econom 33(3):311
Phillips PCB, Moon R (1999) Linear regression limit theory for nonstationary panel data

Chapter 3
Spatial Data Analysis and Econometrics

3.1 Introduction

In Chap. 2 we surveyed key concepts and developments in the econometric analysis of time series, which may be unfamiliar to spatial econometricians, but are essential to the understanding of the econometric analysis of nonstationary spatial panel data. In the present chapter, we survey key concepts in the econometric analysis of spatial data, which may be unfamiliar to time series econometricians, but are essential to the understanding of the econometric analysis of nonstationary panel data. Just as we suggested that Chap. 2 may be skipped by time series practitioners, so we suggest that the present chapter may be skipped by those familiar with spatial econometrics. We note, however, that whereas practitioners of spatial econometrics typically have some familiarity with the econometrics of time series, practitioners of time series econometrics usually have no familiarity with spatial econometrics for reasons given in Chap. 1. Indeed, spatial econometricians have incorporated advances in times series analysis to improve their understanding of concepts such as spatial dependence and spatial scale. The current explosion in computing power and geo-coded information has put space and distance squarely back on the agenda such that notions of 'the death of distance' (Cairncross 1997) have been greatly exaggerated.

The intellectual moorings of spatial econometrics is probably Cliff and Ord's (1969) seminal paper on 'The Problem of Spatial Autocorrelation'. This marked the collaboration of statistics with geography in an attempt to apply statistical theory to spatial data. Over time, this fusion spawned two sub disciplines. Within statistics, the emergence of the field of spatial statistics was marked by the publication of volumes by Ripley (1981) and Cressie (1993). These were concerned with the analysis of spatial patterns and spatial stochastic variation using implicitly spatial (geo-referenced) data. In the world of econometrics, the sub-field of spatial econometrics began to take root at roughly the same time as evinced by Paelinck and Klaassen's *Spatial Econometrics* in 1979. They defined the new field as concerned

M. Beenstock, D. Felsenstein, *The Econometric Analysis of Non-Stationary Spatial Panel Data*, Advances in Spatial Science,
https://doi.org/10.1007/978-3-030-03614-0_3

with spatial dependence and spatial asymmetries in economic relationships between places, and the explicit incorporation of space in urban and regional modeling. Intellectual histories of spatial econometrics consider the publication of this book as a watershed event (Anselin 2010; Florax and van der Vlist 2003).

The academic antecedents of the synthesis of time series and spatial analysis is harder to trace. Bartlett (1955) and Whittle (1954) observed that notions from time series could be extended to the analysis of spatial data, but they drew attention to conceptual differences between time and space. Most importantly, whereas time is linear, sequential and unidirectional because time moves forward in equal steps, space is nonlinear, non-sequential and multi-directional because space has no ordering, it has several dimensions (north-south, east-west), and it is usually not measured in equal steps. In time series data there is only one coordinate (t); t − 1 occurs before t and the difference between t − 1 and t is always 1. By contrast, spatial data need at least two coordinates, latitude (m) and longitude (n), there is no sequencing within and between m and n and the distance between them is variant. Moreover, spatial data consist of areas rather than points in space. Because these areas vary by shape and size the distance between them is not constant.

Perhaps the first attempt at synthesizing spatial analysis and time series can be attributed to Bennett (1979) with the publication of *Spatial Time Series*. The preface of the volume articulates a goal of serving as a 'bridging function . . . between spatial analysis procedures and the wider fields of engineering, econometrics and statistics for which most of the theory of non-spatial systems has been developed to date' (p. ii). The volume then proceeds to present a systems-analytic approach to understanding environmental and socio-economic systems that operate over both space and time such as geomorphological change on the one hand and labor market processes on the other. While the book is cognizant of spatial and temporal dependence, the treatment of these issues and those of spatial non-stationarity and spatial heterogeneity is very different to that of modern-day spatial and time series econometrics and reflects the 'pre unit-root econometrics' era. Furthermore, the volume is strangely silent on the issue of spatial panel data in which distinct spatial patterns may arise due to both local clustering and pervasive common factors such as climate or macroeconomic developments. The former represents weak spatial (cross sectional) dependence between units while the latter indicates strong, aggregate dependence generated by shocks that affect the spatial units differentially. Bennett implicitly assumed that the data are stationary, both temporally and spatially as did many other authors writing before the "unit root revolution" of the 1980s.

3.2 The Nature of Spatial Data

Spatial data are inherently 'messy' especially in the social sciences. In the natural sciences surfaces may be measured by two dimensional grids, or by three dimensional blocs e.g. the atmosphere in meteorology and oceans in oceanography. In the social sciences spatial data come in all sorts of shapes and sizes due to the chaotic development of the spatial economy. Spatial data are collected from 'the field' be that the archive, the survey, or the social media. As such, they do not neatly adhere to the conventions of classic statistical measurement for stochastic modeling, thereby violating iid assumptions made in standard statistical inference and hypothesis testing. As mentioned, spatial data are generally not equally spaced as are time series data. Spatial observations may be aggregates, such that the dependence structure in the data may change as new observations are added, thereby inducing spatial nonstationarity. Moreover, the locations that form the building blocks of spatial data may be endogenous since the locational choices of households and firms may not be independent of the characteristics of these locations, including their physical and socioeconomic amenities, such as climate, quality of schools and government incentives. The same applies to the realm of non-geographic space. Firms locate in a particular product space in order to maximize profits. Their 'location' is therefore endogenous. Instrumenting for this choice of location and its 'distance' from other product locations is difficult. It is for this reason that locational choice is mainly considered exogenous, and the characteristics of places are considered as given.

Units of time are fundamentally different in these respects from units of space. The realization of a variable during time t does not depend on how time is measured in the way that the realization of a variable in spatial unit i may depend on how space is measured. For example, annual GDP is simply the sum of quarterly GDP. Time aggregation does not involve conceptual issues in the measurement of GDP. Matters are different when spatial units are aggregated. Combining spatial units A and B inevitably conceals migration between A and B, and may also conceal differences in the structure of economic activity e.g. agriculture versus manufacturing.

On the other hand, spatial data may have econometric advantages. Pinske and Slade (2010) note that while endogeneity issues may pervade spatial data, they tend also to offer more instrumental variables for handling these issues because, as already noted, higher order spatial lags are imperfectly correlated with their lower order counterparts. The first order spatial lag for unit i ($\tilde{y}_i$) is imperfectly correlated with its second-order spatial lag ($\tilde{\tilde{y}}_i$), hence the latter can be used as an instrumental variable for the former. For example, higher order spatial lags of exogenous variables may serve as instrumental variables for the spatial lag of house prices.

Additionally, spatial data are unlikely to be spatially stationary. Spatial stationarity, as discussed in Chap. 5, arises when the sample moments in spatial cross-section data are independent of where in space they are measured. Weak spatial stationarity applies when first (means) and second (variances and covariances) moments are independent of space. Strong spatial stationarity applies when higher order moments are also independent of space. Many spatial processes exhibit highly irregular (non-smooth) behavior in their covariance structure. For example, boundaries between different locations or geomorphological patterns based on non-uniform geology may induce sharp changes in covariances across space, thereby inducing spatial nonstationarity. Although Tobler's First Law of Geography implies that spatial covariances tend to zero with the distance between them, this is not a sufficient condition for stationarity (as it would be in time series data) as noted by Granger (1969).

As noted in Chap. 1, spatial asymptotics are inherently different to temporal asymptotics. Since infill-asymptotics are not appropriate for socioeconomic data, we focus on increasing-domain asymptotics. Regarding the latter, in Chap. 1 we distinguished between edge effects that are immovable, and edge effects induced by sampling. On the one hand, dependence between spatial units intuitively slows down the rate of asymptotic convergence relative to independent cross-section data. On the other hand, as we shall see in Chap. 5, the higher dimensionality of spatial data makes it easier to detect spurious correlation in nonstationary spatial data than in nonstationary time series data. As noted by Cressie (1993), matters are different when the data are stationary; in two-dimensional space the central limit theorem may cease to apply. Moreover, for national datasets such as US states, the edges of space are immovable in which case increasing-domain asymptotics are no longer applicable (Cressie 1993; Wooldridge 2010; Elhorst 2014). Whereas T is conceptually infinite, matters are different regarding space, which is inherently fixed if edges are immovable, and especially as far as social sciences are concerned where borders are created through physical barriers, geopolitics, language, religion and culture.

Spatial data differ from time series data in that the area over which they are compiled may be configured in many arbitrary ways. This gives rise to the "modifiable areal unit problem" (MAUP) first identified by Yule and Kendall (1950) and discussed further below. MAUP posits that statistical results can vary depending on the way data are apportioned to spatial units of different sizes (the scale issue). In addition, even when base areal units are of similar size or scale, variation in results can arise due to the topology or zoning system used. MAUP therefore comprises two related issues driven by the nature of spatial data.

The analysis of spatial data requires attention to spatial heterogeneity, spatial dependence and spatial scale. All three are mutually connected: the appropriate modeling of spatial heterogeneity depends on choice of scale and the correct choice of scale increases prediction accuracy and mitigates spatial dependence.

3.3 Spatial Connectivity

Spatial dependence is characterized through the connectivity matrix (W), which is specified exogenously. If there are N spatial units, W is an $N \times N$ matrix with elements w_{ij} where $i = 1,2,\ldots,N$. These elements express the spatial relation between unit i and j. Since unit i cannot have a spatial relationship with itself $w_{ii} = 0$, i.e. the leading diagonal of W is zero. There are many ways of specifying W. For example, if only contiguous units are related, w_{ij} is zero if units i and j are not contiguous. In this case W is a sparse matrix because most of its elements are zero. If spatial connectivity is defined in terms of the distance between units i and j d_{ij}, W will no longer be sparse but it will be symmetric, i.e. $w_{ij} = w_{ji}$ because $d_{ij} = d_{ji}$. If spatial connectivity takes account of the relative sizes of units i and j so that w_{ij} depends on the size of unit i relative to the size of unit j, W will be asymmetric because w_{ij} does not equal w_{ji}. A key issue in spatial econometrics involves the specification of W (LeSage and Pace 2014; Qu and Lee 2015). We shall have more to say about this matter in Chap. 4, where we discuss specification tests for alternative definitions of W, and where we consider whether W can be estimated instead of being specified exogenously.

W is usually normalized so that its row elements sum to one, i.e. $\sum_{j \neq 1}^{N} w_{ij} = 1$. The spatial lag of y_i is defined as $\tilde{y}_i = \sum_{j \neq i}^{N} w_{ij} y_j$, which is a weighted average of y in spatial units outside unit i. The N-vector of spatial lags may be written as $\tilde{y} = Wy$. Powers of W express higher order spatial lags. For example, $W\tilde{y} = W^2 y = \tilde{\tilde{y}}$ denotes the second order spatial lag of y.

3.4 The Spatial Lag Model

Let y be an N-vector of observations on the dependent variable in a cross-section of N spatial units, X is a K × N matrix of observations on the independent variables (including an intercept), and ε is a vector of iid errors. The basic spatial model is:

$$y = X\beta + \lambda\tilde{y} + \tilde{X}\delta + u \tag{3.1a}$$

$$u = \rho\tilde{u} + \varepsilon \tag{3.1b}$$

Spatial variables are denoted by tildes. For example, $\tilde{x} = Wx$. In Eq. (3.1a) λ denotes the "spatial autoregressive" or SAR coefficient, and δ denotes the vector of "spatial Durbin" coefficients. In Eq. (3.1b) ρ denotes the "spatial autocorrelation" or SAC coefficient. The SAR coefficient induces spatial spillover because y_i depends on y_j unless $\lambda = 0$. The SAC coefficient induces a second type of spatial spillover because u_i depends on u_j unless $\rho = 0$. The spatial Durbin coefficient induces a third type of spatial spillover because y_i depends on x_{kj} unless $\delta_k = 0$.

The general solution for y is obtained by substituting $\tilde{y} = Wy$ in Eq. (3.1a) and $\tilde{u} = Wu$ in Eq. (3.1b), and then solving the result y:

$$\begin{aligned} y &= AX\beta + C\tilde{X}\delta + D\varepsilon \\ C &= AW \\ A &= (I - \lambda W)^{-1} \\ B &= (I - \rho W)^{-1} \\ D &= AB \end{aligned} \tag{3.2}$$

According to Eq. (3.2) the partial derivative of y_i with respect to x_k in spatial unit j is:

$$\frac{\partial y_i}{\partial x_{kj}} = \beta_k a_{ij} + \delta_k c_{ij} \tag{3.3}$$

where a and c are elements of A and C. The first component is induced by the spatial lagged dependent variable; an increase in x_k in unit j affects y_j through β_k, which spills-over onto y_i. The second component is induced by the spatial Durbin lag; an increase in x_{kj} spills over directly onto y_i through δ_k. If the SAR coefficient (λ) is positive a_{ii} exceeds unity; an increase in x_k in unit i affects y_i directly, which in turn affects y_j. The latter reverberates back onto y_i hence the multiplier exceeds 1. If the SAR coefficient is negative a_{ii} is less than 1.

Because a_{ij} and c_{ij} vary by i and j, they are spatially state dependent. Investigators might be interested in three aggregations of Eq. (3.3). The first refers to the average own impulse response (when j = i):

$$\frac{1}{N}\sum_{i=1}^{N}\frac{\partial y_i}{\partial x_{ki}} = \beta_k \frac{1}{N} traceA + \delta_k \frac{1}{N} traceC \tag{3.4a}$$

Equation (3.4a) includes the direct effect of an increase in x_k in unit i on y_i, which equals β_k in all units, as well as the indirect effects via the spatial lag coefficient (λ) and the spatial Durbin lag coefficient (δ_k). Therefore, the average indirect effect is Eq. (3.4a) minus β_k. This average indirect effect has become a standard feature in most spatial econometric software.

The second refers to the average spatial impulse response for unit i when x_k increases globally and not just locally:

$$\frac{1}{N}\sum_{j=1}^{N}\frac{\partial y_i}{\partial x_{kj}} = \beta_k \sum_{j=1}^{N} a_{ij} + \delta_k \sum_{j=1}^{N} c_{ij} \tag{3.4b}$$

Whereas Eq. (3.4a) refers to the average own impulse response for all spatial units when x_k increases locally, Eq. (3.4b) refers to the average impulse response for region i when x_k increases globally. If β, δ and λ are positive, Eq. (3.4b) must be larger than Eq. (3.4a). The third aggregate refers to the average effect for all spatial units when x_k increases globally. It is the average of Eq. (3.4b):

$$\frac{1}{N^2}\sum_{i=1}^{N}\sum_{j=1}^{N}\frac{\partial y_i}{\partial x_{kj}} = \beta_k S_A + \delta_k S_C \tag{3.4c}$$

where S_A and S_C sum the elements in A and C.

Equations (3.4a–3.4c) define the spatial impulse responses of y_i with respect to x_{kj}. Another type of spatial impulse response is with respect to the innovations (ε). The counterpart to Eq. (3.3) is:

$$\frac{\partial y_i}{\partial \varepsilon_j} = d_{ij} \tag{3.5}$$

Whereas the spatial impulse responses in Eqs. (3.4a–3.4c) do not depend on ρ, matters are different in the case of Eq. (3.5). See e.g. LeSage and Pace (2009) for further discussion of these impulse responses.

In non-spatial models ρ, λ and δ are assumed to be zero. If λ and δ are not zero, Eq. (3.2) is simply $y = X\beta + u$, and will be misspecified. OLS estimates of β will be biased and inconsistent because of omitted variables. Note also, that if λ is not zero, OLS is biased and inconsistent because the spatial lag of y must be correlated with u. The OLS estimate of λ is biased upward if positive and biased downward if negative. Furthermore, the OLS estimate of λ is biased and inconsistent because of ρ. Spatial autocorrelation induces dependence between the spatial lag of y in Eq. (3.1a) and u since $\tilde{y}$ depends on $\tilde{u}$ and u depends on $\tilde{u}$.

The specification of spatial Durbin lags does not have adverse econometric implications for OLS. If X is exogenous, so are spatial lags of X. Therefore, OLS estimates of β and δ are unbiased and consistent provided $\lambda = 0$. If, however, ρ is not zero, these OLS estimates continue to be unbiased and consistent, but they cease to be efficient.

Since OLS is biased, inconsistent and inefficient, Eq. (3.2) is usually estimated by maximum likelihood (ML) by IV or GMM. The former takes into account the spatial dependence between y and the spatial lag of u by using the Jacobian matrix $J = \partial\varepsilon/\partial y$, which according to Eq. (3.2) is equal to D^{-1}. The log likelihood function includes the logarithm of the determinant of D^{-1} ($\ln|D^{-1}|$), and the ML estimates of ρ and λ are solved using the first order conditions with respect to ρ and λ:

$$\frac{\partial \ln |D^{-1}|}{\partial \rho} = -W(I - \lambda W) traceD = 0 \tag{3.6a}$$

$$\frac{\partial \ln |D^{-1}|}{\partial \lambda} = -W(I - \rho W) traceD = 0 \tag{3.6b}$$

Since W is exogenous, Eqs. (3.6a and 3.6b) depend only on ρ and λ. Equation (3.6a) uses the fact that $\partial D^{-1}/\partial \rho = -W(I - \lambda W)$.

IV estimators use Eq. (3.2) as the reduced form for y. OLS estimation of Eq. (3.2) generates $\hat{\hat{y}} = W\hat{y}$ as the instrumented spatial lag of y, which is substituted into Eq. (3.1a) for $\tilde{y}$. Note that since $A = I + \rho W + \rho^2 W^2 + \ldots$,

$$\hat{\hat{y}} = W\hat{y} = \sum_{k=1}^{K} \hat{\beta}_k \left(\tilde{x}_k + \lambda \tilde{\tilde{x}}_k + \lambda^2 \tilde{\tilde{\tilde{x}}}_k + \ldots\right) + \sum_{k=1}^{K} \delta_k \left(\tilde{\tilde{x}}_k + \lambda \tilde{\tilde{\tilde{x}}}_k + \lambda^2 \tilde{\tilde{\tilde{\tilde{x}}}}_k + \ldots\right) \quad (3.7)$$

Equation (3.7) clarifies that the instrumental variables consist of higher order spatial lags of the exogenous variable. Since λ is a fraction, the higher order terms in parentheses tend to zero. In practice, the polynomial for A is truncated. If the model includes spatial Durbin lags as in Eq. (3.1a) the IVs must include second order spatial lags and above. Otherwise, they must include first order spatial lags and above. See e.g. Anselin (1988) for further details and discussion.

3.5 Spatial Autocorrelation

The spatial autocorrelation coefficient (ρ) in Eq. (3.1b) would only be justified if the error terms (u) in Eq. (3.1a) happened to be spatially autocorrelated. Spatial autocorrelation arises when georeferenced data are correlated. This association can arise due to technical reasons, for example, data incongruence between the spatial extent of the phenomenon of interest and the institutional units for which it is available. It can also arise for substantive reasons, in particular spillovers and unobserved pervasive phenomena that induce correlation across space. If error terms happen to be spatially autocorrelated, u in Eq. (3.1a) ceases to be iid. Testing for spatial autocorrelation in error terms may reveal model misspecification, and spatial heterogeneity. Due to the multi-directional nature of space, testing for spatial autocorrelation is not a spatial variant of the Durbin–Watson statistic commonly used for testing for temporal autocorrelation. Nevertheless, the basic principles are similar.

We introduce various approaches for measuring spatial autocorrelation in error terms, and their associated significance tests.

Moran's I

Moran's I (Moran 1950) is commonly used to measure spatial autocorrelation. It is defined as:

$$I = \frac{1}{\sum_i \sum_j w_{ij}} \times \frac{\sum_i \sum_j w_{ij} \hat{u}_i \hat{u}_j}{\frac{1}{N} \sum_i \hat{u}_i^2} \quad (3.8a)$$

i.e. it is the spatially weighted covariance between the error terms divided by their variance. Equation (3.8a) is more transparent if W is row-summed to unity, so that $\sum_i \sum_j w_{ij} = N$ in which event Eq. (3.8a) becomes:

$$I = \frac{\sum_i \sum_j w_{ij} \hat{u}_i \hat{u}_j}{\sum_i \hat{u}_i^2} \tag{3.8b}$$

If $u_i = u_j$ the error terms are perfectly positively correlated, in which case $I = 1$ according to Eq. (3.8b). If at the other extreme $u_i = -u_j$ the error terms are perfectly negatively correlated in which case $I = -1$. If the error terms are uncorrelated $I = 0$.

To test whether I is significantly different from zero it is standardized by subtracting its expected value under the null hypothesis that it is zero, and dividing the result by its standard deviation under the null:

$$z = \frac{I - E(I)}{sd(I)} \sim N(0, 1) \tag{3.9a}$$

Where the expected value of I is:

$$E(I) = -\frac{1}{N-1} \tag{3.9b}$$

which tends to zero with N. The variance of I is defined as:

$$var(I) = E(I^2) - E(I)^2 \tag{3.9c}$$

The first term of Eq. (3.9c) is complicated and is defined as:

$$E(I^2) = \frac{NS_4 - S_3 S_5}{(N-1)(N-2)(N-3)\sum_i \sum_j w_{ij}} \tag{3.9d}$$

$$S_1 = \frac{1}{2} \sum_i \sum_j (w_{ij} + w_{ji})^2$$

$$S_2 = \sum_i \left(\sum_j w_{ij} + \sum_j w_{ji} \right)^2$$

$$S_3 = \frac{\frac{1}{N} \sum_i \hat{u}_i^4}{\left(\frac{1}{N} \sum_i \hat{u}_i^2 \right)^2}$$

$$S_4 = (N^2 - 3N + 3) S_1 - NS_2 + 3 \left(\sum_i \sum_j w_{ij} \right)^2$$

$$S_5 = (N^2 - N) S_1 - 2NS_2 + 6 \left(\sum_i \sum_j w_{ij} \right)^2$$

If z exceeds its critical value of 1.96 ($p = 0.5$) the error terms are positively spatially autocorrelated. See Cressie (1993) for a full articulation.

Moran's I may be decomposed into local components. Local Moran's I for spatial unit i is defined as:

$$I_i = \frac{\hat{u}_i \sum_{j \neq i} w_{ij} \hat{u}_i \hat{u}_j}{\frac{1}{N} \sum_i \hat{u}_i^2} \tag{3.10a}$$

Where global Moran's I is equal to the weighted average of its local components:

$$I = \frac{1}{N} \sum_i I_i \tag{3.10b}$$

The absence of global spatial autocorrelation (I = 0) might conceal local spatial autocorrelation, or what appears to be global spatial autocorrelation might in fact be induced by pockets of local spatial autocorrelation.

In spatial panel data Moran's I may be calculated for each time period and averaged:

$$\bar{I} = \frac{1}{T} \sum_{t=1}^{T} I_t \tag{3.11a}$$

To test for spatial autocorrelation in panel data the standardized panel average has a standard normal distribution:

$$\frac{\bar{I}}{V} \sim N(0, 1) \tag{3.11b}$$

where

$$V^2 = \frac{N^2 \sum_i \sum_j w_{ij}^2 + 3\left(\sum_i \sum_j w_{ij}\right)^2 - N \sum_i \left(\sum_j w_{ij}\right)^2}{T\left(N^2 - 1\right)\left(\sum_i \sum_j w_{ij}\right)^2} \tag{3.11c}$$

An alternative formulation to Moran's I is based on computing the sum of squared differences and dividing by the variance adjusted for the spatial configuration, yields a contiguity ratio, known as Geary's C:

$$C = \frac{(N-1) \sum_i \sum_j w_{ij} \left(\hat{u}_i - \hat{u}_j\right)^2}{2 \sum_i \sum_j w_{ij} \sum_{i=1}^{N} \hat{u}_i^2} \tag{3.12}$$

Perfect positive correlation arises when $u_i = u_j$ in which case C = 0. Perfect negative correlation arises when $u_i = -u_j$ in which case C = 2. There is no spatial autocorrelation when C = 1. By focusing on differences between u_i and u_j rather than their products, C is more sensitive to local spatial autocorrelation than Moran's I.

In contrast to Moran I and C statistics, Getis and Ord (1992) introduced a spatial autocorrelation statistic (the G statistic) that indicates the degree to which low and high values in the data are spatially clustered. This is generally used as a local indicator of spatial autocorrelation whereby the weight matrix is row-adjusted to 1 and the row-multiplier uses N − 1 instead of N. Strictly speaking G measures spatial concentration rather than spatial autocorrelation, and resembles a spatial Gini coefficient. Therefore, unlike Moran I and C, which are meaningful measures of spatial autocorrelation in error terms, G is more sensibly applied to measuring the spatial concentration in variables such as crime, income etc. The G statistic is a scale invariant (but not location invariant) statistic applicable to variables that are positive and have a natural origin. The distribution of the statistic in terms of z and p values indicates spatial clustering. For this reason it is popularly portrayed in GIS packages as a 'hot spot' statistic. Large and significant z scores for G indicate clustering of high values (hot spots). Significant clustering of low value z scores indicates cold spots.

G is calculated as the sum of the weighted covariances divided by the sum of the unweighted covariances:

$$G = \frac{\sum\limits_i \sum\limits_j w_{ij}\left(\hat{u}_i \hat{u}_j\right)}{\sum\limits_i \sum\limits_j \left(\hat{u}_i \hat{u}_j\right)} \quad i \neq j \tag{3.13}$$

Under complete spatial randomness, the expected value of G would be:

$$E(G) = \frac{\sum\limits_i \sum\limits_j w_{ij}}{N(N-1)} \quad i \neq j$$

which tends to zero with N when w is row-summed to 1.

Lagrange Multiplier Statistic

In Lagrange multiplier (LM) tests the null hypothesis is assumed to be false, and the model is estimated ignoring the null hypothesis. Subsequently, an auxiliary equation is estimated to test the null hypothesis. The auxiliary equation usually controls for the variables specified in the model. It also specifies the omitted variables generated by the null hypothesis. If the LM test statistic rejects the null hypothesis, no damage was induced by ignoring it. If, on the other hand, the null hypothesis is not rejected by the LM test, the null hypothesis should not have been ignored in the first place. Since in many situations the null hypothesis is ignorable, LM tests have become increasingly popular. It saves the bother of allowing for potential restrictions, which might prove to be irrelevant.

In our present context Eq. (3.1a) is initially estimated ignoring the null hypothesis of SAC expressed in Eq. (3.1b). The auxiliary equation for the LM test is:

$$\hat{u} = a + Xb + \tilde{X}c + d\tilde{y} + e\tilde{u} + v \tag{3.14}$$

where v is a vector of iid error terms. The auxiliary equation specifies all the covariates used to estimate Eq. (3.1a) as well as the null hypothesis to be tested. If e is not significantly different from zero, no harm was done by ignoring ρ in Eq. (3.1b). If e = 0 the R^2 of Eq. (3.14) must be zero because b = c = d = 0 by definition. Regressing error terms on the covariates, which generated them, must deliver zero goodness-of-fit. The LM statistic is NR^2 which is distributed χ_1^2. If the LM statistic is less than its critical value, ignoring SAC did no harm. If instead LM exceeds its critical value it must be because e is significantly different from zero, in which event SAC was not ignorable.

Equation (3.14) cannot be estimated by OLS for the same reasons that Eq. (3.1b) cannot be estimated by OLS; the spatial lags of y and u are not independent of v. The preferred method of estimation is ML.

3.6 Spatial Heterogeneity

Spatial heterogeneity is a special case of observed heterogeneity relating to variation over space. It arises when the effects of covariates on dependent variables vary by location. Geographical patterns that correlate across space may not just be statistical nuisances to be treated by including additional variables, but might express spatial heterogeneity. In contrast to spatial dependence and spillover discussed above, coping with spatial heterogeneity does not call on special estimation techniques. It can be incorporated by using spatially distinct units between which model parameters vary or by allowing model parameters to vary over space as in geographically weighted regression (see below).

Spatial heterogeneity is particularly challenging since it is often difficult to distinguish it from spatial dependence (Anselin 2010). This 'linear inverse problem' arises when trying to reconstruct an object (function) from indirect observations (Kirsch 1996). Solving this problem means recovering the function from noisy observations. This is akin to inversely deriving data from parameters of a model instead of vice versa. In the context of distinguishing between spatial heterogeneity and spatial dependence this problem is confounded by the blurred distinction between true and apparent spatial clustering. The essence of the problem is that cross-sectional data, while allowing the identification of clusters and patterns, do not provide sufficient information to identify the processes that led to these patterns. As a result, it is impossible to distinguish between the case where spatial patterns are due to structural change (apparent clustering) or follow from a true inherently spatial process of change.

In practice, this is further complicated because each form of misspecification may suggest the other form in diagnostics and specification tests. For example, tests against spatial autocorrelation have power against heteroscedasticity, and tests against heteroscedasticity have power against spatial autocorrelation (Anselin and Griffith 1988). Spatial heterogeneity provides the basis for the specification of the structure of the heterogeneity in a spatial model. Ignoring spatial heterogeneity leads to estimation inefficiency but not to estimation bias.

Geographically Weighted Regression

In spatial analysis, heterogeneity is commonly addressed thorough spatial filtering (Griffith 2003) as discussed further below, or geographically weighted regression (GWR) (Fotheringham et al. 2002). Both techniques have not attracted much attention in the econometrics community and are described briefly here.

In nonparametric regression the parameter estimates vary according to the data in the vicinity of the observations. Hence, for observation i, β_i depends on the data in the vicinity y_i and x_i. GWR deals with spatial heterogeneity because it allows β_i to vary with the data in the vicinity of spatial unit *i*. Typically, linear regression applied to spatial data assumes a spatially stationary process in that a particular shock will elicit the same response across space regardless of where it occurs. This is patently unreasonable as sampling variation may cause relationships to vary across space. Furthermore, intrinsic differences across places (cultural, political and behavioral practices) may elicit different responses to common shocks. Finally a global formulation may misspecify a model that is inherently local.

GWR considers a subset of the input data and estimates a series of weighted least squares regressions allowing for continuously changing response functions. The standard GWR model is:

$$y_i = \alpha_i + \sum_{k=1}^{K} \beta_{ki} x_{ki} + \varepsilon_i \tag{3.15a}$$

in which the parameters α and β vary by location. Unlike Eq. (3.1a), Eq. (3.15a) states that there are no spatial spillovers, but the effects of the covariates on the dependent variable vary by i. The same also applies to Eq. (3.1a) because in Eq. (3.3) a_{ii} and c_{ii} vary by i. However, the mechanism in GWR is non-spatial, and is induced instead by spatial heterogeneity. Anselin (2010) has remarked that it may be difficult to distinguish between spatial heterogeneity as in GWR and spatial dependence as in Eq. (3.1a). However, GWR assumes that y_i is independent of x_j and ε_j, whereas Eq. (3.1a) does not. Since Eqs. (3.1a and 3.15a) are non-nested, non-nested tests (discussed in Chap. 4) should be able to distinguish between them.

Vectorizing Eq. (3.15a) and denoting the parameter vector for unit i by $\theta_i = (\alpha_i\ \beta_{ki})'$ the GWR estimator for θ_i is:

$$\hat{\theta}_i = (X'V_iX)^{-1}X'V_iy \tag{3.15b}$$

where X is an $N \times K + 1$ matrix of observations (including intercept) on the covariates and V_i is a symmetric $N \times N$ matrix with spatial weights v_{ij} and $v_{ii} = 1$. Because these weights depend exclusively on distance, we distinguish them from their counterparts in W. This is why $w_{ii} = 0$ but $v_{ii} = 1$. A popular specification of V_i is the exponential distribution:

$$v_{ij} = \exp\left[-0.5\left(d_{ij}/h\right)^2\right] \quad (3.15c)$$

where h represents the kernel bandwidth. As h increases, the gradient of the kernel becomes less steep and more data points are included in the local calibration. The choice of bandwidth involves a tradeoff between bias and variance. Too small a bandwidth leads to large variances in estimates of β_i since only a small number of observations are considered in each local regression. If too large a bandwidth is selected this creates large bias in the local estimates. This will tend to iron-out the variance in the data points and create a bias by masking local characteristics shrinking the estimates to the size of their global counterparts. To find the optimal value of h, bandwidth optimization strategies are preferred to an ad hoc selected bandwidth (Fotheringham et al. 2002; Páez et al. 2011). GWR estimates are relatively insensitive to the choice of weighting function as long as it is a continuous distance-based function. However, they are sensitive to the degree of distance-decay.

3.7 Modifiable Areal Unit Problem (MAUP)

The MAUP framework addresses the issue of the sensitivity of empirical estimation to the selection of geographic units and particularly their arbitrary nature. Yule and Kendall (1950) observed that correlation coefficients could vary depending on how space is aggregated. This observation involves three separate issues: does the number of spatial units affect the results? Does their size (scale) and shape (topology or configuration) have any effect? Since the number of units varies inversely with their size and perhaps their shape, we focus on size and shape. Size effects arise from choosing a spatial resolution (disaggregating or re-aggregating) from a given set of data. Shape effects arise from choosing the relevant data (defining the shape of spatial units) given a level of spatial resolution.

Suppose that rich and poor people are distributed randomly across space so that in truth there is no spatial inequality. Suppose an investigator aggregates these data into circular areas of fixed diameter. The investigator could create artificial spatial inequality by selectively drawing circles around random spatial concentrations of rich and poor. The investigator could generate yet more spurious inequality if he changes the shapes of his spatial units by grouping poor and rich in separate spatial units. The more freedom allowed in choosing shapes, the more artificial inequality may be generated from the data.

The effect of spatial size is not just a statistical issue but also a practical one. With much policy emphasis being directed towards generating ‘agglomerations’ and ‘clusters’, getting size ‘right’ empirically would seem to have important implications with respect to knowing what works. A common approach is to use simulated experiments. Using three experiments Openshaw and Taylor (1979) investigate how different sized units influence the relationship between the percentage of Republican voters and the share of the population over the age of 60 for 99 counties in Iowa. They report clear differences between size and shape and relate this to the interaction of contiguity inherent in the former with the spatial autocorrelation in the data. A Monte Carlo type experiment with random allocation of values and their allocation to geo-referenced points across different sized grids conducted by Amrhein (1995) has shown that size and shape have little effect and that changes in variance are influenced only by number of units.

More recently, Briant et al. (2010) illustrate how differentiating various French zoning systems by size and shape only marginally affects determinants of wages and trade. They find MAUP-based distortions across six different zoning systems, but in general they conclude that size and shape are of secondary importance compared with estimation issues. Overall, spatial size is a more cogent issue than spatial shape in distorting estimates of trade than of wages. They suggest that gravity models of trade use variables aggregated under different spatial configurations to those of wage models. For example, in trade estimation both sides of the regression may not be treated uniformly (i.e. averaged) as is likely in wage models. As MAUP distortions are related to whether the distribution of variables is preserved, they are more potent in trade estimations than in wage estimations.

At first sight, the issue of spatial shape seems deceptively innocuous and has been considered of 'third order' importance in handling spatial data aggregation (Briant et al. 2010). In fact it consists of two separate but often-confounded issues: spatial zoning representing the arrangement of contiguous polygons, and spatial grouping which expresses the arrangement of non-contiguous polygons. Zoning is really a special case of grouping with a contiguity constraint and represents the most common form of spatial arrangement. For the purpose of spatial econometric analysis the issue of contiguity however is critical as it is this arrangement that facilitates spatial spillover.

Spatial datasets typically comprise discrete units that are administrative or geo-political creations. They are thus exposed to distortions that can arise from edge effects. For example, spatial units on the edge of a square lattice are less exposed to spatial spillover because they have three neighbors instead of four, and in the corners of the lattice they are even less exposed because they only have two neighbors. In oblong lattices there is less spatial dependence than in square lattices because spatial units are closer to the edge in the former. Surprisingly, seminal discussions of the MAUP (Openshaw and Taylor 1979), Fotheringham and Wong (1991) have overlooked this issue. We address this issue in Chap. 5 where we develop unit root tests for SAR coefficients for different topologies.

In contrast, Briant et al. (2010) have tested different spatial topologies such as administrative, grid and random zoning configurations ignoring the implications of spatial spillovers. In parallel to topology they have looked at whether the nature of the information to be allocated to spatial topologies (summed or aggregated information) is sensitive to spatial shape. In the extreme case, this assumes that values in one spatial unit are independent of adjacent or surrounding units, i.e. spatial autarchy is imposed. Shape is found to be of small importance. Smaller more regular units (grid cells) reduce variance and impose homogeneity. Larger units increase volatility and increase heterogeneity. While this seems to indicate MAUP-like bias, spatial dependence is ignored.

3.8 Spatial Filtering

Spatial filtering is frequently used to remove spatial autocorrelation from variables in spatial models. The spatially filtered data are subsequently used to test the hypothesis of interest. To simplify matters, suppose that in Eq. (3.1a) $\rho = \delta = 0$, i.e. the model is $y = X\beta + u$, but u is spatially autocorrelated according to Eq. (3.1b). Since $u = B\varepsilon$, where $B = (I - \rho W)^{-1}$, the model may be expressed in terms of spatially filtered variables by substituting $B\varepsilon$ for u in the model, and then multiplying both side by B^{-1} to obtain:

$$
\begin{aligned}
y^* &== X^*\beta + \varepsilon \\
y^* &= (I - \rho W)y \\
X^* &= (I - \rho W)X
\end{aligned}
\tag{3.16a}
$$

$$
y = X\beta - \rho\tilde{X}\beta + \rho\tilde{y} + \varepsilon \tag{3.16b}
$$

Notice that in Eq. (3.16a) ε is iid, in which case β may be estimated by OLS given ρ, which is estimated first. A crucial assumption in spatial filtering is that ρ is a nuisance parameter that can be concentrated out of the likelihood function. This would be permissible if ρ and β were independent. Although $p \lim \hat{\beta}$ is independent of ρ, matters are different in finite samples. Consequently, in finite samples spatial filtering might induce bias in the estimates of ρ as well as β. The obvious less radical alternative to spatial filtering is to estimate ρ and β jointly by ML.

Spatial filtering treats $(I - \rho W)$ as a common factor that applies to y and X. A rival specification is Eq. (3.1a) in which u is assumed to be spatially uncorrelated. Equation (3.16a) imposes the restrictions $\lambda = \rho$ and $\delta = \rho\beta$, as may be seen in Eq. (3.16b). Since Eq. (3.16b) is nested in Eq. (3.1a) a likelihood ratio test of the two models may be used to determine which model is preferable. Since Eq. (3.16b) imposes two restrictions the likelihood ratio test is distributed χ^2_2. The common factor (spatial filtering) cannot be rejected if $2LR < \chi^2_2$, otherwise Eq. (3.1a) is preferable.

In summary, spatial filtering treats spatial autocorrelation as a nuisance parameter rather than as a diagnostic device for detecting model misspecification. Evidence of spatial autocorrelation may indicate that the model is misspecified in terms of its spatial dynamics. In Chap. 2 we noted that serially correlated errors in time series models typically imply that the model is dynamically misspecified. We also tend to think that spatially autocorrelated errors typically imply that the model is misspecified in terms of its spatial dynamics. If, indeed, the correct model happens to have spatially autocorrelated error terms, spatially filtered OLS is consistent.

However, it may be biased in finite samples. Either way, the justification for spatial filtering is questionable.

Spatial Eigenvectors

The rank of a matrix is equal to the number of its non-zero eigenvalues. Since W is N $\times$ N its rank is N. However, many of its eigenvalues are most probably small, especially when N is large. The eigenvalues are labelled by n = 1,2,. . .,N in terms of their size, where n = 1 is the largest and n = N the smallest. From the spectral decomposition theorem of a matrix $W = \Gamma\Lambda\Gamma'$, where Λ is a diagonal N $\times$ N matrix with the eigenvalues on the leading diagonal, and Γ is the associated matrix of eigenvectors with elements γ_{nj}. Since $\Gamma\Gamma' = I_N$ the eigenvectors are orthonormal, i.e. they are independent of each other. Griffith (1996) showed that W can be decomposed into N orthogonal spatial components using the eigenvectors, as in principal components analysis. The most important of these components is for n = 1 and the least important is for n = N. These spatial components may be used to characterize the spatial dependence generated by W in terms of peripherality, regionality and other spatial attributes that might be geographically meaningful.

Griffith suggested that an alternative to spatial filtering in Eq. (3.16a) is to regress y and x on the eigenvectors of W:

$$y_i = a + \sum_{n=1}^{M} \theta_n \gamma_{ni} + y_i^* \tag{3.17a}$$

$$x_i = b + \sum_{n=1}^{M} \varphi_n \gamma_{ni} + x_i^* \tag{3.17b}$$

Observation i has an eigenvector element for each of the N eigenvectors. However, only M < N eigenvectors will be used, which are derived from the M largest eigenvalues, because the smallest eigenvalues contribute little to the spatial correlation in the data. The generated error terms y* and x* are subsequently used to estimate β by OLS:

$$y_i^* = x_i^* \beta + \varepsilon_i \tag{3.17c}$$

Because the eigenvectors are orthogonal, there is no collinearity between their M covariates. Consequently, investigators may rapidly determine the optimal specification of Eq. (3.17a) in terms of exclusion restrictions for some and even many of the M eigenvectors. For example, Getis and Griffith (2002) use house price data in which N = 48, M = 14 and the final number of included eigenvectors is only 3. An advantage over Eq. (3.17c) is that Eq. (3.17a) is less parametric in the sense that the only the empirically relevant eigenvalues of W are retained.

Substituting Eqs. (3.17a and 3.17b) into Eq. (3.17c) gives:

$$y_i = x_i\beta + \sum_{n=1}^{M} \phi_n \gamma_{ni} + \varepsilon_i$$
$$\phi_n = \theta_n - \beta\varphi_n \tag{3.17d}$$

Equation (3.17d) is the counterpart to Eq. (3.16a) when β and ρ are estimated jointly in that β and ϕ are estimated jointly. However, whereas the estimation of β and ρ is by ML, Eq. (3.17d) may be estimated by OLS.

3.9 Spatial Panel Data

This chapter has been exclusively concerned with spatial cross-section data. On the whole, no new major econometric issues are involved in spatial panel data, provided that they are stationary. Textbooks on panel data usually include a chapter on spatial data (Baltagi 2013; Pesaran 2015). See e.g. Elhorst (2014) on static and dynamic spatial panel data econometrics when the data are stationary. If instead the data are nonstationary, radical changes are involved in the econometric analysis of spatial panel data as well as spatial cross-section data. In Chap. 5 we address the issue of nonstationarity in spatial cross-section data. In Chaps. 7–9 we address the issue of spatio-temporal nonstationarity in spatial panel data. Recently, attention has been drawn to the difference between strong and weak cross-section dependence in stationary as well as nonstationary panel data. This issue is addressed in Chap. 10.

The literature on the econometric analysis of spatial panel data dates back at least to Anselin (1988, Chap. 10). See also Chap. 6 below for a historical review. However, empirical work using spatial panel data developed slowly. An early contribution is Elhorst (2003) who considered the case of temporally static models with spatial dynamics induced by spatial lagged endogenous variables with fixed spatial effects. As in cross-section data, the presence of spatial lagged endogenous variables in panel data affects the identification of SAR coefficients. The econometric solutions discussed above regarding cross-section data (ML, IV, GMM) are directly applicable to temporally static panel data, provided that these data are stationary. Elhorst follows ML procedures used for non-spatial panel data by concentrating out the regional fixed effects from the likelihood function by demeaning the data. Panel counterparts for Moran I and LM statistics for testing for spatial autocorrelation in the residuals have been developed too. Procedures for this are available, for example, in Stata using the xsmle command, in Matlab's econometric toolbox, and in R.

In dynamic panel data models the "incidental parameter problem" is expressed by the fact that the estimated fixed effects are consistent but biased in finite samples. Moreover, concentrating out fixed effects by demeaning or differencing the data induces inconsistency. Since Arellano and Bond (1991) the standard solution to this inconsistency problem has been to use higher order lagged differences of the endogenous variable as instrumental variables for their first order lagged difference.

Subsequently, GMM versions of this solution were developed. The availability of these solutions in econometric software packages has made them popular relative to the alternatives.

The main alternative is bias correction (Hahn and Kuersteiner 2002) of the aforementioned biased estimates induced by the incidental parameter problem. Since the bias is known analytically (as explained in Chap. 6), it is straightforward to correct it. Although bias correction has not proved popular in dynamic panel data econometrics in general, the opposite has been the case in spatial econometrics. Yu et al. (2008) developed quasi ML (QML) methods for panel data models with spatiotemporal dynamics using a two-step procedure. In the first step, they concentrate out the fixed effects and estimate the model ignoring the incidental parameter problem. In the second step they bias-correct the parameter estimates from the first step. A similar two-step procedure was used by Beenstock and Felsenstein (2007) and is discussed in Chap. 6.

Since Pesaran (2006) the spatial econometric analysis of panel data has been challenged by a rival interpretation of cross-section dependence. According to this rival cross-section independence is induced by common factors that have spatially heterogeneous factor loadings. Cross-section dependence stems from the differential effects of shared common factors. Whereas spatial dependence is based on proximity, its common factor rival is not. Subsequently, spatial dependence has been referred to as weak cross-section dependence, and dependence induced by common factors has been referred to by strong cross-section dependence. In Chap. 10 we discuss these issues in detail, and join the growing consensus that the two types of cross-section dependence are not mutually exclusive.

This brief overview of developments in the econometric analysis of spatial panel data refers exclusively to stationary panel data. It certainly does not apply to nonstationary panel data. Indeed, as noted in Chap. 1, there is no literature on the econometric analysis of nonstationary spatial panel. Perhaps the only exception is Yu et al. (2012) who consider the case where the data are nonstationary and are known to be cointegrated. They assume what we seek to test; in practice we do not know that the data are indeed cointegrated. To these ends we follow the methodological path trod by our predecessors in non-spatial panel data (see Chap. 2). We develop the asymptotic theory for testing for the presence of spatiotemporal unit root tests in which N is fixed and $T \to \infty$. We then use simulation methods to compute critical values under the null hypothesis that a spatiotemporal unit root is present. Then we develop the asymptotic theory for testing for spatial panel cointegration where the variables contain spatiotemporal unit roots. Here too N is fixed and $T \to \infty$. Finally, we use simulation methods to compute critical values for spatial panel cointegration tests.

This chapter has presented some of the key ideas in spatial data analysis that are pertinent to time series econometricians. Where applicable, we have highlighted the time series roots of current spatial econometrics. For example, the SAR model is derived from the simple time series autoregressive models and spatial filtering is a variant of time series differencing. Despite these commonalities, there are still many differences. These derive from the unique nature of spatial data and impact on some of the key issues in handling spatial data for econometric time series analysis. The challenges of spatial heterogeneity, dependence, and MAUP, which arise in spatial data do not have any counterparts in time series data. The 'messy' nature of spatial data noted above has manifested itself in the 'problem' of spatial (observational) autocorrelation and dependence (Cliff and Ord 1969) that plagues econometric model specifications. Spatial data can also be 'noisy' typically characterized by stochastic errors and underlying time trends (non stationarity).

Furthermore, spatial data can also be 'dirty' containing corruptions and inconsistencies. A plethora of dedicated techniques have emerged to mitigate some of these excesses. These harness advances in computational sciences and the increasing availability of spatial panel data. The toolbox serving the spatial econometrician has been continually extended through new forms of spatial data interpolation and imputation techniques, extensions to impulse response modeling through spatial filtering, reducing error propagation through GIS and so on. Manipulating these data via smoothing techniques or partitioning into polygons needs to be cognizant of the spatial dependence present in the data. Cross-product statistics such as Moran's I, Geary's C, Getis and Ord's G and other geo-statistical measures for evaluating dependence such as clustering algorithms, rest on an evaluation of the degree to which the data are spatially heterogeneous. Other techniques such as interpolation or surface smoothing via filtering are also grounded in the nature of trends in the data and the specification of a structure for spatial dependence. As time series econometrics gets increasingly involved in cross sectional dependence (both strong and weak), it cannot continue to be oblivious of these issues.

We devote the next chapter to the spatial connectivity matrix, which is the hallmark of the spatial econometric analysis of cross-section data and panel data, and which has been a key focus in the present chapter.

References

Amrhein CG (1995) Searching for the elusive aggregation effect: evidence from statistical simulations. Environ Plan A 27:105–119

Anselin L (1988) Spatial econometrics: methods and models. Kluwer Academic, Dordrecht

Anselin L (2010) Thirty years of spatial econometrics. Pap Reg Sci 89(1):3–25

Anselin L, Griffith DA (1988) Do spatial effects really matter in regression analysis? Pap Reg Sci Assoc 65:11–34

Arellano M, Bond S (1991) Some tests of specification for panel data: Monte Carlo evidence and an application to employment equations. Rev Econ Stud 58:277–297

Baltagi BH (2013) Econometric analysis of panel data, 5th edn. Wiley, Chichester

Bartlett MS (1955) An introduction to stochastic processes. Cambridge University Press, Cambridge

Beenstock M, Felsenstein D (2007) Spatial vector autoregressions. Spat Econ Anal 2:167–196

Bennett RJ (1979) Spatial time series: analysis, forecasting, control. Pion, London

Briant A, Combes PP, Lafourcade M (2010) Dots to boxes: do the size and shape of spatial units jeopardize economic geography estimations? J Urban Econ 67(3):287–302

Cairncross F (1997) The death of distance: how the communications revolution is changing our lives. Harvard Business School Press, Boston, MA

Cliff A, Ord J (1969) The problem of spatial autocorrelation. In: Scott AJ (ed) Studies in regional science, London papers in regional science. Pion, London, pp 25–55

Cressie NAC (1993) Statistics for spatial data. Wiley, New York

Elhorst JP (2003) Specification and estimation of spatial panel data models. Int Reg Sci Rev 26:244–268

Elhorst JP (2014) From spatial cross-section data to spatial panel data. Springer, Berlin

Florax RJGM, van der Vlist AJ (2003) Spatial econometric data analysis: moving beyond traditional models. Int Reg Sci Rev 26(3):223–243

Fotheringham AS, Wong DWS (1991) The modifiable areal unit problem in multivariate statistical analysis. Environ Plan A 23:1025–1044

Fotheringham AS, Brunsdon C, Charlton M (2002) Geographically weighted regression: the analysis of spatially varying relationships. Wiley, London

Getis A, Griffith DA (2002) Comparative spatial filtering in regression analysis. Geogr Anal 32:131–140

Getis A, Ord JK (1992) The analysis of spatial association using distance statistics. Geogr Anal 24:189–206

Granger CWJ (1969) Spatial data and time series analysis. In: Scott A (ed) Studies in regional science, London papers in regional science. Pion, London, pp 1–24

Griffith DA (1996) Spatial autocorrelation and eigenfunctions of the geographic weights matrix accompanying geo-referenced data. Can Geogr 40(4):351–367

Griffith DA (2003) Spatial autocorrelation and spatial filtering: gaining understanding through theory and scientific visualization. Springer, Berlin

Hahn J, Kuersteiner G (2002) Asymptotically unbiased inference for a dynamic panel model with fixed effects when both N and T are large. Econometrica 70:1639–1657

Kirsch A (1996) An introduction to the mathematical theory of inverse problems. Springer, New York

LeSage JP, Pace RK (2014) The biggest myth in spatial econometrics. Econometrics 2(4):217–249

LeSage JP, Pace RK (2009) Introduction to spatial econometrics. CRC, Boca Raton, FL

Moran PAP (1950) Notes on continuous stochastic phenomena. Biometrika 37:17–23

Openshaw S, Taylor PJ (1979) A million or so correlation coefficients: three experiment on the modifiable areal unit problem. In: Wrigley N (ed) Statistical applications in the spatial sciences. Pion, London, pp 127–144

Paelinck J, Klaassen L (1979) Spatial econometrics. Saxon House, Farnborough

Páez A, Farber S, Wheeler D (2011) A simulation-based study of geographically weighted regression as a method for investigating spatially varying relationships. Environ Plan A 43 (12):2992–3010

Pesaran MH (2006) Estimation and inference in large heterogeneous panels with a multifactor error structure. Econometrica 74:967–1012

Pesaran MH (2015) Time series and panel data econometrics. Oxford University Press, Oxford

Pinske J, Slade ME (2010) The future of spatial econometrics. J Reg Sci 50(1):103–117

Qu X, Lee L (2015) Estimating a spatial autoregressive model with an endogenous spatial weight matrix. J Econ 184(2):209–232

Ripley BD (1981) Spatial statistics. Wiley, New York

Whittle P (1954) On stationary processes in the plane. Biometrika 49:434–449

Wooldridge JM (2010) Econometric analysis of cross section and panel data, 2nd edn. MIT Press, Cambridge, MA

Yu J, de Jong R, Lee L-F (2008) Quasi-maximum likelihood estimators for spatial dynamic panel data with fixed effects with both N and T large. J Econ 146:118–134

Yu J, de Jong R, Lee L-F (2012) Estimation for spatial dynamic panel data with fixed effects: the case of spatial cointegration. J Econ 167:16–37

Yule GU, Kendall MG (1950) An introduction to the theory of statistics. Charles Griffin, London

Chapter 4
The Spatial Connectivity Matrix

4.1 Introduction

In the previous chapter we explained that unlike time, which is unilateral and unidirectional, space is multilateral and multidirectional. Time is unilateral because tomorrow follows today, and it is unidirectional because what happens tomorrow may depend on what happens today, but not the other way around. Science fiction writers have speculated about a world in which time machines enable us to go back in time. In such a world, time would be rather like space. Space is multilateral because of its north-south and east-west dimensions, and it is multidirectional because spatial units may be mutually influential. It is for this reason that spatial dependence is much more complex than temporal dependence. We also explained that due to this complexity in spatial dependence, spatial econometricians are forced to specify a spatial connectivity matrix, commonly denoted by W, which defines how spatial units are related. W cannot be estimated.

Ever since its inception in the 1970s the spatial connectivity matrix has been imposed exogenously based on a general notion of how distance affects connectivity. In principle, goodness-of-fit tests may be used to choose between rival definitions of W. In practice, however, most researchers impose W without testing its restrictions empirically. If W is misspecified, parameter estimates are likely to be biased and inconsistent in models containing spatial lags (Stakhovych and Bijmolt 2008). Cuaresma and Feldkircher (2013) have shown how estimates of income convergence across European regions may be biased upwards by up to 100%, depending on the specification of W. The need to specify W is a perennial problem in spatial econometrics.

In this chapter we argue that although W cannot be estimated using spatial cross-section data, and therefore must be specified exogenously, matters may be different in spatial panel data, especially in long panels where the number of time series observations (T) exceeds the number of cross-section observations (N). In short

M. Beenstock, D. Felsenstein, *The Econometric Analysis of Non-Stationary Spatial Panel Data*, Advances in Spatial Science,
https://doi.org/10.1007/978-3-030-03614-0_4

Table 4.1 Typology of W

Metric of association	Nature of W	Role of matrix	Approach
Spatial proximity measures			
Distance decay-based • ($1/d^2$) • Bandwidth distance decline • Social interaction indicators (pop size, commuting)	Imposed on data	Explanatory-predictive	Guided by broad theoretical notions but inherently data-driven
Geometry-based			
• Rook/Queen • nth nearest neighbor distance • Lengths of shared borders, perimeters			
Geostatistical models			
• AMOEBA • Spatial filtering • Maximum entropy • Autocovariance matrix derived from spatial error model • Bayesian estimation • Latent variable modeling	Estimated from data	Descriptive-estimation limited by scale of reference	Theoretical and model driven

panels where N is greater than T, W must be specified in advance as with cross-section data unless restrictions are imposed on W.

In Table 4.1 we distinguish between two approaches to specifying W. Under the spatial proximity approach, W is imposed exogenously based on some general notion of how distance affects connectivity. This approach is broadly theoretical and is driven by a gravity-type notion of how proximity affects spatial interaction. Any metric of distance decay may be used, such as inverse distance raised to a power (Getis and Aldstadt 2004) or bandwidth distance decline (Fotheringham et al. 2002). A variant on this theme is geometry-based in which W is specified exogenously in terms of contiguity and contagion (Rey and Montouri 1999). Here the geometry of spatial units is important and W reflects the geometric configuration of the cells. The data-driven matrix that is derived assumes a connectivity structure based on the Tobler's (1970) 'first rule of geography', i.e. closer neighbors have more effect than distant ones.

In theory, alternative specifications of W may be tested empirically. To fix ideas let W_1 and W_2 be alternative specifications of W. We distinguish between two possibilities. In the first, W_2 is nested in W_1 in the sense that W_2 is a restricted version or a special case of W_1. For example, all the elements of W_2 are identical to the elements of W_1 except for the fact that some elements of W_2 are zero. In this nested case, we may compare goodness-of-fit measures for the model based on W_2 with the model based on W_1. For example, if the likelihood of the former (model 2) is significantly greater than the latter (model 1), we would prefer W_2 to W_1.

Matters are less straightforward if W_1 and W_2 are non-nested, i.e. neither is a special case of its rival. For example, W_1 is specified in terms of contiguity and W_2 is specified in terms of distance, or commuting times. In this case the rival hypotheses about spatiality may be tested using non-nested tests in terms of the encompassing principle (Greene 2012, Sect. 5.8; Davidson and MacKinnon 2009, pp. 671–672). Suppose the hypothesis to be tested is:

$$y = X\beta + \lambda Wy + \varepsilon \tag{4.1}$$

where y is an N-vector of cross-section data, X is a K × N matrix of exogenous variables, β denotes a K-vector of parameters, λ denotes the SAR coefficient and ε is an N-vector of iid error terms.

Let $\hat{y}_1$ denote the predicted value of y when Eq. (4.1) is estimated using W_1 and let $\hat{y}_2$ denote the predicted value when W_2 is specified. The encompassing J test involves estimating the following:

$$y = X\beta_1 + \lambda_1 W_1 y + \theta_1 \hat{y}_2 + \varepsilon_1 \tag{4.2a}$$

$$y = X\beta_2 + \lambda_2 W_2 y + \theta_2 \hat{y}_1 + \varepsilon_2 \tag{4.2b}$$

where $\hat{y}_1$ is the prediction of y when Eq. (4.1) is estimated using W_1 and $\hat{y}_2$ is its counterpart when Eq. (4.1) is estimated using W_2. The encompassing JA test involves estimating:

$$y = X\beta_1 + \lambda_1 W_1 y + \phi_1 \hat{y}_{12} + \varepsilon_1 \tag{4.2c}$$

$$y = X\beta_2 + \lambda_2 W_2 y + \phi_2 \hat{y}_{21} + \varepsilon_2 \tag{4.2d}$$

where $\hat{y}_{12}$ is the prediction of $\hat{y}_1$ when Eq. (4.1) is estimating using $\hat{y}_1$ as the dependent variable instead of y and W_2 is used, and $\hat{y}_{21}$ is the prediction of $\hat{y}_2$ when Eq. (4.1) is estimated using W_1 and the dependent variable is $\hat{y}_2$. The JA test has better finite sample properties than the J test.

There are four possible outcomes:

(i) Model 1 encompasses model 2 because model 1 explains observations that model 2 fails to explain as well as the observations model 2 explained. But model 2 does not explain observations that model 1 fails to explain even if it explains observations that model 1 explains. Therefore, W_1 is empirically superior to W_2. This occurs when θ_1 or ϕ_1 are statistically significant according to a t-test but θ_2 or ϕ_2 are not.

(ii) Model 2 encompasses model 1, in which case W_2 is empirically superior. This occurs when θ_2 or ϕ_2 are statistically significant according to a t-test but θ_1 or ϕ_1 are not.
(iii) Neither model encompasses its rival because model 2 explains observations unexplained by model 1, and model 1 explains observations unexplained by model 2. Therefore, neither specification of W is empirically superior, in which event there is no preferred definition of W. This occurs when θ_1 and θ_2 or ϕ_1 and ϕ_2 are statistically significant. This outcome suggests that a combination of W_1 and W_2 is superior to W_1 and W_2 individually.
(iv) Neither model encompasses its rival because model 1 fails to explain the observations that model 2 fails to explain, and vice-versa. Therefore, neither specification of W is superior. This arises when both θ_1 and θ_2 or ϕ_1 and ϕ_2 are not statistically significant.

In Eqs. (4.2) it is assumed that the εs are iid and are therefore spatially uncorrelated. If they are spatially correlated matters are more complicated as noted by Kelejian (2008) and Mur et al. (2015). LeSage and Pace (2009, Chap. 6) suggest that Bayesian methods may be used to compare non-nested models. If the posterior probability of model 1 is greater than the posterior probability of model 2 then W_1 is preferable to W_2. Since there must be a winner or loser it is not clear how their proposal is consistent with the encompassing principle according to which there may be no winners (case iii) and two losers (case iv).

We illustrate the application of these non-nested tests with an empirical example for cross-section data on house prices in Greater Tel Aviv. In the model average house prices per square meter in 283 statistical areas (defined by the Israel Central Bureau of Statistics) in 2008 are hypothesized to depend on population, average income and a spatial lagged dependent variable. In model 1 W_1 is defined in terms of first order contiguity, and in model 2 W_2 is defined by the reciprocal of distance. In both models W is row summed to 1. The spatial lag coefficient (λ) is estimated by maximum likelihood.

In both models the sign of population is negative and the sign of income is positive. The former may seem surprising but the models do not take account of housing stocks because these data are not available. Since housing stocks and population are positively correlated, and the effect of housing stocks on house prices is expected to be negative, this may explain why the sign of population is negative. The main point, however, is that the SAR coefficients of the two models are very different. Indeed, the SAR coefficient for model 2 is close to unity. Since the statistical areas are small and Greater Tel Aviv is only about 80 km × 20 km, the SAR coefficient for model 2 is naturally larger than for model 1, because nowhere is far from anywhere else. By implication first order contiguity in model 1 is too restrictive.

Both non-nested tests indicate that the non-nested test result is case iii since θ and ϕ are mutually significant. Model 1 does not encompass model 2, and model 2 does not encompass model 1. Since neither model encompasses the other, this means that W_2 and W_1 are not substitutes for each other. The direct effects differ; the coefficient on population is more negative with W_1 than with W_2, and the coefficient on income is larger with W2 than with W1. The average total effect (direct + indirect effect using the trace of $(I_N - \lambda W)^{-1}$) is −0.845 for population with W_1 and −0.686 with W_2. For income these effects are 0.153 for W_1 and 0.196 for W_2.

In summary, the specification of W matters in contrast to the claims of LeSage and Pace (2014). The specification matters for goodness-of-fit, and direct and indirect effect sizes. Because neither model encompassed the other, most probably a combination of the two would do better than either, in which both contiguity and distance are specified. However, we do not pursue this matter here.

Spatial Autoregressive Conditional Heteroscedasticity (SpARCH)

We concluded Chap. 2 by describing ARCH (autoregressive conditional heteroscedasticity) models in time series data. We noted that whereas unconditional heteroscedasticity constitutes a violation of the classical assumptions, matters are different in the case of ARCH as far as linear models are concerned. The spatial counterpart to ARCH was introduced by Beenstock and Felsenstein (2016) where the variance of error terms in spatial unit i is related to the variance of error terms in the neighborhood of i:

$$\varepsilon_i^2 = a + b\tilde{\varepsilon}_i^2 + e_i \tag{4.2e}$$

where b is the SpARCH coefficient, and e is iid. The conditional variance for unit i is expected to be $a + b\tilde{\varepsilon}_i^2$, which varies by i. The unconditional variance may be obtained by vectorising Eq. (4.2e):

$$\varepsilon^2 = ai + bW\varepsilon^2 + e \tag{4.2f}$$

where ε^2 is an N-vector of squared error terms, from which the vector of unconditional variances is expected to be:

$$\begin{aligned} \sigma^2 &= \Psi a \\ \Psi &= (I_N - bW)^{-1} i \end{aligned} \tag{4.2g}$$

The unconditional variance in unit i is expected to be $\sigma_i^2 = \psi_i a$ where ψ_i is an element of Ψ. Since W is row summed to 1, $\psi_i = 1/(1 - b)$, hence the unconditional variances are homoscedastic and equal $a/(1 - b)$.

The SpARCH test involves estimating Eq. (4.2e) and determining whether the estimate of b is statistically significant according to a Lagrange multiplier test, where $LM = NR^2$ has a chi square distribution with df = 1, and where R^2 refers to the auxiliary regression (Eq. 4.2e). For example, for Model 1 in Table 4.2, where W is defined in terms of contiguity, ML and OLS estimates of Eq. (4.2e) are reported in Table 4.3.

The LM statistics in Table 4.3 greatly exceed their critical values (3.84). Therefore, the SpARCH coefficients (b) are statistically significant. The error term variance in statistical area i varies directly with the error term variance in its neighbors. As expected the OLS estimate exceeds its ML counterpart. However, the estimates of the unconditional variance (σ^2) turn out to be similar as do the LM statistics. Tests

Table 4.2 Non-nested tests of W

	Intercept	Population	Income	λ
W_1	8717.70 (6.67)	−824.95 (−3.95)	0.1493 (4.045)	0.3753 (5.0838)
W_2	−990.87 (−1.51)	−556.32 (−3.374)	0.1593 (5.496)	0.998 (121.6)
J-test θ	W2 v W1: 2.2668 (20.73)		W1 v W2: 0.726 (5.2055)	
JA-test ϕ	W2 v W1: 4.433 (8.213)		W1 v W2: 1.2176 (5.737)	

Note: z-statistics in parentheses

Table 4.3 SpARCH models for house prices

	ML	OLS
a	0.057	0.038
b	0.403	0.603
σ^2	0.095	0.097
LM	34.57	37.49

for SpARCH may be based on OLS, but consistent estimates of b are obtained by ML.

In nonlinear models ARCH has econometric implications. Since the models in Table 4.2 are estimated nonlinearly by ML, the evidence of SpARCH casts doubt on the consistency of these estimates. Unfortunately, it is difficult to determine the direction of this inconsistency. The solution to this problem is to estimate Eqs. (4.1 and 4.2e) jointly so that the estimates of the parameters in Eq. (4.1) take account of b in Eq. (4.2e).

The spatial counterpart of GARCH models discussed in Chap. 2 (SpGARCH) would include higher order spatial lags. For example, the specification of $\tilde{\tilde{\varepsilon}}_i^2$ in Eq. (4.2e) would constitute a SpARCH (2) model, and the specification of σ^2 would constitute a SpGARCH (1,1) model.

Estimating W

These tests would be unnecessary if W could be estimated instead of being imposed exogenously. Although exogenizing W is by far the most common approach to specifying spatial connectivity, a second and more recent approach infers W from the data using various geostatistical modeling techniques (Table 4.1). Getis and Aldstadt (2006) propose an algorithm which searches for spatial clustering in the vicinity of selected seeds. The algorithm (AMOEBA) is based on the local statistics model in Getis and Aldstadt (2004) and constructs a data-driven empirical representation of W. In an empirical application they report that the t-statistic on the SAR coefficient is only 1.63 when W is based on contiguity but it is 98.79 when W is derived through their algorithm. Critics may argue that because their algorithm mines the data, the goodness-of-fit was bound to be superior to its rivals'.[1] Paelinck

[1]Their SAC coefficient is 0.97 which implies the residuals contain a spatial unit root.

(2007) too does something similar by grouping correlation coefficients using an optimization algorithm so that observations that are correlated are also related spatially.

A second geostatistical technique is the spatial filtering methodology originally proposed by Griffith (1996). As discussed in Chap. 3, the principle eigenvector of W provides a measure of the relative positioning of each spatial unit and expresses the general degree of connectivity between spatial units. Other eigenvectors, or spatial filters, express different aspects of spatial connectivity, including regional basins, core–periphery, etc. Several authors have investigated which spatial filters are statistically significant (Getis and Griffith 2002; Tiefelsdorf and Griffith 2007; Dray et al. 2006). If all spatial filters are statistically significant then W is correctly specified. If not, they suggest using the significant filters only, which is equivalent to modifying the specification of W in light of the data. The methodology is semi-parametric because W itself is parametric. Results obtained by this methodology naturally depend on how W was parameterized in the first place. If W was incorrectly specified, the spatial filters will be misspecified too, and suffer from pre-test bias.

A third technique uses the covariance matrix from a spatial regression and is based on a remark by Anselin (1988, p. 176): "When observations are available over time as well as across space, these constraints (on W) can be relaxed. In the particular case where the time dimension is larger than the spatial dimension, a spatial weight matrix is no longer necessary..." In this case, where T is larger than N, W may be estimated from spatial panel data.

This idea has been followed-up by Meen (1996) in the spatial dynamics of house prices, by Beenstock and Felsenstein (2012) and by Bhattacharjee and Jensen-Butler (2013). Bhattacharjee and Jensen-Butler obtain spatial weights from the estimated covariance matrix of the spatial errors (i.e. from the observed pattern of spatial autocorrelation). They use this method to study the diffusion of housing demand across UK regions. Their results show significant heterogeneity in regional housing markets indicating that not just physical distance matters, but also social and cultural distance between areas seems to be important. Beenstock and Felsenstein use the variance-covariance matrix of spatial panel data to solve for the spatial connectivity matrix (W) and heterogeneous panel SAR coefficients, as explained in detail below. However, there is an identification problem because there are more unknown elements of W than there are pairwise correlations between the panel units.

Bailey et al. (2016) estimate W for the case in which W is sparse, T is smaller than N, and T is at least 80. They calculate the $\frac{1}{2}N(N-1)$ correlations between the panel units, which are ranked in ascending order in terms of their p-values. If for simplicity $N = 3$ there are three p-values: $PV_1 < PV_2 < PV_3$. Let PV^* denote a predetermined p-value below which the null hypothesis that this family of correlation is zero cannot be rejected. If $PV_1 \leq PV^*/3$ the first correlation (with the lowest p-value) cannot be assumed to be zero. If $PV_2 \leq PV^*/2$ the first two correlations cannot be assumed to be zero. If, for example, this rule implies that r_{12} and r_{13} are significantly different from zero but r_{23} is not, $w_{12} = 1$ if $r_{12} > 0$, $w_{13} = -1$ if $r_{13} < 0$, and $w_{23} = 0$. This procedure resolves the identification problem by defining w discretely rather than continuously. Since W is sparse, many elements are zero and elements which are not zero are assumed to be 1 or -1.

Folmer and Oud (2008) use structural equation modeling (SEM) in which spatial lags are treated as latent variables. In SEM, the structural component of a model represents that causal relations between the latent variables, and the measurement component models the relationship between the latent variables and their observable indicators. They show in an empirical illustration that estimates of W by SEM turn out to be similar to their exogenously specified counterparts. However, their latent variable estimator is naturally more flexible than when W is imposed exogenously.

Finally, the general maximum entropy (GME) model has been used to estimate W empirically (Fernandez-Vazquez et al. 2009) in contexts where the spatial panel data are short (N larger than T). Invariably, in estimating a SAR model, insufficient data necessitates the imposition of W. GME estimates the elements of W jointly with the error terms of the model parameters by allowing for the estimation of unknown probability distributions in situations with limited data. In typically row-standardized, non-negative W matrices, each row can be considered as having a probability distribution. GME identifies unknown probability distributions by choosing the most uniform distribution in light of the limited data. This can be done for parameters and errors in standard models and for W in SAR models.

LeSage and Pace (2014) have argued that concerns about the mispecification of W are "the biggest myth in spatial econometrics". They claim that alternative specifications of W make little difference to the predictions of dependent variables and to estimated direct and indirect effects of covariates. For example, when $N = 1000$ LeSage and Pace report that predictions based on contiguity are correlated 0.9817 with 5 nearest neighbors and are correlated 0.9644 with 30 nearest neighbors. This suggests that the number of neighbors does not matter. Even if predictions happen to be similar, their differences might be statistically significant. Indeed, according to Fisher's test, the difference between these correlations is in fact highly significant ($z = 7.51$). Even the difference between 5 and 10 nearest neighbors is significant ($z = -2.31$). As correlations approach 1 even small differences between correlations tend to be statistically significant. In any case, the non-nested tests reported in Table 4.2 indicate that the specification of W makes a difference.

In this chapter we describe and extend our proposal (Beenstock and Felsenstein 2012) to estimate W. This proposal is based on the method of moments, in which the spatial moments generated by the data are used to estimate W non-parametrically. Out of the geostatistical techniques that have been reviewed, our methodology has most in common with Bhattacharjee and Jensen-Butler (2013). Specifically, we hypothesize a SAR model to be estimated from spatial panel data. We infer W directly from the covariance matrix for the data, from which we also infer heterogeneous SAR coefficients. We show that W and the SAR coefficients are typically under-identified because there are insufficient moment conditions in the data. When W is symmetric the identification deficit turns out to be 1. The number of moment conditions increases if instead of the conventional Pearson covariance matrix, which is symmetric, the Gini covariance matrix is used, which is asymmetric. We show that in this case the identification deficit is not closed because W has to be asymmetric; the number of moment conditions increases, but so does the number of unknown elements of W.

We suggest an interesting special case in which W and the SAR coefficients are exactly identified. Moreover, this special case turns out to be numerically and computationally tractable. We present an empirical application for this special case using spatial panel data for house prices in Israel. We also estimate a "reduced rank" version of the model using the statistically significant principal components of the covariance matrix.

4.2 Methodology

The Data Generating Process

Spatial units are labeled by i = 1,2,. . .,N and time periods by t = 1,2,. . .,T. Let y_t denote a column vector of length N of outcomes in time period t for each spatial unit. The panel SAR model may be written as:

$$y_t = \alpha + \Lambda W y_t + \varepsilon_t \tag{4.3a}$$

where α is an N × 1 vector of common or fixed effects, and Λ is a diagonal matrix of SAR coefficients with diagonal elements λ_i. If these SAR coefficients are homogeneous so that $\lambda_i = \lambda$, Λ is replaced by a scalar λ in Eq. (4.3a). The variance covariance matrix $\Sigma = E(\varepsilon\varepsilon')$ is assumed to be time invariant (temporal homoscedasticity), diagonal (no spatial autocorrelation between ε_i and ε_j) but may be spatially heteroscedastic so that the variance of $\varepsilon(\sigma^2{}_i)$ may vary between spatial units. The spatial Wold representation of Eq. (4.3a) is:

$$\begin{aligned} y_t &= A(\alpha + \varepsilon_t) \\ A &= (I_N - \Lambda W)^{-1} \end{aligned} \tag{4.3b}$$

Invertibility requires that the determinant of $I_N - \Lambda W$ be non zero, i.e. the rank of $I_N - \Lambda W$ equals N. If, for example, $\lambda_i = \lambda = 1$ and the elements of W are row-summed to 1, $I_N - \lambda W$ is not invertible as discussed in the next chapter. $I_N - \Lambda W$ is invertible provided the SAR coefficients are less than 1. Let $V = yy'$ denote the population covariance matrix of the y's. Substituting Eq. (4.3b) into V for y gives:

$$V = A\Sigma A' = H \tag{4.4}$$

Note that if A is symmetric $A = A'$. Since V is symmetric it contains ½N(N + 1) independent elements. If W is symmetric and $\Sigma_j w_{ij} = 1$ (row sum equals unity) there are ½(N − 2)(N − 1) unknown w_{ij} elements of W. There are also N unknown SAR coefficients and N unknown variances (diagonal elements of Σ), making ½N(N + 1) + 1 unknown parameters altogether. Therefore, there is an identification deficit of one; the number of population moments in V is one less than the number of unknown parameters. If W is asymmetric the identification deficit increases to ½N(N + 1). It increases further if ε happens to be spatially autocorrelated.

Notice that even if W is symmetric, ΛW and therefore A are generally asymmetric. If the SAR coefficients are homogeneous, i.e. $\lambda_i = \lambda$, A would be symmetric if W is symmetric. Nevertheless, H is symmetric. As mentioned, the identification deficit is smallest and equal to one when W is symmetric. In this case it might be tempting to exogenize one element of W or Λ so that all the parameters are exactly identified. However, it is of course impossible to test the validity of such arbitrary identifying restrictions. Therefore, we do not exogenize parameters because this goes against the spirit of our proposal.

Aquaro et al. (2015) too consider the case in which the SAR coefficients are heterogeneous in spatial panel data. However, unlike us they assume that W is exogenous. Unlike us, they assume that I − ΛW is invertible because it is strictly diagonal dominant. If N = 2, and $w_{12} = w_{21} = 1$, A is:

$$A = \begin{bmatrix} 1 & -\lambda_1 \\ -\lambda_2 & 1 \end{bmatrix}^{-1} = \frac{1}{1 - \lambda_1 \lambda_2} \begin{bmatrix} 1 & \lambda_1 \\ \lambda_2 & 1 \end{bmatrix} \tag{4.5}$$

which is not invertible if $\lambda_1\lambda_2 = 1$. Therefore, λ_1 may exceed 1 provided λ_2 is sufficiently smaller than 1, in which case I − λW does not need to be strictly diagonal for invertibility. More generally, invertibility requires $\prod_{i=1}^{N} \lambda_i < 1$.

A Special Case: Heterogeneous Mutuality

The identification deficit disappears in a special case in which ΛW = C happens to be a symmetric matrix, which implies that W is asymmetric, but the direct effect of shocks between spatial units are mutual. In this special case the direct effects of shocks in unit i on unit j are assumed to equal the direct effects of shocks in unit j on unit i. This mutuality is heterogeneous; it varies between spatial units. The leading diagonal of C is zero, hence $c_{nn} = 0$. The off-diagonal elements have the property $c_{ni} = -\beta_n w_{nj} = c_{nj} = -\beta_j w_{jn}$, which implies that:

$$\frac{\lambda_i}{\lambda_j} = \frac{w_{ji}}{w_{nj}} \tag{4.6}$$

In this case Λ, W and Σ are exactly identified. H comprises ½(N − 1)(N − 2) unknown elements of C and N diagonal elements of Σ, which are exactly equal to the ½N(N + 1) independent elements of V.

Using the row sum constraints it is possible to identify the SAR coefficients since:

$$\sum_{j\neq i}^{N} c_{ij} = \lambda_i \sum_{j\neq i}^{N} w_{ij} = \lambda_i \tag{4.7}$$

which in turn may be used to solve for the spatial weights:

$$w_{ij} = -\frac{c_{ij}}{\lambda_i} \tag{4.8}$$

This special case is amenable to solution because the solution for V = H has a hierarchical mathematical structure. First, C and Σ are solved by Eq. (4.4). Then Λ is solved by Eq. (4.7). Finally, W is solved by Eq. (4.8).

The first step is facilitated by using $V^{-1} = (I_N - C)\Sigma^{-1}(I_N - C)$. If, for illustrative purposes N = 3:

$$V^{-1} = \begin{bmatrix} \left(\frac{1}{\sigma_1^2}+\frac{c_{12}^2}{\sigma_2^2}+\frac{c_{13}^2}{\sigma_3^2}\right) & \left(-\frac{c_{12}}{\sigma_1^2}-\frac{c_{12}}{\sigma_2^2}+\frac{c_{13}c_{23}}{\sigma_3^2}\right) & \left(-\frac{c_{13}}{\sigma_1^2}+\frac{c_{12}c_{23}}{\sigma_2^2}-\frac{c_{13}}{\sigma_3^2}\right) \\ \left(-\frac{c_{12}}{\sigma_1^2}-\frac{c_{12}}{\sigma_2^2}+\frac{c_{13}c_{23}}{\sigma_3^2}\right) & \left(\frac{c_{12}^2}{\sigma_1^2}+\frac{1}{\sigma_2^2}+\frac{c_{23}^2}{\sigma_3^2}\right) & \left(\frac{c_{12}c_{13}}{\sigma_1^2}-\frac{c_{23}}{\sigma_2^2}-\frac{c_{23}}{\sigma_3^2}\right) \\ \left(-\frac{c_{13}}{\sigma_1^2}+\frac{c_{12}c_{23}}{\sigma_2^2}-\frac{c_{13}}{\sigma_3^2}\right) & \left(\frac{c_{12}c_{13}}{\sigma_1^2}-\frac{c_{23}}{\sigma_2^2}-\frac{c_{23}}{\sigma_3^2}\right) & \left(\frac{c_{13}^2}{\sigma_1^2}+\frac{c_{23}^2}{\sigma_2^2}+\frac{1}{\sigma_3^2}\right) \end{bmatrix} \tag{4.9a}$$

The six independent elements of V^{-1} solve for the six unknown parameters c_{12}, c_{13}, c_{23}, σ_1, σ_2 and σ_3. The six independent elements in Eq. (4.9a) are nonlinear quadratic equations in the unknown parameters, which are solved in terms of the sample moments (denoted by v) in Eq. (4.9b).

$$V^{-1} \equiv \frac{1}{\det}\begin{bmatrix} v_2^2v_3^2 - v_{23}^2 & v_{23}v_{13} - v_{12}v_3^2 & v_{12}v_{23} - v_2^2v_{13} \\ v_{23}v_{13} - v_{12}v_3^2 & v_1^2v_3^2 - v_{13}^2 & v_{12}v_{13} - v_1^2v_{23} \\ v_{12}v_{23} - v_2^2v_{13} & v_{12}v_{13} - v_1^2v_{23} & v_1^2v_2^2 - v_{12}^2 \end{bmatrix} \tag{4.9b}$$

$$\det = v_1^2\left(v_2^2v_3^2 - v_{23}^2\right) - v_{12}\left(v_{12}v_3^2 - v_{13}v_{23}\right) + v_{13}\left(v_{12}v_{23} - v_2^2v_{13}\right) \tag{4.9c}$$

For example v_1 denotes the standard deviation of y_1 and v_{12} denotes the covariance between $y_1$and y_2. The first element in Eq. (4.9a) equals the first element in Eq. (4.9b) as determined by the data, i.e.:

$$\frac{1}{\hat{\sigma}_1^2}+\frac{\hat{c}_{12}}{\hat{\sigma}_2^2}+\frac{\hat{c}_{13}^2}{\hat{\sigma}_3^2} = \frac{v_2^2v_3^2 - v_{23}^2}{v_1^2\left(v_2^2v_3^2 - v_{23}^2\right) - v_{12}\left(v_{12}v_3^2 - v_{13}v_{23}\right) + v_{13}\left(v_{12}v_{23} - v_2^2v_{13}\right)} \tag{4.10}$$

The second element in Eq. (4.9a) equals the second element in Eq. (4.9b) and so on.

The elements of V^{-1} involve products of the variances and covariances of the data. The determinant of V^{-1} therefore involves products of fourth moments of the data. Subsequently the variances of the estimates of C and Σ involve eighth moments of the data. Consequently, eighth moments of the data are assumed to be finite. Note that if the data are normally distributed their eighth moment equals $105\sigma^8$.

Consistent Estimates of B, W and Σ

In this section we discuss how the population parameters (B, W and Σ) can be estimated for the special case from a sample of T observations on panel data for N spatial units. In contrast to non-spatial panel data, N is naturally fixed in spatial panel data since it usually comprises all the spatial units in the country or region. In the empirical illustration below N = 9 since there are nine regions which cover the entirety of Israel. In larger countries or geopolitical units, such the EU, N will naturally be larger. The sample size varies with T. Given N, the sample covariance matrix estimated from T observations, $\hat{V}_T$, equals the estimate of $A\Sigma A'$, which requires that T > N. Since the probability limit of a product is equal to the product of the probability limits, Eq. (4.4) implies:

$$p\lim(\hat{V}_T) = p\lim(\hat{A}_T)p\lim(\hat{\Sigma}_T)p\lim(\hat{A}_T)' \tag{4.11}$$

Therefore, if:

$$p\lim(\hat{V}_T) = V \tag{4.12}$$

we may conclude therefore that $p\lim(\hat{A}_T) = A$ and $p\lim(\hat{\Sigma}_T) = \Sigma$. The main parameters of interest are B and W, which according to Eq. (4.4) are related to A nonlinearly. According to the Slutzky Theorem[2] the probability limit of a nonlinear function of x equals the nonlinear function of the probability limit of x. Therefore, since $p\lim(\hat{A}_T) = A$, the Slutzky Theorem states that $p\lim(\hat{B}_T) = B$ and $p\lim(\hat{W}_T) = W$. In short, consistency requires that Eq. (4.12) be valid.[3]

If the panel data are independent, Eq. (4.12) is obviously valid. However, they are dependent for two reasons. First, under the null hypothesis the units in the panel are spatially dependent. Secondly, the data may be temporally dependent. For example, y_{nt} might be temporally autocorrelated within and perhaps between spatial units.[4] If N is fixed the former dependence is not important for consistency of $\hat{V}$. However, the latter dependence is obviously important. The conditions for consistency[5] due to the latter are:

---

[2]The Slutzky Theorem states that plim[f(x)] = f[plim(x)]. Also plim(A′) = plim(A)′.

[3]Since the Slutzky Theorem implies $p\lim(\hat{V}^{-1}) = V^{-1}$ Eq. (4.7) implies $p\lim(\hat{C}) = C, p\lim(\hat{\Sigma}) = \Sigma$.

[4]In Eq. (4.1) ε_{it} might be correlated with ε_{it-1} and ε_{kt-1}.

[5]See e.g. Spanos (1986) and Davidson and MacKinnon (2009).

(i) The panel data are temporally stationary, i.e. the unconditional sample moments are independent of t.
(ii) The panel data are ergodic, i.e. events that are separated far enough in time are asymptotically independent.

We therefore test for these conditions using panel unit root tests. If N is not fixed because it is a sample of spatial units rather than the population, conditions i and ii must also apply spatially. This means that the data are spatially stationary, isotropic and ergodic. The former means that the sample moments do not depend on where they are measured in space. If in addition the sample moments do not depend on the orientation between units, the data are isotropic. Spatial ergodicity means that more distant spatial units are asymptotically independent. However, here N is fixed. Therefore, provided we check for conditions i and ii we may ascertain whether Eq. (4.10) is valid, in which case the moment estimator is consistent[6] for B and W, and the estimate of Σ is consistent.

If the data are temporally autocorrelated the long-run covariance matrix (V_{LR}) differs from V. In this case Eq. (4.1) includes temporal lags as well as spatial lags as in Chap. 3 where V_{LR} is defined. Since V_{LR} is the asymptotic tendency of the covariance matrix, we should use V_{LR} rather than V if the data happen to be temporally autocorrelated. If the data are not autocorrelated we may use the sample covariance matrix V.

In conventional SAR models in which W is imposed the SAR coefficients cannot be estimated by OLS because Wy_t in Eq. (4.3a) is endogenous; it is not independent of ε_t. Instead the SAR coefficients have to be estimated by the methods of maximum likelihood or instrumental variables. This endogeneity problem does not arise[7] with our proposed estimator because Eq. (4.5) is not affected by the endogeneity of Wy_t. This convenient property results from the fact that Eq. (4.2) is the spatial reduced form of the SAR model. Therefore, the population moments of V exactly identify B, W and Σ in the special case. Estimation error is induced in the usual way because in practice these parameters are estimated from sample moments. Analytical solutions for the variances of the estimates of W and B are not available because these estimates are nonlinear functions of the sample moments. However, they may be obtained numerically by panel-bootstrapping $\hat{V}_T$.

Spatial Gini Covariance

Whereas Pearson's covariance matrix (V) is necessarily symmetric, the Gini covariance matrix (V_G) is asymmetric (Yitzhaki and Schechtman 2013). The Gini covariance between i and j is defined as cov(y_{it}, R_{jt}) where R_{jt} denotes the rank out of T of y_{jt}. The largest value of y_j has rank T and the smallest value has rank 1. Since cov(y_{jt}, R_{it}) generally differs from cov(y_{it}, R_{jt}) the Gini covariance matrix is asymmetric and V_G contains N^2 independent elements in contrast to V which contains only ½N (N + 1) independent elements. Gini covariances are symmetric like their Pearson

[6]The finite sample properties of the moment estimator may be derived using Monte Carlo methods.

[7]Obviously the estimates of B and W depend upon the data. This is true of any estimate. However, this does not mean that the estimates are affected by simultaneous equations bias.

counterparts when y_i and y_j are exchangeable, i.e. when the shapes of the marginal distributions for y_i and y_j are the same. The Gini counterpart of Eq. (4.5) is:

$$V_G = A\Sigma_G A' = H_G \tag{4.13}$$

where Σ_G denotes the Gini covariance matrix for ε. If Σ_G is diagonal it may be shown that V_G must be symmetric in which case all the variates are exchangeable. If V_G is asymmetric it must be because Σ_G is asymmetric, which in turn means that Σ_G is not diagonal. The off-diagonal elements of Σ_G are induced by SAC in ε such that SAC between ε_i and ε_j is asymmetric. Since Σ_G is generally asymmetric it contains N^2 independent elements. Therefore, although the Gini covariance matrix increases the number of moments by ½N(N − 1) the number of unknown SAC parameters increases even more by N(N − 1). Indeed, if in the data V_G is asymmetric it must be because Σ_G is asymmetric in which event the SAR model is misspecified and a SARMA specification is required instead.

Principal Components

We suggest that more robust estimates of the SAR model parameters may be obtained by applying Eq. (4.5) to the statistically significant principal components of V. These principal components contain information on spatial dependence in the data. If there are K < N statistically significant principal components the rank of V is equal to K. The N − K = p statistically insignificant principal components do not contain useful information on spatial dependence in the data. We use the eigenvalue test due to Schott (1991) to determine p where the eigenvalues of V are denoted by λ:

$$S = \frac{pT}{2}\left[\frac{p^{-1}\sum_{i=1+K}^{N}\lambda_i^2}{\left[p^{-1}\sum_{i=1+K}^{N}\lambda_i\right]^2} - 1\right] \approx \chi^2_{\frac{p(1+p)}{2}-1} \tag{4.14}$$

If S is smaller than the critical value of chi square we cannot reject the hypothesis that the p smallest eigenvalues are not significantly different from the K'th.

The spectral decomposition of V is $V = G\Lambda G'$ where Λ is the N × N eigenvalue matrix of V and G is the N × N matrix of its eigenvectors. The N × 1 principal component vector is equal to $P = G'y$. Let Λ^* denote the K × K eigenvalue matrix formed by the statistically significant principal components, let G^* denote its N × K matrix of eigenvectors, and let $P^* = G^{*\prime}y$ be the K × 1 vector of significant principal components. Finally, we denote $y^* = \Lambda P^*$ where Λ is an N × K matrix of loadings obtained[8] using the generalized inverse of $G^{*\prime}$: $\Lambda = G^{*\prime +} = (G^*G^{*\prime})^{-1}G^*$. The variance covariance matrix formed by the statistically significant principal components is $V^* = y^*y^{*\prime}$. Using V^* rather than V eliminates statistically insignificant spatial dependence in the data, thereby increasing the robustness of the estimates of the SAR model.

[8]We used the PCA procedure in Matlab.

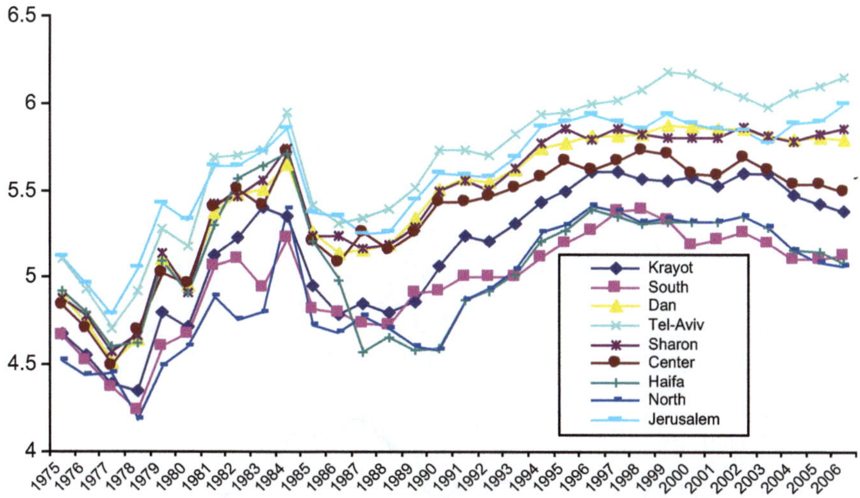

Fig. 4.1 Regional house prices in Israel logs at 1991 prices

4.3 Empirical Application

The Data

To illustrate the methodology we use spatial panel data for the logarithm of regional house prices (measured in constant prices, see Fig. 4.1) in Israel observed annually between 1975 and 2006 for nine regions mapped in Map 4.1. The panel unit root test statistic (IPS) due to Im et al. (2003) is −1.74 and its common factor counterpart (CIPS) due to Pesaran (2007) is −1.902. Therefore, the data are nonstationary. However, the data are stationary in first differences since the IPS and CIPS statistics are −6.029 and −4.216 respectively. These panel unit root tests ignore spatial dependency. However, as noted in Chap. 7, they are reliable provided the spatial dependence is not too strong. In any case these unit root tests fall within the critical values[9] provided in Table 7.1.

The correlation matrices for the levels ($d = 0$) and first differences ($d = 1$) of the log of real house prices are given in Table 4.4. Not surprisingly, the correlations are larger in levels ($d = 0$) than in first-differences ($d = 1$). However, even in the latter case the correlations are large and positive and range between 0.225 and 0.95. Because the data are stationary in first differences, the correlation matrix is a consistent estimate for the case when $d = 1$. We assume for the meanwhile that the correlation matrix implies that the cross-section dependence in the data is induced by spatial dependence and is not induced by common factors as discussed in Chap. 10. In fact the average correlation (0.728) is much higher than its critical value of 0.12 for weak (spatial) cross-section dependence.

[9]In the empirical illustration $N = 9$ and $T = 31$. Table 7.1 does not include this particular case.

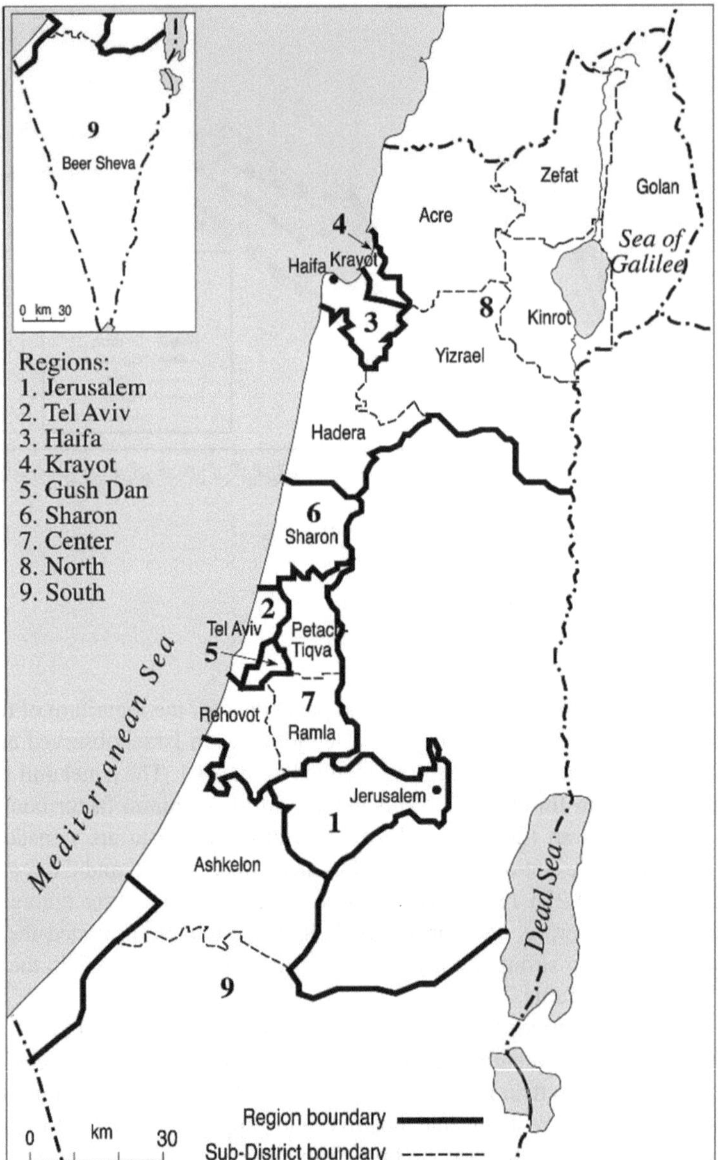

Map 4.1 Geographic regions of Israel

To compute the long-term covariance or correlation matrix we estimated a first order panel vector autoregression (PVAR) in which the first difference of the log of house prices is regressed the lagged first differences of house prices within and between regions. To our surprise, the 81 VAR parameters were not statistically

Table 4.4 Correlation matrix for regional house prices

	d	South	Dan	Tel Aviv	Sharon	Center	Haifa	North	Jerusalem
Krayot	0	0.959	0.978	0.967	0.977	0.953	0.733	0.770	0.956
	1	0.711	0.888	0.797	0.865	0.755	0.824	0.225	0.748
South	0		0.954	0.943	0.953	0.959	0.709	0.918	0.028
	1		0.797	0.751	0.800	0.806	0.703	0.670	0.698
Dan	0			0.991	0.994	0.972	0.638	0.793	0.971
	1			0.950	0.947	0.891	0.817	0.391	0.907
Tel Aviv	0				0.987	0.961	0.648	0.774	0.980
	1				0.914	0.886	0.715	0.413	0.940
Sharon	0					0.971	0.662	0.779	0.975
	1					0.855	0.910	0.395	0.888
Center	0						0.667	0.765	0.948
	1						0.638	0.549	0.802
Haifa	0							0.469	0.708
	1							0.322	0.730
North	0								0.737
	1								0.326

Table 4.5 Gini correlation matrix for regional house prices (d = 1)

	Krayot	South	Dan	Tel Aviv	Sharon	Center	Haifa	North	Jerusalem
Krayot	1	0.632	0.828	0.671	0.769	0.715	0.830	0.536	0.672
South	0.557	1	0.690	0.603	0.693	0.743	0.611	0.696	0.628
Dan	0.835	0.702	1	0.937	0.905	0.890	0.818	0.453	0.912
Tel Aviv	0.700	0.602	0.927	1	0.845	0.820	0.685	0.419	0.929
Sharon	0.801	0.695	0.905	0.851	1	0.805	0.800	0.452	0.887
Center	0.647	0.708	0.836	0.778	0.769	1	0.601	0.516	0.713
Haifa	0.763	0.656	0.760	0.574	0.744	0.564	1	0.447	0.693
North	0.114	0.804	0.474	0.420	0.398	0.619	0.400	1	0.342
Jerusalem	0.644	0.553	0.869	0.933	0.853	0.716	0.667	0.317	1

significant. This is also true if only the nine within lags are specified. This means that logs of house prices are indistinguishable from random walks. It also means that the long-term covariance matrix (V_{LR}) equals V in the present illustration.

We report in Table 4.5 the Gini correlation matrix for the first difference in the logarithm of house prices. The Gini correlation coefficient between y_i and y_j is defined as:

$$r_{Gij} = \frac{\mathrm{cov}\left(y_{it}R_{jt}\right)}{\mathrm{cov}(y_{it}R_{it})} \tag{4.15}$$

where R_i refers to the rank of y_i in its distribution. Whereas Table 4.4 is symmetric, Table 4.5 is asymmetric. For example, the Pearson correlation coefficient between the change in log house prices in the Krayot and the South is 0.711 in Table 4.4. According to Table 4.5 the Gini correlation between Krayot and the South is 0.632 while between the South and Krayot it is 0.557. The Gini correlations range between 0.11 and 0.93. In most cases the Gini correlations turn out to be asymmetric. In some cases, e.g. Krayot and North the Gini correlations are highly asymmetric whereas in other cases the correlation are almost symmetric, e.g. between Tel Aviv and Dan. Table 4.5 suggests that imposing symmetry distorts the correlations between regional house prices because the marginal distributions of regional house prices are not "exchangeable".

Results

In this section, we report for the special case estimates of W and the SAR coefficients using Eq. (4.4) for the covariance matrix of the log differences of regional house prices. We use differences rather than levels because the levels are nonstationary. Therefore, estimates of $C = BW$ are consistent because the covariance matrix is consistent. Since, as noted in Sect. 4.2 the solution to the special case has a three-step hierarchical structure, this greatly simplifies the computational burden. We have no reason to believe that our proposed methodology for the special case would not be feasible if N happens to be larger than 9. However, if N is relatively large T must be correspondingly larger since the moment estimator requires that T be greater than N. This means that the moment estimator is most probably not feasible if N is large.

The estimated W for the special case is reported in Table 4.6. The elements of the estimated W matrix range between −0.159 and 0.561 and estimated W is asymmetric. In some cases there is near symmetry, e.g. between South and Krayot, but in most cases the estimated elements of W are asymmetric. For example, the weight of Jerusalem for Tel Aviv is 0.404 and the weight of Tel Aviv for Jerusalem is 0.561. Therefore, Jerusalem is more connected to Tel Aviv than is Tel Aviv to Jerusalem. Notice that these asymmetric weights are correlated; if one is larger then so is the other. Notice also that some elements are negative suggesting negative spillovers rather than positive ones. Meen (1996), Bhattacharjee and Jensen-Butler (2013) and Bailey et al. (2016) also report negative estimates of elements of W. We see no reason why spatial weights must be positive since spatial units may have "good" neighbors and "bad" neighbors. There is no pair, however, in which w_{ij} has the opposite sign to w_{ij}, although there is no inherent reason why this should not arise.

Neither here nor elsewhere do we try to interpret the relative orders of magnitude of the estimated elements of W since our main purpose is to demonstrate the methodology. According to Table 4.6 the strongest spatial connectivity occurs between Jerusalem and Tel Aviv, between Haifa and Krayot and between North and South. This suggests that imposing W a priori in terms, for example, of distance and contiguity would have been quite inappropriate and misleading. Letting the data "speak for themselves" seems to lead to quite different estimates of W than distance alone might suggest.

Table 4.6 Spatial connectivity matrix ($d = 1$)

	Krayot	South	Dan	Tel Aviv	Sharon	Center	Haifa	North	Jerusalem
Krayot		−0.058	0.279	0.037	0.249	0.111	0.365	0.123	−0.096
South	−0.059		0.127	−0.056	0.158	0.294	0.175	0.362	−0.002
Dan	0.214	0.097		0.295	0.119	0.176	0.120	−0.093	0.074
Tel Aviv	0.026	0.039	0.273		0.125	0.199	−0.046	0.058	0.404
Sharon	0.177	0.111	0.110	0.126		0.125	0.146	0.026	0.179
Center	0.095	0.249	0.196	0.241	0.150		−0.099	0.130	0.038
Haifa	0.343	0.163	0.147	−0.061	0.193	−0.109		0.188	0.166
North	0.148	0.470	−0.159	0.108	0.048	0.198	0.210		−0.032
Jerusalem	−0.094	−0.002	0.095	0.561	0.248	0.044	0.173	−0.024	

Table 4.7 Estimates of SAR coefficients and standard errors of estimate

	Krayot	South	Dan	Tel Aviv	Sharon	Center	Haifa	North	Jerusalem
SAR	0.726	0.721	0.949	1.027	1.023	0.848	0.772	0.554	0.739
$\sigma(\varepsilon)$	0.072	0.075	0.027	0.043	0.056	0.077	0.117	0.159	0.057

Table 4.7 reports the SAR coefficients and the variances of ε for each of the nine regions. The SAR coefficients range between 0.55 and 1.03. Since spatial weights are row-summed to 1, SAR coefficients must be less than 1 for stationarity and for the invertibility of I − BW. As mentioned in Sect. 2.1, invertibility does not require that all the SAR coefficients be less than 1. In any case the panel unit root tests clearly indicated that the data are stationary in log first differences. The standard errors of estimate range between 0.027 and 0.159. Since the data are logarithms these standard errors are approximately percentages. The SAR model fits best in Dan and worst in the North. There is substantial heterogeneity in the SAR coefficients, and some of the SAR coefficients exceed 1. However, the fact that the majority of SAR coefficients are less than one ensures that the data as a whole are stationary. Indeed, the product of the SAR coefficients equals 0.14, which is smaller than 1 as required.

Although the spatial weights are asymmetric, spatial impulse responses are symmetric by definition in the special case. For example, the spatial weight of Jerusalem for Tel Aviv is 0.404 and the weight of Tel Aviv for Jerusalem is 0.561. However, the SAR coefficient for Tel Aviv is greater than the SAR coefficient for Jerusalem. Using Eq. (4.5), the direct impulse effect of Tel Aviv on Jerusalem is $0.739 \times 0.561 = 0.4145$ which is equal to the direct impulse of Jerusalem on Tel Aviv.

Bootstrapping

Had the population covariance matrix (V) been known, its ½N(N − 1) elements would solve for the unknown population parameters in the special case (BW and Σ). The population variances of BW may be calculated in the normal way using Σ. We use the panel-bootstrap[10] to compute the standard errors of the estimated components of W and the SAR coefficients for the case when $d = 1$. This procedure draws samples from the residuals of the estimated SAR model (ε). Since these residuals are spatially uncorrelated we do not have to take direct account of spatial dependence in the bootstrap since this is taken into consideration by the SAR model itself. Therefore, the spatial dependence in the sample data is appropriately incorporated into the bootstrapping exercise. We used 1000 replications.[11] Because the bootstrapped means differ slightly from the estimates reported in Tables 4.5 and 4.6, we report in Table 4.8 and 4.9 the means as well as the standard deviations of the bootstrapped parameters.

[10]Bootstrapping is simpler here than in Bhattacharjee and Jensen-Butler (2013) because apart from W they estimate other structural model parameters. However, they do not use the panel-bootstrap.

[11]See Andrews and Buchinsky (2000) regarding the desirable number of bootstrap replications.

Table 4.8 Bootstrapped means and standard deviations of W

	Krayot	South	Dan	Tel Aviv	Sharon	Center	Haifa	North	Jerusalem
Krayot		−0.098	0.267	0.019	0.264	0.119	**0.378**	0.118	−0.069
		0.188	*0.138*	*0.120*	*0.157*	*0.193*	*0.173*	*0.168*	*0.161*
South	−0.102		0.140	−0.057	0.149	**0.361**	0.148	**0.369**	−0.007
	0.193		*0.143*	*0.128*	*0.180*	*0.162*	*0.179*	*0.131*	*0.204*
Dan	0.212	0.107		**0.332**	0.106	0.133	0.152	−0.109	0.068
	0.114	*0.105*		*0.124*	*0.110*	*0.102*	*0.082*	*0.072*	*0.118*
Tel Aviv	0.009	−0.045	**0.308**		0.119	0.186	−0.048	0.053	**0.416**
	0.089	*0.089*	*0.106*		*0.096*	*0.101*	*0.067*	*0.054*	*0.091*
Sharon	0.191	0.103	0.101	0.118		0.155	0.130	0.014	0.188
	0.105	*0.124*	*0.104*	*0.095*		*0.111*	*0.113*	*0.076*	*0.103*
Center	0.110	**0.305**	0.152	0.224	0.182		−0.075	0.075	0.026
	0.177	*0.129*	*0.118*	*0.120*	*0.128*		*0.189*	*0.144*	*0.177*
Haifa	**0.353**	0.150	0.182	−0.068	0.177	−0.097		0.172	0.130
	0.123	*0.172*	*0.0837*	*0.092*	*0.149*	*0.210*		*0.142*	*0.150*
North	0.195	**0.515**	−0.191	0.101	0.028	0.120	0.251		−0.019
	0.321	*0.210*	*0.124*	*0.106*	*0.146*	*0.245*	*0.209*		*0.185*
Jerusalem	−0.076	−0.010	0.096	**0.576**	0.252	0.033	0.135	−0.005	
	0.159	*0.198*	*0.161*	*0.131*	*0.130*	*0.203*	*0.161*	*0.125*	

Notes: Special case, d = 1. Standard errors reported in italics. Bold items exceed two standard errors

Table 4.9 Bootstrapped means and standard deviations of B

Krayot	South	Dan	Tel Aviv	Sharon	Center	Haifa	North	Jerusalem
0.763	0.727	0.957	1.022	1.001	0.847	0.778	0.540	0.740
0.138	0.087	0.069	0.081	0.096	0.099	0.133	0.124	0.103

Table 4.8 indicates that the elements of W are estimated imprecisely. Indeed, most of the elements of W are not statistically significant. We highlight in bold the eight elements of W that have means that are at least twice as large as their standard deviation. Notice that none of the negative spatial weights is statistically significant. By contrast all the SAR coefficients reported in Table 4.9 are statistically significant.

Principal Components Estimates

We use Eq. (4.14) to test the statistical significance of the eigenvalues of the covariance matrix. Since N = 9 in our example we test the hypothesis that the p smallest eigenvalues of the covariance matrix V are equal to the N-p-1'th eigenvalue. If the null hypothesis cannot be rejected we determine the rank of V to be k = N-p-1. When d = 0 we find that the rank of the covariance matrix is 9 (full rank). However, when d = 1, k = 4 according Schott's test.

Using these first four principal components we compute V* from which we derive the following nonparametric estimates of the W matrix and the SAR coefficients for the special case.

Table 4.10 should be compared with Table 4.6 and Table 4.11 should be compared with Table 4.7. The reduced rank estimate of W has a wider range than its counterpart in Table 4.6. On the whole, the elements in Table 4.10 are quite different to their counterparts in Table 4.6. However, Table 4.11 indicates that the SAR coefficients are similar to their counterparts in Table 4.7, and the goodness-of-fit in Table 4.11 is clearly superior. The reduced rank SAR models are especially accurate in the South, Dan, Tel Aviv, Sharon and Center. The model continues to fit poorly in the North.

In this chapter we focused on the specification of the spatial connectivity matrix W in two contexts: cross-section data and panel data. In cross-section data there is no alternative to specifying W exogenously. Nevertheless, alternative specifications of W may be tested empirically. Since alternative specifications of W are non-nested, we proposed non-nested test procedures to distinguish between rival specifications of W. In an empirical example for Israel concerning cross-section data for house prices, we showed that specifying W in terms of first order contiguity generates very different results to when W is specified in terms of inverse distance. Moreover, because neither specification encompasses the other there is no preferred specification.

We also proposed a non-parametric moment estimator, designed for spatial panel data, to estimate the spatial connectivity matrix W in heterogeneous SAR models. Normally, W is imposed by the investigator rather than estimated. Our proposal joins recent suggestions to estimate W rather to impose it. However, our proposal differs from these suggestions. The basic insight is that the variance-covariance matrix of

Table 4.10 Estimate of W using four principal components

	Krayot	South	Dan	Tel Aviv	Sharon	Center	Haifa	North	Jerusalem
Krayot		−0.383	0.297	−0.160	0.130	0.359	0.622	0.241	−0.102
South	−0.344		0.018	−0.334	0.093	0.769	0.530	0.356	0.098
Dan	0.203	0.014		0.182	0.084	0.311	0.146	−0.093	0.152
Tel Aviv	−0.104	−0.240	0.170		0.305	0.326	−0.042	0.077	0.509
Sharon	0.083	−0.066	0.077	0.299		0.305	0.249	0.002	0.050
Center	0.226	0.540	0.284	0.318	0.303		−0.444	−0.058	−0.170
Haifa	0.454	0.431	0.154	−0.048	0.286	−0.513		0.065	0.171
North	0.373	0.614	0.207	0.183	0.005	−0.142	0.138		0.036
Jerusalem	−0.094	0.101	0.203	0.726	0.074	−0.248	0.216	0.021	

Table 4.11 Estimates of SAR coefficients and σ(ε) using four principal components (d = 1)

	Krayot	South	Dan	Tel Aviv	Sharon	Center	Haifa	North	Jerusalem
SAR	0.677	0.753	0.978	1.048	1.066	1.073	0.927	0.436	0.733
σ(ε)	0.060	0.045	0.001	0.002	0.003	0.002	0.081	0.169	0.043

the panel data contains information on their spatial dependence. We used panel data for regional house prices in Israel to illustrate the methodology.

If W is symmetric there is an identification deficit of one, because there are insufficient moment conditions in the data to identify all the parameters in the SAR model. However, in a "special case" of mutual heterogeneity the parameters are exactly identified. We therefore present results for the special case. Solving the parameters from the moment conditions involves finding solutions to a relatively large number of simultaneous equations that happen to be nonlinear polynomials. However, thanks to the recursive structure of the special case, we find no difficulty in obtaining solutions.

We have illustrated how W may be estimated from spatial panel data in SAR models in which there are no covariates. The methodology may be extended to SAR models in which covariates are specified, i.e. where instead of Eq. (4.1) the model is:

$$y_t = \alpha + BWy_t + X_t\gamma + \varepsilon_t \tag{4.16a}$$

where X is an N × k matrix of covariates and γ is a k-vector of parameters to be estimated. We suggest an iterative two step method for estimating these parameters. In step 1 γ is initialized at γ_0 and $y_t - X_t\gamma_0 = \breve{y}_{0t}$ is calculated. In step 2 $\breve{y}_{0t}$ is used to estimate B_1 and W_1 as described in this chapter. In iteration 1 γ_1 is estimated in step 1 by regressing spatially-filtered y_t on X_t:

$$y_t - B_1W_1y_t = \alpha_1 + X_t\gamma_1 + \varepsilon_{1t} \tag{4.16b}$$

In step 2 B_2 and W_2 are estimated using $y_t - X_t\hat{\gamma}_1 = \breve{y}_{1t}$. Iterations continue until the estimates of γ, B, W and α converge.

In the next chapter, we focus on the issue of nonstationarity in spatial cross-section data. This issue is important for a variety of reasons. First, spatial econometricians have been concerned with unit roots and cointegration in spatial cross-section data. Second, some spatial cross-section data may be nonstationary. Third, in nonstationary spatial panel data, unit roots can be induced by spatial as well as temporal phenomena. Chap. 5 explains why.

References

Andrews DWK, Buchinsky M (2000) A three-step method for choosing the number of bootstrap replications. Econometrica 68:23–51

Anselin L (1988) Spatial econometrics: methods and models. Kluwer Academic, Dordrecht

Aquaro M, Bailey N, Pesaran MH (2015) Quasi maximum likelihood estimation of spatial models with heterogeneous coefficients. Mimeo, University of Warwick

Bailey N, Holly S, Pesaran MH (2016) A two stage approach to spatiotemporal analysis with strong and weak cross-section dependence. J Appl Economet 31(1):249–280

Beenstock M, Felsenstein D (2012) Nonparametric estimation of the spatial connectivity matrix using spatial panel data. Geogr Anal 44(4):386–397

Beenstock M, Felsenstein D (2016) Chapter 11: Double spatial dependence in gravity models: migration from the European Neighborhood to the European Union. In: Patuelli R, Arbia G (eds) Spatial econometric interaction modelling. Springer, Cham

Bhattacharjee A, Jensen-Butler C (2013) Estimation of the spatial weights matrix under constraints. Reg Sci Urban Econ 43:617–634

Cuaresma JC, Feldkircher M (2013) Spatial filtering, model uncertainty and the speed of income convergence in Europe. J Appl Economet 28(4):720–741

Davidson R, MacKinnon JG (2009) Econometric theory and methods. Oxford University Press, New York

Dray S, Legendre P, Peres-Neto PR (2006) Spatial modeling: a comprehensive framework for principal coordinate analysis of neighbour matrices. Ecol Model 196:483–493

Fernandez-Vazquez E, Mayor-Fernandez M, Rodriguez Valez J (2009) Estimating spatial autoregressive models by GME-GCE techniques. Int Reg Sci Rev 32(2):148–172

Folmer H, Oud J (2008) How to get rid of W: a latent variables approach to modelling spatially lagged variables. Environ Plan A: Econ Space 40(10):2526–2538

Fotheringham AS, Brunsdon C, Charlton M (2002) Geographically weighted regression: the analysis of spatially varying relationships. Wiley, London

Getis A, Aldstadt J (2004) Constructing the spatial weights matrix using a local statistic. Geogr Anal 36:90–104

Getis A, Aldstadt J (2006) Using AMOEBA to create a spatial weights matrix and identify spatial cluster. Geogr Anal 38(4):327–343

Getis A, Griffith DA (2002) Comparative spatial filtering in regression analysis. Geogr Anal 32:131–140

Greene WH (2012) Econometric analysis. Prentice Hall, Upper Saddle River, NJ

Griffith DA (1996) Some guidelines for specifying the geographic weights matrix contained in spatial statistical models. In: Arlinghaus SL (ed) Practical handbook of spatial statistics. CRC, Boca Raton, FL

Im K, Pesaran MH, Shin Y (2003) Testing for unit roots in heterogeneous panels. J Econ 115:53–74

Kelejian H (2008) A spatial J-test for model specification against a single or a set of non-nested alternatives. Lett Spat Resour Sci 1:3–11

LeSage JP, Pace RK (2014) The biggest myth in spatial econometrics. Econometrics 2(4):217–249

LeSage JP, Pace RK (2009) Introduction to spatial econometrics. CRC, Boca Raton, FL

Meen G (1996) Spatial aggregation, spatial dependence and predictability in the UK housing market. Hous Stud 11:345–372

Mur J, Herrera M, Ruiz M (2015) Selecting the W matrix: parametric v nonparametric approaches. Working Paper, University of Zaragoza

Paelinck THP (2007) Deriving the W-matrix via p-median correlation analysis. George Mason University School of Public Policy

Pesaran MH (2007) A simple panel unit root test in the presence of cross section dependence. J Appl Economet 22(2):265–310

Rey S, Montouri B (1999) US regional income convergence: a spatial econometric perspective. Reg Stud 33:143–156

Schott JR (1991) A test for a specific principal component of a correlation matrix. J Am Stat Assoc 86:741–751

Spanos A (1986) Statistical foundations of econometric modelling. Cambridge University Press, Cambridge

Stakhovych S, Bijmolt THA (2008) Specification of spatial models: a simulation study on weights matrices. Pap Reg Sci 88:389–409

Tiefelsdorf M, Griffith DA (2007) Semiparametric filtering of spatial autocorrelation: the eigenvector approach. Environ Plan A 39:1193–1221

Tobler W (1970) A computer movie simulating urban growth in the Detroit region. Econ Geogr 46 (2):234–240

Yitzhaki S, Shechtman E (2013) The Gini methodology: a primer on statistical methodology. Springer, New York

Chapter 5
Unit Root and Cointegration Tests in Spatial Cross-Section Data

5.1 Introduction

In Chap. 2 we recalled that one of the major developments in the econometric analysis of time series in the last quarter of the twentieth century involved nonstationary time series. Specifically, tests for unit roots and cointegration have become standard features in intermediate as well as advanced textbooks in econometrics. In principle, the same issues and problems arise in spatial data. Indeed, in our review of spatial econometrics in Chap. 3, mention of unit roots and nonstationarity in spatial data was notably absent. Spatial data are stationary when their sample moments are independent of space. This means that the sample moments generated by data from the north-west regions should be similar to those generated by data from the south-east regions, etc. Granger (1969 p. 15) thinks that spatial data are inherently nonstationary. "All the possible methods developed so far rely heavily on an assumption of stationarity, that is, an assumption that the relationship between values of the processes is the same for *every* pair of points whose *relative* positions are the same. Thus, for example, if direction did not matter, the degree to which these variables were related would depend only on the distance between the points. The relationship between values measured at Oxford and London will be the same as between two Lincolnshire villages 55 or so miles apart. The correlation between unemployment figures in New York and Philadelphia would be the same as between two small mid-western towns roughly 100 miles apart. The assumption of stationarity on the plane is completely unrealistic for economic variables."

Maybe. Perhaps matters would be different for conditional rather than the unconditional stationarity to which Granger refers. The correlation for unemployment between cities and between towns or villages might differ. In our opinion Granger might have been too pessimistic. Nevertheless, spatial econometricians often assume

M. Beenstock, D. Felsenstein, *The Econometric Analysis of Non-Stationary Spatial Panel Data*, Advances in Spatial Science,
https://doi.org/10.1007/978-3-030-03614-0_5

that spatial data are stationary. The central motivation of this chapter is to emphasize the need for prior validation of this critical assumption.

If the data are stationary the spatial propagation of shocks weakens with distance. If they are nonstationary not only does spatial propagation fail to weaken with distance, it may even increase. In this case the world should be chaotic; the butterfly wings that proverbially flapped in Japan create storms in South Africa and Patagonia. Because the world is not chaotic storms tend to remain localized. This is as true for economic systems as it is for meteorology. Therefore, we think that spatial economic data are inherently stationary in the global sense. By contrast, economic time series tend to be temporally nonstationary. However, spatial cross-section data may appear to be spatially nonstationary in a local sense. Therefore, in specific national contexts the data may be spatially nonstationary.

Fingleton (1999) was the first to demonstrate that if the data generating processes (DGP) for spatial cross-section data happen to contain spatial unit roots, the estimated regression coefficients may be spurious. Strictly speaking, Fingleton referred to "nonsense" regression rather than "spurious" regression. The latter arises when y and x are independent random walks with drift. Drift causes the means of y and x to increase over time, which induces spurious correlation. As discussed in Chap. 2, nonsense regression arises when y and x are driftless random walks, and is induced by the fact that the variances of y and x increase over time. The spatial DGPs studied by Fingleton have zero spatial drift, hence the correct adjective is "nonsense" rather than "spurious". By contrast the DGP in Mur and Trivez (2003) has spatial drift, so that the adjective "spurious" is appropriate in their case. Fingleton suggested that the concept of cointegration proposed by Engle and Granger (1987) to test for nonsense and spurious regression in time series data may be extended to spatial data. Therefore, if the DGPs of y and x happen to embody spatial unit roots, the regression coefficient of y on x will be genuine rather than nonsense provided y and x are spatially cointegrated. If, on the other hand y and x are not spatially cointegrated, the regression coefficient is nonsense or spurious. This happens when the error terms contain a spatial unit root.

Fingleton did not provide a spatial unit root test to determine whether the DGPs of spatial data contain spatial unit roots and are therefore spatially nonstationary. Nor did he propose a spatial cointegration test to determine whether parameter estimates are nonsense or not. In this chapter we describe our efforts (Beenstock and Felsenstein 2012; Beenstoch et al. 2012) to develop a test statistic for unit roots in spatial cross-section data, as well as to develop cointegration tests for spatially nonstationary cross-section data. Specifically, we derive the distribution of the SAR coefficient under the null hypothesis of a spatial unit root. We obtain critical values for the spatial counterpart to the well-known Dickey–Fuller statistic described in Chap. 2. Second, we develop a test statistic for spatial cointegration in which the data happen to contain spatial unit roots. In doing so we apply to spatial cross section data concepts developed by Engle and Granger (1987) for nonstationary time series data described in Chap. 2. Specifically, spatial cointegration requires that the model error terms be stationary, and that their spatial autocorrelation coefficient (SAC) be less than one. Spurious and nonsense regression phenomena arise when this null hypothesis that SAC $=1$ cannot be rejected. If, however, the null hypothesis is rejected the data are spatially cointegrated.

Lauridsen and Kosfeld suggested two types of cointegration tests for nonstationary spatial data. Our approach is similar to Lauridsen and Kosfeld (2004) who test the null hypothesis that the model error terms contain a spatial unit root. They calculate the distribution of the Wald test under the null hypothesis that the error terms contain a spatial unit root. Strictly speaking, they calculate critical values for cointegration tests when there are two variables in the model. In contrast, we calculate the spatial counterpart to the Dickey–Fuller statistic. Lauridsen and Kosfeld (2006, 2007) also suggested a two stage Lagrange multiplier (LM) test for spatial unit roots. In the first stage, the LM SAC statistic is calculated for the residuals. If the LM statistic is not significant, the residuals must be stationary. If the LM statistic is significant, the second stage is intended to determine whether SAC = 1 by estimating the model with spatially differenced data. If SAC = 1 the LM statistic for the residuals in the second stage should not be significant. The LM statistic is only valid for stationary residuals.

The difficulty with this proposal is that if the model is cointegrated, the second stage is misspecified; it should be a spatial error correction model. If the model is $y = \beta x + u$ and u is stationary, the spatial ECM in the second stage should be $\Delta y = \delta \Delta x + \rho W u + e$ where ρ is the spatial error correction coefficient, $\Delta = I - W$ is the spatial difference operator, and e is iid. Lauridsen and Kosfeld (2006) ignore ρ. Their test implicitly assumes that Δx and u are independent. More generally, as pointed out in Chap. 2, LM tests assume stationarity under the null. Rejection of the null does not necessarily imply nonstationarity when differences are fractional. This criticism does not apply to tests where the null is nonstationarity. Fractional differencing in spatial cross-section data remains an unexplored issue.

Since cointegration theory is derived from unit root theory, we begin with the latter. To fix ideas we consider the case of a spatial unit root when space is lateral, i.e. spatial units are located on an infinite line with first-order neighbors to the east and west. We show analytically in this case that as the SAR coefficient approaches ½ there is a spatial unit root, spatial impulse responses approach infinity and cease to vary inversely with distance, and the variance of y tends to infinity. Matters are different when the line is finite. In this case a spatial unit root arises when the SAR coefficient exceeds ½ by a value that varies inversely with number of spatial units. We show that this difference is induced by edge effects; units on the edge of space are less spatially connected than units within space. More generally, edge effects induce a phenomenon to which we refer to by "pseudo spatial nonstationarity" because even though units share a common SAR coefficient, which is less than ½, the variance of y depends on where it is measured. Recall that spatial stationarity requires that the moments of y should be independent of where they are measured. We also show that as the number of spatial units increases, the variance of y increases as a result of the greater scope for spatial interaction. This phenomenon is unique to spatial data and has no parallel in time series data. We use simulation methods to extend the discussion to unit roots in multilateral space, e.g. when spatial units have neighbors to their north and south as well as their east and west. The greater scope for spatial interaction lowers the SAR coefficient that induces a unit root by the order of 1/n where n is the number of neighbors.

Next, we show that under the null hypothesis of a spatial unit root OLS estimates of SAR coefficients are not just consistent, they are super-consistent (see Chap. 2). We conclude the discussion of spatial unit roots by simulating the critical values for spatial unit root tests under the null. These critical values are the counterpart for spatial cross-section data to the Dickey–Fuller statistic for time series data discussed in Chap. 2. At first, we assume that space is a square rook lattice and that the spatial connectivity matrix (W) is sparse with $w_{ij} = 1$ for contiguous spatial units and zero otherwise. We calculate critical values for this case. Subsequently, we vary the tessellation for oblong spaces, rook-queen lattices, and for specific locations, such as Columbus, Ohio and NUTS2. We do so because we show that spatial impulse responses depend on topology; they are stronger in square lattices than in oblong ones, and they are stronger in queen lattices than in rook ones. It turns out, however, that the critical values are closer to unity than critical values for time series. The reason for this difference is that because space is multilateral and multidimensional, whereas time is unilateral and unidirectional, we learn much more rapidly from spatial data than from time series data. In other words, it is easier to detect nonstationary in space than it is in time.

If spatial cross-section data happen to be nonstationary, parameter estimates of covariates (x), spatial Durbin lags and spatial lagged dependent variables obtained by standard spatial econometric methods designed for stationary data will be spurious or nonsense if their error terms (u) are nonstationary. If, however, the error terms are stationary, these parameter estimates will be genuine. Indeed, we show that they will be super-consistent and may consequently be estimated by OLS rather than IV, GMM and ML. To determine whether the error terms are stationary we simulate critical values under the null hypothesis that they contain a spatial unit root. These critical values are naturally stricter than their counterparts for y because u is an estimate and degrees of freedom have been used to estimate them. If the unit root hypothesis for u is rejected, the variables in the model (covariates, spatial lags and spatial Durbin lags) are spatially cointegrated with y.

Fingleton (1999) and Mur and Trivez (2003) assumed for convenience that there is an unconnected spatial unit, which may affect other spatial units but which are not influenced by them. We explain below that this contrivance was intended to introduce into spatial data a beginning or starting point as is natural in time series data. Time has a natural beginning whereas space does not. Also, space typically has immovable edges whereas time does not. Our proposed spatial unit root test takes topology and edge effects into consideration without resorting to the artificial contrivance of unconnected spatial units. We note, in this context, that the standard practice of normalizing spatial weights to sum to unity ignores the fact that spatial units along the edges and in the corners of the lattice are less connected.

Lee and Yu (2009) consider the spurious regression problem when the DGPs for y and x contain spatial roots that are near but less than unity. In fact, like us, they attribute this nearness to the finiteness of N; as N increases spatial unit roots tend to 1. Also, like us they dispense with unconnected spatial units, and distinguish SAR process with and without spatial drift. They show that if y and x are generated by independent SAR processes, the regression coefficient between y and x may not be zero. Moreover, its t-statistic may exceed ±1.96 and appear to be significant. They argue that R^2 tends to zero, and like us, the spurious regression residuals have a spatial unit root. Our main contribution is to obtain the distribution of SAC under the null that SAC = 1. If SAC is less than its critical value, the null of spurious or nonsense regression may be rejected.

We have already mentioned in Chap. 3 that the analogy between space and time turns out to be weak for several reasons. First, whereas time progresses so that y_{t-1} is determined before y_t the same does not happen in spatial data. There are no analogous concepts to past and future in space. Therefore, y_s and y_{s+1} may be mutually influential and dependent since s is s + 1's neighbor's neighbor. This means that space cannot be conveniently treated as a progression like time. There is a natural one-way direction in time but not in space. Secondly, there are only two directions to time, backwards or forwards, whereas space involves many directions. Apart from the directions of the compass, neighbors may be above or below. Imagine time series analysis if what happened at time t affected what happened at time t − 1, i.e. if the past depended upon the present and not just the other way around.

All this sounds as though the econometric analysis of spatial data must be more complex than the econometric analysis of time series data. However, the opposite is true in the present context. Because spatial data interact forwards and backwards, as well as upwards and downwards spurious regression reveals itself more clearly in spatial data than in time-series data. This makes spatial unit root testing easier than temporal unit root testing. It also makes spatial cointegration testing easier than temporal cointegration testing.

The fact that space is finite does not undermine the asymptotic theory of the econometric analysis of spatial cross-section data. ML, IV and GMM estimators of spatial lag models using cross-section data are consistent (as N tends to infinity) but are biased in finite samples. These properties are not peculiar to spatial cross-section data since these estimators are known to be biased in finite samples more generally. At the point in time when non-spatial cross-section data are sampled, the population is inherently finite too. Nevertheless, asymptotic theory proceeds as if N can be infinite. We repeat a quotation from Chap. 1. "In order to define consistency we have to specify what it means for the sample size N to tend to infinity. . .At first sight this may seem like a very odd notion. After all, any given dataset contains a fixed number of observations. . .In the case of a model with cross-section data, we can pretend that the sample is drawn from a population of infinite size, and we can imagine drawing more and more observations from that population." (Davidson and MacKinnon 2009 p. 92). This virtual reality also applies to spatial cross-section data. Indeed, it is a virtual reality with which econometricians have lived with comfortably for close to a century. Therefore, the finiteness of space does not undermine the foundations of the econometric theory of spatial cross-section data any more than do finite populations undermine the foundations of the econometric theory of cross-section data in general.

5.2 Data Generating Processes

In what follows there are N spatial units labeled by i and spatial lags are labeled by tilde. The hypothesis of interest is that y depends on x:

$$y_i = \gamma + \beta x_i + u_i \tag{5.1a}$$

$$u_i = \rho \tilde{u}_i + v_i \tag{5.1b}$$

where e.g. $\tilde{u}_i = \sum_{j \neq i}^{N} w_{ij} u_j$ denotes the spatially weighted average value of u among the neighbor's of i with weights summing to unity, and ρ is the SAC coefficient of u. The v's are iid random variables.

The data generating processes (DGP) for y and x are assumed to be first-order SAR models:

$$y_i = \lambda_y \tilde{y}_i + \varepsilon_i \tag{5.2a}$$

$$x_i = \lambda_x \tilde{x}_i + e_i \tag{5.2b}$$

where ε and e are iid random variables with correlation r. A variable is defined to be strongly stationary if all its moments are finite and are independent of location or space. It is weakly (covariance) stationary if the first two moments are finite and are independent of space. Spatial covariances should depend "…only upon the relative position of different locations, as determined by their relative orientation (angle) and respective distances. Since the orientation between two points in two (or more) dimensions still leaves a great number of different situations (potentially over a 360 degree rotation), the stricter notion of isotropy is imposed as well." (Anselin 1988, p. 43). Since regression does not use higher order moments we focus on covariance stationarity.

In Fig. 5.1 space has two dimensions F and G. The line connecting points A and B expresses the juxtaposition between A and B as represented by its length and angle.

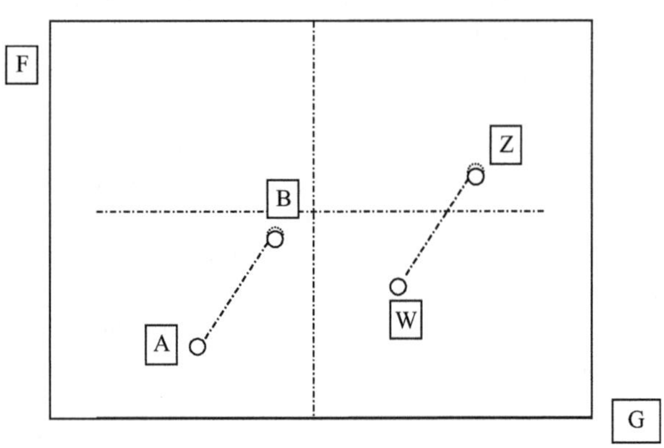

Fig. 5.1 Spatial stationarity and ergodicity

Initially the sample consists of observations in the bottom left-hand quadrant. In this quadrant there are many other data points with the same juxtaposition. The correlation between such points is denoted by c. W and Z have the same juxtaposition as A and B but are outside the original sample. Stationarity requires that the correlation between points such as W and Z is equal to c. Spatial correlations are the same regardless of where they are measured.

Spatial ergodicity requires that the correlation between points such as A and Z is smaller than the correlation between A and B because Z is more remote from A than B. As Z becomes infinitely remote from A the correlation between A and Z should tend to zero if the data are stationary.

A variable is spatially integrated of order d when its d'th spatial difference is spatially stationary. Therefore y $\sim$ SI(1) and x $\sim$ SI(1) when $\lambda_y = \lambda_x = 1$. If u $\sim$ SI (1) because $\rho = 1$, Eq. (5.1a) is a nonsense regression, which happens if ε and e are independent i.e. $r = 0$. If u $\sim$ SI(0) because $\rho < 1$, Eq. (5.1a) is not nonsense as pointed out by Fingleton (1999). This happen because $r \neq 0$, i.e. because ε and e are jointly distributed random variables.

This suggests that the cointegration test statistic for spatial cross section data should focus on rejecting the null hypothesis that $\rho = 1$. The same applies to spatial unit root tests for λ_y and λ_x. We use Monte Carlo simulation to derive the distributions of λ_y and λ_x under the null hypothesis that these parameters are equal to unity. These distributions provide critical values for rejecting the null hypothesis that the data contain a spatial unit root. Subsequently, we use Monte Carlo simulation to compute critical values for spatial cointegration tests when the data contain spatial unit roots and when $\rho = 1$ under the null hypothesis. If the calculated value of ρ is less than its critical value, we may reject the hypothesis that the result is spatially spurious.

Let y denote a column vector of length N with elements y_j. W is an irregular but isotropic N $\times$ N spatial connectivity matrix in which connectivity may vary between spatial units. Equation (5.2a) may be vectorized as:

$$y = \lambda_y W y + \varepsilon \tag{5.3}$$

If $I_N - \lambda W$ is invertible, the spatial Wold representation of Eq. (5.3) is:

$$y = A\varepsilon \tag{5.4a}$$

$$A = \left(I_N - \lambda_y W\right)^{-1} = I_N + \lambda_y W + \lambda_y^2 W^2 + \ldots \tag{5.4b}$$

Invertibility requires that the elements of A be finite which is satisfied when powers of $\lambda_y W$ are convergent. Also, $r_{\min}^{-1} < \lambda_y < r_{\max}^{-1}$ for invertibility, where r_{min} and r_{max} are the smallest and largest eigenvalues of W. The spatial variance-covariance matrix generated by Eq. (5.4a) is expected to be:

$$\Sigma = E(yy') = \sigma_\varepsilon^2 B_N \tag{5.5a}$$

$$B_N = AA' \tag{5.5b}$$

According to Eq. (5.4a) the first moment of y is finite and is independent of N since E(y) = 0. Matters are quite different in the case of second moments because according to Eq. (5.5a) Σ may depend on N. Since $I - \lambda_y W$ is invertible $\det(I - \lambda W)$ must be finite, which guarantees that det(Σ) is finite. Therefore, the second moments are finite. However, the second moments will depend upon N if B_N varies with N. According to Eq. (5.4b) this depends on W and λ_y.

Normalizing $\sigma_\varepsilon = 1$, the variance of y_i with N units is b_{ii} and its covariance with y_j is b_{ij}. Suppose that the sample increases by 1 from N to M and location M is remote from i and j. Stationary requires that b_{ii} and b_{ij} remain unchanged. These conditions require that shocks in remote spatial units have no repercussions on units i and j, e.g. $\lambda_y^{M-i} W_M^{M-i}$ tends to zero. Therefore, stationarity requires that $\lambda_y W_M$ be convergent. y is isotropic if adding a remote spatial unit makes no difference to the connectivity between incumbent units. Therefore, when y is isotropic, convergence does not depend on W, it depends on $\lambda_y < 1$. We do not consider the more general case in which the data are not isotropic. However, we investigate critical values for spatial unit roots for different topologies, including irregular topologies in which the number of neighbors is not the same for all spatial units.

5.3 Spatial Impulse Responses

In this section, we show that spatial unit roots asymptotically induce spatial impulse responses that do not die out with distance. If spatial cross-section data are stationary, shocks occurring remotely from i have no effect on i. If, however, spatial cross-section data are nonstationary, such remote shocks affect i as if they occurred in i itself. This result is established analytically for lateral space i.e. where space is an infinite line that has no beginning and end, and spatial units have neighbors on two sides only.

In multilateral space, there are more than two neighbors. For example, in bilateral space (rook lattice) each spatial unit has four sides and neighbors. Unfortunately, we are unable to obtain analytical solutions for this more relevant case. We therefore simulate spatial impulse responses numerically. Because of computational constraints we are forced to assume that space is finite, which means that we cannot obtain asymptotic impulse responses as we do in the lateral case. We think that this may be advantageous because space is inherently finite. We show that in finite space impulse responses die out with distance even in the presence of a spatial unit root. This happens because peripheral spatial units are less connected than core spatial units. Indeed, this core–periphery effect may create the misleading impression that the data are spatially stationary when the opposite is true.

Infinite Lateral Space

Spatial units are assumed to be located laterally (along an axis representing west and east or north and south) so that each unit has a neighbor on either side. Units continue to be labeled by $i = -\infty, \ldots, \infty$. There is an infinite number of spatial units and unit $i + 1$ is unit i's neighbor to the left or west and unit $i - 1$ is its neighbor to the right or east. The assumption that N is infinite is made for two reasons. The first is to show what might hypothetically happen if space was infinite and lateral. This abstraction is heuristic because space is not lateral, and because in reality space is typically fixed because of immovable edges. An alternative to lateral space might be to assume that space is a circle on which there is a fixed number of spatial units. Had space been a circle rather than a line, spatial units would eventually become their own neighbors through circularity. This circularity does not arise when space is lateral. The second and main reason is to compare spatial impulse responses when N is infinite with spatial impulse responses when N is fixed.

Cressie (1993, p. 438) considers a similar idea to circular space. "Another possibility is to wrap a $U \times V$ lattice on a torus; however, the donut-shaped space may be distasteful to those who object having, for example, (1, v) and (U, v) as nearest neighbors." A torus is a circle rotated in three dimensional space. The distasteful nearest neighbors would be, for example, diagonal white and black rooks.

Spillovers are assumed to be first-order, i.e. they occur between immediate neighbors. The SAR model in this case is:

$$y_i = \lambda\left(y_{i+1} + y_{i-1}\right) + \varepsilon_i \tag{5.6}$$

where λ denotes the spatial spillover coefficient and ε is an iid random variable with variance equal to σ_ε^2.

Equation (5.6) is a second order stochastic spatial difference equation. Let S denote a spatial lag operator such that $S^j y_i = y_{i-j}$ where j may be positive (west of i) or negative (east of i). Multiplying Eq. (5.6) by S and rewriting the result in terms of the spatial lag operator gives:

$$\left(1 - \lambda^{-1}S + S^2\right)y_i = -\lambda^{-1}\varepsilon_{i-1} \tag{5.7}$$

The characteristic equation of Eq. (5.7) is:

$$\omega^2 - \lambda^{-1}\omega + 1 = 0 \tag{5.8}$$

If $0 < \lambda < ½$ the roots of Eq. (5.8), denoted by ω_1 and ω_2, are real and positive and are reciprocally related because $\omega_1 = 1/\omega_2$. The roots will be complex if $4\lambda^2 > 1$ which arises when $\lambda > ½$. When $\lambda = ½$ both roots are equal to unity. When $0 < \lambda < ½$ one root is positive and less than one (ω_1) while the other (ω_2) is positive and greater than one, since the roots come in reciprocal pairs. Because $(1 - \omega_1 S)(1 - \omega_2 S) = (1 - \lambda^{-1} S + S^2)$ the general solution[1] to Eq. (5.6) is:

$$y_i = -\frac{\lambda^{-1}\varepsilon_{i-1}}{(1-\omega_1 S)(1-\omega_2 S)} + A_1\omega_1^d + A_2\omega_2^d \tag{5.9}$$

where A_1 and A_2 are arbitrary constants of integration and d denotes distance from i. To obtain a particular solution it is necessary to determine A_1 and A_2 using data on y for two spatial units. Since in what follows we have no interest in the particular solution we ignore it by setting these arbitrary constants to zero. Using partial fractions[2] we note that:

$$\frac{1}{(1-\omega_1 S)(1-\omega_2 S)} = \frac{1}{\omega_1 - \omega_2}\left[\frac{\omega_1}{1-\omega_1 S} - \frac{\omega_2}{1-\omega_2 S}\right] \tag{5.10}$$

We also note that[3]:

$$\frac{1}{1-\omega_1 S} = \sum_{d=0}^{\infty} \omega_1^d S^d \tag{5.11}$$

If $\omega_1 < 1$ Eq. (5.9) is convergent because ω_1^d tends to zero with d. Since the roots come in reciprocal pairs, applying Eq. (5.11) to ω_2 would induce a divergent process because ω_2^d tends to infinity with d, and because $\omega_2 > 1$ if $\omega_1 < 1$. This would imply unreasonably that despite the fact that $\lambda < ½$ y is spatially explosive and divergent. The solution to this problem is to note that $(1 - \omega_2 S)^{-1}$ has two polynomial inversions, one that is the counterpart of Eq. (5.11) and another which is:

$$\frac{1}{1-\omega_2 S} = -\frac{(\omega_2 S)^{-1}}{1-(\omega_2 S)^{-1}} = -\frac{\omega_1 S^{-1}}{1-\omega_1 S^{-1}} = -\sum_{i=1}^{\infty} \omega_1^{d+1} S^{-d} \tag{5.12}$$

Equation (5.12) is the "forward" inversion whereas Eq. (5.11) is a "backward" inversion. Substituting $\omega_2 = \omega_1^{-1}$ into the forward inversion generates Eq. (5.12) which is convergent because it depends on ω_1^d. Equation (5.11) operates "westwards" since $d = i - j \geq 0$ and Eq. (5.12) operates "eastwards" since $d = i - j < 0$.

Substituting Eqs. (5.10–5.12) into Eq. (5.9) gives the general solution for y as:

[1] See e.g. Sargent (1979, Chap. 9).

[2] Ibid p. 179.

[3] Ibid p. 176.

$$y_i = \frac{\lambda^{-1}}{\omega_1^{-1} - \omega_1}\left[\sum_{d=1}^{\infty}\omega_1^d \varepsilon_{i-d} + \sum_{d=0}^{\infty}\omega_1^d \varepsilon_{i+d}\right] \tag{5.13}$$

Equation (5.13) is the spatial Wold representation of Eq. (5.6) since it expresses y_i in terms of the stochastic shocks in all units to the east and west of unit i as well as in unit i itself. Equation (5.13) is also the spatial impulse response function. If $\omega_1 < 1$ Eq. (5.13) states that closer units to i have a greater effect on i than more remote units. The spatial impulse responses are symmetric, as expected, since ε_{i+d} has the same effect on y_i as ε_{i-d}:

$$\frac{\partial y_i}{\partial \varepsilon_{i-d}} = \frac{\partial y_i}{\partial \varepsilon_{i+d}} = \frac{\lambda^{-1}\omega_1^d}{\omega_1^{-1} - \omega_1} \tag{5.14}$$

Equation (5.14) also shows that the impulses tend to zero as the distance between spatial units (i) tends hypothetically to infinity. This means that shocks that occurred infinitely far from unit i have no effect on y_i. In addition, Eq. (5.14) shows, as expected, that the largest impulse is for shocks that occur in region i itself ($d = 0$).

Finally, ω_1 varies directly with λ. For example, when $\lambda = 0.1$ $\omega_1 = 0.1015$ in which case the impulse response from immediate neighbors ($d = 1$) according to Eq. (5.14) is equal to 0.103 and the local impulse response ($d = 0$) is 1.0207. Notice that the local impulse exceeds 1 because there is a spatial echo; shocks in unit i propagate back onto it via other spatial units. When $\lambda = 0.2$ ω_1 increases as expected to 0.2087 and the impulse response from immediate neighbors increases as expected to 0.225 and the own impulse increases to 1.091 because the spatial echo varies directly with λ. When $\lambda = 0.498$ these impulse responses jump to 10.24 and 11.19 respectively. As λ approaches ½, ω_1 approaches 1 and the impulse responses approach infinity. When $\lambda = ½$ both roots equal 1, the impulse responses explode and no longer depend on distance. In time series the impulse responses do not explode and tend to 1 because y_{t+1} cannot feedback onto y_t whereas in lateral space y_{i+1} and y_i feedback onto each other, i.e. time series data are uni-directional, whereas spatial data are multi-directional.

According to Eq. (5.13) $E(y_i) = 0$ because the expected value of the ε's are all zero by definition. Therefore, the first moment is independent of i. The unconditional variance of y from Eq. (5.13) is equal to:

$$\mathrm{var}(y) = \frac{\lambda^{-2}\left(1 + \omega_1^2\right)}{\left(1 - \omega_1^2\right)\left(\omega_1^{-1} - \omega_1\right)^2}\sigma_\varepsilon^2 \tag{5.15}$$

which is finite since $0 \le \omega_1 < 1$ and it does not depend on i. Therefore if $0 < \lambda < ½$ the first and second moments of y_i are finite and independent of i. Matters are different when $\lambda = ½$. Since $\omega_1 = 1$, the denominator of Eq. (5.15) is zero and the variance of y is therefore infinite.

Finite Lateral Space

On several occasions we have remarked that space, unlike time, is inherently finite. In this subsection we consider the previous discussion when N is finite instead of infinite. If N = 2 both spatial units are mutual neighbors. Matters are different when N exceeds 2. For example, when N = 3 units 1 and 3 have only one neighbor (unit 2) whereas unit 2 has units 1 and 3 for neighbors. When N = 2:

$$y_1 = \lambda y_2 + \varepsilon_1 \tag{5.16a}$$

$$y_2 = \lambda y_1 + \varepsilon_2 \tag{5.16b}$$

Their solutions are:

$$y_1 = \frac{\varepsilon_1 + \lambda\varepsilon_2}{1 - \lambda^2} \tag{5.16c}$$

$$y_2 = \frac{\varepsilon_2 + \lambda\varepsilon_1}{1 - \lambda^2} \tag{5.16d}$$

If $0 \leq \lambda < 1$ the expected values of y_1 and y_2 are zero and their variances are equal to:

$$\sigma_y^2 = \frac{1 + \lambda^2}{\left(1 - \lambda^2\right)^2}\sigma_\varepsilon^2 \tag{5.16e}$$

Because the first two moments are finite and are the same in both units (do not depend on where they are measured) y is spatially stationary. Notice also that the impulse responses vary inversely with distance because $1/(1 - \lambda^2) > \lambda/(1 - \lambda^2)$, i.e. the own impulse response exceeds the cross impulse response. As λ increases towards 1, these impulses and the variance of y become increasingly large. When λ = 1 they become infinite. Since covariance stationarity requires finite first and second moments, y ceases to be stationary when λ = 1. Also the impulse responses cease to vary inversely with distance because they are infinite.

Matters are different if N > 2 in lateral space because of edge effects. For example, if N = 3 unit 2 is more spatially connected than units 1 and 3, as noted. Units 1 and 3 are located on the edge of space. The counterparts of Eqs. (5.16a and 5.16b) are:

$$y_1 = \lambda y_2 + \varepsilon_1 \tag{5.17a}$$

$$y_2 = \lambda(y_1 + y_3) + \varepsilon_2 \tag{5.17b}$$

$$y_3 = \lambda y_2 + \varepsilon_3 \tag{5.17c}$$

The counterparts of Eqs. (5.16c and 5.16d) are:

$$y_1 = \frac{(1-\lambda^2)\varepsilon_1 + \lambda\varepsilon_2 + \lambda^2\varepsilon_3}{1-2\lambda^2} \tag{5.17d}$$

$$y_2 = \frac{\lambda\varepsilon_1 + \varepsilon_2 + \lambda\varepsilon_3}{1-2\lambda^2} \tag{5.17e}$$

$$y_3 = \frac{\lambda^2\varepsilon_1 + \lambda\varepsilon_2 + (1-\lambda^2)\varepsilon_3}{1-2\lambda^2} \tag{5.17f}$$

The counterparts to Eq. (5.16e) are:

$$\sigma_{yi}^2 = \frac{1+\lambda^4}{(1-2\lambda^2)^2}\sigma_\varepsilon^2 \tag{5.17g}$$

$$\sigma_{y2}^2 = \frac{1+2\lambda^2}{(1-2\lambda^2)^2}\sigma_\varepsilon^2 \tag{5.17h}$$

$$\sigma_{y3}^2 = \sigma_{y1}^2 \tag{5.17i}$$

If $1 \leq 2\lambda^2 < 1$ the expected values of y_1, y_2 and y_3 are zero, and the variances of y_1 and y_2 are equal, but smaller than the variance of y_2. The latter means that the variance of y depends upon where it is measured. It is smaller if units 1 and 3 are sampled than if all units are sampled. Since the sample moments of stationary data should be independent of where they are measured, the data appear to be nonstationary despite the absence of a spatial unit root. The reason for this is straight forward; because space is finite units 1 and 3 have smaller variances because they are located on the edge of space. This is also the reason why the spatial impulse responses for units 1 and 3 tend to be smaller than their counterparts for unit 2. As expected, the impulse responses vary inversely with distance. For example, the impulse responses between units 1 and 3 are smaller than the impulse responses between units 1 and 2.

This phenomenon has no counterpart in time series data. In Chap. 2 we saw that if temporal data are stationary the sample moments are expected to be the same regardless of when they are measured. The reason for this is that time does not have an edge in the way that space has an edge. Alternatively, because the future cannot affect the past, and only the past can affect the future, all temporal units have the same time series properties. If the future could affect the past, edge effects would arise in time series data as they do in spatial data.

A related matter concerns the spatial impulse responses when N = 3 compared to those with N = 2. The former are larger than the latter because there is more spatial interaction between three units than between two. More generally, spatial impulse responses and variances vary directly with the number of spatial units. Nor does this phenomenon arise in time series data; the sample moments of stationary time series do not change as the observation period increases.

The impulse responses and variances tend to infinity as $2\lambda^2$ tends to 1. Therefore, the condition for a spatial unit root is $\lambda = \sqrt{\frac{1}{2}} = 0.7071$ instead of 1 in the case when N = 2. More generally, the coefficient of λ^2 in the denominator of Eqs. (5.17d–5.17f) equals the number of first-order neighbors away from the edge of space, which is 2 when space is lateral. If $\lambda < 0.7071$ the first two moments of y are finite, in which case y is spatially stationary. If $0.5 < \lambda < 0.7071$ edge effects ensure that y is stationary despite the fact that asymptotically y is nonstationary. This pseudo stationarity is induced by edge effects because impulse responses and variances of units on the edge of space are naturally smaller than their counterparts in the middle of space. Edge effects also increase the unit root condition for λ. This phenomenon has no counterpart in time series data.

Bilateral Space

When space is multilateral and spatial units have more than two neighbors the critical value for λ that gives rise to a spatial unit root is $\lambda^* = 1/n$. If space is a rook lattice each spatial unit has four neighbors in which case $\lambda^* = ¼$, and if it is a queen lattice $\lambda^* = ⅛$. In bilateral space spatial units have four neighbors. The use of lattices in spatial statistics has a long history (Cressie, Chap. 7). They have also been extensively used in spatial econometrics. For example, Florax et al. (2003) use regular two dimensional lattices and Stakhovych and Bijmolt (2008) use irregular two dimensional lattices. Because lattices have edges, it might be argued that they artificially impede asymptotic analysis. Insofar as spatial edges are immovable (in the sense of Chap. 1), we see this an advantage rather than a criticism. Insofar as spatial edges are induced by sampling, we study the implications of increasing N by enlarging the lattice.

The bilateral counterpart to Eq. (5.6) may be written familiarly as the SAR model:

$$y = \lambda W y + \varepsilon \tag{5.18a}$$

where W is a sparse N × N matrix with elements $w_{ij} = 1$ if i and j are neighbors and $w_{ij} = 0$ otherwise, and y and ε are vectors of length N. In the lateral case, N is infinite and space has no immovable edge. However, in the bilateral case N is assumed to be fixed, in which case space has an edge, as it typically does in practice. For islands such as the United Kingdom, Australia and New Zealand the edges are coasts. For countries such as Mali and Algeria the edges are deserts. For many countries such as Israel and its Arab neighbors the edges are geopolitical. This was also the case for East and West Germany until re-unification. Although chessboard lattices are artificial, they nevertheless illustrate the role of edge effects in the generation of spatial impulses and their influence on spatial stationarity. We think that immovable edges are inherent to human space because of social, physical, cultural, ethnic and political reasons Earth is fractured, and human beings do not have unfettered open access to all its parts. Whereas Earth is not a seamless planet as far as humans are concerned, matters may be different in the physical sciences. For example, climate models treat the atmosphere, oceans and land mass as seamless interconnected phenomena in three dimensional space. It is for this reason that the chessboard is a more realistic idiom than the circle or sphere. The human world is flat rather than round. For the physical world, which is round rather than flat the two dimensional chessboard will be less appropriate than the three dimensional torus.

Fingleton (1999) normalized the row-sum weights (w) to unity, and normalized $\lambda = 1$. This means that within a lattice spatial units have four neighbors with $w_{ij} = ¼$, at the corners of the lattice there are two neighbors with $w_{ij} = ½$, and at the edge of the lattice where there are three neighbors $w_{ij} = ⅓$. We therefore prefer to normalize $w_{ij} = 1$ in which case the sum of weights is 4 and $\lambda^* = ¼$ because this does not artificially inflate spatial spillover at the corners of the lattice and along its edges. Another difference is that unlike Fingleton we do not assume the existence of an "unconnected spatial unit", which attributes a "beginning" to space. In our lattice all units are mutually connected.

In this context we wish to draw attention to the inherent differences between space and time that were raised in Chap. 1. In dynamic time series models the initial values of the data are left unexplained. For example, in a first order autoregression for y observed during $t = 1,\ldots,T$, the residual for y_1 cannot be estimated. If the error terms are serially independent, this does not matter for estimation because y_1 is weakly exogenous for the AR parameter. However, there would be an initial value problem if the error terms were serially dependent. The same applies in dynamic panel data. If the error terms are iid there is no initial value problem. In the absence of serial correlation in the error terms, the initial value y_1 is weakly exogenous because time is sequential; y_1 precedes y_2 and does not depend on subsequent values of y.

In spatial cross-section data there is no natural counterpart to initial values because unlike time series data, spatial data have no beginning. Hence, in spatial data all observations are mutually determined. Perhaps in some spatial datasets unconnected spatial units exist, but in general they do not. Indeed, this is what makes spatial data so interesting and different from time series data. The spatial counterparts to the initial value problem in time series are edge effects induced by sampling under increasing-domain asymptotics. Such edge effects induce bias in finite samples of space. However, unlike immovable edge effects, these edge effects do not concern us here.

The Wold representation of Eq. (5.18a) is:

$$y = A\varepsilon$$
$$A = (I_N - \lambda W)^{-1} = I_N + \sum_{d=1}^{\infty} \lambda^d W^d \tag{5.18b}$$

where $W^d\varepsilon_d$ denotes ε among d'th order neighbors. If λ is normalized to 1 and W is row-summed to 1, the matrix $I_N - \lambda W$ is not invertible regardless of N. If instead $\lambda = 1/n$ and the row-sum restriction is not applied, $I_N - \lambda W_N$ is invertible if N is finite. In fact $\det(I_N - \lambda W_N)$ is O(1/N) so that as space becomes infinitely large, edge effects are asymptotically unimportant.

The spatial impulse responses are:

$$\frac{dy_i}{du_i} = a_{ii} \tag{5.18c}$$

$$\frac{dy_i}{du_j} = a_{ij} \tag{5.18d}$$

We expect a_{jj} to vary directly with the number of spatial units because this gives rise to more scope for spatial spillover, and we expect a_{ij} to vary inversely with the distance between j and i. If, however, there is a spatial unit root, the impulses a_{ji} will not tend to zero as the distance between j and i tends to infinity. We use Matlab to calculate A for square lattices containing N spatial units in which n = 4 and λ* = ¼. To investigate asymptotics we ideally wish to let N tend to infinity, but this is not computationally feasible. We therefore make N as large as practically possible (approximately 1000) given computing constraints.

Because N is finite, A is inevitably affected by edge effects. Since the lattice is chessboard in design, spatial units on the edge are less exposed to spatial spillover because they have only three neighbors instead of four. Spatial units in the four corners of the lattice only have two neighbors. We expect a_{ii} and a_{ij} to be greater the closer is unit i to the epicenter i* of the lattice because there is more scope for spatial interaction in the center than at the periphery. We do not expect a_{ij} to be symmetrical unless i = i* because only at the epicenter is the distance to the edge of the square lattice the same in all four directions.

In Fig. 5.2 we plot impulse responses for a_{i*j} when N = 961. Since the lattice is square it is 31 × 31, and the distance from its epicenter to the edge is therefore 15. The impulse responses are measured along the vertical, and Euclidean distance from i* is measured along the horizontal. The 15th value of i is on the edge of the lattice and the 30th value is at the corner of the lattice, hence the dog-leg at spatial lag 15. Higher spatial lags than 30 are obtained by cumulating the distance by travelling up and down rows or columns of the lattice. Since N = 961 the maximal distance e.g. from the top left corner of the lattice to the bottom right corner is 960.

Figure 5.2 shows, as expected, that a_{ij} varies directly with λ, and varies inversely with the spatial lag. The impulse responses die away more slowly the larger is λ. It might have been expected that when λ = λ* = ¼ all impulse responses should be infinite. We expect this to happen as N tends to infinity, as in the case of lateral space. It does not happen in Fig. 5.2 because N is finite and space has an edge. Nevertheless, Fig. 5.2 clearly shows that when λ = ¼ there is a qualitative difference and the impulses linger longer in space than when λ = 0.2, and the impulse responses are larger by an order of magnitude, if not infinite.

As indicated in Eq. (5.18c) the diagonal of A measures the direct and indirect effects of a shock in unit i on itself. We refer to these as "local impulses", which are plotted in Fig. 5.3 for different values of λ according to the distance of i from the epicenter of the lattice. The local impulses exceed unity because when a shock occurs in unit i, it affects i's neighbors which feedback onto i. This echo or boomerang effect

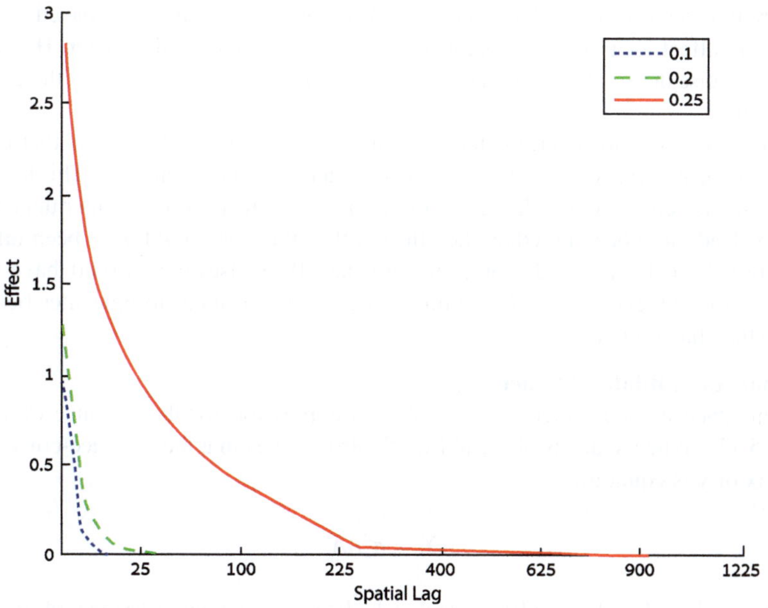

Fig. 5.2 Spatial impulses

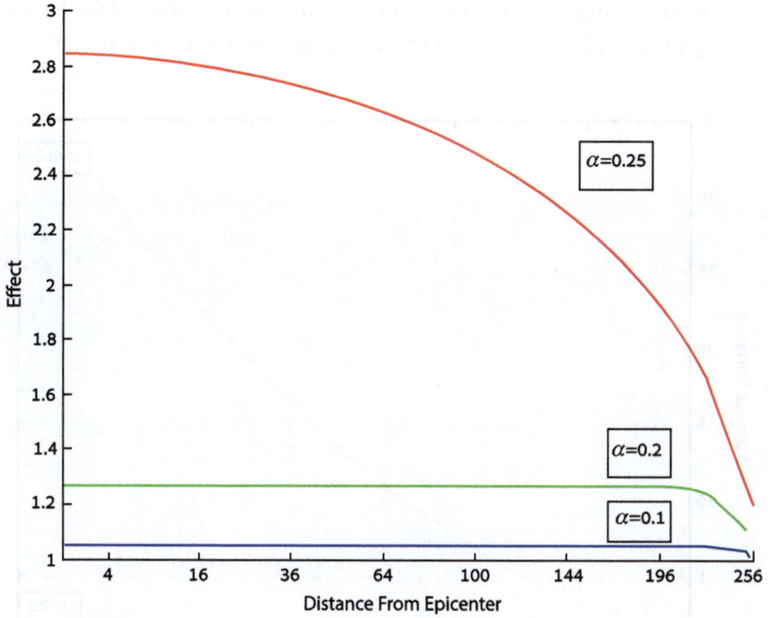

Fig. 5.3 Local impulses

naturally varies directly with λ. Figure 5.3 also shows that when $\lambda < \lambda^*$ the edge effect does not affect local impulses because the echo does not extend very far. Hence the local impulse does not depend upon distance from the epicenter, except at the edge of the lattice.

When $\lambda = \lambda^*$, however, matters are quite different. Figure 5.3 shows that in this case the local impulses vary inversely with distance from the epicenter. This happens because the echo resounds far; close to the epicenter the echo is stronger than at the edges. Had there been no edge, the effect at the epicenter would have been infinity because the echo resounds for ever, and the effect elsewhere would have been infinite too. Indeed, when N is infinity there is no meaning to epicenter because the lattice has no borders.

Variances in Bilateral Space

When space is lateral there is an analytical expression for the variance of y, see Eq. (5.15). When space is bilateral Eq. (5.18b) implies that the variance-covariance matrix of y is equal to:

$$\Sigma = \sigma_{\varepsilon}^{2} AA' \tag{5.19}$$

We follow Fingleton (1999) and calculate the average variance of y as N increases, which equals trace (Σ)/N. Unlike Fingleton we do not fix y at the epicenter. We use 10,000 Monte Carlo simulations instead of 1000, and we do not arbitrarily inflate spatial weights at the corners and along the edges of the lattice. The results are plotted on Fig. 5.4, which shows that as λ increases towards $\lambda^* = ¼$, the

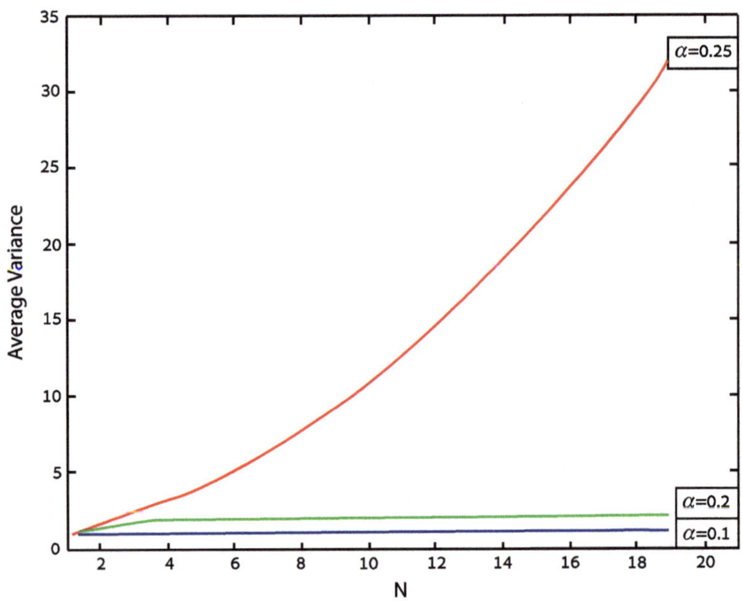

Fig. 5.4 Relationship between variance and number of spatial units

variance of y varies directly with N^{ψ} where $\psi > 1$. Figure 5.4 clearly establishes that the variance depends upon N as λ increases towards λ^*. Indeed, the variance increases nonlinearly with N. This happens because as N increases there is more scope for spatial interaction, which increases the variance among the incumbent $N - 1$ units. However, when $\lambda < \lambda^*$, the variance does not depend upon N, as should be the case if the data are stationary. Stationarity requires that the variance should not depend on the sample size.

Irregular Lattices

In regular lattices the number of neighbors is the same for all spatial units except along the edges and in the corners. In irregular lattices the number of neighbors varies between spatial units even if they are located in the core of the lattice. It is conceptually unclear how to define spatial unit roots in irregular lattices. One intuitive conjecture is that if $w_{ji} = 1$ for contiguous units λ should be normalized to equal the reciprocal of the average number of neighbors. This conjecture is based on the principle that $\lambda^* = 1/n$ in regular lattices. For example, in NUTS2 the number of contiguous neighbors ranges between 1 and 11 with a mean of 4.714. Setting $\lambda^* = 0.212$ turns out to be incorrect because the mean of λ in the Monte Carlo simulations is 0.186 and none of the 10,000 estimates exceeds 0.212. Therefore, this conjecture is incorrect.

A tempting solution to this problem is set $\lambda^* = 1$ and to restrict W to be row-sum = 1. In this case the number of neighbors does not matter from a technical point of view. This solution assumes unreasonably that spatial connectedness is independent of the number of neighbors, so that the NUTS2 unit with one neighbor is just as spatially connected as the unit with 11 neighbors. This solution also ignores edge effects.

We suggest a third solution based on the idea that as N tends to infinity, λ^* should ensure that spatial impulse responses cease to vary inversely with distance. If W_0 is an irregular (sparse) spatial weight matrix for N_0 units and λ^* denotes the spatial unit root, edge effects guarantee that $I_N - \lambda^* W_0$ is invertible and spatial impulses die out. If λ^* is correctly defined these impulses should cease to die out as N tends to infinity. Let W_1 be an irregular weights matrix when $N_1 > N_0$. Because N has increased, some or all of the edge units in W_0 will lose their edge status. Suppose that W_1 is irregular in the same way that W_0 was irregular (otherwise it is difficult to make asymptotic arguments). Impulses induced by $\lambda^* W_1$ should die away more slowly than those induced by $\lambda^* W_0$, and so on for W_2 etc. If $\lambda < \lambda^*$ these impulses will die out too rapidly. Therefore, λ^* is selected to ensure that impulses do not die out at all as N tends to infinity.

Just as we saw in Fig. 5.2 that λ^* induced a qualitative change in the persistence of spatial impulses, and in Fig. 5.3 it induced explosive tendencies in own impulses, so we suggest that λ^* may be calculated for each irregular lattice. For example, in the case of NUTS2 where the number of neighbors ranges between 1 and 11 we find, by simulation, that $\lambda^* = 0.167$. For $\lambda < 0.167$ spatial impulses do not persist and own impulses are damped. However, if $\lambda = 0.167$ spatial impulses become persistent and own impulses cease to be damped. For Columbus Ohio we find by simulation that $\lambda^* = 0.17$.

5.4 Spatial Unit Root Tests

Suppose a SAR model for y is estimated with cross-section data for N spatial units, W_N is row-summed to one, and the estimate of λ is 0.5. If this estimate is not statistically significantly smaller than λ*, the null hypothesis that y is spatially nonstationary cannot be rejected. It is straightforward to test $\lambda = 0$ using a t-test because y is stationary under the null and $\hat{\lambda}$ is asymptotically normally distributed. By contrast, $\hat{\lambda}$ does not have a standard distribution under the null $\lambda = \lambda^*$. Therefore, a t-test for $\hat{\lambda} - \lambda^*$ would be invalid. In Chap. 2 we saw that the same problem arose with estimates of AR coefficients in time series model. Dickey and Fuller provided the solution to this methodological problem.

Econometric Theory

The SAR model is:

$$y_i = \lambda \tilde{y}_i + \varepsilon_i \tag{5.19a}$$

The OLS estimate of λ is:

$$\hat{\lambda} = \frac{\sum y_i \tilde{y}_i}{\sum \tilde{y}_i^2} = \lambda + b \tag{5.19b}$$

$$b = \frac{\frac{1}{N}\sum \tilde{y}_i \varepsilon_i}{\frac{1}{N}\sum \tilde{y}_i^2} \tag{5.19c}$$

If y is stationary it is well known that $\hat{\lambda}$ is attenuated, and $b > 0$ if $\lambda > 0$. Matters are different if y is nonstationary. The asymptotic properties of $\tilde{y}$ are the same as those for y. In lateral space the numerator of b according to Eq. (5.13) is:

$$\frac{1}{N}\sum \tilde{y}_i \varepsilon_i = \frac{2\omega_1}{\lambda\left(\omega_1^{-1} - \omega_1\right)}\sigma_\varepsilon^2 \tag{5.19d}$$

And its denominator is:

$$\frac{1}{N}\sum \tilde{y}_i^2 = \frac{6}{\lambda^2\left(\omega_1^{-1} - \omega_1\right)^2\left(1 - \omega_1^2\right)}\sigma_\varepsilon^2 \tag{5.19e}$$

Therefore:

$$b = \frac{1}{3}\lambda\omega_1\left(\omega_1^{-1} - \omega_1\right)\left(1 - \omega_1^2\right) \tag{5.19f}$$

It may be shown that b varies inversely with λ and tends to zero as λ approaches ½. If $\lambda = 0.4$ $b = 0.075$. If $\lambda = 0.499$ $b = 0.00235$. Alternatively, since ω_1 tends to 1 as λ approaches ½, b tends to zero according to Eq. (5.19f). This establishes that the OLS estimate of λ is consistent if y is nonstationary.

In Eq. (5.19f) N is infinite by assumption. It is more difficult to evaluate the properties of $\hat{\lambda}$ as N approaches infinity. However, we may evaluate them using the results for finite bilateral space. According to Fig. 5.4 the denominator of b is $O_p(N^\Psi)$ where $\psi > 1$. Since ε is stationary by definition, the numerator is $O_p(1)$ according to Eq. (2.2). Since b tends to zero with N, $\hat{\lambda}$ is super-consistent. If ε is normally distributed the numerator and denominator of b are asymptotically normally distributed. However, the ratio between them is not normally distributed. The distribution of $\hat{\lambda} - \lambda^*$ has a spatial "Dickey–Fuller" distribution, which has to be simulated numerically.

Monte Carlo Simulation

We set $\lambda = \lambda^* = ¼$ in Eq. (5.18a) and generate 10,000 artificial data sets for y by drawing the ε's using pseudo random numbers from a standard normal distribution for given N. We use these synthetic data sets to estimate by maximum likelihood 10,000 SAR models. Lauridsen and Kosfeld (2006) note that this is, "...in principle doable although hardly practical in simulation studies..." (page 367). We use the ML procedure in Matlab's Econometric Toolbox, but allow the SAR coefficient to range between −2 and 2 instead of the default of −1 and 1. The distribution of the 10,000 estimates of the SAR coefficients is plotted in Fig. 5.5 for the case when N = 400 spatial units in a square lattice.

Not surprisingly the mean estimate of the SAR coefficient is almost 0.25 (0.2498) and the mode is around 0.25 (0.2520). However, some estimates exceed 0.25. The distribution is clearly skewed to the left. Since the null hypothesis is $\alpha = 0.25$, it is no surprise that some estimates exceed 0.25. This also happens in time series, see Hendry (1995) page 104. Indeed, the general "Dickey–Fuller" shape of Fig. 5.5 is similar to its time series counterpart, but it is less diffuse. According to Fig. 5.5, when N = 400 there is a 95% chance of getting a SAR coefficient that is greater than SAR* = 0.243. Therefore, the critical value for the SAR coefficient is 0.243 at p = 0.05.

In Table 5.1 we report SAR* for different values of N and p. If the estimated SAR coefficient is greater than SAR* the spatial cross-section data contain a spatial unit root. For example, when N = 100 and p = 0.05 SAR* is 0.225. If SAR is greater than SAR* we cannot reject the null hypothesis of a spatial unit root. Therefore, if the SAR estimate is, for example, 0.2 we may reject the hypothesis of a spatial unit root. SAR* naturally varies inversely with p and it varies directly with N, or the sample size.

The computations reported in Table 5.1 are inherently random because they depend on the seed used to generate the pseudo random numbers, which is chosen

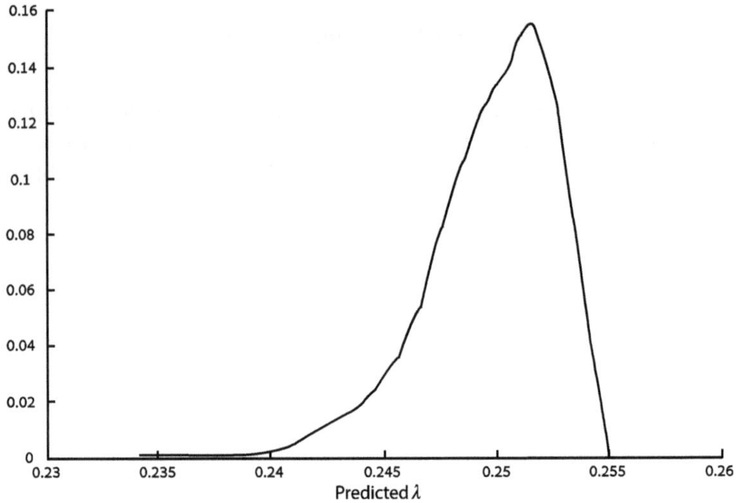

Fig. 5.5 The distribution of SAR coefficient when $\lambda = \frac{1}{4}$

randomly. To obtain some impression of the degree of randomness we reseeded the case for N = 100 500 times and reduced the number of Monte Carlo trials from 10,000 to 5000. The computer time increases exponentially and multiplicatively with the number of trails, the number of seedings and N. For example, when p = 0.05 one standard deviation of the critical value of SAR* is about ½% and SAR* is bounded between 0.224 and 0.226 (Table 5.2). Therefore, the critical values reported in Table 5.1 are reliable.

We also investigated the sensitivity of the computations reported in Table 5.1 to the number of Monte Carlo trials, which in Table 5.1 is 10,000. Here too N = 100. Table 5.3 shows, as expected, that the critical values are not sensitive to the number of trials when p is relatively large. Indeed, in this case even 1000 trials would have been sufficient. However, matters are quite different when p is relatively small, e.g. p = 0.01. In this case the critical value of SAR* varies directly with the number of trials. Clearly, to dig into the tail of the distribution requires increasing the number of trials.

We saw that spatial impulses are affected by topology especially when there is a spatial unit root. This suggests that spatial unit root tests might vary by topology. In Table 5.4 we therefore report critical values for different topologies when the number of spatial units is 400. We also report critical values for irregular topologies in Columbus, Ohio and the European Union[4] (NUTS 2). Case 1 in Table 5.4 is identical to the case in Table 5.1. We normalize the spatial unit root to unity for ease of comparison. For example, in case 1 each unit has four neighbors, therefore the normalized critical value is $4 \times 0.243 = 0.972$ at p = 0.05. Changing the lattice from

[4]We thank Bernard Fingleton for supplying these data.

Table 5.1 Spatial unit root test statistics for square rook lattice: SAR*

	N		
P	25	100	400
0.01	0.071	0.209	0.24
0.05	0.139	0.225	0.243
0.1	0.161	0.231	0.244

Table 5.2 Confidence intervals for Table 5.1 (N = 100)

	Mean	Variance	Std.	Min	Max	Mode
Mean	0.2456	1.68E – 08	1.30E – 04	0.2452	0.246	0.2456
Mode	0.249	1.81E – 08	1.35E – 04	0.2489	0.252	0.2489
1%	0.2086	4.32E – 06	0.0021	0.204	0.215	0.209
5%	0.2249	2.88E – 07	5.37E – 04	0.224	0.226	0.225
10%	0.2308	1.10E – 06	1.00E – 03	0.228	0.233	0.231

Table 5.3 Sensitivity of Table 5.1 to the number of trials (N = 100)

	Trials				
	500	1000	5000	10,000	15,000
Mean	0.2454	0.2454	0.2456	0.2452	0.2456
Mode	0.25	0.248	0.249	0.244	0.249
1%	0.193	0.208	0.2059	0.209	0.211
5%	0.22	0.225	0.224	0.225	0.225
10%	0.228	0.23	0.231	0.2309	0.2319
Truncated	32.2	30.3	32.04	32.74	31.2667

Table 5.4 Critical values for spatial unit roots for different tessellations (p = 0.05)

Case	Critical value: SAR*
1. Square (20 × 20) rook lattice	0.972
2. Oblong (10 × 40) rook lattice	0.944
3. Square (20 × 20) queen lattice	0.960
4. Columbus, Ohio	0.953
5. NUTS 2	0.988

a square to an oblong reduces the critical value slightly to 0.944 from 0.972. Since in an oblong the average distance between spatial units is greater than in the case of a square, there is correspondingly less spatial interaction. This makes it more difficult to estimate the SAR coefficient, and as a result, its critical value is less.

In case 3 each unit has eight neighbors instead of four, which increases the scope for spatial interaction. However, despite the fact that there is more spatial interaction in case 3 than in case 1 it is harder to reject the null hypothesis of a spatial unit root (the critical value in case 3 is 0.96 whereas in case 1 it is 0.972). The reason for this is that edge effects are stronger in case 3 than in case 1. In case 3 corner and edge units have three and five neighbors respectively instead of eight neighbors, whereas in case 1 they have two and three neighbors respectively instead of four.

Cases 4 and 5 differ to the previous cases in that they do not refer to artificial topologies in which the lattices are regular. Case 4 refers to Anselin's (1988) spatial connectivity matrix for Columbus, Ohio, and case 5 refers to NUTS 2. Using the methodology described above for determining unit roots when W is irregular through simulation, we find that the unit root for Columbus is 0.17 and for NUTS2 it is 0.167. If, for example, in the case of Columbus $\alpha = 0.168$ the spatial impulses are damped. However, when $\alpha = 0.17$ these impulses become explosive. The critical values have been normalized to unity for purposes of comparison. Because the critical value is higher for NUTS2 than for Columbus, it is easier to reject the null hypothesis in the case of NUTS2 than in the case of Columbus. The critical values at $p = 0.01$ are 0.964 for NUTS2 and 0.853 for Columbus. This shows that the MC distribution for the SAR coefficients is tighter for NUTS2 than it is for Columbus.

Table 5.4 shows that critical values are not sensitive to topography. It is tempting to say that if estimated SAR coefficients are less than 0.9, one may be reasonably confident in rejecting the hypothesis of a spatial unit root regardless of topography. Critical values for spatial unit roots are larger than their time series counterparts. For example, if there are 100 observations the critical value for ρ at $p = 0.05$ is 0.863 according to Dickey and Fuller. Therefore, it is easier to reject unit roots in spatial data than in time series data. We conjecture that this is because space is multi-directional whereas time only moves forward.

5.5 Spatial Cointegration Tests

Fingleton (1999) observed that if the DGPs for y and x contain spatial unit roots, estimates of β in Eq. (5.1a) may be "nonsense" in the sense of Yule (1926). If $\beta = 0$ in Eq. (5.1a) and $y \sim SI(1)$ then it must be the case that $u \sim SI(1)$ so that $\rho = 1$ in Eq. (5.1b). If, however, y and x are spatially cointegrated u must be stationary in which case $\rho < 1$.

Econometric Theory

Suppose the null hypothesis to be tested is:

$$y_i = \alpha + \beta x_i + \lambda_0 \tilde{y}_i + u_i \tag{5.20a}$$

$$u_i = \rho \tilde{u}_i + e_i \tag{5.20b}$$

Where y and x are nonstationary because they contain a spatial unit toot. If u is nonstationary because $\rho = 1$, Eq. (5.20a) is a nonsense regression. Suppose $\rho < 1$ so that the variables in Eq. (5.20a) are spatially cointegrated. The OLS estimates of β and λ_0 are:

$$\hat{\beta} = \beta + b_\beta$$

$$b_\beta = -\frac{\frac{1}{N}\sum (x_i - \bar{x})\tilde{y}_i \frac{1}{N}\sum \tilde{y}_i u_i}{\frac{1}{N}\sum (x_i - \bar{x})^2 \frac{1}{N}\sum (\tilde{y}_i - \bar{\tilde{y}})^2 - \left[\frac{1}{N}\sum (x_i - \bar{x})\tilde{y}_i\right]^2} \tag{5.20c}$$

$$\hat{\lambda}_0 = \lambda_0 + b_\lambda$$

$$b_{\lambda_0} = \frac{\frac{1}{N}\sum (x_i - \bar{x})^2 \frac{1}{N}\sum \tilde{y}_i u_i}{\frac{1}{N}\sum (x_i - \bar{x})^2 \frac{!}{N}\sum (\tilde{y}_i - \bar{\tilde{y}})^2 - \left[\frac{1}{N}\sum (x_i - \bar{x})\tilde{y}_i\right]^2} \tag{5.20d}$$

If space is lateral and infinite, it may be shown that Eqs. (5.13 and 5.20b) imply that the covariance between $\tilde{y}$ and u is:

$$\frac{1}{N}\sum_{i=1}^{\infty} \tilde{y}_i u_i = \frac{2(\omega + \omega_\rho)}{\lambda\rho(\omega^{-1} - \omega)(\omega_\rho^{-1} - \omega_\rho)(1 - \omega\omega_\rho)} \sigma_{e\varepsilon_y} \tag{5.20e}$$

where σ_{ε_y} denotes the covariance between e in Eq. (5.20b) and ε_y in Eq. (5.13), ω denotes ω_1 in Eq. (5.13) and ω_ρ denotes the eigenvalue of Eq. (5.20b), which is obtained in the same manner as ω. If e and ε_y happen to be independent b_β and b_θ are zero because Eq. (5.20e) is zero, in which case $\hat{\beta}$ and $\hat{\theta}$ are unbiased. In general, however, e and ε_y are unlikely to be independent in which case OLS is not unbiased as expected.

Under the null hypothesis of cointegration, matters are different. In this case we show that b_β and b_λ tend to zero as λ tends to ½ so that $\hat{\beta}$ and $\hat{\lambda}_0$ are generally unbiased. We simplify by assuming the SAR coefficients for y and x are the same, hence $\lambda_y = \lambda_x = \lambda$. This means that ω is the same for y and x. Recall that $\omega = 1$ when $\lambda = ½$. We also assume that ε_y and ε_x share the same variance with covariance σ_{yx}. From Eq. (5.15) the variance of x is:

$$\text{var}(x) = \frac{(1 + \omega^2)}{\lambda^2(1 - \omega^2)(\omega^{-1} - \omega)^2} \sigma_\varepsilon^2 \tag{5.20f}$$

Using Eq. (5.13) for $\tilde{y}$ and x, the covariance between x and $\tilde{y}$ is:

$$\text{cov}(\tilde{y}x) = \frac{4\omega}{\lambda^2(\omega^{-1} - \omega)^2(1 - \omega^2)} \sigma_{xy} \tag{5.20g}$$

Substituting Eqs. (5.19e and 5.20e–5.20g) into (5.20d) gives:

$$b_{\lambda_0} = \left[\frac{2\lambda(1+\omega^2)(1-\omega^2)(\omega+\omega_\rho)}{\rho\left(\omega_\rho^{-1}-\omega_\rho\right)(1-\omega\omega_\rho)}\sigma_\varepsilon^2\sigma_{\varepsilon\varepsilon_y}\right]\left[\frac{\omega^{-1}-\omega}{6(1+\omega^2)(\omega^{-1}-\omega)\sigma_\varepsilon^4 - 16\omega^2\sigma_{yx}^2}\right] \quad (5.20h)$$

Since ω tends to 1 as λ tends to ½, b_θ tends to zero because the numerators of the square brackets are zero. A similar result applies to b_β. Consequently, $\hat{\beta}$ and $\hat{\lambda}_0$ are unbiased. The intuition behind this result is straightforward. When λ = ½ y, $\tilde{y}$ and x cease to be stationary. However, u is stationary because $0 \le \rho < 1$; otherwise these variables would not be cointegrated. As ω approaches 1 their variances and covariances tend to infinity because they contain $(1-\omega^2)(\omega^{-1}-\omega)$ in their denominators. According to Eq. (5.20e) the covariance between $\tilde{y}$ and u tends to infinity more slowly because its denominator contains $\omega^{-1}-\omega$ alone.

Thus far we have established that OLS estimates of cointegrating vectors are unbiased when N is infinite. Although consistency is a weaker concept than unbiasedness, it may be of interest to establish that OLS estimators of cointegrating vectors are consistent. If estimates of cointegrating vectors are unbiased when N is infinite, it does not necessarily mean that they are also consistent. We have already noticed in the case of OLS estimates of SAR coefficients that when N is finite, edge effects may create the misleading impression that there is no unit root. However, this impression decreases with N, and disappears completely as N tends to infinity. The same phenomenon applies to estimates of ρ in Eq. (5.20b). Suppose the true value of ρ is ½ in lateral space, i.e. the variables in Eq. (5.20a) are not spatially cointegrated. If N is finite and $\hat{\rho} = \frac{1}{2}$, the spatial impulse responses for u with respect to e will be finite and vary inversely with distance just as they did in Figs. 5.2 and 5.3 with respect to λ. However, just as we showed that this misleading impression varies inversely with N in the case of λ, it also varies inversely with N in the case of ρ. Just as OLS estimates of λ are super-consistent, so are OLS estimates of ρ super-consistent.

According to Fig. 5.4 the variances and covariances of y, $\tilde{y}$ and x are $O_p(N^\Psi)$ where ψ > 1. Since u is stationary by definition, the covariance between $\tilde{y}$ and u must be $O_p(N^\zeta)$ where ζ < ψ. This means that in Eq. (5.20c):

$$b_\beta = \frac{O_p\left(T^{\psi+\zeta}\right)}{O_p\left(T^{2\omega}\right)} = O_p\left(T^{\zeta-\psi}\right) \quad (5.20i)$$

Hence the OLS estimate of β is (ψ − ζ)T super-consistent. The same applies to b_θ and the OLS estimate of θ.

Monte Carlo Simulation

In this subsection we consider the estimation of β in Eq. (5.20a) under the assumption that θ = 0. Since β = 0 under the null, and y ~ SI(1), θ is trivially equal to λ*. We generate 10,000 artificial datasets for y and x with λ* = ¼ because each unit has four

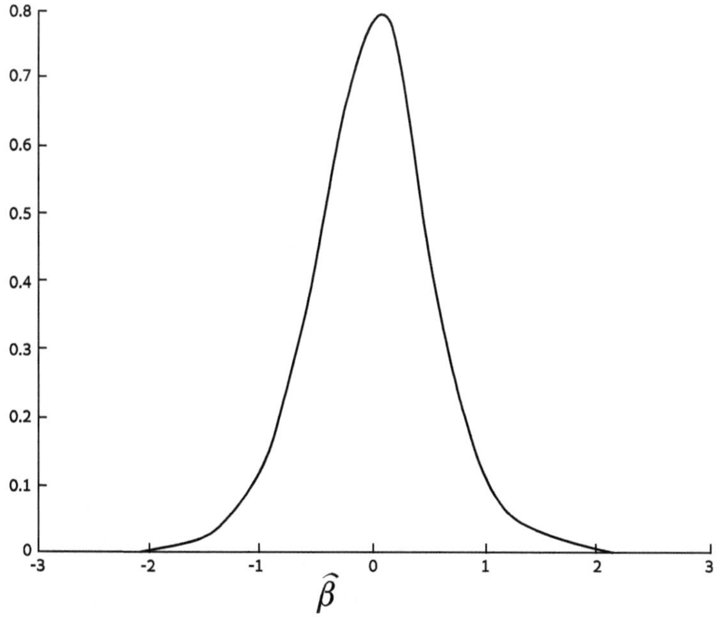

Fig. 5.6 The distribution of the spatial nonsense regression coefficient

immediate neighbors. The random numbers used to generate y and x are independent, hence we expect $\beta = 0$ in each draw. We use these datasets to generate 10,000 OLS estimates of β. The distribution of these estimates is plotted in Fig. 5.6 for $N = 400$. The distribution in Fig. 5.6 is approximately normal, and is qualitatively similar to its time series counterpart (Hendry 1995, p. 124).The mean is a non-zero random variable which in Fig. 5.6 is 0.006 and the mode is -0.0088.There are positive as well as negative estimates of β. The residuals from these nonsense regressions are used to estimate 10,000 estimates of SAC (ρ) with ρ normalized to ¼ instead of 1, which are plotted on Fig. 5.7. As in Fig. 5.5, Fig. 5.7 has the shape of a "Dickey–Fuller" distribution.

The mode in Fig. 5.7 is 0.2527 and the mean is 0.2482. However, there are estimates that are below and above ¼. When $p = 0.05$ Fig. 5.7 implies that $SAC^* = 0.241$. If $SAC < SAC^*$ the OLS estimate of β is not nonsense in which event y and x are spatially cointegrated. If, on the other hand, $SAC > SAC^*$ we cannot reject the hypothesis that the residuals contain a unit root. The estimate of β is "nonsense" and y and x are not spatially cointegrated.

Lauridsen and Kosfeld (2004) calculate critical values for the Wald statistic under the null hypothesis that the residuals are nonstationary. They assume in Eqs. (5.1a and 5.1b) that $\gamma = \beta = 1$, $x \sim U(0,1)$, $\rho = 1$, and $v \sim N(0,1)$. Based on 1000 trials they calculate (rook case, $p = 0.05$) $\chi^2(1) = 4.83$ for $N = 25$. The Wald statistic must exceed this critical value to reject the null hypothesis of no cointegration. Surprisingly, their critical values increase with N. One would think that with more data it

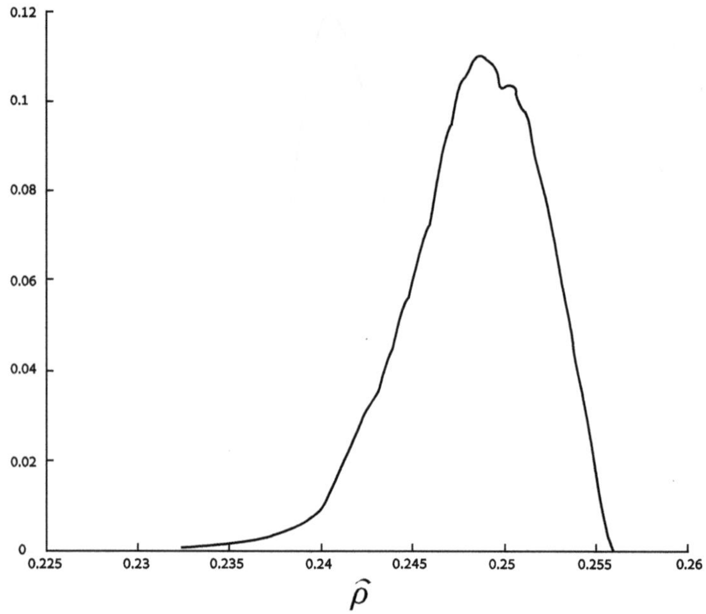

Fig. 5.7 The distribution of $\hat{\rho}$ for spatial nonsense regressions

Table 5.5 Spatial cointegration test statistics: SAC* (k = 2)

	N		
p	25	100	400
0.01	0.0450	0.198	0.239
0.05	0.107	0.215	0.243
0.1	0.1400	0.224	0.245

would be easier to reject the null hypothesis. Since ours is not a Wald test, it is difficult to compare our results with theirs.

Table 5.5 records the critical value of SAC* in the bivariate case (k = 2). Note that SAC* in Table 5.5 is typically smaller than SAR* in Table 5.1. This difference reflects the loss in degrees of freedom since SAC* is based on estimated residuals rather than true residuals. As expected, SAC* varies directly with N and p.

Table 5.6 records critical values for SAC* for different values of k when p = 0.05. As expected SAC* varies inversely with k, especially the smaller is N, because there are fewer degrees of freedom.

In this chapter, we describe some recent methodological results concerning spatial cross-section data that are nonstationary. We investigate spatial impulse responses for the SAR model in the presence and absence of spatial unit roots. We show that asymptotically space has an "infinite spatial memory" when there is a spatial unit root such that infinitely remote shocks impact on spatial units as if distance did not matter. By contrast, finite space has natural edges, so that spatial memory ceases to be infinite and spatial impulses dissipate. Hence, topology

Table 5.6 Spatial cointegration test statistics: SAC* (p = 0.05)

k	N		
	25	100	400
2	0.107	0.215	0.243
3	0.073	0.205	0.240
4	0.034	0.197	0.238

matters. However, there is a qualitative difference in the presence of unit roots; spatial impulses tend to be more persistent. In contrast to time series, spatial impulses "echo" and "boomerang" because each unit is its neighbor's neighbor. This induces forward and backward linkages between spatial units. Here too, we show that there is a qualitative difference between SAR processes with and without unit roots.

We show analytically that if space is lateral and infinite OLS estimates of SAR coefficients are unbiased under the null of a spatial unit root. We conjecture that this property also applies to multilateral space. To establish super-consistency, we use simulation methods for finite bilateral space by successively increasing N.

We also compute critical values for SAR coefficients when under the null hypothesis there is a unit root in spatial cross-section data. Our Monte Carlo computations follow procedures previously used by Dickey and Fuller who computed critical values for temporal unit roots. Critical values for spatial unit roots tend to be larger than their time series counterparts. Indeed, they are very close to unity. This qualitative difference is explained by the fact that because there is more scope for interaction in spatial data than in time series data, it is easier to reject the null hypothesis of a spatial unit root than a temporal unit root. Indeed, this intuition is brought out in the critical values calculated for different symmetric topologies. For example, the critical value is smaller for oblong topologies than square topologies because there is more scope for interaction in squares than in oblongs that have the same number of spatial units.

If the DGPs for spatial cross-section data happen to be spatially nonstationary, the nonsense regression phenomenon arises in spatial cross-section data as pointed out by Fingleton (1999). Spatial regressions cease to be nonsense if their residuals are spatially stationary, i.e. their SAC coefficient is significantly smaller than its unit root counterpart. In this event the variables in the model are spatially cointegrated. We prove for infinite lateral space that OLS estimates of spatial lag models are unbiased under the null of spatial cointegration. We conjecture that this result also applies to multilateral space. We use simulation methods for finite bilateral space to establish super-consistency. We report critical values for spatial cointegration in spatial cross-section data. These critical values are designed to distinguish between genuine and nonsense regressions. Here too we follow procedures already developed for time series data. Specifically, we derive critical SAC values since we follow Engle and Granger in using residual-based cointegration test statistics.

Critical values for spatial unit roots tend be an order of magnitude larger than their temporal counterparts. For example when N = 100 and p = 0.05 the critical value for the SAR coefficient (λ) is approximately 0.9. Typically, empirical SAR coefficients are much smaller than 0.9, suggesting that spatial cross-section data tend to be stationary. If they were not, spatial cross-section data would be chaotic. Shocks that occurred at the edge of space would impact upon its epicenter as if distance did not matter. Indeed, Tobler's first law of geography would have been broken. Empirically, however, Tobler's law is safe and salient. It might reasonably be asked why we bothered to write this chapter. Our answer is threefold. First, as noted, spatial econometricians have been concerned with unit roots and cointegration in spatial cross-section data. Second, there may be spatial cross-section data that are nonstationary. Third, and most importantly, in nonstationary spatial panel data, which are discussed in Chap. 7, unit roots are induced by spatial as well as temporal phenomena. Hopefully, the present chapter will deepen understanding of the contribution of spatial dependence in the generation of spatiotemporal unit roots and nonstationarity.

Just as a variety of cointegration tests have been developed for time series data, we do not wish to suggest that residual-based test statistics are uniquely suited for testing spatial cointegration. We see no reason why Johansen-type tests and error correction tests for cointegration mentioned in Chap. 2 cannot be developed for spatial cross-section data. Johansen's reduced rank regression methodology could be applied to spatially filtered data, and spatial error correction models could form a basis for testing spatial cointegration. However, we hope the present chapter has made a useful start by considering residual-based spatial cointegration tests.

Until now, we have been concerned with conceptual issues in the econometric analysis of time series and cross-section data. In the remaining chapters, our focus is upon nonstationary spatial panel data. In the next chapter we begin this odyssey by introducing the spatial vector autoregression.

References

Anselin L (1988) Spatial econometrics: methods and models. Kluwer Academic, Dordrecht

Beenstock M, Felsenstein D (2012) Nonparametric estimation of the spatial connectivity matrix using spatial panel data. Geogr Anal 44(4):386–397

Beenstock M, Feldman D, Felsenstein D (2012) Testing for unit roots and cointegration in spatial cross-section data. Spat Econ Anal 7(2):203–222

Cressie NAC (1993) Statistics for spatial data. Wiley, New York

Davidson R, MacKinnon JG (2009) Econometric theory and methods. Oxford University Press, New York

Engle R, Granger CWJ (1987) Co-integration and error correction: representation, estimation and testing. Econometrica 35:251–276

Fingleton B (1999) Spurious spatial regression: some Monte Carlo results with spatial unit roots and spatial cointegration. J Reg Sci 39:1–19

Florax RJGM, Folmer H, Rey SJ (2003) Specification searches in spatial econometrics: the relevance of Hendry's methodology. Reg Sci Urban Econ 33:557–559

Granger CWJ (1969) Spatial data and time series analysis. In: Scott A (ed) Studies in regional science, London papers in regional science. Pion, London, pp 1–24

Hendry DF (1995) Dynamic econometrics. Oxford University Press, Oxford

Lauridsen J, Kosfeld R (2004) A Wald test for spatial nonstationarity. Estudios de Economia Aplicada 22:475–486

Lauridsen J, Kosfeld R (2006) A test strategy for spurious spatial regression, spatial nonstationarity, and spatial cointegration. Pap Reg Sci 85:363–377

Lauridsen J, Kosfeld R (2007) Spatial cointegration and heteroscedasticity. J Geogr Syst 9:253–265

Lee L-F, Yu J (2009) Spatial nonstationarity and spurious regression: the case with a row-normalized spatial weights matrix. Spat Econ Anal 4:301–327

Mur J, Trivez FJ (2003) Unit roots and deterministic trends in spatial econometric models. Int Reg Sci Rev 26:289–312

Sargent TJ (1979) Macroeconomic theory. Academic, New York

Stakhovych S, Bijmolt THA (2008) Specification of spatial models: a simulation study on weights matrices. Pap Reg Sci 88:389–409

Yule GU (1926) Why do we sometimes get nonsense-correlations between time series? A study in sampling and the nature of time series. J R Stat Soc 89:1–64

Chapter 6
Spatial Vector Autoregressions

6.1 Introduction

Regional scientists have shown that spatial dependence in economic data may alter, and even reverse, the results of standard time-series models. For example, Rey and Montouri (1999) showed that beta convergence tests depend upon spatial spillovers in the US. A similar finding is reported by Badinger et al. (2004) for the EU. These and other studies establish the importance of integrating spatial and temporal lags in the econometric analysis of regional data. Badinger et al. (2004) have suggested that dynamic panel data econometrics developed for spatially uncorrelated data may be applied to spatially correlated data if the data are first spatially filtered. This two-stage procedure assumes that spatial dependencies in the data are nuisance parameters, which are entirely independent of the underlying "spaceless" model to be estimated. If this is not the case, their two-stage procedure may filter away important components in the underlying model.[1] Just as it is inadvisable to use seasonally filtered data in dynamic time series models (Hendry 1995), we think it is inadvisable to use spatially filtered data in dynamic spatial panel data models. Instead, we take the view that spatial lags and spatial autocorrelation should be estimated jointly with temporal lags and temporal autocorrelation in dynamic panel data models. This motivates what we refer to as a "spatial vector autoregression" or SpVAR for short, in which spatial dynamics and temporal dynamics are estimated jointly.

The present chapter focusses on SpVAR methodology in which the panel data happen to be temporally stationary and their cross-section dependence is assumed to be weak or spatial. If the cross-section dependence happened to be strong, spatial

[1]Yu et al. (2008) have suggested that the non-spatial parameters be concentrated out of the likelihood function, and that the spatial parameters be estimated from the concentrated likelihood function. This proposal like that of Badinger et al. (2004) is equally problematic.

M. Beenstock, D. Felsenstein, *The Econometric Analysis of Non-Stationary Spatial Panel Data*, Advances in Spatial Science,
https://doi.org/10.1007/978-3-030-03614-0_6

models would have been inappropriate, as explained in Chap. 10. The VAR methodology, described in Chap. 2, requires the data to be temporally stationary. SpVARs are VARs in which the data happen to be spatial. For example, in a bivariate VAR model there are two variables y and x, which are observed over T time periods. In a bivariate SpVAR, y and x are observed over T time periods in N spatial units. Whereas VARs refer to time series data, SpVARs refer to spatial panel data. Indeed, SpVARs are in effect panel VARs in which there is weak cross-section dependence between the panel units.

The complexity of SpVARs is much greater than the complexity of VARs for time series data for two reasons. First, spatial lags induce boomerang effects as explained in Chaps. 3 and 5. Second, the number of roots or eigenvalues in SpVARs is N times larger than in VARs. For example, in first-order bivariate VARs the number of roots is 2. In SpVARs the number roots is 20 if $N = 10$. This happens because the number of variables in the SpVAR is N times larger than in the corresponding VARs.

SpVARs differ from VARs in that they incorporate spatial as well as temporal dynamics, and they differ from spatial models because they incorporate temporal dynamics. SpVARs contain two types of spatial dynamics. Variables at time t may depend upon contemporaneous spatial lags as in spatial models for cross-section data discussed in Chaps. 3 and 5. In addition, variables at time t may depend upon spatial lags at time $t - \tau$ ($\tau > 0$). We refer to the latter awkwardly as "temporally-lagged spatial lags". In the absence of spatial lags, SpVARs are identical to VARs, and in the absence of temporal lags SpVARs are identical to spatial panel models.

We ask whether SpVARs identify all the structural parameters to be estimated. These parameters include the model's underlying parameters in addition to its spatial and temporal lag coefficients. Since it is well known (see Chap. 2) that structural VAR models (SVARs) generally fail to identify all the structural parameters, it is not surprising that the same applies to SpVARs. However, in univariate SpVARs matters are different; all the structural parameters are identified. We also show that the eigenvalues in SpVARs depend upon spatial and temporal dynamics, therefore stationarity depends upon both types of dynamics, as noted by Mur and Trivez (2003).[2]

We distinguish between SpVARs with and without spatial autocorrelation (SAC) in the innovations (error terms). We compare SpVARs in which there are no spatial lags but the innovations are spatially correlated, with SpVARS in which there are spatial lags but the innovations are spatially uncorrelated. The former is nested in the latter and a common factor test may be used to distinguish empirically between them. We also show that the impulse responses of SpVARs with spatial autocorrelation are a simple transformation of the impulse responses in which regional shocks are assumed to be uncorrelated.

Because SpVARs are complex, we begin by presenting a two-region first-order VAR with a single state variable. This simple "toy" model illustrates the key issues

[2]Stationarity here is defined temporally rather than spatially as in Fingleton (1999).

involved with SpVARs. Subsequently, we extend the toy model to N regions. Finally, we generalize the latter to include several state variables.

We illustrate the SpVAR methodology with an application to regional data for Israel. The estimated SpVAR contains four variables in nine regions over 18 years. The SpVAR is estimated as a homogeneous stationary panel data model in which regions are specified to have specific effects, and within-variable shocks are assumed to be spatially correlated. Panel unit root tests are used to determine the order of differencing in the SpVAR to ensure that the data used to estimate the SpVAR are stationary. Finally, the impulse responses of the estimated SpVAR are calculated under the assumption that regional shocks are independent, and under the assumption that they are spatially correlated.

6.2 SpVAR Theory

Terminology

In what follows spatial units are labeled by $i = 1,2,\ldots,N$, time periods are labeled by $t = 1,2,\ldots,T$, state variables are labeled by y_m where $m = 1,2,\ldots,M$, exogenous variables are labeled by x_k where $k = 1,2,\ldots,K$, and innovations are denoted by ε_{mit}, assumed to be iid and uncorrelated unless otherwise stated. Temporal lag orders are labeled by $p = 1,2,\ldots,P$, and spatial lags are labelled by tilde; e.g. $\tilde{y}$ is the first-order spatial lag of y and $\tilde{\tilde{y}}$ denotes the second-order spatial lag. The vectors y_{mt} and x_{kt} stack the observations on y_{mit} and x_{kit} by spatial unit and are therefore vectors of length N. The contemporaneous vector of innovations is denoted by ε_{mt}. Note that first-order spatial lags are defined as $\tilde{y}_{mt} = Wy_{mt}$ and second-order spatial lags are defined as $\tilde{\tilde{y}}_{mt} = W^2 y_{mt}$, where W denotes the $N \times N$ connectivity matrix. Y_t is an MN vector of all the current observations of the state variables stacked by m, i.e. the first N elements ordered by i refer to $m = 1$ and the last N elements refer to $m = M$. The spatial lag of Y_t is $\tilde{Y}_t = (I_M \otimes W)Y_t = \tilde{W}Y_t$. Finally, L denotes a temporal lag operator e.g. $y_{t-j} = L^j y_t$.

Contemporaneous SAR coefficients are denoted by λ. Lagged SAR coefficients (temporally-lagged spatial lags) are denoted by ϕ. Temporal AR coefficients are denoted by π. Simultaneous structural parameters between endogenous (state) variables are denoted by γ. Coefficients of the exogenous variables are denoted by β. Λ, Π, Θ, and Γ are $N \times N$ diagonal matrices with elements λ_i, π_i, ϕ_i and γ_i on the leading diagonal.

Toy SpVAR

To set the scene we illustrate the simplest SpVAR in which there are only two spatial units ($N = 2$), there is only one state variable ($M = 1$), the temporal dynamics are first-order ($P = 1$), and $w_{12} = w_{21} = 1$ because the two spatial units are mutual neighbors. There are no exogenous variables ($K = 0$). This toy model transparently conveys all the key features of SpVARs. For further simplicity, the structural model is symmetric in parameters:

$$y_{1t} = \lambda y_{2t} + \pi y_{1t-1} + \phi y_{2t-1} + \varepsilon_{1t} \tag{6.1a}$$

$$y_{2t} = \lambda y_{1t} + \pi y_{2t-1} + \phi y_{1t-1} + \varepsilon_{2t} \tag{6.1b}$$

There are mutual spatial spillovers between the two spatial units via λ, and lagged spatial spillovers via ϕ. The temporal lag coefficient is denoted by π. Notice that γ does not feature in Eqs. (6.1a and 6.1b) because there is only one state variable (M = 1). Equations (6.1a and 6.1b) are simultaneous, dynamic equations in y_{1t} and y_{2t}. They may be rewritten as:

$$\begin{bmatrix} 1-\pi L & -(\lambda+\phi L) \\ -(\lambda+\phi L) & 1-\pi L \end{bmatrix} \begin{bmatrix} y_{1t} \\ y_{2t} \end{bmatrix} = \begin{bmatrix} \varepsilon_{1t} \\ \varepsilon_{2t} \end{bmatrix} \tag{6.1c}$$

Equation (6.1c) is an SpVAR because y_{1t} and y_{2t} depend on y_{1t-1} and y_{2t-1}. The determinant of the coefficient matrix is $1 - \lambda^2 - 2(\pi+\phi\lambda)L+(\pi^2 - \phi^2)L^2$ which is quadratic in L. Its characteristic equation is therefore:

$$\left(1-\lambda^2\right)\omega^2 + 2(\pi+\phi\lambda)\omega + \pi^2 - \phi^2 = 0 \tag{6.1d}$$

The characteristic equation solves for two eigenvalues or roots, ω_1 and ω_2:

$$\omega_1 = \frac{(\pi+\phi\lambda)+(\phi+\lambda\pi)}{1-\lambda^2} \tag{6.1e}$$

$$\omega_2 = \frac{(\pi+\phi\lambda)-(\phi+\lambda\pi)}{1-\lambda^2} \tag{6.1f}$$

Stationarity requires these roots be less than unity in absolute value. It is obvious that stationarity does not simply depend upon π as it would in the absence of spatial effects ($\phi = \lambda = 0$). Indeed, the absolute value of π may be less than unity, but y may nonetheless be nonstationary. The following results are easily established:

1. If $\pi = 1$ y is nonstationary regardless of λ and ϕ (unless these parameters are negative). Therefore, if a variable is temporally nonstationary it remains so when spatial dynamics are present.
2. If $\pi + \phi + \lambda = 1$ one of the roots equals 1 in which case y is nonstationary.
3. If $\lambda = 0$ the eigenvalues are $\omega = \pi \pm \phi$. Therefore if $\phi = 1$ y must be nonstationary regardless of $\pi > 0$.
4. If $\pi = 0$ the eigenvalues are $\omega = (\lambda\phi \pm \phi)/(1 - \lambda^2)$ in which case y is nonstationary if $\phi + \lambda = 1$.

Assuming stationarity, the general solution for y_{1t} is:

$$y_{1t} = \frac{\varepsilon_{1t} - \pi\varepsilon_{1t-1} + \lambda\varepsilon_{2t} + \phi\varepsilon_{2t-1}}{(1-\omega_1 L)(1-\omega_2 L)} + A_1\omega_1^t + A_2\omega_2^t \tag{6.1g}$$

where the arbitrary constants A_1 and A_2 are determined by initial conditions. Since the roots lie within the unit circle these terms tend to zero over time. Inverting the lag polynomials by partial fractions in Eq. (6.1g) gives the Wold representation between y_{1t} and current and lagged innovations:

$$y_{1t} = \frac{1}{\omega_1 - \omega_2}\sum_{p=1}^{\infty}\left[\left(\omega_1^{1+p} - \omega_2^{1+p}\right)\left(\varepsilon_{1t-p} - \pi\varepsilon_{1t-p-1} + \lambda\varepsilon_{2t-p} + \phi\varepsilon_{2t-p-1}\right)\right] + C_1\omega_1^t + C_2\omega_2^t \tag{6.1h}$$

where the C's are arbitrary constants determined by initial conditions. According to Eq. (6.1h) current and lagged innovations in region 2 reverberate onto region 1. Since the structural model is symmetric the counterparts of Eqs. (6.1g and 6.1h) for y_{2t} may be obtained by interchanging ε_1 and ε_2.

In Table 6.1 we distinguish between three types of impulse response for y_1 with respect to the innovations ε_1 and ε_2. The impact impulse response refers to the instantaneous effect of the innovations on the current value of y_1. Notice that the own impulse response exceeds 1, as expected, due to spatial "echo" or "boomerang" effects. The cross impact impulse due to ε_2 exceeds 1 when λ is greater than 0.618. The long run impulses refer to permanent increases in the innovations. These impulses vary directly with π, ϕ and λ and exceed their impact counterparts. Had these shocks been temporary, the long run effect is of course zero due to stationarity. This is also implied by the formula in Table 6.2 for intermediate impulse responses, by setting $P = \infty$. Finally, the intermediate impulse responses refer to temporary

Table 6.1 SpVAR impulse responses for y_1 toy model

Case	ε_1	ε_2
Impact	$\frac{1}{1-\lambda^2} > 1$	$\frac{\lambda}{1-\lambda^2}$
Long run	$\frac{1-\pi}{(1-\pi)^2-(\phi+\lambda)^2}$	$\frac{\phi+\lambda}{(1-\pi)^2-(\phi+\lambda)^2}$
Intermediate	$\frac{(\omega_1-\pi)\omega_1^P - (\omega_2-\phi)\omega_2^P}{\omega_1-\omega_2}$	$\frac{(\phi+\lambda\omega_1)\omega_1^P - (\phi+\lambda\omega_2)\omega_2^P}{\omega_1-\omega_2}$

Table 6.2 SpVAR roots for toy model

Case	π	λ	ϕ	ω_1	ω_2
1	0.5	0.2	0.3	1	0.166`
2	0.5	0.1	0.3	0.88`	0.1818
3	0.5	0	0.3	0.8	0.2
4	1	0.2	−0.8	0.25	1.5

increases in the innovations. They are inevitably smaller than their impact counterparts because impulses vary inversely with p.

The first three cases in Table 6.2 refer to different parameter values for which we calculate their roots. In the first case one of the roots equals one as expected because the coefficients sum to one. In cases 2 and 3 the roots are less than one. In case 3 there is no instantaneous spatial lag ($\theta = 0$), but there is a temporally-lagged spatial lag. In case 4 even though the sum of the coefficients is less than one, the second root exceeds one. This happens because $\pi = 1$.

Finally, in Table 6.3 we report the impulse responses for cases 2 and 3 in Table 6.2. The own impact impulse response for case 2 exceeds one as expected (1.0101) but only slightly because the spatial lag coefficient is small ($\lambda = 0.1$). The cross impulse response is small because of λ. Notice that in case 3 the own impulse response is 1 because $\lambda = 0$ and the cross impulse response is zero.

The long run impulse responses are naturally much larger than their impact counterparts. The own impulse responses are larger (5.55) than their cross counterparts (4.44). In case 3 these impulses are lower because spatial spillover is less in case 3 than in case 2. The intermediate impulse responses are calculated for $p = 4$. In case 2 the own intermediate impulse response is 0.344, which is naturally smaller than its impact counterpart, but is naturally larger than its counterpart in case 3. Notice, however, that the cross impulses exceed their impact counterparts. In case 2 the intermediate cross impulse response is 0.304 whereas the impact impulse response is 0.091. The reason for this is obvious from case 3 where the cross impact response must be zero, but the intermediate impulse response is 0.214. A temporary increase in ε_2 increases y_2, which subsequently affects y_1 through the lagged spatial lag effects (π).

Univariate SpVAR

In this subsection the number of spatial units is increased to $N > 2$, but M and P continue to equal 1. We also introduce an exogenous variable and no longer assume symmetry. In summary, $M = P = K = 1$, i.e. there is one state variable (y), one exogenous variable (x), and the temporal dynamics are first-order. The structural model is:

$$y_{it} = \alpha_i + \beta_i x_{it} + \lambda_i \tilde{y}_{it} + \pi_i y_{it-1} + \phi_i \tilde{y}_{it-1} + \varepsilon_{it} \tag{6.2a}$$

where the αs denote specific effects of the spatial units, the βs refer to the direct effects of x on y, the λs are contemporaneous spatial lag or SAR parameters, the πs

Table 6.3 Illustrative SpVAR impulse responses

Case (Table 6.2)	Impulse type	ε_1	ε_2
2	Impact	1.0101	0.091
2	Long run	5.55`	4.44`
2	$p = 4$	0.344	0.304
3	Impact	1	0
3	Long run	3.125	1.875
3	$p = 4$	0.215	0.214

are temporal lag or AR parameters, and the ϕs are the temporally-lagged spatial lag or SAR parameters. There are 5N structural parameters in Eq. (6.2a) because the parameters are assumed to be heterogeneous. Had they been assumed to be homogenous there would only have been four structural parameters (β, λ, ϕ and π) plus N specific effects.

Vectorizing Eq. (6.2a) gives:

$$y_t = \alpha + \mathrm{B}x_t + \Lambda W y_t + \Pi y_{t-1} + \Phi W y_{t-1} + \varepsilon_t \tag{6.2b}$$

where y and x are N-vectors, B, Λ, Φ and Π are diagonal matrices of the structural parameters and α is vector of specific effects. The solution for y_t is:

$$y_t = A[\alpha + Bx_t + (\Phi W + \Pi) y_{t-1} + \varepsilon_t] \tag{6.2c}$$

where $A = (\mathrm{I}_N - \Lambda W)^{-1}$ with elements a_{ij}.

Equation (6.2c) is a univariate spatial vector autoregression in which the innovations are dependent through A. Although M = 1, Eq. (6.2c) contains N variables. The structural parameters in Eq. (6.2a) are identified. There are two econometric problems to be solved in estimating Eq. (6.2a). The first concerns the λ coefficients, which may be estimated by maximum likelihood or instrumental variables (see Chap. 3). The second concerns the ϕs and πs. If these coefficients are assumed to be homogeneous they may be estimated using the methodology proposed by Arellano and Bond (1991). These two estimation problems have been combined by Yu et al. (2008) so that λ and π are estimated jointly.

The spatiotemporal impulse responses for the univariate SpVAR may be obtained as follows. Gathering terms in y_t, Eq. (6.2c) may be rewritten as:

$$\begin{aligned}[\mathrm{I}_N - CL] y_t &= A[\alpha + Bx_t + \varepsilon_t] \\ C &= A(\Phi W + \Pi)\end{aligned} \tag{6.2d}$$

where L denotes the temporal lag operator. Therefore, y_t is:

$$y_t = (I_N - C)^{-1} A\alpha + ABx_t + A\varepsilon_{t-1} + \sum_{\tau=1}^{\infty} C^{\tau} A(Bx_{t-\tau} + \varepsilon_{t-\tau}) \tag{6.2e}$$

The current spatial impulse responses from Eq. (6.2e) are:

$$\frac{dy_t}{dx_t} = AB \tag{6.2f}$$

From which:

$$\frac{dy_{it}}{dx_{jt}} = \beta_i a_{ij} \tag{6.2g}$$

The spatiotemporal impulse responses are:

$$\frac{dy_t}{dx_{t-\tau}} = C^{\tau}AB \tag{6.2h}$$

From which:

$$\frac{dy_{it}}{dx_{jt-\tau}} = \beta_i f_{\tau ij} \tag{6.2i}$$

where $f_{\tau ij}$ is an element of $C^{\tau}A$. Since the elements of C are fractions due to stationarity, $f_{\tau ij}$ varies inversely with τ; the spatiotemporal impulse responses tend to zero over time.

Bivariate SpVAR

In bivariate SpVARs $M = 2$, i.e. there are two state variables. Multivariate SpVARs are qualitatively different to univariate SpVARs because the structural parameters in multivariate SpVARs include γ parameters, which cannot be identified. The reasons are essentially the same as those given in Chap. 2 for standard VARs. The structural equations for the state variables are assumed to be:

$$y_{1t} = \alpha_1 + \gamma_1 y_{2t} + \lambda_{11}\tilde{y}_{1t} + \lambda_{12}\tilde{y}_{2t} + \pi_{11}y_{1t-1} + \pi_{12}y_{2t-1} + \phi_{11}\tilde{y}_{1t-1} + \phi_{12}\tilde{y}_{2t-1} + \varepsilon_{1t} \tag{6.3a}$$

$$y_{2t} = \alpha_2 + \gamma_2 y_{1t} + \lambda_{21}\tilde{y}_{1t} + \lambda_{22}\tilde{y}_{2t} + \pi_{21}y_{1t-1} + \pi_{22}y_{2t-1} + \phi_{21}\tilde{y}_{1t-1} + \phi_{22}\tilde{y}_{2t-1} + \varepsilon_{2t} \tag{6.3b}$$

where y_{1t} is an N-vector with elements y_{1it} and y_{2t} is an N-vector with elements y_{2it}. In the structural model the two state variables (y_1 and y_2) depend on each other in both current and lagged time periods through the γ and π parameters respectively, and they are spatially dependent both currently and lagged though the λ and ϕ parameters respectively. In contrast to the univariate SpVAR these parameters are assumed to be homogeneous for expositional simplicity, e.g. π_1 is the same for all spatial units. Since the exogenous variables are not central to our argument we have dropped them from Eqs. (6.3a and 6.3b) for convenience, so $K = 0$.

Equations (6.3a and 6.3b) are simultaneous at time t because of the γ and spatial lag coefficients (λ). We begin by solving them for the current time period:

$$
\begin{aligned}
y_{1t} = {} & \kappa_1 + (\pi_{11} + \gamma_1\pi_{21})y_{1t-1} + (\pi_{12} + \gamma_1\pi_{22})y_{2t-1} \\
& + (\phi_{11} + \gamma_1\phi_{21} - \lambda_{12}\pi_{21} - \lambda_{22}\pi_{11})\tilde{y}_{1t-1} \\
& + (\phi_{12} + \gamma_1\phi_{22} - \lambda_{22}\pi_{12} - \lambda_{12}\pi_{22})\tilde{y}_{2t-1} \\
& - (\lambda_{22}\phi_{11} + \lambda_{12}\phi_{21})\tilde{\tilde{y}}_{1t-1} - (\lambda_{22}\phi_{12} + \lambda_{12}\pi_{22})\tilde{\tilde{y}}_{2t-1} \\
& + \varepsilon_{1t} - \lambda_{22}\tilde{\varepsilon}_{1t} + \gamma_1\varepsilon_{2t} - \lambda_{12}\tilde{\varepsilon}_{2t}
\end{aligned} \tag{6.3c}
$$

$$
\begin{aligned}
y_{2t} = {} & \kappa_2 + (\pi_{21} + \gamma_2\pi_{11})y_{1t-1} + (\pi_{22} + \gamma_2\pi_{12})y_{2t-1} \\
& + (\phi_{21} + \gamma_2\phi_{11} - \lambda_{11}\pi_{21} - \lambda_{21}\pi_{11})\tilde{y}_{1t-1} \\
& + (\phi_{22} + \gamma_2\phi_{12} - \lambda_{11}\pi_{22} - \lambda_{21}\pi_{12})\tilde{y}_{2t-1} \\
& - (\lambda_{11}\phi_{21} + \lambda_{21}\phi_{11})\tilde{\tilde{y}}_{1t-1} + (\lambda_{11}\phi_{22} + \lambda_{21}\phi_{12})\tilde{\tilde{y}}_{2t-1} \\
& + \varepsilon_{2t} - \lambda_{21}\tilde{\varepsilon}_{2t} + \gamma_2\varepsilon_{1t} - \lambda_{11}\tilde{\varepsilon}_{1t}
\end{aligned} \tag{6.3d}
$$

Equations (6.3a and 6.3b) constitute an SpVAR involving first-order temporal lags in the state variables, and first-order and second-order lagged spatial lags. Note that the SpVAR innovations are correlated and are spatially autocorrelated. Note also that whereas there are 18 structural parameters in Eqs. (6.3a and 6.3b) comprising 2 αs, 2 γs, 4 λs, 4 πs, 4 ϕs, $\sigma_{\varepsilon 1}$ and $\sigma_{\varepsilon 2}$, there are only 15 independent SpVAR parameters (14 SpVAR parameters plus the covariance between the SpVAR innovations). As expected from the discussion of VARs in Chap. 2, there is an identification deficit of three. This identification deficit was zero in the univariate case ($M = 1$), and would have been larger for $M > 2$.

Next, we solve the SpVAR to obtain its spatio-temporal impulse responses with respect to its innovations (e):

$$e_{1t} = \varepsilon_{1t} - \lambda_{22}\tilde{\varepsilon}_{1t} + \gamma_1\varepsilon_{2t} - \lambda_{12}\tilde{\varepsilon}_{2t} \tag{6.3e}$$

$$e_{2t} = \varepsilon_{2t} - \lambda_{21}\tilde{\varepsilon}_{2t} + \gamma_2\varepsilon_{1t} - \lambda_{11}\tilde{\varepsilon}_{1t} \tag{6.3f}$$

Equations (6.3c and 6.3d) may be rewritten as:

$$
\begin{bmatrix} I_N - \Omega_{11}L & -\Omega_{12}L \\ -\Omega_{21}L & I_N - \Omega_{22}L \end{bmatrix}
\begin{bmatrix} y_{1t} \\ y_{2t} \end{bmatrix} =
\begin{bmatrix} \kappa_1 + e_{1t} \\ \kappa_2 + e_{2t} \end{bmatrix} \tag{6.3g}
$$

$$
\begin{aligned}
\Omega_{11} &= (\pi_{11} + \gamma_1\pi_{21})I_N + (\phi_{11} + \gamma_1\phi_{21} - \lambda_{12}\pi_{21} - \lambda_{22}\pi_{11})W \\
&\quad - (\lambda_{22}\phi_{11} + \lambda_{12}\phi_{21})W^2 \\
\Omega_{12} &= (\pi_{12} + \gamma_1\pi_{22})I_N + (\phi_{12} + \gamma_1\phi_{22} - \lambda_{22}\pi_{12} - \lambda_{12}\pi_{22})W \\
&\quad - (\lambda_{22}\phi_{12} + \lambda_{12}\pi_{22})W^2 \\
\Omega_{21} &= (\pi_{21} + \gamma_2\pi_{11})I_N + (\phi_{21} + \gamma_2\phi_{11} - \lambda_{11}\pi_{21} - \lambda_{21}\pi_{11})W \\
&\quad - (\lambda_{11}\phi_{22} + \lambda_{21}\phi_{12})W^2 \\
\Omega_{22} &= (\pi_{22} + \gamma_2\pi_{12})I_N + (\phi_{22} + \gamma_2\phi_{12} - \lambda_{11}\pi_{22} - \lambda_{21}\pi_{12})W \\
&\quad - (\lambda_{11}\phi_{22} + \lambda_{21}\phi_{12})W^2
\end{aligned}
$$

Notice that the Ωs contain terms in W^2 as well as W. Hence the solutions to Eq. (6.3g) will include second order spatial lags as well as their first order counterparts that are specified in the structural model (Eqs. 6.3a and 6.3b). The same applies to the temporal dynamics of the model. The solutions to Eq. (6.3g) will include second order temporal lags in addition to their first order counterparts specified in the structural model. This result is generated by the determinant of the coefficient matrix in Eq. (6.3g):

$$\begin{vmatrix} I_N - \Omega_{11}L & -\Omega_{12}L \\ -\Omega_{21}L & I_N - \Omega_{22}L \end{vmatrix} = I_N - (\Omega_{11} + \Omega_{22})L + (\Omega_{11}\Omega_{22} - \Omega_{12}\Omega_{21})L^2 \quad (6.3h)$$

which contains L^2 in addition to L.

The solution for y_{1t} from Eq. (6.3g) is:

$$\begin{aligned} y_{1t} &= B[(I_N - \Omega_{22})\kappa_1 + \Omega_{12}\kappa_2 + e_{1t} - \Omega_{22}e_{1t-1} + \Omega_{12}e_{2t-1}] \\ B &= \left[I_N - (\Omega_{22} + \Omega_{11})L + (\Omega_{11}\Omega_{22} - \Omega_{12}\Omega_{21})L^2\right]^{-1} \end{aligned} \quad (6.3i)$$

As expected from Chap. 2, although the structural model and the SpVAR entail first-order temporal dynamics, Eq. (6.3i) entails second-order temporal and spatial dynamics. This is because these dynamic orders equals NP, which in the present case is $2 \times 1 = 2$. In second order systems with $P = 2$, Eqs. (6.3a and 6.3b) would have involved second-order temporal lags, in which case B would have been a fourth order polynomial in L. The term in square brackets is a second-order polynomial in the temporal lag operator (L), which factorizes into $(I_N - R_1L)(I_N - R_2L)$, where $R_1 + R_2 = \Omega_{11} + \Omega_{12}$ and $R_1R_2 = \Omega_{11}\Omega_{22} - \Omega_{12}\Omega_{21}$. Using a decomposition based on partial fractions, B may be expressed more conveniently by:

$$B = (R_1 - R_2)^{-1}\left[R_1(I_N - R_1L)^{-1} - R_2(I_N - R_2L)^{-1}\right] \quad (6.3j)$$

where the polynomial expansions of the terms in square brackets may be obtained using:

$$(I_N - RL)^{-1} = I_N + \sum_{p=1}^{\infty} R^p L^p$$

Finally, the spatio-temporal impulse responses for y_{1t} with respect to the SpVAR innovations are generated by:

$$y_{1t} = (R_1 - R_2)^{-1}\left[\sum_{p=0}^{\infty}\left(R_1^{1+p} - R_2^{1+p}\right)\left(e_{1t-p} - \Omega_{22}e_{1t-1-p} + \Omega_{12}e_{2t-1-p}\right)\right] \tag{6.3k}$$

From which the impulse response vectors for y_1 with respect to e_1 and e_2 are:

$$\frac{\partial y_{1t}}{\partial e_{1t-p}} = (R_1 - R_2)^{-1}\left[R_1^{1+p} - R_2^{1+p} - \Omega_{22}\left(R_1^p - R_2^p\right)\right] = \Theta_{1p} \tag{6.3l}$$

$$\frac{\partial y_{1t}}{\partial e_{2t-p}} = (R_1 - R_2)^{-1}\Omega_{12}\left(R_1^p - R_2^p\right) = \Theta_{2p} \tag{6.3m}$$

where Θ_{1p} and Θ_{2p} are $N \times N$ matrices with elements θ_{1pij} and θ_{2pij}, which vary inversely with p. Finally, the impulse responses of y_{1it} with respect to the structural innovations ε_{1jt-p} and ε_{2t-p} are obtained by substituting Eqs. (6.3e and 6.3f) into Eqs. (6.3l and 6.3m):

$$\frac{\partial y_{1it}}{\partial \varepsilon_{1jt-p}} = \theta_{1pij}\left(1 - \lambda_{22}w_{ij}\right) + \theta_{2pij}\left(\gamma_2 - \lambda_{11}w_{ij}\right) \tag{6.3n}$$

$$\frac{\partial y_{1it}}{\partial \varepsilon_{2jt-p}} = \theta_{1pij}\left(\gamma_1 - \lambda_{12}w_{ij}\right) + \theta_{2pij}\left(1 - \lambda_{22}w_{ij}\right) \tag{6.3o}$$

In a similar fashion we may obtain the spatiotemporal impulse responses for y_{2it} with respect to ε_{1jt-p} and ε_{2jt-p}.

Multivariate SpVAR

Finally, we generalize the SpVAR to the case where M and N are unrestricted. The structural equation for variable m is in unit i is:

$$y_{mit} = \alpha_{mi} + \sum_{n \neq m}^{M}\gamma_{mn}y_{nit} + \sum_{n=1}^{M}\pi_{mn}y_{mit-1} + \sum_{n=1}^{M}\lambda_{mn}\tilde{y}_{nit} + \varepsilon_{mit} \tag{6.4a}$$

where α_{mi} denotes the fixed effect for variable m in unit i. Each variable depends on the current values of all other variables via the γ coefficients, the lagged dependent variables via the π coefficients and the current spatial lagged variables via the λ coefficients. For simplicity we have omitted the temporal lags of these spatial dependent variables by setting the ϕ coefficients to zero. Stacking by spatial units Eq. (6.4a) may be vectorized where y denotes an NM vector in which the first N elements refer to the first unit, and the last N elements refer to unit N:

$$y_t = \alpha + \Gamma \otimes I_N y_t + \Pi \otimes I_N y_{t-1} + (\Lambda \otimes I_N)(W \otimes I_M) y_t + \varepsilon_t \tag{6.4b}$$

where α is an MN vector of fixed effects stacked by m, Γ denotes the $M \times M$ coefficient matrix with elements γ_{mn} and zeros along the leading diagonal, and Λ and Π denote $M \times M$ coefficient matrices with elements λ_{mn} and π_{mn}. The SpVAR is given by the solution of Eq. (6.4b) for y_t:

$$\begin{aligned} y_t &= A(\alpha + \Pi \otimes I_N y_{t-1} + \varepsilon_t) \\ A &= [I_{NM} - \Gamma \otimes I_N - (\Lambda \otimes I_N)(W \otimes I_M)]^{-1} \end{aligned} \tag{6.4c}$$

The Wold representation for Eq. (6.4c) is:

$$\begin{aligned} y_t &= (I_{NM} - \Omega)^{-1} A\alpha + A\varepsilon_t + \sum_{\tau=1}^{\infty} \Omega^{\tau} A (\Pi \otimes I_N) A \varepsilon_{t-\tau} \\ \Omega &= A(\Pi \otimes I_N) \end{aligned} \tag{6.4d}$$

From which the MN spatiotemporal impulse responses of all variables with respect to all variables in all spatial units over all temporal lags may be derived.

6.3 Econometric Issues

The Incidental Parameter Problem

If spatial fixed effects are specified in first order dynamic panel data models of the type:

$$y_{it} = \alpha_i + \pi y_{it-1} + u_{it} \tag{6.5a}$$

the "incidental parameter problem" induces bias in the estimates of π. The econometric implications of estimating fixed effects in dynamic panels have attracted much attention in the literature (Baltagi 2013, Chap. 8). The basic problem is that estimates of π are biased downwards when T is finite, with the bias being $O(T^{-1})$. Hsiao (1986) showed that in AR(1) models as in Eq. (6.5a) the bias is equal to:

$$b = -\frac{\frac{1+\pi}{T-1}\left(1 - \frac{1-\pi^T}{T(1-\pi)}\right)}{\left(1 - \frac{2\pi}{(1-\pi)(T-1)}\left(1 - \frac{1-\pi^T}{T(1-\pi)}\right)\right)} \tag{6.5b}$$

The bias tends to zero as T tends to infinity so $\text{plim}(\hat{\pi}) = \pi$. If the panel is short (T is small) this bias may not be negligible. In Fig. 6.1 we use Eq. (6.5b) to plot the relationship between $\hat{\pi}$ and π for various values of T. As expected the plotted schedules approach the 45° line from below as T increases. In our empirical example $T = 16$. Equation (6.5b) implies in this case that the asymptotic bias is –0.0991

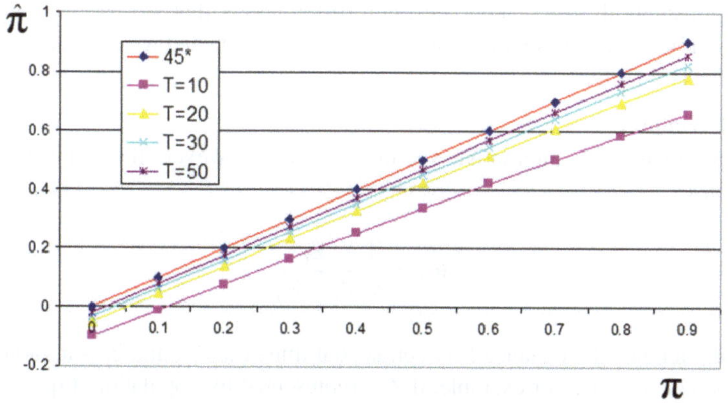

Fig. 6.1 The inconsistency of the panel autoregressive coefficient

when $\pi = 0.5$, in which case $\hat{\pi} = 0.4009$. If $\pi = 0$ the asymptotic bias is -0.06, in which case $\hat{\pi} = -0.06$. Also, the bias varies directly with. For example, when $\pi = -0.5$ the bias is -0.031, which is a third of its counterpart when $\pi = 0.5$.

The most popular solution to the incidental parameter problem (Arellano and Bond 1991; Blundell and Bond 1998) is based on instrumental variable estimation or GMM, where sufficiently lagged values of Δy_j are used to instrument Δy_{jt-1}. See e.g. Badinger et al. (2004). Apart from the "weak instrument" problem, there is a further problem since the autoregressive order (P) in Eq. (6.5a), which has been assumed to be 1, is unknown in practice. If P = 1, as is typically assumed, matters are easier. But P is unknown as is the autocorrelation structure of the error term (u) in Eq. (6.5a). The larger is the autoregressive order (P) and the more autocorrelated are the error terms, the less reasonable it is to use lagged dependent variables to solve the incidental parameter problem. We are therefore skeptical about the Arellano–Bond–Blundell (ABB) solution to this problem.

Kiviet (1995) and Hahn and Kuersteiner (2002) have suggested bias-correction as an alternative to the ABB solution. Since ML and GMM require the specification of instrumental variables whereas bias-correction does not, bias-correction is a practical and attractive alternative to ABB.[3] However, it has not proved to be as popular as ABB, perhaps because ABB has been readily available and accessible in Stata and Eviews, whereas bias correction has not. We suggest using Eq. (6.5b) to bias-correct estimates of π. For example, if T = 16 and the estimate of π is 0.4009 the bias-corrected estimate would be 0.5.

Like us, Yu et al. (2008) prefer bias correction over ABB. They concentrate out spatial fixed effects from the likelihood function by demeaning the data, and estimate Λ, Γ, and Π by QML. Subsequently, they bias-correct these estimates as well as the estimated fixed effects. The bias-corrected estimates continue to be biased, but the

[3]Hahn and Kuersteiner (2002) show that a simpler bias correction than Eq. (6.5b) is not outperformed by GMM in finite samples.

bias is substantially mitigated. The main difference is that we use IV rather than QML, and because N is small we do not demean the data and we estimate the spatial fixed effects directly.

Spatial Weights

We experiment with alternative spatial weights. However, the main results we present use:

$$w_{ij} = \frac{1}{d_{ij}} \frac{Z_i}{Z_i + Z_j} \tag{6.6}$$

where d_{ij} denotes the distance between spatial units i and j, and Z is a variable that captures scale effects. For example, if Z is represented by population, Eq. (6.6) states that the importance of unit j in unit i varies directly with the population in unit j relative to unit i. Spatial weights are therefore larger for bigger neighbors, and smaller for smaller neighbors. This spatial weighting scheme is asymmetric unless $Z_i = Z_j$, i.e. the units are of equal size. Other asymmetric weighting schemes include e.g. commuting weights, which reflect rates of commuting between regions i and j. The weights are row-summed to one.

If the spatial lag coefficients are estimated by ML and the W matrix is symmetric, the estimated variance-covariance matrix of the parameters is symmetric. This result does not extend, however, to the case where W is asymmetric.[4] If, however, the spatial lag coefficients are estimated by IV rather than ML it does not matter that W is asymmetric.

Fixed Versus Random Effects in Spatial Panels

The choice between fixed and random effects in spatial panel data models is not trivial. Several issues have been raised in the literature. First, if the data happen to be a random sample of the population, unconditional inference about the population necessitates estimation with random effects. If, however, the objective is limited to making conditional inferences about the sample, then fixed effects should be specified. Since researchers are usually interested in making unconditional inferences about the population, the default option should be random effects. This line of reasoning[5] implies that if the sample happened to be the population, specific effects should be fixed because each panel member represents itself and has not been sampled randomly.

In household panels the sample is small relative to the population. However, in spatial panels the data typically cover the entire population of spatial units. For example, the Penn World Tables cover all the countries in the world and NUTS2 covers all the regions in the European Union. Our data cover all the regions of Israel. Since none of the regions is sampled, estimation should be with fixed effects. "For

[4]See Anselin (1988) p 79 footnote 14.

[5]See e.g. Hsiao (1986) p 43, Maddala (2001) p 576, Baltagi (2013) p 14 and Cameron and Trivedi (2005) p 717.

example, an inter-country comparison may well include the full set of countries for which it is reasonable to assume that the model is constant." (Greene 2012, p. 411). Matters would be different if the spatial units in the data were a random sample of the spatial units in the population, such as a sample of cities or counties. "This view would be appropriate if we believed that sampled cross-sectional units were drawn from a large population." (Greene 2012, p. 411.)

A second issue raised in the literature concerns dependence between random effects and the covariates in the model. Such dependence, if it exists, typically induces bias in the parameter estimates of the model. Mundlak (1978) has argued in this case that the fixed effects estimator would be observationally equivalent to the random effects estimator. Indeed, this is the line adopted by Wooldridge (2010) who suggests specifying fixed effects if the covariates and random effects happen to be dependent. This argument would only be relevant if the spatial panel dataset was a sample rather than the population.

A third issue is practical. If the number of units in the panel is large, estimating fixed effects consumes degrees of freedom and reduces the variation in the data. Also, LSDV does not allow the estimation of parameters that vary in the cross section but which do not vary over time. These problems do not arise when random effects are specified. In spatial data the number of spatial units tends to be relatively small, so that this issue is not of major importance. In our case the number of spatial units is nine. However, in some spatial panel data sets such as NUTS 2 the number of spatial units runs into the hundreds. In this case Mundlak's estimator might be attractive in practice.

Seemingly Unrelated Regression (SUR)

In Chap. 10 we note that cross-section dependence in the error terms in spatial panel data models may assume three forms. First, the dependence may be spatial; the error terms are spatially autocorrelated. Second, the dependence may be induced by unspecified common factors. Third, the error terms may simply be seemingly unrelated; they do not have spatial or common factor structures. In the first case, the cross-section dependence might be eliminated by specifying spatial lagged dependent variables in the model, as discussed in Chap. 2. In the second case, the cross-section dependence might be eliminated by specifying common correlated effects (Pesaran 2006). In the third case, the solution is to estimate the spatial panel data model by SUR. Since the three cases are not mutually exclusive, it makes sense to estimate the SpVAR by SUR. Indeed, estimation is by SUR in Chaps. 8, 9 and 10. Notice that SUR should not be confused with the spatial SUR estimator where $N > T$, and separate cross-section models are estimated for each time period (Anselin 1988, Chap. 10; Elhorst 2014, Chap. 3).

6.3.1 Data

Sources and Definitions

For our empirical application of SpVAR we use annual panel data for nine regions in Israel (see Map 4.1) for the period 1987–2004. The vector comprises four variables: real earnings, population, real house prices and the stock of housing. The latter is measured in 1000's of square meters. Hence, $T = 18$, $N = 9$, $M = 4$ and $K = 0$. Since these observations are too few to estimate individual models for each region, we pool the time series and cross-section data for purposes of estimation. We note that the IPS panel unit root tests proposed by Im et al. (2003) report critical values for $T \geq 10$, in which case we feel that it is meaningful to use 18 years of data. Calculations by IPS show that when $T = 18$ and $N = 9$ the size of the unit root test is about 0.05 and its power is about 0.2. This means that the probability of incorrectly rejecting the null hypothesis when it is true is about 5%, and the probability of correctly rejecting it when it is false is about 20%. The latter would have been 26% with $T = 25$ and 75% with $T = 50$. In our opinion, what matters is the length of the observation period and not merely the number of data points. 18 monthly or even quarterly data points would not have been adequate because the observation period would have been only a year and half in the former case and four and half years in the latter. These periods would have been too short for observing convergence phenomena, whereas 18 years is in our opinion a sufficiently long period for these purposes.

At this stage, we do not present a formal economic model, which relates these four variables, (as we do in Chap. 8). Such a model might predict that house prices vary directly with the demand for housing services in the region, which in turn varies directly with income and population, and they vary inversely with the supply of housing services as measured by the stock of housing.[6] It might also predict that the regional distribution of the population depends upon house prices and earnings; people prefer to live in regions where earnings are higher and housing is cheaper. It might further predict regional spillover effects. For example, if house prices happen to become more expensive in neighboring regions house buyers will prefer to move into regions where housing is cheaper, which would tend to raise house prices in the region. Therefore, there is sufficient reason to believe that the SpVAR will not be vacuous. However, we stress that we do not use the SpVAR to test structural hypotheses about regional housing and labor markets. Our main motivation is to apply SpVAR, and to illustrate the methodology.

Real earnings in region i time t have been constructed by us from the Household Income Surveys of the Central Bureau of Statistics (CBS) and are deflated by the national consumer price index (CPI). The population in region i at the beginning of time t (POP_{it}) is published by CBS. CBS also publishes indices of house prices for the nine regions (see Chap. 4), which are based on transactions data and which we deflate by the CPI. Finally, we have constructed the stock of housing in region i at

[6] See Bar-Nathan et al. (1998).

the beginning of time t (H_{it}), which is measured in (gross) square meters. We use data on housing completions in the nine regions measured in square meters, published by CBS. The change in the stock of housing is defined as completions minus our estimates of demolitions. The level of the housing stock is inferred from data in the 1995 census.

Panel Unit Root Tests
The data are plotted in Fig. 6.2. Not surprisingly, all four variables have grown over time, hence they cannot be stationary. It should be noted that the 1990s witnessed mass immigration from the former USSR, which had major macroeconomic implications, especially for labor and housing markets (Beenstock and Fisher 1997). The population grew in all regions, but particularly in the South where housing was cheaper. In Table 6.4 we report panel unit root tests (t-bar) due to Im et al. (2003), which is the average of the first-order augmented Dickey-Fuller statistics for variable m in the nine regions. When $d = 0$ the absolute value of t-bar is below its critical value in the case of earnings and the housing stock, so these variables are clearly non-stationary. Surprisingly, however, Table 6.4 suggests that population and house prices are stationary in log levels. When $d = 1$ absolute t-bar is greater than its critical value for all variables, hence all four variables are difference stationary. Although Table 6.4 suggests that earnings and the housing stock are I(1) while population and house prices are I(0), we specify the SpVAR in log first differences.

Spatial dependence in the data may distort the empirical size of the IPS test, as noted above and discussed in detail in Chap. 7. However, the data plotted in Fig. 6.3 are clearly trending, so that the conclusion that $d = 1$ is not controversial despite potential size distortions in Table 6.4.

6.4 Results

Our main objective is to estimate Eq. (6.4a). However, Γ is not identified by the SpVAR parameters in Eq. (6.4b). We begin by estimating Eq. (6.4b) in the first stage. Then we use the predicted values of y_t to serve as instrumental variables for $\tilde{y}_t$ in Eq. (6.4a), i.e. we estimate Eq. (6.4a) using $\tilde{\hat{y}}_t = W\tilde{y}_t$ instead of $\tilde{y}_t$. This two stage procedure delivers consistent estimates of Λ, Θ and Π under the unavoidable assumption that $\Gamma = 0$, provided that the SpVAR innovations are serially independent. If they are serially independent, y_{t-1} and the lagged spatial lag ($\tilde{y}_{t-1}$) are weakly exogenous for Λ.

Estimating the SpVAR's Reduced Form
Since $T = 18$ the SpVAR is limited to first-order spatial and temporal lags. There are insufficient degrees of freedom to justify higher order lags. In any case the panel DW statistics and other tests do not suggest that higher order temporal lags are required. There are also insufficient degrees of freedom to estimate heterogeneous models in which the parameters vary by region and/or by time period since $N = 9$ and $T = 18$. Therefore, the SpVAR is homogeneous.

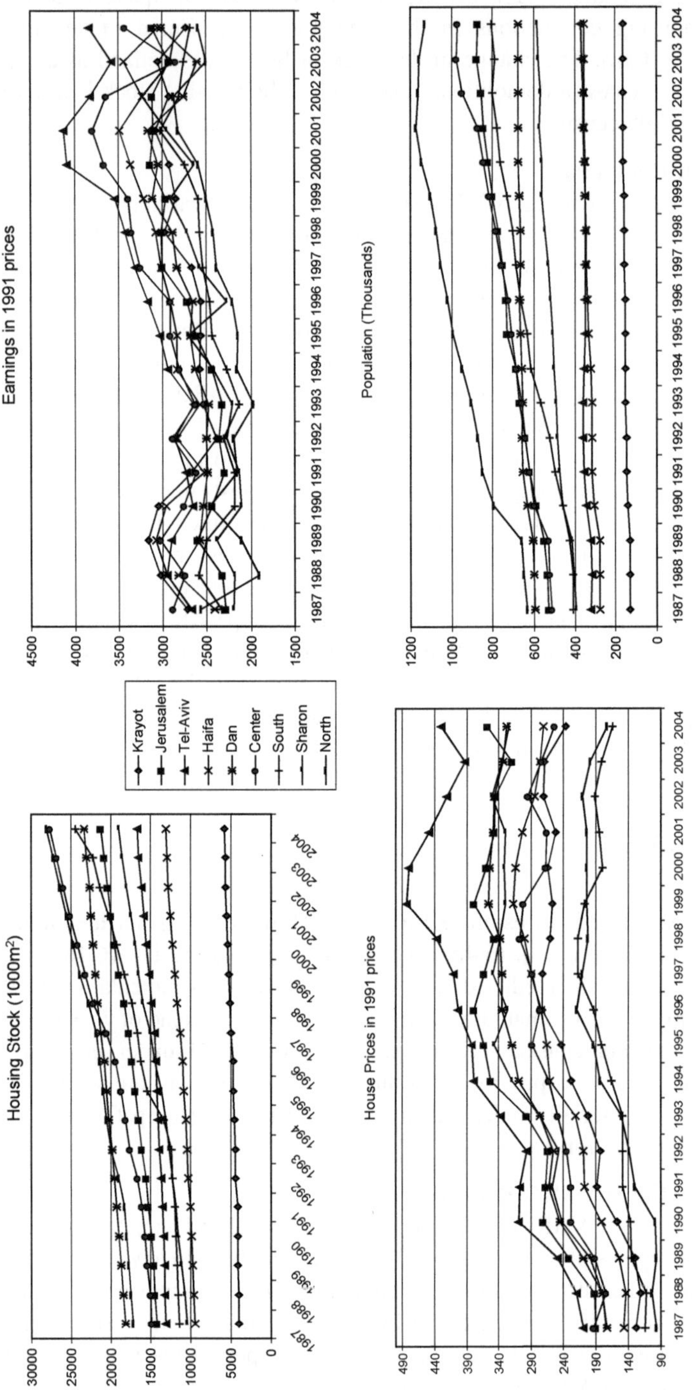

Fig. 6.2 Regional panel data

Table 6.4 Panel unit root tests

(t-bar)			
Ln(Y_j)	d = 0	d = 1	d = 2
Earnings	−1.205	−3.503	−5.079
Population	−2.707	−2.531	−6.603
House prices	−3.030	−2.537	−5.321
Housing stock	−0.092	−2.227	−3.410

Auxiliary regression: $\Delta^d \ln Y_{knt} = \alpha_{kn} + \lambda_{kn}\Delta^{d-1}\ln Y_{knt-1} + \delta_{kn}\Delta^d \ln Y_{knt-1} + \varepsilon_{knt.}$ The critical values of t-bar with N = 9 and T = 18 are −2.28 at p = 0.01 and −2.17 at p = 0.05

Because the SpVAR includes 36 separate relationships (nine regional relationships for each of the four variables), we simplify by estimating each variable as a separate bloc consisting of nine regional panel relationships. For example, the earnings bloc specifies first order temporal and lagged spatial lags for earnings, but it also specifies first order temporal and lagged spatial lags for each of the other three variables. This implies, for example, that current earnings in Jerusalem may be affected by lagged house prices in Tel Aviv as well as in the neighborhood of Jerusalem. Each of the four blocs is estimated separately, which implies that spatial correlation exists within state variables but not between them. For example, earnings shocks in Jerusalem may be correlated with earnings shocks in Tel Aviv, but they are assumed to be uncorrelated with population shocks in Tel Aviv. To have specified spatial correlation between variables would have greatly increased the burden of estimation.

Each region in the bloc is specified to have a specific effect and the regional shocks within the bloc are assumed to be contemporaneously correlated (spatially correlated). The method of estimation in each of the four blocs is therefore SUR, which provides estimates of the spatial correlation coefficients for the bloc. Finally, the regional specific effects are assumed to be fixed for the bloc and are estimated by LSDV.

An unrestricted first-order SpVAR based on Eq. (6.4a) is reported in Table 6.5. In the unrestricted SpVAR the panel DW statistics do not indicate the presence of first-order temporal serial correlation in the residuals. In the unrestricted model several parameters are not statistically significant. We applied the "general-to-specific" methodology (Hendry 1995) to estimate a restricted model, which is also reported in Table 6.5. Restrictions are acceptable when the multivariate SBC (Schwarz Bayesian Criterion) is minimized and the residuals remain serially independent. Both of these conditions are fulfilled for the restricted model reported in Table 6.5.

Recall that all the variables that feature in the SpVAR are first differences of logarithms. In the case of the first difference in the logarithm of earnings all temporal lags with the exception of population are statistically significant in the unrestricted model. The autoregressive coefficient for earnings is negative (−0.357). As discussed above, this coefficient is biased downwards. Using Eq. (6.5b) to bias-correct this estimate implies that the true estimate is about −0.31. Additionally, earnings vary directly with lagged housing stock and inversely with the lagged house

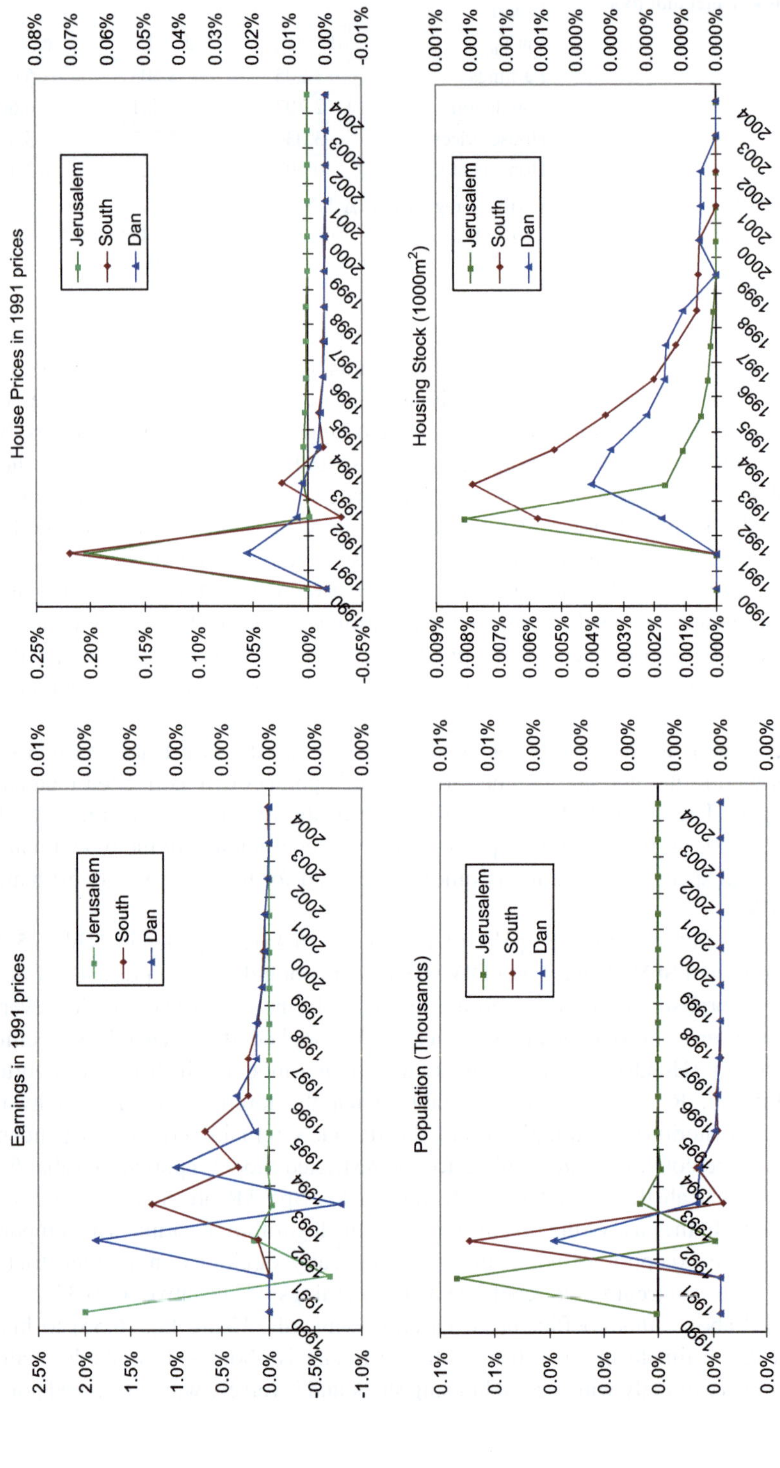

Fig. 6.3 Impulse responses: 2% earnings shock in Jerusalem

Table 6.5 Parameter estimates of the SpVAR's reduced form: Eq. (6.4b)

	Earnings		Population		House prices		Housing stock	
	Unrestricted model	Restricted model	Unrestricted model	Restricted model	Unrestricted model	Restricted model	Unrestricted model	Restricted model
Temporal lag								
Earnings	−0.357	−0.332	0.038	0.037	0.104	0.102	0.006**	–
Population	−0.311*	–	0.112**	–	0.678	0.672	0.059	0.060
House prices	−0.148	−0.104	0.0004**	–	−0.006**	–	0.016	0.018
Housing stock	0.970	1.019	−0.078**	–	0.0003	–	0.396	0.389
Lagged spatial lag								
Earnings	0.131**	–	0.018**	–	0.233	0.235	0.0003**	–
Population	−0.314**	−0.497	0.037**	–	−0.593*	−0.605*	−0.064	−0.068
House prices	0.205**	0.196**	0.104	0.103	0.493	0.403	0.003**	–
Housing stock	1.836	2.174	−0.359	−0.458	−0.790	−0.810	0.172	0.170
R^2 adjusted	0.146	0.148	0.297	0.312	0.091	0.107	0.464	0.474
Panel DW	2.235	2.176	2.116	1.866	1.843	1.861	1.641	1.639
SAC (δ)		0.794		0.836		0.853		0.952
Lagged SAC γ		0.118**		−0.040**		−0.007**		−0.060**
TAC (ρ)		−0.147*		−0.034**		0.009**		0.044**
Det Σ		0.0049		0.0003		0.0001		0.0014
F statistic		0.847		0.393		0.000		0.019

SBC unrestricted: −814.88

SBC restricted: −818.97

All variables are first differences in logarithms. Bloc estimation by SUR with fixed effects and residual covariance matrix Σ. The number of observations (NT) per bloc is 144. The estimation period including lags is 1987–2004. All parameter estimates have p-value < 0.05. Asterisked parameters have p-value between 0.05 and 0.1. Double asterisked parameters have p-value > 0.1. SAC and TAC respectively denote the spatial and temporal autocorrelation coefficients for the residuals. The F-statistic is a Wald test of the restricted model within blocs, and SBC is the Schwarz Bayesian Criterion for testing the restricted model within and between blocs prices. None of the lagged spatial lags are significant with the exception of housing stock which is positively related to current earnings. The restricted model tells very much the same story. The only exception being the (negative and significant) effect of spatially lagged population. This implies that population growth in neighboring regions reduces current wage growth. The opposite applies to the rate of growth in the housing stock in neighboring regions.

In the restricted model for the rate of population growth there is a small temporal lag on the rate of growth of earnings, but no autoregressive effect. Equation (6.5b) suggests that when the estimated autoregressive coefficient is zero, the bias-corrected coefficient is approximately 0.06. Two lagged spatial lag coefficients are statistically significant, implying a spillover effect to population growth from the growth in house prices in neighboring regions. The opposite applies to the rate of growth in the housing stock in neighboring regions.

The current growth in real house prices varies directly with the lagged rates of growth in earnings and population, but as in the case of population growth, there is no autoregressive effect, hence the bias-corrected coefficient is 0.06. All four lagged spatial lag coefficients are statistically significant. The growth in house prices varies directly with lagged house price growth in neighboring regions, and inversely with the growth in the housing stock in these regions. There is also a lagged spillover effect from earnings growth in neighboring regions. Finally, the rate of growth of the housing stock varies directly with its own lag. Equation (6.5b) suggests that the bias-corrected autoregressive coefficient is about 0.48. There is also a positive spillover effect from lagged housing growth in neighboring regions.

We make no systematic attempt at interpreting the coefficients of the SpVAR's reduced form in terms of economic theory. Our view, as mentioned in Chap. 2, is that VAR modeling does not constitute a sound methodological basis for hypothesis testing, especially when the data happen to be nonstationary as here. The main reason for this is that economic theory refers to relationships between levels of variables whereas VARs typically refer to changes in their levels. Establishing empirically that Y and X happen to be related in first differences does not necessarily mean that they are related in levels. We think that hypothesis testing with non-stationary panel data such as ours should be carried out using panel cointegration (Kao 1999) as discussed in Chap. 7. Nevertheless, VAR modeling requires no methodological justification and should be viewed as a statistical tool for understanding the dynamic structure between variables, especially when economic theory is often vague about the nature of these dynamics (Sims 1980). This applies *a fortiori* in the case of SpVARs when economic theory is vague about spatial dynamics as well as temporal dynamics.

Spatial Correlation

Table 6.6 indicates that the residuals are spatially correlated. Indeed, the SAC coefficient ranges between 0.794 and 0.952. Since Table 6.6 refers to the reduced form, these SAC coefficients are not a major concern; they do not affect the consistency of the reduced form parameter estimates. More important is the fact that the lagged SAC coefficients and the temporal autocorrelation coefficients are not

Table 6.6 Spatial autocorrelations: SUR estimates

	Jerusalem	Tel Aviv	Haifa	Krayot	Dan	Center	South	Sharon
Tel Aviv								
Earnings	0.4689							
Population	0.0592							
Housing	0.4681							
Prices	0.8367							
Haifa								
Earnings	0.5258	0.4885						
Population	0.6395	0.3769						
Housing	0.4465	0.1443						
Prices	0.5760	0.7259						
Krayot								
Earnings	0.3261	−0.0986	0.3123					
Population	0.3571	0.7532	0.6699					
Housing	0.3628	−0.0947	0.7005					
Prices	0.1686	0.1560	0.4088					
Dan								
Earnings	0.4624	0.6346	0.2150	−0.1596				
Population	0.4381	0.7662	0.6846	0.6268				
Housing	0.1188	0.2435	0.0275	−0.0042				
Prices	0.9057	0.8092	0.7621	0.3445				
Center								
Earnings	0.6940	0.7720	0.4029	−0.0672	0.7591			
Population	0.3192	0.4450	0.6501	0.6314	0.3945			
Housing	0.5693	0.5025	0.5410	0.6675	0.4096			
Prices	0.4371	0.3631	0.2653	0.1329	0.4384			

(continued)

Table 6.6 (continued)

	Jerusalem	Tel Aviv	Haifa	Krayot	Dan	Center	South	Sharon
South								
Earnings	0.3180	0.6475	0.5510	0.1060	0.3680	0.5494		
Population	0.2908	0.2860	0.2584	0.5066	0.2959	0.2491		
Housing	−0.3851	−0.2398	−0.4762	−0.2845	−0.4985	−0.4704		
Prices	0.3490	0.1425	0.2024	0.1480	0.4834	0.4808		
Sharon								
Earnings	0.1975	0.0748	0.2110	0.1117	0.0491	0.2969	0.6222	
Population	0.3651	0.6995	0.7510	0.7970	0.7944	0.4116	0.3496	
Housing	−0.1399	0.1156	0.2709	0.4803	0.3213	0.5398	−0.2150	
Prices	0.6307	0.5167	0.6013	0.4715	0.7682	0.5781	0.3371	
North								
Earnings	0.4529	0.2913	0.3333	0.1053	0.2991	0.4946	0.2078	0.2438
Population	0.6555	0.4359	0.8813	0.7927	0.6439	0.5445	0.5638	0.7686
Housing	0.6104	0.5999	0.4791	0.4058	−0.0860	0.5896	−0.2150	0.0463
Prices	0.1364	−0.0331	0.3159	0.5648	0.1499	−0.1297	0.1607	0.1653

significantly different from zero, for otherwise the variables in the model could not serve as weakly exogenous instrumental variables for estimating Eq. (6.4a) and identifying the contemporaneous spatial lag coefficients (Λ). Finally, Table 6.5 reports the determinant of the residual variance-covariance matrix estimated by SUR (detΣ). If the residuals between regions are independent det$\Sigma = 1$. The greater the regional dependence between residuals the closer to zero will be detΣ. The estimates of detΣ are clearly less than unity, and are quite close to zero, suggesting a high degree of correlation between the residuals of different regions for all four variables in the model.

In Table 6.6 we report the spatial autocorrelation coefficients estimated by SUR. For example, the correlation between earnings shocks in Tel-Aviv and Jerusalem is 0.47, while the correlation between population shocks in these two regions is 0.06. Table 6.6 reveals that almost every element in the SUR matrix is statistically significant. Most of the spatial autocorrelations are less than 0.5 in absolute value. However, a few exceed 0.8 and the largest in absolute value is 0.91 (between house price shocks in Tel-Aviv and Dan). We make no attempt at interpreting these coefficients. Recall that these spatial correlations have been estimated by SUR within blocs but not between them. Therefore, the spatial correlations between variables are zero by construction. This means, for example, that earnings shocks in Jerusalem are uncorrelated with population shocks in Tel Aviv.

Impulse Responses

We illustrate the properties of the reduced form SpVAR by reporting spatio-temporal impulse response simulations. In a temporal VAR the impulse responses refer to the dynamic effects of shocks to a certain variable upon itself as well as the other variables that feature in the model. In SpVARs the impulse responses refer to the effects of shocks that occur in a specific region and to a certain variable upon the following:

1. The shocked variable in the region in which the shock occurred.
2. Other variables in the region in which the shock occurred.
3. The shocked variable in other regions.
4. Other variables in other regions.

The impulse responses in SpVARs therefore include the temporal dynamic effects as in a regular VAR as well as the ricochet effect between regions and across variables induced by the spatial specification of the model. The latter include the spatial lag structure of the restricted model as given in Table 6.5 as well as its spatial autocorrelation structure as given in Table 6.6. For these purely illustrative purposes, we use the autoregressive coefficients as reported in Table 6.5 rather than their bias-corrected counterparts.

We begin by temporarily shocking earnings in Jerusalem and investigating the effects of this shock upon the four dimensions mentioned in the previous paragraph. At first we assume that regional shocks are uncorrelated, i.e. we ignore the spatial autocorrelation structure of the model as given in Table 6.6. This means that the earnings shock in Jerusalem is entirely idiosyncratic. It also means that the impulse responses stem entirely from the spatial and temporal lag structures featured in Table 6.5. Subsequently, we assume that regional shocks are spatially correlated, i.e. we calculate the impulse responses using the parameters in Tables 6.5 and 6.6. This means that earnings shocks in Jerusalem are not entirely idiosyncratic; an earnings shock in Jerusalem is accompanied by earnings shocks elsewhere through the model's spatial autocorrelation structure.

To compute the impulse responses, we first carry out a full dynamic simulation (FDS) of the entire SpVAR starting in 1990 and terminating in 2004, which takes as its initial conditions the values of the state variables as of 1989. This provides base-run values in levels for all the variables during 1990–2004. Because the SpVAR is estimated in the first differences of logarithms we shock earnings in Jerusalem by 0.02 (2%) in 1990 followed by an antithetic shock of −0.02 in 1991, so that the level of the variables in the model are preserved in the long run. We compute new dynamic solutions for all the variables in levels during 1990–2004. The impulse responses are defined as the differences between these new solutions and their base run (FDS) values. We expect the impulse responses to die out over time. Since the model is loglinear the impulse responses are not base dependent, i.e. they are independent of when they occur.

Figure 6.3 plots the impulses generated by a 2% earnings shock occurring in the region of Jerusalem in 1990 for all four variables in the model in three of the nine regions. (To have included all nine regions would have been too confusing.) The upper left panel in Fig. 6.3 plots the impulse for earnings in the three regions. Note that in all panels, the local impulses are measured on the left vertical and the external impulses are measured on the right vertical, which has a smaller scale. Initially the level of earnings in Jerusalem necessarily increases by 0.02 (2%), but in 1991 it falls by nearly 1% relative to the base-run. This overshooting happens because the temporal autoregressive coefficient for earnings is negative (Table 6.5). The impulses die down quite rapidly. The spatial lag structure implies that the increase in earnings in Jerusalem in 1990 spills over onto other areas in 1991. The spatial lag coefficient is 0.131 in Table 6.5, hence we expect these spillover effects to be positive. However, we do not expect them to be identical across regions since the spatial weighting matrix is not uniform. Jerusalem has a greater impact on the South than it does on the Dan region. This is why from 1993 onwards, the earnings impulse in the South is more positive than it is in the Dan region. Subsequently these impulses oscillate but eventually die out, as expected.

These regional spillovers cannot, of course, arise in a standard VAR. They are the distinctive contribution of SpVARs. Shocks that occur in one region spillover to other regions provided that the spatial lag coefficient is non-zero. The differential force of these spillovers depends on the spatial weighting matrix. The force will be stronger in regions in which Jerusalem is relatively more important. Recall that we have defined these spatial weights asymmetrically using Eq. (6.6). Therefore, the force will be stronger in regions closer to Jerusalem and in which the population is smaller than Jerusalem's.

The other three panels in Fig. 6.3 plot the impulses for the three other variables in the three regions. The impulses for Jerusalem are standard because they would arise in a standard VAR. For example, the top right panel shows that following the earnings shock in Jerusalem in 1990, house prices rise in Jerusalem in 1991 reflecting the positive (0.104) temporal lag, reported in Table 6.5, of earnings on house prices. Subsequently these impulses die out as expected. The novel feature in this panel is the spatial spillover of earnings shocks in Jerusalem onto house prices in other regions. These spillovers are positive because the spatial lag for earnings on house prices is positive (0.233) in Table 6.5. The spillover is greater in the South than in the Dan region because the spatial weight for the South is larger. Subsequently, the impulses on both regions die out as expected.

The remaining (lower left and right) panels in Fig. 6.3 plot the impulses for population and housing stock. They show that earnings shocks in Jerusalem spill-over onto population and the housing stocks in other regions. In general, the impulses in Fig. 6.4 die out quite rapidly, within about 4 years for population and slightly longer for housing stock. In the short run, however, they are non-zero within and between regions. Note that had we shocked earnings in say Tel-Aviv instead of Jerusalem we would not have got the same impulses reported in Fig. 6.3, because the spatial spillovers are not independent of where the shocks occur. The spillover from Tel-Aviv to the South is not the same as the spillover from Jerusalem to the South. Indeed, because of the use of asymmetric spatial weights, the spillover from Jerusalem to Tel-Aviv is not the same as the spillover from Tel Aviv to Jerusalem. In short, direction matters as does the geographical distribution of shocks.

In Fig. 6.4 we plot the impulses for a 2% population shock in Tel-Aviv. The upper right panel plots the population impulses for Tel Aviv, Dan region and the Krayot. Note that according to Table 6.5 the spatial lag for population is positive (0.037) in which case we expect population shocks in Tel-Aviv to spillover positively onto population in other regions. This expectation is confirmed. The spatial lag coefficient on population for earnings is negative (−0.314), so that the increase in the population in Tel-Aviv in 1990 should spillover negatively onto earnings elsewhere in 1991 (but positively in Tel-Aviv). This upper left panel shows that this is what happens in 1991. The same applies to both house prices in the lower left panel and housing stock in the lower left panel. In both cases, the impulses for Dan region and the Krayot are negative, because the population spatial lags are negative, (0.593 and −0.064 respectively).

In the interest of space, we do not report impulses for shocks to house prices and the housing stocks. Here too there are spatial spillovers. The nature of these spillovers may be seen in Table 6.5. For example, in the case of house prices the spatial spillover onto house prices elsewhere is positive (0.493), and the spatial spillover onto population elsewhere is also positives but smaller (0.104).

Impulses with Spatially Correlated Shocks

Recall that the impulses in Figs. 6.2 and 6.3 refer to uncorrelated shocks and ignore the spatial correlation structure in Table 6.6. In this section we calculate impulses in which the shocks are assumed to be spatially correlated according to Table 6.6. It may be shown that the correlated impulses are a simple matrix transformation of their uncorrelated counterparts. Let $\varepsilon_t = \mathbf{A}\varepsilon_t + \mathbf{e}_t$ be the spatial autocorrelation model

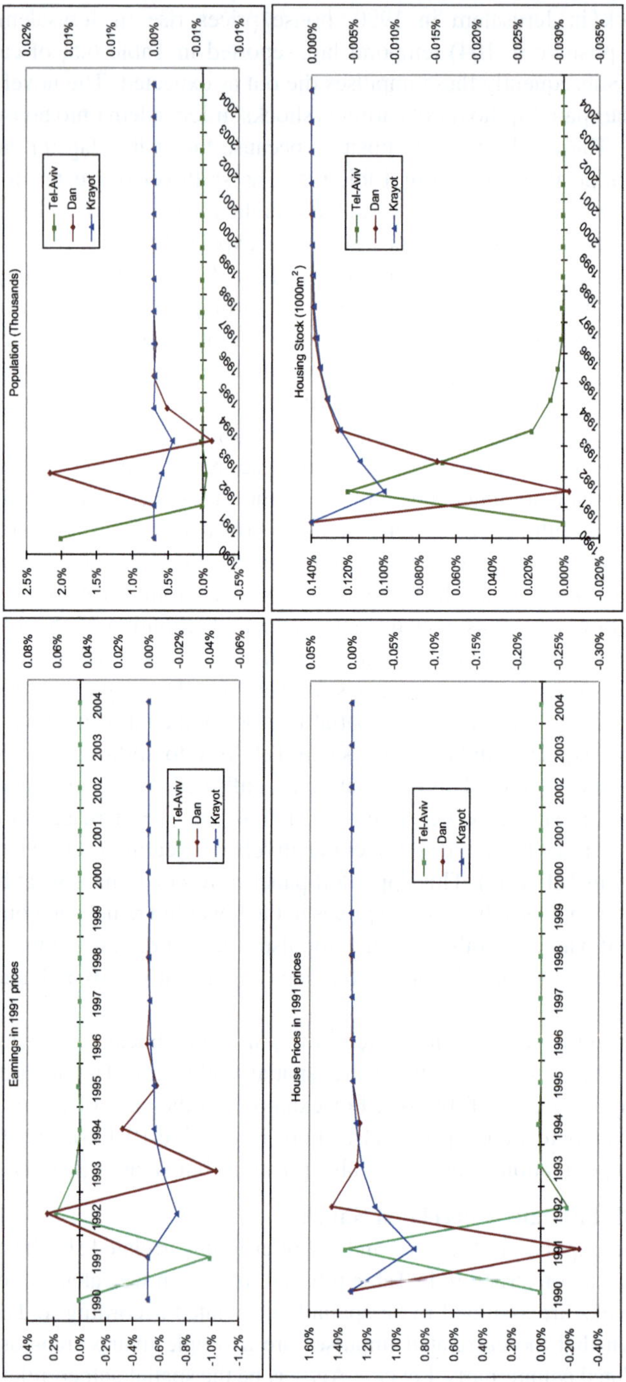

Fig. 6.4 Impulse responses: 2% population shock in Tel Aviv

in which **ε** is a column vector of regional shocks, **e** is a vector of idiosyncratic shocks, and **A** is a lower triangular matrix of spatial correlation coefficients. In our SpVAR **A** is given by Table 6.6. We may solve for the ε's in terms of the e's as: $\boldsymbol{\varepsilon}_t = (\mathbf{I} - \mathbf{A})^{-1}\mathbf{e}_t$. Figures 6.2 and 6.3 are calculated assuming $\mathbf{A} = \mathbf{0}$ in which case $\boldsymbol{\varepsilon}_t = \mathbf{e}_t$. Therefore, to transform uncorrelated impulses into correlated impulses we simply have to multiply the former by $(\mathbf{I} - \mathbf{A})^{-1}$. This means that the correlated impulses are a weighted average of their uncorrelated counterparts.

Table 6.6 implies that when there is a positive shock to earnings in Jerusalem of 2%, there is a positive shock to earnings in Tel-Aviv of 0.94% (=2 × 0.4689) and a positive shock in Haifa of 1.05%, etc. For example, the correlated impulses for an earnings shock in Jerusalem on earnings in the South is just a weighted average of the uncorrelated impulses in the nine regions. We compare the impulses generated in 1991 from a 2% shock inserted a year earlier in both the Jerusalem and Tel-Aviv. The Jerusalem simulation addresses an earnings shock and the Tel-Aviv simulation relates to a population shock (Table 6.7). We limit ourselves to reporting the correlated and uncorrelated impulses on the same regions represented in Figs. 6.3 and 6.4.

Table 6.7 shows that allowing for spatial correlation can make a difference to the magnitudes of the impulses. For example, in the case of a 2% earnings shock in Jerusalem, the correlated impulse effect on house prices in all other regions is consistently larger than in the uncorrelated case. The same can be seen for the impact of a 2% population shock in Tel-Aviv. The uncorrelated impulse response with respect to housing supply and house price in other regions is consistently smaller than in the correlated case. In some instances, spatial correlation can even reverse the sign of the impulse. This can be seen with respect to the correlated

Table 6.7 Comparing impulses in 1991 with and without spatial correlation: (a) 2% earnings shock in Jerusalem, (b) 2% population shock in Tel Aviv

	Earnings	Population	Prices	Housing
(a)				
Jerusalem	−0.00664	0.00073	0.00421	0.00000
	−0.00664	0.00073	0.00203	0.00000
Dan	−0.00307	0.00043	0.00370	0.00000
	0.00000	0.00000	0.00021	0.00000
South	−0.00211	0.00023	0.00328	0.00000
	0.00000	0.00000	0.00071	0.00000
(b)				
Tel Aviv	−0.00994	0.00000	0.01968	0.00155
	−0.00993	0.00000	0.01345	0.00119
Dan	0.00630	0.00000	−0.00801	−0.00053
	0.00000	0.00000	−0.00272	−0.00031
Krayot	−0.00098	0.00000	0.00083	0.00004
	0.00000	0.00000	−0.00078	−0.00008

The upper number refers to the spatially correlated case and the lower number refers to the spatially uncorrelated case. Impulses have been multiplied by 100 impulse response on both house prices and housing supply in the Krayot region. These results, however, come as no surprise. The spatial autocorrelation structure may obviously reinforce or offset the impulses obtained when the shocks are assumed to be spatially uncorrelated.

Estimating the Contemporaneous Spatial Lag Coefficients

Finally, we turn to the estimation of Eq. (6.4a), which includes contemporaneous spatial lag (SAR) coefficients for the state variables. The spatial lag variables ($\tilde{y}$) are instrumented using their predicted values from the restricted model in Table 6.5. As mentioned, these predicted values are weakly exogenous because the residuals in Table 6.6 are neither temporally autocorrelated nor is there lagged spatial autocorrelation. Results are reported in Table 6.8.

The contemporaneous SAR or spatial lag coefficients are statistically significant for three of the four variables, the exception being population growth. In the case of the housing stock the SAR coefficient is −0.397 and for earnings it is 0.7834. Note that despite the specification of spatial lags, the SAC coefficients are statistically significant. This means that SAC does not result from dynamic spatial misspecification. Note also that determinant of the residual correlation matrix ($\det\Sigma$) is close to zero for all four variables even after allowing SAC. This means that the residual correlation matrix is not simply due to SAC and that residuals are correlated between regions because shocks happen to be correlated for reasons unrelated to SAC. With the exception of earnings, the lagged SAC and temporal autocorrelation coefficients are not statistically significant. Many temporal lag coefficients are not significantly different from zero[7] with the exception of the housing stock. Finally, an F-test shows that the fixed effect coefficients are not statistically significant for earnings and house prices, but they are very significant for population and the housing stock.

In this chapter we have tried to integrate time series econometrics with spatial econometrics by estimating spatial and temporal dynamics jointly. Moreover, we use vectors of variables rather than single variables. We refer to this kind of modeling of spatial panel data as SpVAR, or spatial vector autoregressions. SpVARs contain such features as temporal lags, spatial lags, temporally-lagged spatial lags, spatially autocorrelated errors and spatially correlated errors that are not autocorrelated. The latter are estimated by SUR and measure the correlation between shocks in different regions. Spatial autocorrelation imposes restrictions on the spatial correlation matrix. Whereas in cross-section data only spatial autocorrelation can be identified, in spatial panel data both types of correlation may be estimated.

We have illustrated these issues by estimating a SpVAR using annual data for Israel over the period 1987–2004 for nine regions and four variables. We show that in addition to temporal lags, there is evidence of temporally-lagged spatial lags as

[7]There is only one autoregressive coefficient in Table 6.5 (for the housing stock). Its bias-corrected counterpart is 0.64. The other bias-corrected autoregressive coefficients are 0.06, since their biased counterparts are zero.

Table 6.8 Parameter estimates of the SpVAR: Eq. (6.4a)

	1. Earnings		2. Population		3. House prices		4. Housing stock	
	Coefficient	Standard error	Coefficient	Standard error	Coefficient	Standard error	Coefficient	Standard error
Temporal lag								
Earnings			0.0348	0.0114				
Population							0.0889	0.0204
House prices							0.0258	0.0060
Housing stock	0.4830	0.0995					0.5265	0.0760
Lagged spatial lag								
Earnings								
Population					−0.4955	0.2325	−0.1038	0.0250
House prices			0.1012	0.0301	0.5163	0.0557		
Housing stock			−0.4638	0.1420			0.2408	0.0431
Spatial lag	0.7833	0.0530	0.0229	0.1566	0.5844	0.0600	−0.3973	0.1280
R^2 adjusted	0.1677		0.3081		0.1170		0.4761	
Panel DW	2.2608		1.8710		1.7962		1.6661	
detΣ	0.001325		0.00004		0.00011		0.002	
SAC (δ)	0.7974	0.0026	0.8364	0.0023	0.8491	0.0015	0.9705	0.0140
Lagged SAC γ	0.1883	0.0659	0.0401	0.0734	−0.0118	0.0661	−0.1094	0.0830
TAC (ρ)	−0.2458	0.0827	−0.0347	0.0874	0.0215	0.0778	0.0699	0.0844

See notes to Table 6.6

well as spatially correlated errors.[8] We use the estimated SpVAR to simulate impulse responses, which propagate within and between regions and within and between variables. These impulse responses show that innovations propagate over time and across space. For example, an innovation in a single region not only propagates over the variables in that region, but also between regions and over time. In turn these reverberations feedback onto the source region. As expected for stationary spatial panel data, these shocks eventually die out after about 4 years.

We distinguish between correlated and uncorrelated shocks. In the former case, innovations in one region are correlated with innovations elsewhere according to the spatial correlation matrix estimated in the SpVAR. Such correlated shocks inevitably induce more regional turbulence than their uncorrelated counterparts.

Without formulating a formal economic model, we have statistically tested the temporal and spatial dynamics relating to those leading variables that contribute to disparities between regions: earnings, house prices, housing demand (represented by population distribution) and housing supply (regional housing stock). We estimate SpVAR models with first-order temporal and spatial lags. Spatial effects are estimated using asymmetric spatial weights based on distances and population sizes. For inter-regional impulse effects, these give more weight to closer and larger, more populated regions.

Finally we use the estimated SpVAR to estimate contemporaneous spatial lag coefficients by the method of instrumental variables, having first established that the latter are weakly exogenous. This model incorporates temporal lags, contemporaneous spatial lags, and temporally-lagged spatial lags.

We have repeatedly mentioned that the SpVAR methodology cannot be used to estimate and test structural models because the structural parameters are not identified. Perhaps this does not matter if the objectives are purely statistical, descriptive or predictive. In Chap. 2 we mentioned that structural VARs (SVAR) have proved very popular, in which untestable restrictions are imposed on the VAR parameters to "identify" structural parameters. Such "immaculate" identification may be applied to SpVARs too. However, we do not encourage such a trend. Such structural SpVARs might generate post-modern narratives about the determinants of spatiotemporal phenomena but there is no way in which the theory behind these narratives can be tested empirically.

The solution to this methodological impasse is introduced in Chap. 7, followed by empirical illustrations in subsequent chapters. This solution is based on the extension of cointegration theory discussed in Chap. 2 to nonstationary spatial panel data.

References

Anselin L (1988) Spatial econometrics: methods and models. Kluwer Academic, Dordrecht

[8]Spatial lags are not estimated separately here. They are implicitly estimated in the lagged spatial lag coefficients.

Arellano M, Bond S (1991) Some tests of specification for panel data: Monte Carlo evidence and an application to employment equations. Rev Econ Stud 58:277–297
Badinger H, Müller WG, Tondl G (2004) Regional convergence in the European Union 1985–1999: a spatial dynamic panel analysis. Reg Stud 38:241–253
Baltagi BH (2013) Econometric analysis of panel data, 5th edn. Wiley, Chichester
Bar-Nathan M, Beenstock M, Haitovsky Y (1998) The market for housing in Israel. Reg Sci Urban Econ 28:21–50
Beenstock M, Fisher J (1997) The macroeconomic effects of immigration: Israel in the 1990s. Rev World Econ 133:330–358
Blundell R, Bond S (1998) Initial conditions and moment restrictions in dynamic panel data models. Econometrica 87:115–143
Cameron AC, Trivedi PK (2005) Microeconometrics. Cambridge University Press, Cambridge
Elhorst JP (2014) From spatial cross-section data to spatial panel data. Springer, Berlin
Fingleton B (1999) Spurious spatial regression: some Monte Carlo results with spatial unit roots and spatial cointegration. J Reg Sci 39:1–19
Greene WH (2012) Econometric analysis. Prentice Hall, Upper Saddle River, NJ
Hahn J, Kuersteiner G (2002) Asymptotically unbiased inference for a dynamic panel model with fixed effects when both N and T are large. Econometrica 70:1639–1657
Hendry DF (1995) Dynamic econometrics. Oxford University Press, Oxford
Hsiao C (1986) Analysis of panel data. Cambridge University Press, Cambridge
Im K, Pesaran MH, Shin Y (2003) Testing for unit roots in heterogeneous panels. J Econ 115:53–74
Kao C (1999) Spurious regression and residual based tests for cointegration in panel data. J Econ 90:1–44
Kiviet J (1995) On bias, inconsistency and efficiency of various estimators in dynamic panel data models. J Econ 68:53–78
Maddala GS (2001) Introduction to econometrics, 3rd edn. Wiley, New York
Mundlak Y (1978) On variable coefficients models, Annales de L'insee, France, Apr–Sept
Mur J, Trivez FJ (2003) Unit roots and deterministic trends in spatial econometric models. Int Reg Sci Rev 26:289–312
Pesaran MH (2006) Estimation and inference in large heterogeneous panels with a multifactor error structure. Econometrica 74:967–1012
Rey S, Montouri B (1999) US regional income convergence: a spatial econometric perspective. Reg Stud 33:143–156
Sims CA (1980) Macroeconomics and reality. Econometrica 58:1–48
Wooldridge JM (2010) Econometric analysis of cross section and panel data, 2nd edn. MIT Press, Cambridge, MA
Yu J, de Jong R, Lee L-F (2008) Quasi-maximum likelihood estimators for spatial dynamic panel data with fixed effects with both N and T large. J Econ 146:118–134

Chapter 7
Unit Root and Cointegration Tests for Spatially Dependent Panel Data

7.1 Introduction

In the previous chapter we noted two major methodological problems with spatial vector autoregressions (SpVAR). The first is that the SpVAR parameters do not identify the parameters of the underlying structural model from which the SpVAR is derived. Specifically, the contemporaneous structural parameters are under-identified. Moreover, the identification deficit increases with the number of state variables. Since the state variables are likely to depend on each other during the current time period, this problem has profound methodological implications. It effectively means that structural hypotheses cannot be tested empirically by SpVARs. SpVARs may nevertheless be useful for prediction, data description, and ex post narratives, but they have little epistemological value.

The second methodological problem is that the state variables in SpVARs must be stationary. Since most economic data are nonstationary, SpVAR practitioners stationarize their data by various means, e.g. first-differencing the data if they are difference stationary, and by detrending them if they are trend stationary. In Chap. 2 we explained that testing hypotheses using first-differenced or detrended data is not equivalent to testing hypotheses regarding the levels relationship between these variables. Since economic theory is mostly about levels rather than differences, this means that even if there were no identification deficit, SpVARs could not be used for purposes of hypothesis testing.

In Chap. 2 we recounted how cointegration theory resolved these methodological impasses, first for nonstationary time series in the late 1980s, and subsequently for nonstationary panel data in the 2000s. In the present chapter we extend cointegration theory to nonstationary spatial panel data. This methodological agenda has two natural parts. In the first, we discuss unit root tests for spatial panel data, which are different from their counterparts in Chap. 2, where it was assumed that the panel units are independent as e.g. in the IPS statistic (Im et al. 2003), or it was assumed

M. Beenstock, D. Felsenstein, *The Econometric Analysis of Non-Stationary Spatial Panel Data*, Advances in Spatial Science,
https://doi.org/10.1007/978-3-030-03614-0_7

that the cross section dependence is strong (Pesaran 2007). What happens when the cross-section dependence is weak and therefore spatial? Surprisingly, the literature is silent on this matter. For example, it is not mentioned by Baltagi (2013, Chap. 13), Elhorst (2014) and Pesaran (2015, Chap. 30). These authors take care to ensure that the data are stationary. For example, Elhorst (Sect. 4.6) discusses the implications of stationarity for invertibility, but he does not discuss the econometric implications of nonstationarity. The second component concerns cointegration tests when the cointegrating vector includes spatial lagged dependent variables. Should such variables be treated as other nonstationary variables, or does their spatial status make them special? Here too the literature is silent. In this chapter we are primarily concerned with filling these methodological voids by developing panel unit root and panel cointegration tests when the data are spatial. In Chaps. 8 and 9 we provide empirical illustrations of these ideas.

Like us, Yu et al. (2012) study spatial panel cointegration when the data are nonstationary. However, their approach is different to ours. They seek to estimate all the parameters in Eq. (6.4a) including the parameters of lagged dependent variables (π) and temporally-lagged spatial lags (ϕ). This agenda requires them to use concentrated likelihoods in which the spatial fixed effects are concentrated out. Since their method of estimation is quasi maximum likelihood (QMLE) they, like us, do not rely on the assumption that the error terms are normally distributed. They use Monte Carlo methods to show that if the variables (y, $\tilde{y}$ and x) are cointegrated, their proposed estimators have satisfactory finite sample properties. However, unlike us, they do not provide statistical tests and associated critical values for spatial panel cointegration, i.e. when the null hypothesis is no cointegration.

In short, Yu, de Jong and Lee assume what we seek to test. They assume that the variables in the model are spatially cointegrated. By contrast, we seek to test whether these variables are indeed spatially cointegrated. In Chap. 9 we explain that there are two natural steps to estimating Eq. (6.4a). The first step involves testing for cointegration between y, x, $\tilde{y}$ and $\tilde{x}$. If they happen to be cointegrated, the second step involves estimating the spatial error correction model between these variables. By assuming that the variables are cointegrated, Yu et al. are concerned with the second step.

We spatialize Pedroni's approach (described in Chap. 2), which is based on OLS, and which does not require the estimation of ϕ and π. This agenda tests for spatial cointegration between y, $\tilde{y}$ and x in Eq. (6.4a). We think that Occam's Razor attaches a premium to less ambitious methods provided, of course, that they test the same hypotheses.

Caveat

There are many empirical examples of panel data models in which T is relatively large. For example, the Penn World Tables cover many countries over many years. When T is large, we think that there is no need to resort to panel data econometrics because there are sufficient observations to test hypotheses for each panel unit. If panel units are homogeneous, it makes no difference if the data are pooled or not. If, as in general, panel units are heterogeneous, pooling the data may enforce homogeneity when it is not appropriate. One size does not fit all. This is especially the case in macroeconomics where models that suit one country do not necessarily suit another. Hypothesis testing with panel data econometrics runs the risk of rejecting hypotheses despite the fact that these hypotheses may be true for some panel units. It also runs the risk of rejecting hypotheses under the assumption of homogeneity when these hypotheses are true under the assumption of heterogeneity.

In our view data pooling only makes sense when T is relatively small. In this case there are insufficient observations to estimate separate models for each panel unit. However, there are NT observations if the data are pooled. It is therefore tempting to pool the data, especially when the alternative is to do nothing at all. The price of pooling is the imposition of homogeneity, even though this may be inappropriate.

7.2 Unit Roots

In Chap. 2 our preferred panel unit root test was Eq. (2.2), which we repeat here for convenience:

$$\Delta y_{it} = \alpha_i + (\pi_i - 1)y_{it-1} + \varepsilon_{it} \tag{7.1}$$

where the ε's are iid and independent across panel units. Notice that Eq. (7.1) allows each panel unit to have a different root (π_i), which is why we prefer it. The null hypothesis in IPS is $\pi_i = 1$. The IPS test statistic (Eq. 2.5) is based on the average of the Dickey–Fuller (DF) statistics estimated for each panel unit. According to the central limit theorem this average tends to be normally distributed as the number of panel units increases. The critical values calculated by IPS take account of the sample sizes in terms of the number of panel units (N) and time periods (T).

The IPS test has been extended to allow for strong cross-section dependence in the ε's (Eq. 2.6). As we explain further in Chap. 10, this dependence is not spatial because it is induced by a common factor, and is therefore unrelated to the distance between panel units. Baltagi et al. (2007) investigated the implications of spatial autocorrelation (SAC) for the size of panel unit root tests, such as IPS, designed for independent panel units. They assumed that:

$$\varepsilon_{it} = \rho_i \tilde{\varepsilon}_{it} + e_{it} \tag{7.2}$$

where ρ_i are SAC coefficients and e is iid. They found that the IPS and other tests become undersized especially when the SAC coefficient exceeds 0.4. Mild but significant spatial autocorrelation does not greatly impair the statistical power of tests such as IPS. However, Baltagi et al. stopped short of suggesting a panel unit root test designed specifically for spatially dependent data.

In this chapter we develop unit root tests for spatial panel data in which the cross-dependence is weak. We provide the asymptotic theory for these tests. In common with other unit root tests, the distribution for the test statistic must be obtained numerically because it does not have an analytical counterpart. We therefore carry out Monte Carlo simulations to compute critical values of panel unit root tests for spatially dependent panel data. However, unlike Baltagi et al. (2007) we assume that spatial dependence is induced by spatial lags (SAR) rather than spatial autocorrelation (SAC). We suggest two DGPs of interest:

$$\Delta y_{it} = \alpha_i + (\pi_i - 1)y_{it-1} + \lambda_i \tilde{y}_{it} + \varepsilon_{it} \tag{7.3a}$$

$$\Delta y_{it} = \alpha_i + (\pi_i - 1)y_{it-1} + \phi_i \tilde{y}_{it-1} + \varepsilon_{it} \tag{7.3b}$$

where ε is assumed to be iid and is therefore spatially independent. In Eq. (7.3a) the SAR coefficient is contemporaneous, whereas in Eq. (7.3b) it is temporally lagged. We take the view that while SAC and SAR may coexist, SAC is likely to be a symptom of misspecification of the spatial dynamics of the model, as discussed in Chap. 3. This view is the spatial counterpart to the principle in time series models that autocorrelation is a symptom of dynamic misspecification (Hendry 1995). Therefore, appropriate SAR specification tends to obviate the need for SAC. Assuming that spatial dependence is induced by SAR rather than SAC complicates our task because OLS estimates of SAR coefficients are typically inconsistent and biased. Specifically, we "spatialize" the IPS panel unit root test in which the parameters of the panel units are assumed to be heterogeneous. Since our proposed test allows for spatial dependence, we refer to it by "SpIPS".

The Case of N = 2

In spatial DGPs such as Eqs. (7.3a and 7.3b) there is a unit root when $\pi + \lambda$ or $\pi + \phi = 1$. This proposition may be demonstrated for Eq. (7.3a) in the simplest symmetric case in which $N = 2$:

$$y_{1t} = \pi y_{1t-1} + \lambda y_{2t} + \varepsilon_{1t} \tag{7.4a}$$

$$y_{2t} = \pi y_{2t-1} + \lambda y_{1t} + \varepsilon_{2t} \tag{7.4b}$$

where ε_1 and ε_2 are iid and mutually independent. The solutions for y_1 and y_2 are:

$$y_{1t} = \frac{\varepsilon_{1t} - \pi\varepsilon_{1t-1} + \lambda\varepsilon_{2t}}{1 - \lambda^2 - 2\pi L + \pi^2 L^2} \tag{7.4c}$$

$$y_{2t} = \frac{\varepsilon_{2t} - \pi\varepsilon_{2t-1} + \lambda\varepsilon_{1t}}{1 - \lambda^2 - 2\pi L + \pi^2 L^2} \tag{7.4d}$$

where L denotes the temporal lag operator. Since the denominator is quadratic, there are two roots, ω_1 and ω_2, which are the solution to the characteristic equation:

$$\left(1 - \lambda^2\right)\omega^2 - 2\pi\omega + \pi^2 = 0 \tag{7.4e}$$

Therefore, the roots are equal to:

$$\omega = \frac{\pi \pm \pi\lambda}{1-\lambda^2} \tag{7.4f}$$

If $\pi + \lambda = 1$ one of these roots is 1 and the other is $\pi/(2 - \pi) < 1$. The same is true in the asymmetric case in which π and λ vary by spatial unit. For example, if $\pi_1 = 0.4$ and $\pi_2 = 0.6$, $\omega_1 = 1$ and $\omega_2 = 0.315$. In general, the number of roots is N, of which one root is 1 and the other roots are less than one in absolute value. The Wold representation for Eq. (7.4a) in the presence of a unit root ($\pi + \lambda = 1$) is:

$$\Delta y_{it} = \frac{\varepsilon_{1t} - \pi\varepsilon_{1t-1} + (1-\pi)\varepsilon_{2t}}{1-\omega L}$$
$$= \sum_{\tau=0}^{t-1} \omega^{\tau}[\varepsilon_{1t-\tau} - \pi\varepsilon_{1t-1-\tau} + (1-\pi)\varepsilon_{2t-\tau}] \tag{7.4g}$$

Equation (7.4g) generates the impulse responses for Δy_{1t} with respect to $\varepsilon_{1t-\tau}$ and $\varepsilon_{2t-\tau}$. Solving Eq. (7.4g) for y_{1t} gives:

$$y_{1t} = e_1 \sum_{i=0}^{t-1} \omega^i + e_2 \sum_{i=0}^{t-2} \omega^i + \ldots + e_t = \frac{1}{1-\omega} \sum_{\tau=1}^{t} (1-\omega^{t+1-\tau}) e_\tau \tag{7.4h}$$
$$e_t = \varepsilon_{it} - \pi\varepsilon_{1t-1} + (1-\pi)\varepsilon_{2t}$$

The first two moments generated by Eq. (7.4h) are:

$$E(y_{1t}) = 0 \tag{7.4i}$$

$$\mathrm{var}(y_{1t}) = t\sigma_e^2 + (t-1)\mathrm{cov}(e_t e_{t-1}) + \mathrm{O}_p\left(\frac{1}{t}\right)$$
$$\sigma_e^2 = (1+\pi^2)\sigma_1^2 + (1-\pi)^2\sigma_2^2 \tag{7.4j}$$
$$\mathrm{cov}(e_t e_{t-1}) = -\pi\sigma_1^2$$

According to Eq. (7.4i) the unconditional expected value of y_{it} is zero regardless of when it is measured. However, according to Eq. (7.4j) its unconditional variance varies directly with time (t) because of the presence of a unit root. The last term in Eq. (7.4j) is induced by the stationary root, and tends to zero with t. Hence, as expected, y_1 and y_2 are nonstationary. Notice that although the temporal autoregressive coefficient (π) may be less than 1, nonstationarity is induced because of the spatial autoregressive coefficient (λ). Indeed, y_1 and y_2 will be stationary when π exceeds 1 provided λ is sufficiently negative. Therefore, spatiotemporal unit roots differ from temporal unit roots discussed in Chap. 2 and spatial unit roots discussed in Chap. 5.

Thus far we have assumed that π and λ are homogeneous. If they are heterogeneous, the roots are:

$$\omega = \frac{\pi_1 + \pi_2 \pm \sqrt{(\pi_1 - \pi_2)^2 + 4\lambda_1\lambda_2}}{2(1 - \lambda_1\lambda_2)} \tag{7.4k}$$

If e.g. $\pi_1 = 0.7$, $\pi_2 = 0.9$, $\lambda_1 = 0.3$ and $\lambda_2 = 0.1$ the roots are 1.031 and 0.619. Therefore, to a close degree of approximation, a unit root is induced if the averages of π and λ sum to one.

The OLS estimators for π and λ are estimated separately for each panel unit:

$$\hat{\pi}_i = \frac{S_{y_i y_{i-1}} S_{\tilde{y}_i \tilde{y}_i} - S_{y_i \tilde{y}_i} S_{\tilde{y}_i y_{i-1}}}{S_{y_{i-1} y_{i-1}} S_{\tilde{y}_i \tilde{y}_i} - S^2_{\tilde{y}_i y_{i-1}}} \tag{7.5a}$$

$$\hat{\lambda}_i = \frac{S_{y_i \tilde{y}_i} S_{y_{i-1} y_{i-1}} - S_{y_i y_{i-1}} S_{\tilde{y}_i y_{i-1}}}{S_{y_{i-1} y_{i-1}} S_{\tilde{y}_i \tilde{y}_i} - S^2_{\tilde{y}_i y_{i-1}}} \tag{7.5b}$$

The probability limits of Eqs. (7.5a and 7.5b) are taken with respect to T alone, since N is fixed in spatial data. These probability limits (dropping subscript i for convenience in S) are:

$$p \lim \hat{\pi}_i = \pi_i + \text{plim} \frac{S_{\varepsilon y_{-1}} S_{\tilde{y}\tilde{y}} - S_{\varepsilon \tilde{y}} S_{\tilde{y} y_{-1}}}{S_{y_{-1} y_{-1}} S_{\tilde{y}\tilde{y}} - S^2_{\tilde{y} y_{-1}}} \tag{7.5c}$$

$$p \lim \hat{\lambda}_i = \lambda_i + \text{plim} \frac{S_{\varepsilon \tilde{y}} S_{y_{-1} y_{-1}} - S_{\varepsilon y_{-1}} S_{\tilde{y} y_{-1}}}{S_{y_{-1} y_{-1}} S_{\tilde{y}\tilde{y}} - S^2_{\tilde{y} y_{-1}}} \tag{7.5d}$$

As discussed in Chap. 2, the summation terms (S) in Eqs. (7.5c and 7.5d) may be expressed in terms of Wiener processes, and have limiting distributions that are asymptotically normal provided they are divided by some power (a) of T. This power denotes the asymptotic order of magnitude in probability of S, which in Chap. 2 is denoted by $O_p(T^a)$. Let $B_i(r)$ denote the Wiener process for y_i. For example:

$$\frac{1}{T} S_{\varepsilon_i y_{i-1}} \Rightarrow \int_0^1 B_i(r) dB_i(r) \sim \frac{1}{2}\left(\chi_1^2 - 1\right) \tag{7.5e}$$

$$\frac{1}{T^2} S_{y_i y_i} \Rightarrow \int_0^1 [B_i(r)]^2 dr \sim N\left(\frac{1}{2}, \frac{1}{6}\right) \tag{7.5f}$$

Equation (7.5e) states that the covariance between ε_i, which is stationary and y_{i-1}, which is nonstationary has a mean of zero [since $E\left(\chi^2_{df}\right) = df$] and a variance of ½ [since $var\left(\chi^2_{df}\right) = 2df$]. It also states that $S_{\varepsilon y_{-1}} \sim O_p(T)$, hence its asymptotic order is 1. According to Eq. (7.5f) $S_{y_{-1}y_{-1}} \sim O_p(T^2)$; its asymptotic order is 2.

Since $\tilde{y}_{it} = \sum_{j \neq i}^{N} w_{ij} y_{jt}$:

$$\frac{1}{T^2} S_{y_{i-1}\tilde{y}_i} \Rightarrow \int_0^1 B_i(r) \sum_{j \neq i}^{N} w_{ij} B_j(r) dr \tag{7.5g}$$

which does not have an analytical distribution, but the asymptotic order of $S_{y_{-1}\tilde{y}}$ is 2. Therefore terms such as $S_{\tilde{y}\tilde{y}}, S_{y_{-1}y_{-1}}$ *and* $S_{\tilde{y}y_{-1}}$ are $O_p(T^2)$, whereas $S_{\varepsilon y_{-1}}$ and $S_{\varepsilon\tilde{y}}$ are $O_p(T)$ because y is nonstationary whereas ε is stationary. Hence, under the null of $\rho_i + \lambda_i = 1$, the OLS estimators for ρ_i and λ_i are T super-consistent because in Eqs. (7.5a and 7.5b):

$$plim \frac{S_{\varepsilon y_{-1}} S_{\tilde{y}\tilde{y}} - S_{\varepsilon\tilde{y}} S_{\tilde{y}y_{-1}}}{S_{y_{-1}y_{-1}} S_{\tilde{y}\tilde{y}} - S^2_{\tilde{y}y_{-1}}} \sim \frac{O_p(T^3) - O_p(T^3)}{O_p(T^4) - O_p(T^4)} = O_p(T^{-1}) \tag{7.5h}$$

$$plim \frac{S_{\varepsilon\tilde{y}} S_{y_{-1}y_{-1}} - S_{\varepsilon y_{-1}} S_{\tilde{y}y_{-1}}}{S_{y_{-1}y_{-1}} S_{\tilde{y}\tilde{y}} - S^2_{\tilde{y}y_{-1}}} \sim O_p(T^{-1}) \tag{7.5i}$$

Under the null, the distributions of these OLS estimates cannot be individually normal for three reasons. Although $S_{y_{-1}y_{-1}}$ and $S_{\varepsilon y_{-1}}$ are asymptotically normal, summations such as $S_{\tilde{y}y_{-1}}$ and $S_{\tilde{y}\tilde{y}}$ are not. Second, as we saw in Chap. 2, products of normally distributed random variables cannot be normally distributed. The same applies to ratios of asymptotically normal random variables. Therefore, these distributions have to be calculated by Monte Carlo simulation methods. However, the cross-section average of the N OLS estimates of π and λ tend to be normally distributed due to the central limit theorem.

Equations (7.4a and 7.4b) do not have intercepts, or specific effects. This explains why the unconditional expected values of y_1 and y_2 are zero in Eq. (7.4i). Had specific effects, α_1 and α_2, been specified in Eqs. (7.4a and 7.4b). Eq. (7.4i) would be:

$$E(y_{1t}) = \left(\frac{\alpha_1 + \lambda\alpha_2}{1 - \omega}\right) t \tag{7.5j}$$

The unconditional expected value depends linearly with time (t) through the fixed effects. Hence, y_1 and y_2 are nonstationary because their means as well as their variances are not independent of time. The specific effects induce drift in the DGPs for y_1 and y_2. Note, however, that the unconditional expected values depend on both specific effects because of the spatial dependence between y_1 and y_2.

In Chap. 2 we saw that drift increases the super-consistency of OLS from T to $T^{1½}$. The same applies here. For example, it may be shown e.g. $S_{yy} \sim O_p(T^3)$ whereas

$S_{\tilde{y}\varepsilon} \sim O_p\left(T^{1\frac{1}{2}}\right)$ so that the Eqs. (7.5h and 7.5i) are $O_p(T^{-1½})$. Hence, the specification of specific effects enhances super-consistency from T to $T^{1½}$-consistency.

The Case with N > 2

In the previous discussion we simplified matters by setting N = 2 in the interest of expositional transparency. The same principles apply in the more general case when N > 2. Equation (7.4a) becomes:

$$y_{it} = \alpha_i + \pi_i y_{it-1} + \lambda_i \tilde{y}_{it} + \varepsilon_{it} \tag{7.6a}$$

Where α_i denote specific effects. Equation (7.6a) vectorizes to:

$$y_t = \alpha + \Pi y_{t-1} + \Lambda W y_t + \varepsilon_t \tag{7.6b}$$

where y and α are N-vectors, and Π and Λ are diagonal N × N matrices with π_i and λ_i on their leading diagonals. The solution for y_t is:

$$\begin{aligned} y_t &= A(\alpha + \Pi y_{t-1} + \varepsilon_t) \\ A &= (I_N - \Lambda W)^{-1} \end{aligned} \tag{7.6c}$$

which is a panel VAR model. The Wold representation for Eq. (7.6c) is:

$$\begin{aligned} y_t &= (I_N - A\Pi L)^{-1} A(\alpha + \varepsilon_t) = B\alpha + A\varepsilon_t + A\Pi A\varepsilon_{t-1} + (A\Pi)^2 A\varepsilon_{t-2} + \ldots. \\ B &= (I_N - A\Pi)^{-1} A \end{aligned} \tag{7.6d}$$

Equation (7.6d) generates the spatiotemporal impulse responses of y_t with respect to ε_{t-p}. The matrix $I_N - A\Pi$ has N roots, which lie inside the unit circle if y is stationary. One of these roots must equal 1 if $\Lambda = I_N - \Pi$ because $\pi_i + \lambda_i = 1$ for all spatial units. More generally a unit root is induced when $\frac{1}{N}trace(\Pi + \Lambda) = 1$, i.e. $\bar{\pi} + \bar{\lambda} = 1$.

In summary, when $\bar{\pi} + \bar{\lambda} = 1$ there must be a unit root in which case the data cannot be stationary. This result was first noted by Elhorst (2001). More precisely, in the homogeneous case the condition for a unit root if $\lambda \geq 0$ is $|\pi| + \lambda\omega_{max} = 1$ where ω_{max} is the maximum eigenvalue of W. If W is row-summed to 1, $\omega_{max} = 1$ and π is positive, the unit root condition becomes $\pi + \lambda = 1$. For non-spatial DGPs there is a unit root when π is 1. By contrast, in spatial DGPs there may be a unit root when π is less than 1. Of course, if λ is sufficiently negative there may not be a unit root even when π exceeds 1. If there happens to be a unit root because $\pi + \lambda = 1$, the functional central limit theorem states that the data must be normalized by root T in which case they are asymptotically normally distributed. OLS estimates of π and λ are super-consistent under the null hypothesis. Indeed, they are T-consistent instead of root T consistent. The specific effects in Eq. (7.6a) imply that OLS estimates of π and λ are $T^{1½}$-consistent. This means that under the null hypothesis of spatiotemporal unit roots, SAR coefficients may be estimated without recourse to ML, instrumental variables or the generalized method of moments. Since analytical solutions are unavailable for the distribution of estimates of π and λ under the null, we resort to numerical simulation methods to obtain them.

Monte Carlo Analysis

In what follows we begin by using Monte Carlo methods to obtain the distribution of $\pi_i = 1$ given λ. This exercise parallels Baltagi et al. (2007) except we assume that there is a spatial lag as in Eq. (7.4a) rather than spatial autocorrelation as in Eq. (7.2). Subsequently, we obtain the distribution of estimates of $\pi_i + \lambda_i$ under the null hypothesis $\pi_i + \lambda_i = 1$. We think that both exercises are of interest. The first is of interest because economic variables tend to grow over time irrespective of spatial dependence. As noted in Chap. 2, the Solow growth model predicts that logarithms of GDP, wages, investment etc. should be trend stationary, whereas endogenous growth theory predicts that these variables should be difference stationary. In either case these variables are nonstationary. Therefore, in spatial panel data we expect that $\pi = 1$ regardless of λ. In addition, for reasons given in Chap. 5, we expect that λ is positive but less than one. For this reason, spatial panel data are expected to have roots that exceed one.

The second exercise is of interest in the context of the "near unit root" critique. The null hypothesis in the panel unit root tests discussed in Chap. 2 is $\pi = 1$. Suppose, instead, that the null hypothesis is $\pi = 0.99$, i.e. there is no unit root. In practice, it is difficult to distinguish between the two. In nonspatial panel data this may be an issue. However, in spatial panel data matters are different because unit roots depend on λ and not just on π. The null hypothesis of $\pi + \lambda = 1$ is less vulnerable, therefore, to the "near unit root" critique. Unit roots in spatial panel data are conceptually different to their counterparts in nonspatial panel data.

Since the original efforts of Dickey and Fuller, unit roots tests have been presented in terms of estimates of $1 - \pi$ divided by the standard deviation of π, i.e. as Student t statistics, which, however, do not have t distributions. This tradition has extended to panel unit root tests. For example, IPS is based on the average of the t statistics for the individual panel units. A less popular but equivalent alternative is to present unit root tests in terms of $T(\pi - 1)$, as in Hamilton (1994, Table B5), where the critical values are based on the percentiles of the distribution of π under the null of $\pi = 1$. We adopt this presentation in what follows. We begin with obtaining the distribution $\overline{\pi} + \overline{\lambda}$ under the null that their sum is 1.

We set $y_0 = \alpha = 0$, $\pi_i = 1$ and $\lambda_i = \lambda$, and draw N independent values of $\varepsilon_t \sim iiN(0,1)$ for $t = 1, 2, \ldots, T$, i.e. NT in all. These draws of ε are used to generate y_t using Eq. (7.6a). W is assumed to be rook-square (as in Chap. 5) with $w_{ij} = ¼$ for contiguous spatial units and zero otherwise. Spatial weights sum to one since each unit has four neighbors, except at the edge and corners of the lattice where the weights sum to ¾ and ½ respectively. This means appropriately that there is less spatial spillover at the corners and along the edges of the lattice than inside the lattice. Topology matters, as it did in Chap. 5. Since the lattice is square, each side is the square root of N. Therefore, if $N = 100$ the lattice is 10×10 and the epicenter of the lattice is 5 spatial units away from its edge. Next, the generated data for y_{it} are used to estimate π_i heterogeneously for all spatial units. These estimates are averaged to obtain $\bar{\pi}$, or π bar. These steps are repeated using 10,000 Monte Carlo trials to obtain the distribution of π bar under the null (π bar = 1).

The Distribution of π + λ

When $\pi = 1$ and $\lambda = 0$ we reproduce the IPS test statistic as expected because this assumes no cross-section dependence. This exercise is based on OLS because it does not involve estimating λ. Matters are different when λ is not zero because, as described in Chap. 3, OLS estimates of spatial lag parameters (λ) are upward biased and not consistent. Although OLS is super-consistent under the null, π_i and λ_i should be estimated by ML or IV if the unit root hypothesis is rejected. We choose IV and instrument the spatial lag $\tilde{y}_{it}$ using y_{it-1} and its first and second order lagged spatial lags $\left(\tilde{y}_{it-1}, \tilde{\tilde{y}}_{it-1}\right)$. These instruments contain identifying information in the temporal lags of unit i's neighbors and its neighbors' neighbors as well as the lagged value of y in unit i's neighbors. In principle, we should also use information on higher order neighbors, but since the lattice is small (10 × 10) we rapidly hit the edge of the lattice when using higher order neighbors. Therefore, we use truncated IV estimation (Lee 2003).

Indeed OLS induces, as expected, positive bias in λ and negative bias in π. However, this bias disappears with truncated IV estimation. For each spatial unit we obtain 10,000 estimates of λ_i and π_i. Their typical distributions are plotted in Figs. 7.1 and 7.2. Figure 7.1 plots the distribution of truncated IV estimates of π at the center of the lattice when $T = 25$, $N = 100$, and $\lambda = 0.1$. Because of edge effects,

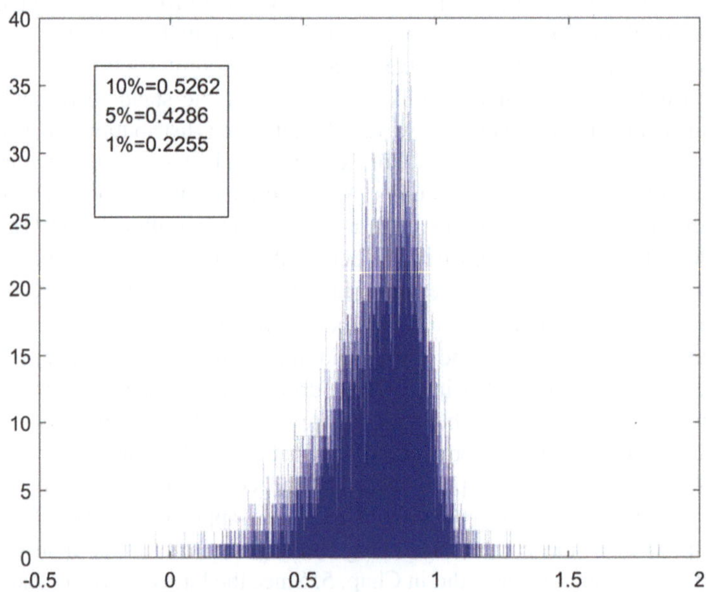

Fig. 7.1 Distribution of π at center: λ = 0.1

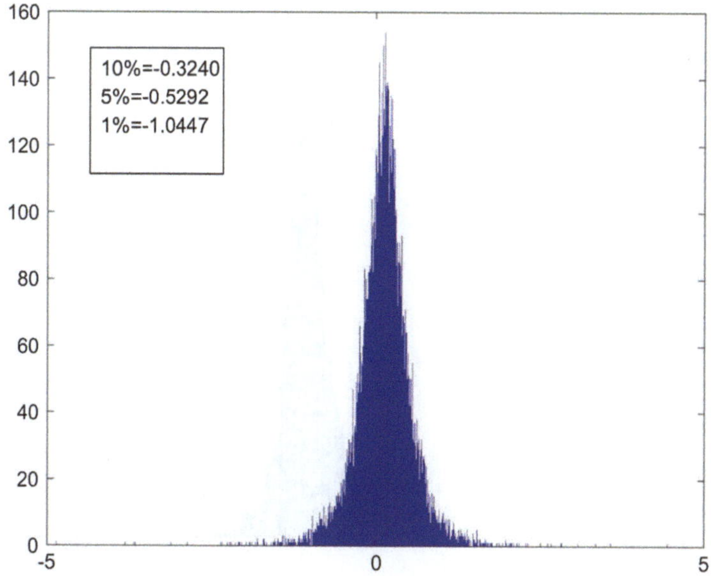

Fig. 7.2 Distribution of λ at center: λ = 0.1

the distribution might be different closer to the edge of the lattice where there is less spatial interaction. It is well known that when the DGP contains a unit root, the distribution is skewed to the left, as in Fig. 7.1. Indeed, the mean (0.774) is substantially smaller than $\pi = 0.9$. This skewness transmits itself to the histogram for the estimates of λ, as may be seen in Fig. 7.2. In fact, at the center the mean estimate of π is 0.774 and the mean estimate of λ is 0.14. By comparison, the distribution for λ is more symmetric. However, had λ been 0.9 instead of 0.1, Fig. 7.2 would have been skewed relative to Fig. 7.1.

Figure 7.3 plots the distribution of $\pi + \lambda$ at the center of the lattice. Not surprisingly, it is less skewed than Fig. 7.1. However, the mean is less than one.

For each Monte Carlo simulation we calculate π-bar, which is the mean of the N estimates of π_i. The distribution of 10,000 estimates of π-bar is presented in Fig. 7.4. Not surprisingly, in contrast to Fig. 7.1, which refers to a single spatial unit, Fig. 7.4 appears to be normally distributed because of the central limit theorem, i.e. it refers to cross-section averages. However, the mean is smaller than the true value of π (0.9) because the distribution of π for each of the N spatial units is skewed to the left. Figure 7.5 plots the distribution of λ, which exceeds its true value of 0.1. This excess compensates to some degree for the under-estimate of π. Figure 7.6 plots the distribution of $\pi + \lambda$ under the null of $\pi + \lambda = 1$. Notice that the mean is less than 1 (0.91) because the means of $\pi + \lambda$ for the individual spatial units are less than 1. Figure 7.6 is used to obtain critical values for $\pi + \lambda$ under the null of $\pi + \lambda = 1$. The 5th percentile in Fig. 7.6 is 0.8309.

When $N = 100$ and $T = 25$ and $\lambda = 0.1$ the critical value for $\pi + \lambda$ is 0.8309 for $p = 0.05$. If the panel mean estimate of $\pi + \lambda$ is greater than 0.8309 the null

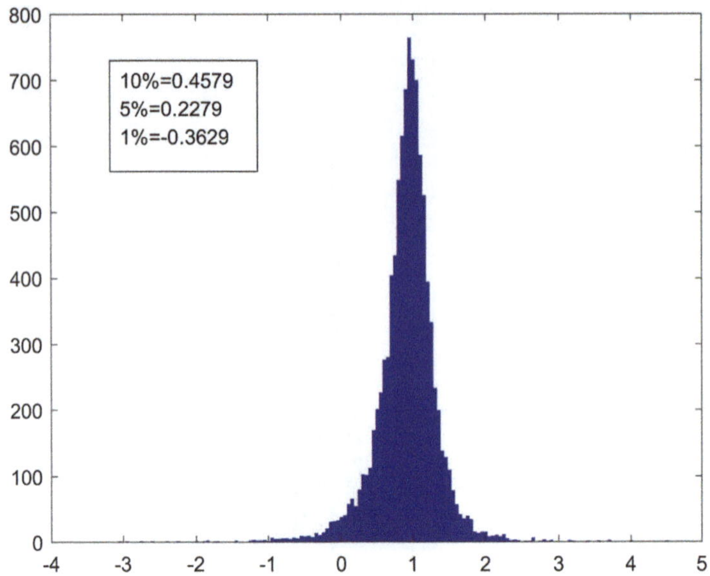

Fig. 7.3 Distribution of $\pi + \lambda$ at center: $\lambda = 0.1$

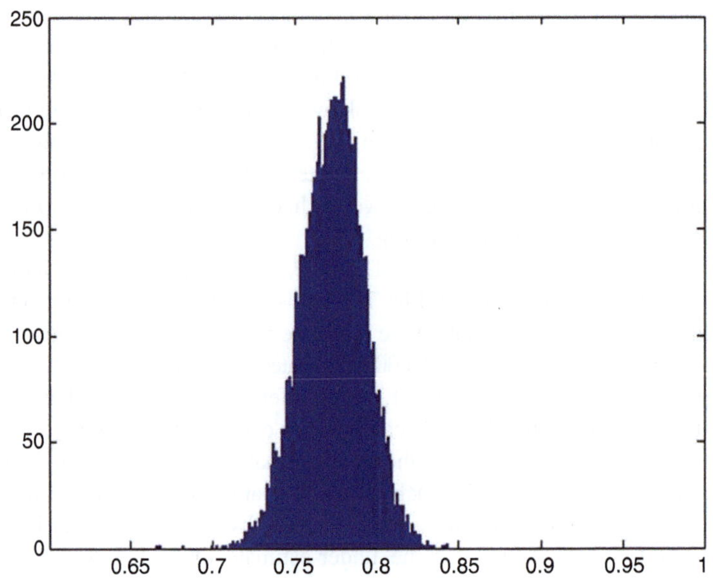

Fig. 7.4 Distribution of π-bar: $\lambda = 0.1$

hypothesis that $\pi + \lambda = 1$ cannot be rejected. If, for example, the panel mean estimate of $\pi + \lambda = 0.8$ we would reject the unit root hypothesis and conclude that the data are stationary at the 95% probability level. However, if we want to be 99%

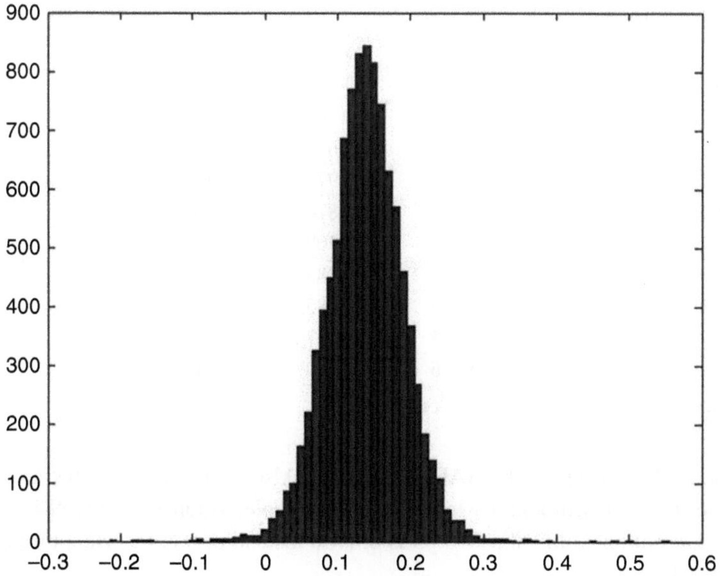

Fig. 7.5 Distribution of λ-bar: $\lambda = 0.1$

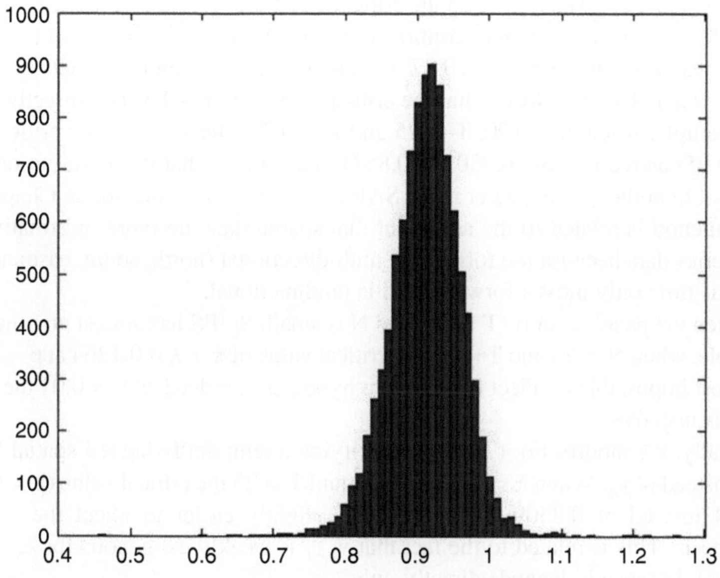

Fig. 7.6 Distribution of $\pi + \lambda$: $\lambda = 0.1$

sure that there is no unit root, we would reach the opposite conclusion because the critical value of $\pi + \lambda$ is 0.7857, which is less than 0.8. Table 7.1 shows that the critical value of $\pi + \lambda$ increases slightly with λ; it is harder to reject the unit root

Table 7.1 Critical values for SpIPS

λ		0.1			0.2	0.4
Percent		1%	5%	10%	5%	5%
N = 25	T = 10	−0.440	0.1264	0.3189		
	T = 25	0.6612	0.7616	0.8042		
	T = 50	0.8655	0.8977	0.9137		
N = 100	T = 10	0.0733	0.3876	0.4938		
	T = 25	0.7858	0.8309	0.8495	0.8521	0.8835
	T = 50	0.9138	0.9283	0.9359		
N = 225	T = 10	0.3016	0.5085	0.5773		
	T = 25	0.8275	0.8577	0.8704		
	T = 50	0.9026	0.9349	0.9415		

Notes: Square 10 × 10 lattice with rook contiguity

hypothesis the greater is the SAR coefficient. Also, the critical values are slightly sensitive to the instrumental variables. For example, when $\lambda = 0.1$, N = 100 and T = 25 the critical value at p = 0.05 is 0.8406 instead of 0.8309 when three IVs are used instead of two.

As expected, the critical values increase towards 1 when either T or N is larger. However, the critical values are more sensitive to T than to N. For example, if N = 100 and T is 50 instead of 25 the critical value at p = 0.05 increases from 0.8309 to 0.9283, i.e. we can be more confident of rejecting the unit root hypothesis. If the panel mean estimate of $\pi + \lambda$ is 0.87 we cannot reject the unit root when T = 25 but we can when T = 50. Notice that the critical value for $\pi + \lambda$ varies directly with λ. For example, when N = 100, T = 25 and $\lambda = 0.2$ instead of 0.1, the critical value (p = 0.05) increases from 0.8309 to 0.8521. This means that it is easier to reject the unit root hypothesis the greater is the SAR coefficient. As explained in Chap. 5, this phenomenon is related to the argument that spatial data are more informative than time series data because the former are multidirectional (north, south, east and west) whereas time only moves forward, and is unidirectional.

When the panel is short (T = 10) and N is small, SpIPS has almost no power. For example, when N = 25 and T = 10 the critical value of $\pi + \lambda$ is 0.1264 at p = 0.05. It is almost impossible to reject the unit root hypothesis. Indeed, at p = 0.01 the critical value is negative.

Finally, we modify Eq. (7.6a) by specifying a temporally-lagged spatial lag, i.e. $\tilde{y}_{it-1}$ instead of $\tilde{y}_{it}$. When $\lambda = 0.1$, N = 100 and T = 25 the critical value (p = 0.05) is 0.8494 instead of 0.8309, i.e. it becomes slightly easier to reject the unit root hypothesis. This is related to the fact that $\tilde{y}_{it-1}$ is weakly exogenous for λ, whereas $\tilde{y}_{it}$ is not, because it depends directly on ε_t.

Designer SpIPS

The critical values in Table 7.1 refer to a square rook-lattice. We saw in Chap. 5 that critical values in spatial cross-section data depend on the parameters of the lattice, which affect spatial connectivity. Therefore, the critical values in Table 7.1 are indicative at best; shape and topology matter. Such matters do not arise in the case of IPS and CIPS where space plays no role. In principle, critical values for SpIPS

Table 7.2 Comparing SpIPS with IPS and CIPS

	IPS		CIPS		SpIPS	
d	0	1	0	1	0	1
House prices	1.622	−2.229	−1.125	−4.290	0.939	0.6170
Housing starts	0.209	−2.936	−2.936	−5.625	1.051	0.6907
Housing stock	−0.878	−0.778	−1.89	−2.768	0.953	0.6080
Population	1.299	−1.439	−1.756	−4.734	0.938	−0.0042
Wages	−4.428	−10.641	−2.371	−3.641	0.892	0.0863
Capital	0.142	4.667	−2.582	−4.105	0.983	0.7896
Critical value p = 0.05	−1.64		−2.25		0.69	

Notes: Logarithms. N = 9, T = 28 (1987–2014). Lag order = 1

should be tailored to the role of space in the data to which they are applied. This issue is related to the MAUP problem discussed in Chap. 3. There are two related aspects to MAUP. First, the way in which spatial units are constructed in terms of their geographical boundaries might matter for inference. In principle, this issue has its counterpart in time series data, where time periods may be aggregated in different ways, e.g. by months, quarters etc. Second, the way in which spatial connectivity (W) is specified might matter for inference as discussed in Chap. 4. The latter implies that unlike IPS and CIPS, SpIPS cannot have universal application because it varies with W.

In Table 7.2 we compare SpIPS test statistics with their IPS and CIPS counterparts for several key spatial panel variables in Israel during 1987–2014. According to SpIPS all the variables are nonstationary since average estimates of $\pi + \lambda$ exceeds their critical value of 0.69 when d = 0. Note that this critical value differs from its counterpart in Table 7.1 because it has been calculated for N = 9, T = 28 and W in which the elements are $w_{ij} = L_j/d_{ij}(L_j+L_i)$ where L denotes built-up land in 1990 and d denotes distance. Since built-up land reflects planning decisions made long before 1990, it is strongly exogenous with respect to the variables featured in Table 7.2. Unfortunately, Table 7.1 does not include the case in which T = 28 and N = 9 for comparison.

According to IPS all the variables are nonstationary with the exception of wages. According to CIPS half the variables are stationary. The difference between IPS and CIPS may be attributed to strong cross-section dependence, which is controlled for in the latter. For example, housing starts, which are visibly nonstationary in Fig. 6.3, are stationary according to CIPS. Alternatively, conditional on a common factor, which accounts for strong cross-section dependence, CIPS rejects the null of a unit root in the case of housing starts. According to SpIPS and CIPS all variables are difference stationary. By contrast, according to IPS capital, population and housing stocks are not difference stationary.

The Conditional Distribution of $\pi = 1$ Given λ

In this sub-section we obtain the distribution of π given λ under the null of $\pi = 1$. This exercise parallels the one in Baltagi et al. (2007) except, we assume the DGP is Eq. (7.6a) whereas they assume the DGP is Eq. (7.1) with spatial autocorrelation in ε. For example, if $\lambda = 0.2$, N = 100 and T = 25 the critical value of π is 0.704. Suppose that the estimate of π from Eq. (7.3a) is 0.6. We may reject the hypothesis that $\pi = 1$. This does not necessarily mean that y is stationary because the eigenvalues depend on π and λ.

Table 7.3 reports critical values for π-bar for different values of N, T and λ. We include the case for $\lambda = 0$ since this is equivalent to the IPS statistic, which serves as a benchmark. As expected, the critical value increases with T and N since more data makes it easier to reject the null hypothesis that $\pi = 1$. Notice that the critical value is more sensitive to T than it is to N. A less obvious result is the effect of λ on the critical values. If λ is small, π-bar is smaller than its IPS benchmark. For example, when $T = 25$, $N = 100$ and $\lambda = 0.04$ π-bar is 0.693, whereas when $\lambda = 0$ it is 0.696. However, when λ is larger the opposite tends to happen. Indeed, π-bar increases towards 1, which makes it easier to reject the hypothesis of a unit root. The insight for this phenomenon is discussed in Chap. 5; spatial unit root tests have more statistical power than their temporal counterparts. These results suggest that if spatial dependence is sufficiently large, it is easier to reject the null hypothesis of $\pi = 1$. The intuitive reason is that although spatial dependence increases noise because shocks spillover between spatial units, it increases the variance disproportionately. In short, spatial spillover makes it easier to reject the null hypothesis because it tends to accentuate shocks, thereby facilitating the revelation of incipient nonstationarity.

When $N = 100$ and $T = 25$ the critical value of rho-bar at $p = 0.05$ is 0.696. The critical value increases slightly to 0.704 when λ is 0.2. In this case, SAR in the DGP makes almost no difference. Matters are quite different, however, when $T = 10$; the critical value falls from 0.427 to 0.302. The same applies when $T = 50$, but the direction is reversed; the critical value increases from 0.842 to 0.958. This pattern also applies for different values of N. Therefore, the effect of SAR on the IPS statistic depends on T rather than N. If the panel is short ($T < 25$), IPS is over-sized because its critical value is too large. The opposite happens when the panel is long ($T > 25$); IPS is under-sized. In the intermediate case IPS is correctly sized.

These critical values assume that ε_{it} in Eq. (7.6a) is iid. Nuisance parameters are induced by serial correlation and spatial autocorrelation. The former may be handled by augmenting Eq. (7.6a) with terms in lagged Δy as in IPS. The latter may be handled by estimating SAC in ε.

7.3 Spatial Panel Cointegration

In Chap. 2 we recalled panel cointegration tests designed to test for spurious and nonsense regression phenomena. These tests, developed in the 1980s were subsequently, extended to panel data (Kao 1999; Pedroni 1999, 2004; Groen and Kleibergen 2003; Westerlund 2007). However, the units in the panel are assumed to be independent. Panel cointegration tests have been developed for panels with strong cross-section dependence (Banerjee and Carrion-I-Silvestre 2017) but they have not been developed for spatial panels with weak cross-section dependence. There are two main aspects to such spatial dependence. Suppose we wish to test the null hypothesis that $\beta = \lambda_0 = 0$:

Table 7.3 Critical values of π-bar given λ

		$\lambda = 0$			$\lambda = 0.04$			$\lambda = 0.2$		
Percent		1%	5%	10%	1%	5%	10%	1%	5%	10%
N = 25	T = 10	0.32784	0.37372	0.39774	0.080784	0.25047	0.30946	0.038446	0.20142	0.25643
	T = 25	0.62973	0.66106	0.67869	0.62378	0.6583	0.67584	0.61848	0.65185	0.6696
	T = 50	0.80901	0.82487	0.8328	0.80444	0.82129	0.82995	0.89654	0.9219	0.93263
N = 100	T = 10	0.4032	0.42749	0.440415	0.282691	0.35152	0.380629	0.238864	0.301863	0.329147
	T = 25	0.67981	0.69633	0.70417	0.67849	0.69338	0.70134	0.688289	0.704241	0.712053
	T = 50	0.83531	0.84227	0.84625	0.83116	0.83931	0.84327	0.950061	0.958088	0.961954
N = 225	T = 10	0.430558	0.447017	0.455387	0.334974	0.386037	0.405381	0.293023	0.335325	0.354018
	T = 25	0.723823	0.731716	0.735764	0.707116	0.717957	0.722995	0.706853	0.717675	0.723132
	T = 50	0.850728	0.855552	0.858108	0.844629	0.849745	0.852316	0.962538	0.967279	0.969512

See notes to Table 7.1. Null hypothesis: $\pi = 1$ given λ

$$y_{it} = \alpha_i + \beta x_{it} + \lambda_0 \tilde{y}_{it} + u_{it} \tag{7.7a}$$

$$u_{it} = \rho_i \tilde{u}_{it} + \tau_i u_{it-1} + v_{it} \tag{7.7b}$$

where y and x are nonstationary, λ_0 is a spatial lag coefficient, ρ is the SAC coefficient and τ is the autocorrelation coefficient. Notice that y and $\tilde{y} = Wy$ share the same time series properties. So if y is difference stationary, so must $\tilde{y}$ be difference stationary. Note also that in general y is not cointegrated with $\tilde{y}$ except in the unlikely event that the spatial difference $y - \tilde{y}$ happens to be stationary. In standard panel cointegration tests the stationarity of u is tested under the assumption that in the DGPs for y and x (Eq. 7.6a), $\lambda = 0$ and $\pi = 1$, i.e. y and x are difference stationary and spatially independent. Also λ_0 is assumed to be zero. The variables in Eq. (7.7a) are cointegrated if its error terms (u) are stationary, i.e. when $\rho + \tau < 1$.

Spatial dependence in Eqs. (7.6a and 7.7a) raises three questions. First, how are standard cointegration tests affected by assuming λ is zero in the data generating processes for y and x in Eq. (7.6a)? Second, how are these tests affected by assuming that λ_0 is zero in Eq. (7.7a)? Third, how are these tests affected by assuming that ρ is zero in Eq. (7.7b)? Moreover, in spatial contexts the taxonomy of cointegration is richer than in non-spatial contexts. Suppose u is I(1) when $\psi = 0$ and u is I (0) otherwise. This means that y and x are not cointegrated unless spatial lags are specified. What are the critical values for panel cointegration in this spatial context? Also, how are these critical values affected by ρ?

There are five main cases:

1. If u ~ I(0), but u ~ I(1) when $\lambda_0 = 0$, y and x are "spatially cointegrated" but not "locally cointegrated", i.e. y and x are not cointegrated (local) but y, x and the spatial lag of y are cointegrated.
2. If u ~ I(0) irrespective of λ_0, y and x are "globally cointegrated", i.e. y and x are cointegrated and y, x and the spatial lag of y are cointegrated.
3. If u ~ I(0) and u ~ I(1) otherwise, y and x are "locally cointegrated" but not "spatially cointegrated".
4. If u ~ I(0) when $\beta = 0$ but u ~ I(1) otherwise, y is cointegrated with its spatial lag. This is a technical possibility.
5. If u ~ I(1) irrespective of λ_0, y and x are not cointegrated.

As mentioned in Chap. 2, Pedroni proposed two test statistics for heterogeneous panel cointegration. The group augmented Dickey–Fuller statistic (GADF) equals the average of the N ADF statistics for the individual panel units, i.e. it is the average of the estimates of $(1 - \tau_i)/\mathrm{sd}(\tau_i)$. The group rho statistic (Grho) is the average of t_i. If GADF or Grho are greater than their critical values (GADF* < 0, Grho*) the null hypothesis of $\tau = 1$ cannot be rejected. GADF and Grho are equivalent tests asymptotically. In what follows we obtain the critical values for SpGrho, which is the spatial counterpart of Grho*, and is based on the distribution of $\rho + \tau$ under the null of $\rho + \tau = 1$.

We use Monte Carlo simulation to generate difference stationary panel data using Eq. (7.6a) for y and x under the assumption that ε_y and ε_x are independent. We generate 10,000 simulated data sets for y and x for different values for N, T and λ using as before a contiguity rook-based spatial weight matrix W for a square lattice. These values of y and x are used to calculate $\tilde{y}$ and $\tilde{x}$. We use these simulated data to estimate Eq. (7.7a) by ML. Since the DGPs for y and x are independent, the variables in Eq. (7.7a) are not cointegrated by construction, and estimates of $\rho + \tau$ are expected to be 1. If T is sufficiently large, we may obtain the distribution for $\hat{\rho}_i + \hat{\tau}_i$ under the null hypothesis for each unit in the panel. This is like a DF cointegration test statistic except for the fact that the panel units are spatially dependent. Alternatively, we may obtain a panel cointegration test statistic by obtaining the mean and variance of $\rho + \tau$. This is equivalent to the group-rho cointegration test suggested by Pedroni (1999) except for the fact that the panel units are spatially dependent and the cointegrating vector contains spatial lags of y and x.

The histogram of 10,000 estimates of β is presented in Fig. 7.7 for the case where $N = 100$, $T = 10$ and $\lambda = 0.2$ and $\lambda_0 = 0$. As demonstrated by Phillips and Moon (1999) these estimates are a random variable such that $E(\beta) \neq 0$ even as T tends to infinity. Indeed, as noted in Chap. 2, in time series data the t-statistics of the estimates of β tend to infinity at the rate of root-T. Figure 7.7 shows that estimated β is sometimes positive and sometimes negative, and although the mean is small it is not exactly equal to zero. This is the spatiotemporal counterpart to the nonsense regression phenomenon discussed in Chap. 2.

Next, the 10,000 sets of residuals, are used to estimate $\rho_i + \tau_i$ for each spatial unit, which makes 10,000 × N estimates in total. These estimates are expected to be 1 since the true value of β is zero. Figure 7.8 plots the histogram of these estimates at the epicenter. They have a "Dickey–Fuller" distribution, which is skewed to the left

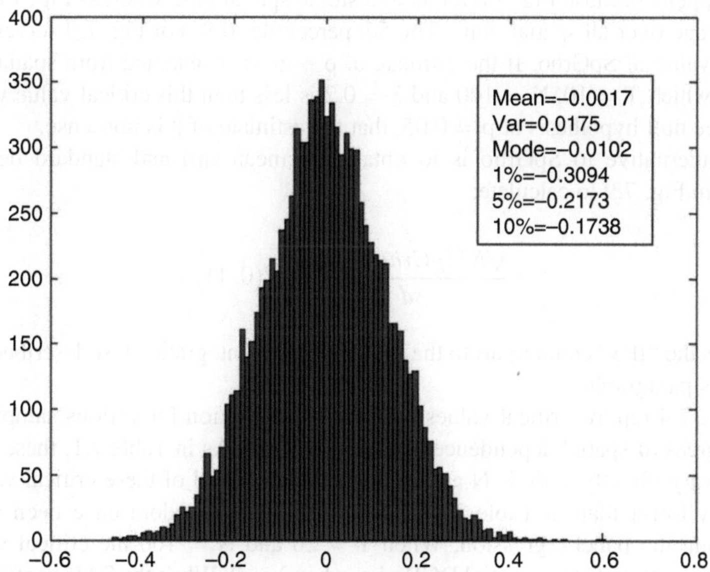

Fig. 7.7 Histogram for panel nonsense regression coefficient

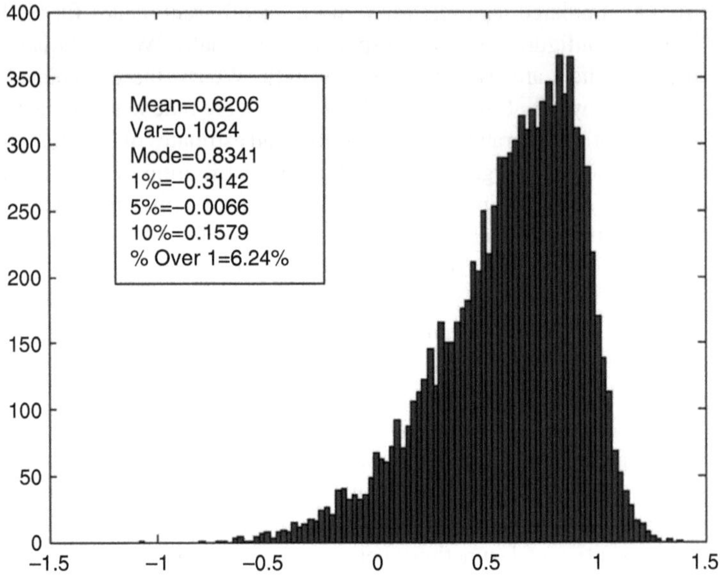

Fig. 7.8 Distribution of $\rho + \tau$ at center: $\lambda = 0.2$

of 1, as in Fig. 7.1. Next we calculate SpGrho, which is the average of the N estimates of $\rho_i + \tau_i$. The histogram for the 10,000 estimates of SpGrho is presented in Fig. 7.9. In contrast to Fig. 7.8, which has Dickey–Fuller type distribution, the distribution in Fig. 7.9 appears normally distributed, due to the central limit theorem. This happens because Fig. 7.8 refers to a single spatial unit, whereas Fig. 7.8 refers the average over all spatial units. The 5th percentile (0.83) of Fig. 7.9 serves as the critical value of SpGrho. If the estimate of $\rho + \tau$—bar obtained from spatial panel data in which T = 10, N = 100 and $\lambda = 0.2$ is less than this critical value we may reject the null hypothesis at $p = 0.05$, that the estimate of β is nonsense.

An alternative to SpGrho is to obtain the mean (m) and standard deviation (sd) from Fig. 7.9 to calculate:

$$\frac{\sqrt{N}(SpGrho - m)}{sd} \approx N(0, 1)$$

which is the "IPS" counterpart to the spatial panel cointegration test described in the previous paragraph.

Table 7.4 reports critical values for local cointegration for various sample sizes and degrees of spatial dependence as measured by λ. As in Table 7.1, these critical values vary directly with T, N and λ. However, the level of these critical values is naturally lower than in Table 7.1 because degrees of freedom have been used in estimating the panel regression. When T = 20 and N = 100 the critical value is 0.717 at $p = 0.05$ for nonspatial DGPs, i.e. when $\lambda = 0$. When the SAR coefficient in the DGP is 0.2 the critical value increases to 0.952. It is therefore easier to reject the

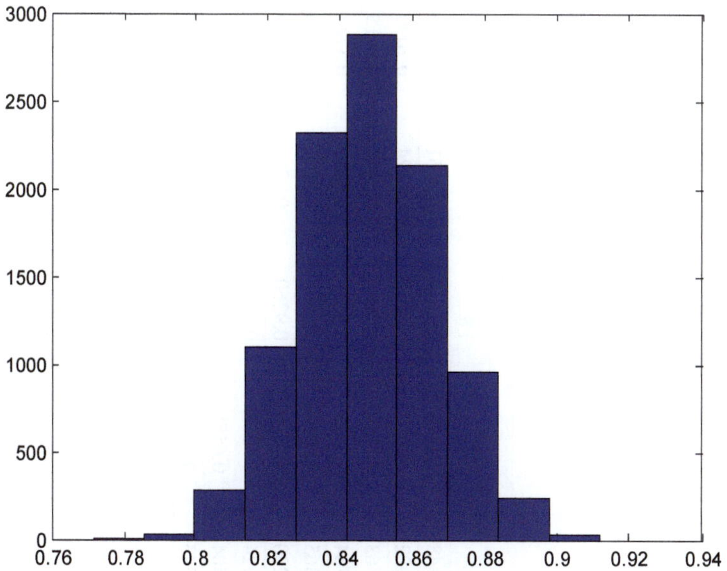

Fig. 7.9 Distribution of $\rho + \tau$: $\lambda = 0.2$

null of no-cointegration when the DGPs are spatial than when they are not. The presence of spatial spillovers in the data accentuates what the data reveal. This result is the spatial counterpart to Engle and Yoo (1991) who noticed that the critical value for the ADF cointegration test statistic (which takes account of autocorrelation) may be larger than its DF counterpart (which ignores autocorrelation).

Table 7.5 reports critical values for SpGrho when $N = 100$, $T = 25$, $\lambda = 0.2$ and k denotes the number of variables hypothesized in the cointegrating vector. These critical values are naturally stricter than their unit root counterparts in Table 7.2 because degrees of freedom have been sacrificed to estimate u. For example, when $T = 25$, $N = 100$, $p = 0.05$ and $\lambda = 0.2$, the critical value in Table 7.1 for a unit root is 0.8521 whereas in Table 7.5 its counterpart is 0.8188. If, for example, $SpIPS = 0.83$ we would reject the null hypothesis of $\pi + \lambda = 1$. If $SpGrho = 0.83$ we could not reject the null hypothesis of $\rho + \tau = 1$. As expected, the critical values become stricter (SpGrho* decreases) as the number of variables in the cointegrating vector gets larger. However, the differences are small as they are in Banerjee and Carrion-I-Silvestre (2017) in the case of strong cross-section dependence.

"Designer" SpGrho

The critical values for panel cointegration in Tables 7.4 and 7.5 refer to regular lattices with rook contiguity. These critical values are indicative at best because space in reality is less accommodating and more complicated. In Table 7.2 we reported tailor-made critical values for SpIPS for Israel. Here we report tailor-made critical values for SpGrho. We begin by plotting in Fig. 7.10 the distribution of $\rho + \tau$ when $N = 9$, $T = 25$, $n = 2$ and W is defined as in Table 7.2.

Table 7.4 Critical values for local cointegration

		$\lambda = 0$			$\lambda = 0.04$			$\lambda = 0.2$		
Percent		1%	5%	10%	1%	5%	10%	1%	5%	10%
N = 25	T = 10	0.3625	0.4101	0.4354	0.3653	0.4148	0.4398	0.4124	0.4661	0.4950
	T = 15	0.5527	0.5867	0.6055	0.5557	0.5902	0.6091	0.6340	0.6824	0.7099
	T = 20	0.6516	0.6817	0.6964	0.6568	0.6863	0.7010	0.7655	0.8142	0.8415
N = 100	T = 10	0.4481	0.4706	0.4827	0.4522	0.4734	0.4858	0.5341	0.5600	0.5743
	T = 15	0.6151	0.6321	0.6409	0.6199	0.6365	0.6454	0.7654	0.7953	0.8100
	T = 20	0.7025	0.7168	0.7236	0.7078	0.7230	0.7299	0.9260	0.9521	0.9680
N = 225	T = 10	0.4743	0.4898	0.4979	0.4777	0.4924	0.5003	0.5710	0.5899	0.6001
	T = 15	0.6345	0.6455	0.6509	0.6389	0.6504	0.6558	0.8123	0.8331	
	T = 20	0.7183	0.7281	0.7327	0.7256	0.7343	0.7395	0.9764	0.9946	1

Table 7.5 Critical values for cointegration: SpGrho

T	N	λ	k	1%	5%	10%
25	100	0.2	2	0.8053	0.8188	0.8250
25	100	0.2	3	0.8028	0.8156	0.8219
25	100	0.2	4	0.7993	0.8120	0.8185
25	100	0.1	2	0.7582		
50	9	0.2	2	0.7229	0.7497	0.7644
25	9	0.2	2	0.6479	0.6969	0.7181
50	9	0.1	2	0.8240		
50	9	0.2	4	0.7036	0.7343	0.7493

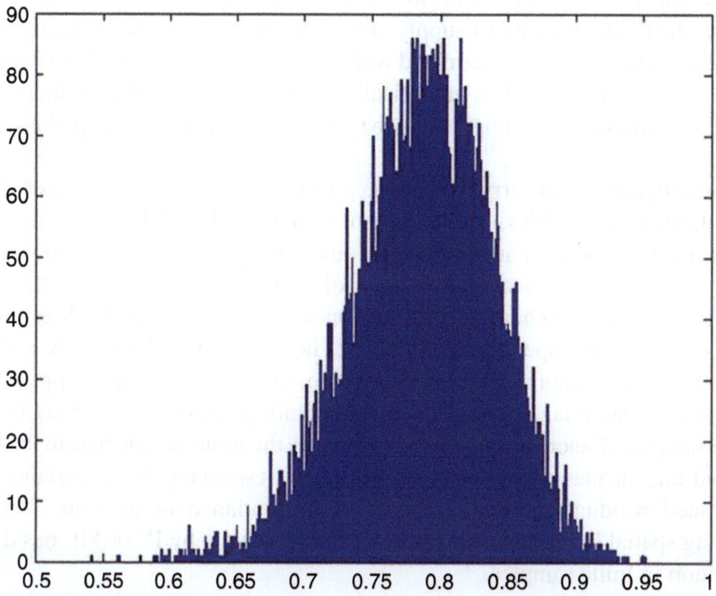

Fig. 7.10 Distribution of $\rho + \tau$: Israel

As expected, the distribution has a mean, which is less than 1. Also, since N is only 9 it is slightly skewed to the left. By contrast, the distribution in Fig. 7.8 is much more symmetric because N = 100. Therefore, the influence of the central limit theorem is stronger in Fig. 7.8 than it is in Fig. 7.10. The 5th percentile of Fig. 7.9 is 0.801, which serves as the critical value of SpGrho for Israel when there are two variables (n = 2). The critical values vary inversely with n, as expected. When n = 4 and 7 SpGrho = 0.776 and 0.748 respectively. Empirical test statistics that are smaller than these critical values reject the null hypothesis of no cointegration. Empirical test statistics greater than these critical values reject the null hypothesis of nonsense regressions.

Super-Consistency

As mentioned in Chap. 2, Stock (1987) was the first to show that OLS estimates of cointegrated vectors are super-consistent; they converge faster in probability than root-T to their population counterparts. Due to super-consistency the parameter estimates of cointegrating vectors are consistent even if the variables in the model happen to be jointly determined. This means that parameter estimates that would not be consistent when the data are stationary, are consistent if the data are nonstationary, provided that the variables concerned are cointegrated.

These properties carry over to nonstationary panel data when N is fixed. Matters are different if N is not fixed (Baltagi 2013, p. 299). Notice that Baltagi's δ_{NT} tends to zero when N is fixed but T tends to infinity. This means that OLS estimates of, for example, the price elasticity of supply and related parameters are consistent despite the fact that price is jointly determined with demand. Conveniently, the determinants of demand may be ignored asymptotically when testing hypotheses about supply, and the determinants of supply may be ignored when testing hypotheses about demand.

These properties also carry over to the estimation of SAR coefficients (of spatial lagged dependent variables). In the case of stationary data, OLS estimates of SAR coefficients are inconsistent because the outcomes of neighbors are jointly determined. In this case, consistent estimation of SAR coefficients is by ML or IV as explained in Chap. 3. When the data are nonstationary, however, OLS estimates of SAR coefficients are super-consistent, as we show. As is well known, IV and GMM are consistent estimators but biased in finite samples. The same applies to the estimation of spatial lag coefficients in cointegrating vectors, which may be biased in finite samples (Banerjee et al. 1993). However, the finite sample bias in the latter is mitigated and in many cases may be negligible, especially if the variance of the cointegrated residuals is small relative to the variance in the data. Therefore, estimating spatial lag parameters in cointegrating vectors by IV or ML has doubtful justification in finite samples.

Suppose the model to be estimated is:

$$y_{it} = \alpha_i + \beta x_{it} + \lambda_0 \tilde{y}_{it} + \gamma h_{it} + u_{it} \tag{7.8a}$$

where x is exogenous, h is endogenous and is therefore dependent on the error terms (u). If y, x and h are stationary OLS estimates of β, λ_0 and γ are obviously biased and not consistent. Matters are different when these variables are difference stationary and cointegrated. This happens because the covariance between nonstationary variables, such as h, and stationary variables, such as u, increases more slowly with T than the variances and covariances between the variables in Eq. (7.8a).

Let the data generating process (DGP) for a difference stationary variable such as h be a random walk with drift α (subscript i is dropped for convenience) so that h has a stochastic trend:

$$\Delta h_t = \theta + \varepsilon_t \tag{7.8b}$$

where $\varepsilon \sim iid(0, \sigma^2)$ without loss of generality. The general solution for h is:

$$\begin{aligned} h_t &= h_0 + \theta t + \breve{\varepsilon}_t \\ \breve{\varepsilon}_t &= \sum_{\tau=1}^{t} \varepsilon_\tau \end{aligned} \tag{7.8c}$$

where $h_0 = 0$ is the initial value for h, and $\breve{\varepsilon}$ is a random walk since $\Delta\breve{\varepsilon}_t = \varepsilon_t$.

According to Eq. (7.8c) h is nonstationary because its first two moments depend on time. Its unconditional mean is αt, and its variance (the variance of $\breve{\varepsilon}$) is $t\sigma^2$.

Suppose u_t is a stationary random variable, as it must be if the variables in Eq. (7.8a) are cointegrated. The covariance between h and u is obtained by multiplying Eq. (7.8b) by u_t, summing, and dividing by T:

$$\mathrm{cov}(hu) = \frac{1}{T}\sum_{t=1}^{T} h_t u_t = \frac{1}{T}\left(\theta \sum_{t=1}^{T} t u_t + \sum_{t=1}^{T} \breve{\varepsilon}_t u_t\right) \tag{7.8d}$$

This covariance has two components. The asymptotic orders in probability of these component are:

$$\frac{1}{T}\sum t u_t \sim O_p\left(T^{1/2}\right) \tag{7.8e}$$

$$\frac{1}{T}\sum \breve{\varepsilon}_t u_t \sim O_p\left(T^0\right) \tag{7.8f}$$

Equation (7.8e) follows from Eq. (2.1f), which concerns the product of t and a stationary random variable. Equation (7.8f) follows from Eq. (2.1) which involves the product of a random walk and a stationary random variable. The asymptotic order of a sum is the largest asymptotic order of its components. Therefore, the covariance of h and u is independent of T if $\alpha = 0$ and it increases with root-T otherwise.

The variances of nonstationary variables such as h increase linearly with T if $\alpha = 0$ and with T^2 otherwise [because the square of h in Eq. (7.8c) depends on t^2)] For similar reasons covariances between difference stationary variables increase with T^2 because their products involve terms in t^2.

These arguments also apply to the spatial lagged dependent variable, because $\tilde{y}$ has the same time series properties as y and h. Therefore, the covariance between $\tilde{y}$ and u is $O_p(T^{1/2})$ and its variance increases with T^2. The probability limits of the OLS estimates of the parameters are equal to:

$$p \lim \hat{\beta} = \beta + p \lim b \tag{7.8g}$$

$$p \lim \hat{\lambda}_0 = \lambda_0 + p \lim l \tag{7.8h}$$

$$p \lim \hat{\gamma} = \gamma + p \lim f \tag{7.8i}$$

where:

$$b = \left[\left(\sigma_{xh}\sigma_{\tilde{y}h} - \sigma_h^2 \right)\sigma_{\tilde{y}u} + \left(\sigma_{x\tilde{y}}\sigma_{\tilde{y}h} - \sigma_{\tilde{y}}^2\sigma_{xh} \right)\sigma_{hu} \right] / d$$
$$l = \left[\left(\sigma_x^2\sigma_{\tilde{y}}^2 - \sigma_{\tilde{y}h}^2 \right)\sigma_{\tilde{y}u} + \left(\sigma_{x\tilde{y}}\sigma_{\tilde{y}h} - \sigma_x^2\sigma_{\tilde{y}h} \right)\sigma_{hu} \right] / d$$
$$f = \left[\left(\sigma_{x\tilde{y}}\sigma_{xh} - \sigma_x^2\sigma_{\tilde{y}h} \right)\sigma_{\tilde{y}u} + \left(\sigma_x^2\sigma_{\tilde{y}}^2 - \sigma_{x\tilde{y}}^2 \right)\sigma_{hu} \right] / d$$
$$d = \sigma_x^2\left(\sigma_{\tilde{y}}^2\sigma_h^2 - \sigma_{\tilde{y}h}^2 \right) - \sigma_{\tilde{y}x}\left(\sigma_{x\tilde{y}} - \sigma_{\tilde{y}h}\sigma_{xh} \right) + \sigma_{xh}\left(\sigma_{x\tilde{y}}\sigma_{\tilde{y}h} - \sigma_{\tilde{y}}^2\sigma_{xh} \right)$$

The asymptotic order in probability of sums of random variables is equal to the largest asymptotic order of one of its components. Hence, if $y = y_1 + y_2$ and y_1 is $O_p(T^a)$ and y_2 is $O_p(T^c)$ the asymptotic order of y is c if c > a. The asymptotic order in probability of products of random variables is equal to the sum of the asymptotic orders of its components. Hence, if $y = y_1y_2$, y is $O_p(T^{a+c})$. Finally, the asymptotic order of quotients is equal to the difference between asymptotic orders. Hence, if $y = y_1/y_2$ the asymptotic order in probability of y is $O_p(T^{a-c})$. Applying these rules means that the numerators of b, l and f are $O_p(T^4) \times O_p(T^{½}) = O_p(T^{4½})$ and d is $O_p(T^6)$ because it involves the products of the variances of x, $\tilde{y}$ and h, each of which is $O_p(T^2)$. Therefore, the probability limits of b, l and f are $O_p(T^{-3/2})$. Consequently, OLS estimates of β, λ_0 and γ are $T^{3/2}$ super-consistent. If $\theta = 0$ in Eq. (7.8b), i.e. the variables are driftless random walks, the OLS estimates turn out to be T consistent, which is still super-consistent relative to root T consistency for stationary data.

In Chap. 2 we mentioned that Banerjee et al. (1993) carried out a Monte Carlo analysis of the finite sample properties of cointegrating vectors in which T ranges between 25 and 200. In general they found that the final sample bias varies inversely with the goodness-of-fit of the cointegrated model, and the noise in the DGPs for h [the variance of ε in Eq. (7.8b)], and it varies directly with the degree of error correction (ρ). With T = 25 the finite sample bias ranges between 2% and 30%. In the case of spatial panel cointegration we expect these finite sample biases to be smaller because the bias is naturally diversified away across the panel units. The bias for region i is unlikely to be perfectly correlated with the bias for region j.

7.4 Spatial Error Correction

In Chap. 2 we explained that cointegration and error correction are two sides of the same coin. Cointegration implies error correction, and error correction implies cointegration. If the variables in Eq. (7.7a) are cointegrated, the spatial error correction model (SpECM) associated with Eq. (7.7a) in its first order form is:

$$\Delta y_{it} = \alpha_i + \pi \Delta y_{it-1} + \beta_0 \Delta x_{it-1} + \phi \Delta \tilde{y}_{it-1} + \xi u_{it-1} + \zeta \tilde{u}_{it-1} + \beta_1 z_t + e_{it} \quad (7.9a)$$

where e are error terms that are assumed to be temporally uncorrelated, but they might be spatial correlated such that $\mathrm{cov}(e_{it}e_{jt}) = \sigma_{ij}$ is non-zero. The local error correction coefficient ξ is expected to be negative, since u_{it-1} is positive when y_{it-1} is greater than its equilibrium value. Therefore, y_{it} is expected to decrease as it corrects itself towards its equilibrium value. In the short run, x may affect y differently to how it affects y in the long-run, hence β_0 might differ from β in Eq. (7.7a). Also, potential short-term inertia in y is captured by π. If there are spatial spillovers in error correction, the dynamics of y will be affected by $\tilde{u}$ among neighbors. Therefore, ζ is the spatial error correction coefficient, and is expected to be have the same sign as ξ. The short-term SAR coefficient ϕ might differ from its long-run counterpart λ in Eq. (7.7a). As in Eq. (7.6a) where α_i is a long-run specific spatial effect, α_{0i} in Eq. (7.9a) is a short-term specific spatial effect. Finally, z is stationary, so it does not affect y in the long-run but it may affect y in the short term via β_1.

Note that when the panel data are difference stationary, all the variables in the SpECM are stationary since u and $\tilde{u}$ are stationary when Eq. (7.6a) is cointegrated. Because all the variables in Eq. (7.9a) are stationary, their parameter estimates have standard distributions. This means that t-tests etc. may be applied in the usual way. Indeed, Eq. (7.9a) may be estimated by standard dynamic panel data methods because it does not include contemporaneous spatial lagged dependent variables $(\tilde{y}_{it})$. If $\xi = \zeta = 0$ Eq. (7.9a) becomes a spatial autoregression since it incorporates temporal lags and spatial lags of Δy and Δx as well as z. When ξ is negative there is local error correction. When ζ is non-zero there is spatial error correction. When both types of error correction occur, we refer to this as "global error correction".

Spatial cointegration does not necessarily imply spatial error correction. If $\tilde{y}$ is specified in the cointegrating vector (λ_0 is statistically significant), the spatial error correction coefficient (ζ) does not have to be statistically significant. In the latter case, the effect of $\tilde{y}$ is expressed through ξ since u_{it-1} and $\tilde{y}_{it-1}$ are dependent. Spatial error correction in fact implies that second order neighbors are also important since according to Eq. (7.7a) the spatial error term is defined as:

$$\tilde{u}_{it} = \tilde{y}_{it} - \alpha_i - \beta \tilde{x}_{it} - \lambda_0 \tilde{\tilde{y}}_{it} \quad (7.9b)$$

where, for example, $\tilde{\tilde{y}}$ denotes a second order spatial lag (neighbors first-removed). So there is no necessary reason why spatial cointegration should induce spatial error correction.

Suppose that cointegration is not spatial because $\lambda_0 = 0$. Equation (7.9b) shows that in this case the spatial error term depends only on $\tilde{y}$ and $\tilde{x}$. Therefore, spatial error correction does not necessarily imply spatial cointegration. In this case spatial lags have only a temporary effect on y since Δy depends on $\tilde{y}$ and $\tilde{x}$. These spatial lags do not have a permanent effect. Note that just because there is no spatial cointegration and error correction ($\lambda_0 = \zeta = 0$), this does not necessarily rule out spatial dynamics. If γ_3 is statistically significant $\Delta\tilde{y}_{it-1}$ affects y temporarily.

7.5 Identification

When the data are stationary parameter identification and consistency are inextricably interwoven. If covariates are correlated with error terms their OLS parameter estimates are biased and cannot be consistent. To solve this problem instrumental variables are required to identify the parameters involved. These instrumental variables must be correlated with the covariates but independent of the dependent variable. Matters are different if the data are nonstationary; identification and consistency are not necessarily related. Indeed, the previous discussion of super-consistency was conducted without any reference to identification. However, this obviously does not mean that identification is irrelevant if the data are nonstationary and cointegrated, especially in multivariate contexts.

To demonstrate this, assume that $\lambda_0 = 0$ in Eq. (7.8a) without loss of generality. We continue to assume that x is exogenous and h is endogenous. Previously the research agenda was univariate because it was solely concerned with Eq. (7.7a). Now the research agenda is extended to the joint determination of y and h. This bivariate example is the simplest of multivariate cases. The null hypotheses are:

$$y_{it} = \alpha_0 + \beta x_{it} + \gamma_0 h_{it} + u_{it} \tag{7.10a}$$

$$y_{it} = \alpha_1 + \gamma m_{it} + \mu h_{it} + v_{it} \tag{7.10b}$$

where y, x, h and m are difference stationary, w is exogenous, and u and v are stationary if the variables in Eqs. (7.10a and 7.10b) are cointegrated. Equation (7.10a) is identical to Eq. (7.8a) with $\lambda_0 = 0$, and Eq. (7.10b) has been normalized with y on the left hand side and h on the right hand side. Recall from Chap. 2 that this normalization is arbitrary if the data are nonstationary; it would not matter asymptotically if h or m had been specified on the left hand side.

By way of motivation let y denote quantity and h denote its price. Equation (7.10a) is the model for demand, in which case γ_0 is expected to be negative, and Eq. (7.10b) is the model for supply, in which case μ is expected to be positive. To identify the demand schedule, m is omitted for Eq. (7.10a). To identify the supply schedule x is omitted from Eq. (7.10b). But for these omitted variables it would have been impossible to distinguish supply from demand. Therefore, x and m have their usual roles as far as identification is concerned, but not as far as consistency is concerned. Equation (7.10a) does not require information on m for consistency. Nor does Eq. (7.10b) require information on x for consistency. The data for y, h, x and m therefore contain two cointegrating vectors. The first comprises y, h and x but excludes m, and the second comprises y, h and m but excludes x. Recall from Chap. 2 that when there are four variables the maximum number of cointegrating vectors is four and the minimum is zero. These cointegrating vectors may be estimated by ML using the methodology of Larsson et al. (2001) or by OLS.

If Eqs. (7.10a and 7.10b) are cointegrated, the spatial vector error correction model (SpVECM) is the vector counterpart to Eq. (7.9a) for two state variables (y and h) instead of one:

$$\begin{aligned}\Delta y_{it} = {} & \gamma_{0i} + \gamma_{11}\Delta y_{it-1} + \gamma_{12}\Delta h_{it-1} + \gamma_{21}\Delta x_{it-1} \\ & + \gamma_{22}\Delta m_{it-1} + \gamma_{31}\Delta \tilde{y}_{it-1} + \gamma_{32}\Delta \tilde{h}_{it-1} + \gamma_{41}\Delta \tilde{x}_{it-1} \\ & + \gamma_{42}\Delta \tilde{m}_{it-1} + \gamma_{51}v_{it-1} + \gamma_{52}u_{it-1} + \gamma_{61}\tilde{v}_{it-1} \\ & + \gamma_{62}\tilde{u}_{it-1} + \gamma_7 z_t + e_{it}\end{aligned} \tag{7.10c}$$

$$\begin{aligned}\Delta h_{it} = {} & \eta_{0i} + \eta_{11}\Delta y_{it-1} + \eta_{12}\Delta h_{it-1} + \eta_{21}\Delta x_{it-1} \\ & + \eta_{22}\Delta m_{it-1} + \eta_{31}\Delta \tilde{y}_{it-1} + \eta_{32}\Delta \tilde{h}_{it-1} + \eta_{41}\Delta \tilde{x}_{it-1} \\ & + \eta_{42}\Delta \tilde{m}_{it-1} + \eta_{51}v_{it-1} + \eta_{52}u_{it-1} + \eta_{61}\tilde{v}_{it-1} \\ & + \eta_{62}\tilde{u}_{it-1} + \eta_7 z_t + d_{it}\end{aligned} \tag{7.10d}$$

where e denotes the innovation for y and d the innovation for h. The SpVECM incorporates six types of parameters: temporal autoregressive (γ_{11}, γ_{12}, η_{11}, η_{12}), spatial autoregressive (γ_{31}, γ_{32}, η_{31}, η_{32}), temporal error correction (γ_{51}, γ_{52}, η_{51}, η_{52}), spatial error correction (γ_{61}, γ_{62}, η_{61}, η_{62}), lagged exogenous (γ_{21}, γ_{22}, η_{21}, η_{22}), and temporally lagged spatial Durbin (γ_{41}, γ_{42}, η_{41}, η_{42}). Inevitably, the taxonomy of cases in SpVECMs is much richer than in SpECMs because error correction may occur between state variables as well as within them. For example, if γ_{52} is statistically significant there is error correction for h to y. If γ_{62} is statistically significant there is spatial error correction from h to y.

So far it has been assumed that x and m are exogenous. However, recall from Chap. 2 that for causality they do not have to be strongly exogenous; they only have to be weakly exogenous. In the present context this means that there is no error correction between x and u, or between m and v. For example, in the former case (first order):

$$\Delta x_{it} = a + b\Delta x_{it-1} + c\Delta y_{it-1} + d\Delta h_{it-1} + fu_{it-1} + e_{it} \tag{7.10e}$$

x is weakly exogenous if the error correction coefficient (f) is not significantly different from zero. If in addition b = c = d = 0, x would be strongly exogenous. More generally, if x and m are included in the SpVECM the counterparts for x and m of the error correction coefficients should be zero for weak exogeneity. If x and m are not weakly exogenous, it would be necessary to treat them as state variables alongside y and h. But identification would then require weakly exogenous variables to identify the parameters in Eqs. (7.10a and 7.10b) which would now include Eq. (7.10e) for x and its counterpart for m. The usual rank and order conditions apply to these weakly exogenous variables.

In Chap. 8 we provide empirical illustrations of unit root tests for spatial DGPs, and cointegration tests for spatial DGPs, which distinguish between local, spatial and global cointegration. We also illustrate spatial error correction modelling. In Chap. 9 we provide empirical illustrations of multivariate state variables and the issues of identification that arise therein, including tests for weak exogeneity of variables such as x and w that are specified for purposes of identification.

7.6 Confidence Intervals

In Chap. 2 we noted that in time series models cointegrating vectors generally have nonstandard distributions, unless the variables concerned happen to be weakly exogenous. This means that t-tests for individual parameter estimates, or F-tests for groups of parameter estimates are invalid. Matters are different in the case of non-spatial panel data because as N becomes large, the central limit theorem induces normality in the distribution of OLS parameter estimates. Indeed, this tendency is visible in Figs. 7.3 and 7.4. In spatial panel data N is fixed. If N is relatively small (as it is in Chap. 8) the central limit theorem cannot be relied upon to induce normality in the distributions of estimated cointegrating vectors. This is not a problem with regard to hypothesis tests regarding the specification of cointegrating vectors. For example, in Eq. (7.7a) the hypothesis that ψ is zero is not tested with reference to its t statistic. Instead, and as noted in Chap. 2, we may reject this hypothesis if the variables in Eq. (7.7a) cease to be cointegrated if this restriction is imposed. The same is true if the p-value of the panel cointegration test is impaired.

Although confidence intervals are not required to test hypotheses about the specification of cointegrating vectors, they may nevertheless be of interest in their own right. We therefore propose a bootstrapping procedure for calculating confidence intervals for cointegrating vectors estimated with nonstationary spatial panel data. We naturally expect that the lower bound of confidence intervals of parameters estimates, such as λ_0, is positive if $\lambda_0 > 0$, and is negative if $\lambda_0 < 0$.

Let the model be:

$$y_{it} = \alpha_i + \beta x_{it} + \lambda \tilde{y}_{it} + u_{it} \tag{7.11a}$$

$$u_{it} = \theta_i u_{it-1} + \rho_i \tilde{u}_{it} + v_{it} \tag{7.11b}$$

$$x_{it} = \alpha_{xi} + \pi_{xi} x_{it-1} + (1 - \pi_{xi})\tilde{x}_{it} + \varepsilon_{xit} \tag{7.11c}$$

$$y_{it} = \alpha_{yi} + \pi_{yi} y_{it-1} + (1 - \pi_{yi})\tilde{y}_{it} + \varepsilon_{yit} \tag{7.11d}$$

where ε_y and ε_x are iid, and $\theta + \rho < 1$ for spatial panel cointegration. The DGPs for y and x contain unit roots. ε_y, ε_x and v are resampled with replacement from their respective empirical distribution functions (EDF) and are denoted by $\breve{\varepsilon}_y$, $\breve{\varepsilon}_x$ and $\breve{v}$. Following Freedman and Peters (1984) $\breve{u}$ and $\breve{v}$ are constructed recursively to preserve their temporal autocorrelation properties:

$$\breve{u}_{it} = \hat{\theta}_i \breve{u}_{it-1} + \hat{\rho}_i \breve{\tilde{u}}_{it} + \breve{v}_{it} \tag{7.11e}$$

$$\breve{x}_{it} = \hat{\alpha}_{xi} + \hat{\pi}_{xi} \breve{x}_{it-1} + \left(1 - \hat{\pi}_{xi}\right) \breve{\tilde{x}}_{it} + \breve{\varepsilon}_{xit} \tag{7.11f}$$

$$\breve{\tilde{y}}_{it} = \sum_{j \neq i}^{N} w_{ij} \left[\hat{\alpha}_{yj} + \hat{\pi}_{yj} \breve{y}_{jt-1} + \left(1 - \hat{\pi}_{yj}\right) \breve{\tilde{y}}_{jt} + \breve{\varepsilon}_{yjt} \right] \tag{7.11g}$$

$$\breve{y}_{it} = \hat{\alpha}_i + \hat{\beta} \breve{x}_{it} + \hat{\lambda} \breve{\tilde{y}}_{it} + \breve{u}_{it} \tag{7.11h}$$

where hats refer to estimates of the various DGP parameters. Note that this procedure differs from Lin et al. (2011) who suggest:

$$\begin{aligned} \breve{y}_t &= A\hat{\alpha} + \hat{\beta} A \breve{x}_t + A \breve{u}_t \\ A &= \left(I - \hat{\lambda} W\right)^{-1} \end{aligned} \tag{7.11i}$$

Their procedure does not ensure that y, x and $\tilde{y}$ are panel cointegrated. For example, if $\beta = 0$ $\breve{y}$ must be stationary because $\breve{u}$ is stationary.

The BS parameters are estimated from repeated estimation of:

$$\breve{y}_{it} = \breve{\alpha}_i + \breve{\beta} \breve{x}_{it} + \breve{\lambda} \breve{\tilde{y}}_{it} + u_{it} \tag{7.11j}$$

which extends to panel data the BS methodology for cointegration proposed by Li and Maddala (1997). The percentile method is used to obtain the confidence intervals and p-values from the bootstrap distributions for $\breve{\beta}$ and $\breve{\lambda}$.

In finite samples consistent estimators might be biased, e.g. $\hat{\beta} \neq \bar{\breve{\beta}}$. The bias corrected estimate (Maddala and Kim 1999, p. 314) is $\beta^* = \hat{\beta} - \left(\bar{\breve{\beta}} - \hat{\beta}\right)$ for which confidence intervals and p values may be obtained by the percentile method. Since the BS distributions may not be symmetric, the confidence intervals are not necessarily symmetric. This BS method is applied in Chap. 8. This method is semiparametric because it makes no parametric assumptions about the distributions of ε_x and v, but it uses parametric estimates of the hatted parameters. A less parametric alternative would be to resample y using equation (7.11d) instead of equation (7.11h) and to resample jointly from the empirical distribution functions for ε_y, ε_x and v.

In Chap. 1 we pointed out that unit root and cointegration tests for spatially dependent panel data constitute a lacuna in spatial econometric theory and practice. In the present chapter, we sought to fill this lacuna. We began by deriving the theoretical distributions of the first and second moments of panel data under the null hypothesis that their data generating processes embody heterogeneous spatiotemporal unit roots. For these purposes we applied the functional central limit and continuous mapping theorems (introduced in Chap. 2) under the assumption that the number of spatial units (N) is fixed and the number of time periods (T) tends to infinity. Next, we used Monte Carlo simulation methods to obtain critical values for spatiotemporal unit root tests, which refer to the sum of the temporal and spatial autoregressive coefficients (AR + SAR). Unlike other unit root tests, spatiotemporal unit root tests depend the specification of the spatial connectivity matrix (W). These critical values were calculated for different values of N, T and W.

Since variables that embody spatiotemporal unit roots may be spuriously correlated, we suggested that if the least squares residuals they generate happen to be stationary, these variables are spatially cointegrated. Specifically, if the variables are integrated to order d, the residuals should be integrated to order $d - 1$. In the standard case $d = 1$, hence the residuals are not integrated ($d - 1 = 0$). This condition is satisfied when the null hypothesis of spatiotemporal unit roots in the residuals is rejected. We derived the theoretical distribution for this spatial panel cointegration test, and we used Monte Carlo simulation methods to calculate critical values under the null for different values of N, T and W.

We distinguished between local cointegration in which the cointegrated variables are not spatial, spatial cointegration in which the cointegrated variables are spatial, and global cointegration in which both types of variables are cointegrated. We noted that the critical values for cointegration tests do not depend on whether the variables are spatial or not.

Since N is fixed, the parameter estimates of cointegrating vectors are in general not asymptotically normal because the central limit theorem does not apply. Consequently, t-tests, F-tests etc., which are derived from the normal distribution, are not applicable. Instead, tests for the statistical significance of variables are carried out using cointegration tests. There is natural interest in the distribution of the parameter estimates of cointegrated vectors. For these purpose we proposed a semiparametric panel bootstrap method for calculating confidence intervals for parameter estimates, which takes account of the spatiotemporal nature of the data generating processes of the variables, and which resample from the empirical distribution functions for their innovations and the residuals.

We demonstrated theoretically that the least squares estimates of parameters obtained using data that embody spatiotemporal unit roots are super-consistent; they converge in probability more rapidly than root-T. We also demonstrated that least squares estimates of SAR coefficients are consistent. This useful property means that the identification problems involved in estimating SAR coefficients using stationary panel data (discussed in Chap. 3) do not arise when the data are nonstationary.

Variables that are cointegrated must be related through error correction, either in whole or in part. We proposed a hierarchy of error correction models. At the lowest level, error correction is local for single variables. At the highest level, error correction is global for vectors of variables. We refer to the latter by the spatial vector error correction model (SpVECM).

Since cointegrating vectors do not imply causal relationships between the variables, we suggested that issues of causality be determined through error correction. Weakly exogenous covariates in error correction models have causal effects on dependent variables. Recall from Chap. 2 that weakly exogenous variables may be dynamically dependent on these dependent variables. Whereas causality and identification are inextricably interwoven when the data are stationary, matters are different when the data are nonstationary. When y and x are nonstationary and cointegrated, these variables are related in the long-run. The causal nexus between them is decided by error correction. One-way error correction from x to y implies causality is from x. Two-way error correction implies mutual causality.

In Table 7.1 we provide empirical examples of our spatiotemporal unit root test. In the next chapter, we provide empirical examples of spatial panel cointegration. In Chap. 9 we provide empirical examples of spatial error correction.

References

Baltagi BH (2013) Econometric analysis of panel data, 5th edn. Wiley, Chichester

Baltagi BH, Bresson G, Pirotte A (2007) Panel unit root tests and spatial dependence. J Appl Economet 22(2):339–360

Banerjee A, Carrion-I-Silvestre JL (2017) Testing for panel cointegration using common correlated effects estimators. J Time Ser Anal 38:610–636

Banerjee A, Dolado JJ, Galbraith JW, Hendry DF (1993) Cointegration, error correction and the econometric analysis of nonstationary data. Oxford University Press, Oxford

Elhorst JP (2001) Dynamic models in space and time. Geogr Anal 33:119–140

Elhorst JP (2014) From spatial cross-section data to spatial panel data. Springer, Berlin

Engle RF, Yoo BS (1991) Cointegrated economic time series: an overview with new results. In: Engle RF, Granger CWJ (eds) Long run economic relationships: readings in cointegration. Oxford University Press, Oxford

Freedman D, Peters S (1984) Bootstrapping a regression equation: some empirical results. J Am Stat Assoc 79:97–106

Groen J, Kleibergen F (2003) Likelihood-based cointegration analysis in panels of vector error-correction models. J Bus Econ Stat 21:295–317

Hamilton J (1994) Time series analysis. Princeton University Press, Princeton, NJ

Hendry DF (1995) Dynamic econometrics. Oxford University Press, Oxford

Im K, Pesaran MH, Shin Y (2003) Testing for unit roots in heterogeneous panels. J Econ 115:53–74

Kao C (1999) Spurious regression and residual based tests for cointegration in panel data. J Econ 90:1–44

Larsson R, Lyhagen J, Löthgren M (2001) Likelihood-based cointegration tests in heterogeneous panels. Econ J 4:109–142

Lee L-F (2003) Best spatial two-stage least squares estimator for a spatial autoregressive model with autoregressive disturbances. Econ Rev 22:307–335

Li H, Maddala GS (1997) Bootstrapping cointegrated regressions. J Econ 80:297–318

Lin K-P, Long Z-H, Ou R (2011) The size and power of bootstrap tests for spatial dependence in linear regression models. Comput Econ 38:153–171

Maddala GS, Kim I-M (1999) Unit roots, cointegration and structural change. Cambridge University Press, Cambridge

Pedroni P (1999) Critical values for cointegration tests in heterogeneous panels with multiple regressors. Oxf Bull Econ Stat 61:653–670

Pedroni P (2004) Panel cointegration: asymptotic and finite sample properties of pooled time series tests with an application to the PPP hypothesis. Economet Theor 20:597–625

Pesaran MH (2007) A simple panel unit root test in the presence of cross section dependence. J Appl Economet 22(2):265–310

Pesaran MH (2015) Time series and panel data econometrics. Oxford University Press, Oxford

Phillips PCB, Moon H (1999) Linear regression limit theory for nonstationary panel data. Econometrica 67:1057–1011

Stock J (1987) Asymptotic properties of least squares estimates of cointegrating vectors. Econometrica 55:1035–1056

Westerlund J (2007) Testing for error correction in panel based data. Oxf Bull Econ Stat 69 (6):709–748

Yu J, de Jong R, Lee L-F (2012) Estimation for spatial dynamic panel data with fixed effects: the case of spatial cointegration. J Econ 167:16–37

Chapter 8
Cointegration in Non-Stationary Spatial Panel Data

8.1 Introduction

In Chap. 6 we argued that spatial VAR models (SpVAR) cannot be used to test structural hypotheses because the structural parameters are under identified. We also argued that structural SpVAR models, like their structural VAR counterparts (SVAR) discussed in Chap. 2, rely on untestable identifying restrictions, and provide at best narratives about the data. Moreover, since the data in VAR models must be stationary, and in practice VAR models are estimated with differenced data, we showed that structural hypotheses cannot be tested using differenced data because economic theory is mainly about levels.

In Chap. 2 we argued that this methodological impasse was resolved by cointegration theory to test hypotheses involving nonstationary time series data in levels. In Chap. 7 we proposed spatial panel cointegration theory to test hypotheses involving nonstationary spatial panel data in levels. In the case of nonstationary spatial panel data, a structural hypothesis is corroborated when the variables concerned are panel cointegrated. In spatial data, the variables concerned include spatial lagged variables. If the variables are cointegrated the structural hypothesis is corroborated. In this event, these variables must be related through error correction. Whereas cointegration is concerned with the long-run temporal relation between the variables concerned, error correction is concerned with the short-term temporal dynamic relations between them. A spatial vector autoregression model (SpVECM) integrates the long-term and short-term relationships between the variables concerned, and therefore provides a complete account of the spatial and temporal relationships between them.

In this and the next chapter, we provide empirical illustrations of the methodological ideas developed in Chap. 7. Our focus in this chapter is on spatial panel cointegration. Our focus in Chap. 9 is on spatial error correction. These empirical illustrations concern the housing market and use nonstationary spatial panel data for

M. Beenstock, D. Felsenstein, *The Econometric Analysis of Non-Stationary Spatial Panel Data*, Advances in Spatial Science,
https://doi.org/10.1007/978-3-030-03614-0_8

Israel. To these ends, we focus on two key variables. The first is concerned with the determination of house prices, and the second is concerned with housing construction. The econometric analysis of national house prices has a long history dating back to the 1960s (Smith 1969). By contrast, the econometric analysis of regional house prices has a much shorter history in which most authors ignore spatial econometric issues (Malpezzi 1999; Capozza et al. 2004; Gallin 2003; Fernandez-Kranz and Hon 2006). Holly et al. (2010) focus upon spatial econometric methodology but there are no spatial dynamics in the hypothesis that they test. Their central specification is that regional house prices vary directly with national house prices, regional income and national income. More recently, Bailey et al. (2016) extended this analysis to the estimation of spatial dynamics.

Cameron et al. (2006), rightly point out, "Regional house price models are not just national house price models with regional data substituted for national data." In their model households take relative house prices between regions into consideration in choosing where to live, thereby inducing spatial dependence in regional house prices. They use regional panel data for UK house prices to estimate error correction models in which lagged regional house prices in contiguous regions spillover temporarily onto house prices in neighboring regions. According to the regional housing model that we propose, these regional spillovers should be permanent and not merely temporary. Indeed, this is one of the key results that we obtain using spatial panel data for house prices in Israel.

As noted by DiPasquale (1999) and many others, the empirical determination of house prices has attracted much more empirical attention than the empirical determination of housing construction. "Virtually every paper written on housing supply begins with the same sentence: While there is an extensive literature on the demand for housing, far less has been written about supply." This asymmetry is puzzling because house prices vary inversely with the supply of housing as measured by the stock of housing (Smith 1969; DiPasquale and Wheaton 1994; Bar-Nathan et al. 1998). Therefore, a complete account of house price behavior requires analysis of both sides of the housing market, the demand for housing and its supply.

The extant research on housing construction has been largely concerned with national housing construction (Ball et al. 2010). We focus here on the determinants of regional housing construction. Indeed, it is possible to reject a hypothesis nationally due to aggregation bias, when the hypothesis is valid regionally. Since regional panel data are inevitably more informative than their national counterparts, it is easier to test hypotheses using regional panel data than national data.

Attention has recently been drawn to local phenomena such as topography, zoning and building regulations in the determination of housing construction (Meen and Nygaard 2011; Saiz 2010; Paciorek 2011). The price elasticity of supply of new housing is expected to vary inversely with the degree of inflexibility in zoning and land use policy as well as with topographical difficulties that raise the cost of construction. Since these parameters are quintessentially local, it makes more sense to estimate local or regional models rather than national models, which ignore local heterogeneity. In our empirical application for Israel, the key local phenomenon of interest is the supply of land rather than topography and building regulation, since the latter is set nationally, while the former is captured by regional specific effects.

As mentioned, regional models are not simply national models applied regionally. This is because regional housing markets are not independent islands. Construction is unlikely to be independent, especially if building contractors operate across locations. Building contractors may choose to operate in locations where profits are higher, or they may have local preferences so that construction in one location is not a perfect substitute for construction in another (Beenstock and Felsenstein 2015). We therefore distinguish between absolute and relative profitability in housing construction. An absolute increase in profitability in a location is hypothesized to increase construction locally. However, an increase in profitability in another location will reduce relative profitability. If construction in different locations are gross substitutes, this will reduce construction locally. On the other hand, if they are gross complements the opposite will apply. Gross complementarity may be induced, for example, by scale economies in which local building costs are affected by construction in other locations, and by advances in building technology, which encourage multi-location operations. In addition, if construction is credit constrained, this constraint may be eased when construction and cash flow increase in other locations.

We distinguish between neighboring locations and other locations since for logistical reasons construction in the former might be related differently to construction between more remote locations. In practice we use spatial econometric methods to estimate spillover effects between neighboring locations, while the latter are specified at the national level. Therefore, our main contribution is to test hypotheses about housing construction using dependent regional panel data.

Since regional housing markets preoccupy us in this and the next two chapters, in the next section we recall the key theoretical building blocks that relate regional housing markets. We present a simple two-region model to make transparent the main properties of the empirical model. This "toy" model is used to determine short-term and steady-state equilibria induced by the gestation lag in construction and the longevity of the housing stock. The toy model is used also to characterize the temporal and spatial diffusion of exogenous shocks to regional housing markets.

We present two types of empirical illustration of regional housing markets. In the first, the analysis refers to a partial equilibrium in which conditioning variables, such as population, income and capital are assumed to be given. In the second, the analysis refers to spatial general equilibrium in which these variables are assumed to be determined along with house prices and housing construction. The latter allows for the fact that house prices may induce inward and outward migration, which in turn will affect wages and capital through internal capital mobility. We think that partial equilibrium analyses are helpful in revealing the underlying forces within regional housing markets, whereas the spatial general equilibrium analysis is essential for studying the relation between housing, labor and capital markets.

8.2 Toy Model

The population (POP) is fixed and lives in two regions A and B, hence $POP = POP_A + POP_B$, where POP_A and POP_B are exogenous. Since the model is symmetric, the specification of the model refers to region A. The housing stocks (H) are quasi-fixed at the beginning of period t and are measured in square meters:

$$H_{At} = \delta H_{At-1} + S_{At-1} \tag{8.1}$$

where S denotes housing construction and δ denotes the rate of depreciation. Housing construction during period $t-1$ is completed by the beginning of period t, i.e. the gestation lag in housing construction is one period. Note that Greek and Latin letters in this section do not conform to the legend in Chap. 1.

Housing construction is hypothesized to vary directly with profitability as measured by house prices minus construction costs. Building contractors decide where to build according to relative profitability in A and B, i.e. there is spatial substitutability in housing construction. Construction during period t is determined according to:

$$S_{At} = \alpha + \beta(P_{At} - C_t) - \gamma(P_{Bt} - C_t) + \psi S_{Bt} \tag{8.2}$$

where P denotes house prices per square meter, C denotes unit construction costs assumed to be the same in A and B, and $\gamma < \beta$ allows for imperfect substitution between construction in A and B. The coefficient $0 < \psi < 1$ captures potential spillover effects in construction from B to A induced by complementarities in construction. For example, capital equipment may be shared by building contractors in A and B, or the delivery of materials to A and B may be dependent. In the "standard" specification in which each housing market is an island unto itself, ψ and γ are zero. Since the model is symmetric Eq. (8.2) also applies to housing construction in B.

The demand for housing space varies directly with population and inversely with house prices per square meter. Although migration is exogenous in the toy model, we assume that if housing is more expensive in B, residents in A are prepared to pay more for their housing. This would obviously makes more sense when migration is endogenous since if house price increase in B this would induce inward migration to A. However, this assumption is not essential. Since the housing stock is quasi-fixed at the beginning of period t, house prices in A vary directly with the population and inversely with the housing stock. They also vary directly with house prices in B:

$$P_{At} = \mu + \pi POP_{At} - \theta H_{At} + \phi P_{Bt} \tag{8.3}$$

where $0 < \phi < 1$. Equation (8.3) also applies to P_B through symmetry.

The model has six state variables (P, S and H in A and B) which are dynamically related because it takes one period to build and the housing stock depreciates. This gestation lag and the stock–flow equilibria induce dynamics in the model despite the fact that structural Eqs. (8.2 and 8.3) are static.

Since by symmetry, Eqs. (8.1–8.3) also apply in B, they solve for six state variables: house prices, housing starts and housing stocks in A and B. It may be shown that their solutions are ARMA(2,2) processes. For example, the solution for the housing stock in A is:

$$H_{At} = (\omega_1 + \omega_2)H_{At-1} - \omega_1\omega_2 H_{At-2} + Z_{At-1} + (a\theta + \delta)Z_{At-2} + \theta b Z_{Bt-2} \quad (8.4)$$

Where:

$$a = \frac{\beta(1+\phi^2) - \gamma(\phi+\psi)}{(1-\phi^2)(1-\psi^2)} > 0 \quad (8.5a)$$

$$b = \frac{\gamma(1+\psi\phi) - 2\beta\phi}{(1-\phi^2)(1-\psi^2)} \gtreqless 0 \quad (8.5b)$$

$$c = \frac{1+\gamma+(1+\psi)\phi^2}{(1-\phi^2)(1-\psi^2)} > 0 \quad (8.5c)$$

where $a > b$, and

$$Z_{At} = (a-b)\mu + a\pi POP_{At} - b\pi POP_{Bt} + c[\alpha + (\gamma - \beta)C_{t-1}] \quad (8.6)$$

ω_1 and ω_2 are the roots of the characteristic equation:

$$\omega^2 + 2(a\theta+\delta)\omega + \left[(a\theta+\delta)^2 - \theta^2 b^2\right] = 0 \quad (8.7)$$

$$\omega_1 = (b-a)\theta + \delta \quad (8.8)$$

$$\omega_2 = -[(b+a)\theta + \delta] \quad (8.9)$$

The roots are real. Since δ is a fraction, stability depends on θ, a and b. Conditional on lagged housing stocks, Eq. (8.4) states that the housing stock in A varies directly with the lagged population in A since $(a - b)\pi > 0$, it varies inversely with the lagged population in B since $(b - a)\pi < 0$, and it varies inversely with the lagged cost of construction since $c(\gamma - \beta) < 0$.

Since the roots are real, convergence to equilibrium is monotonic. This equilibrium is obtained by collapsing the lag structure in Eq. (8.4) to obtain the long-run or stationary-state solution for the housing stock:

$$H_A^* = \frac{(1+a\theta+\delta)Z_A + b\theta Z_B}{(1-\omega_1)(1-\omega_2)} \quad (8.10)$$

Equation (8.10) states that the long run effect of a population increase in A on the housing stock in A is positive since $\frac{(1+a\theta+\delta)(a-b)\pi}{(1-\omega_1)(1-\omega_2)} > 0$, the long run effect of a population increase in B is negative since $\frac{(1+a\theta+\delta)(b-a)\pi}{(1-\omega_1)(1-\omega_2)} < 0$, and the long run effect of an increase in construction costs is negative since $\frac{[1+\delta+(a+b)\theta c(\gamma-\beta)]}{(1-\omega_1)(1-\omega_2)} < 0$.

Solutions for the five remaining state variables have a similar structure to Eq. (8.4), but of course the coefficients (a, b and c) are different. However, the roots ω_1 and ω_2 are the same for all variables. The toy model, simple as it is, illustrates the potential for complexity in the spatial and temporal dynamics of housing markets. Although the housing market clears instantaneously and the gestation lag is only one period, solutions for the state variables involve second order autoregressive dynamics as well as second order moving average dynamics in the exogenous variables. Also, the parameters of these equations embody domino and boomerang effects. The former include the coefficients of lagged values of POP_B, and the latter include the coefficients of the current and lagged values of POP_A. These phenomena arise in the empirical model reported below.

Since the empirical model is panel cointegrated and expectations of house prices are assumed to have no long-run effect on outcomes in the housing market, it is conveniently unnecessary to specify expectations in the model. Because house prices are nonstationary, so must expectations of house prices be nonstationary, and errors in expectations must be stationary regardless of whether they are rational or adaptive. If they are rational, errors in expectations must be random. If they are adaptive, errors in expectations must be autocorrelated. However, in either case these errors are stationary. Therefore, although expectations naturally affect the short-term dynamics of housing markets, they have no long-term effects. Consequently, the role of expectations of house prices has been ignored in the toy model, and it is also ignored in the empirical model.

The empirical model presented below differs from the toy model in several ways. First, in the toy model the gestation period for housing construction is one period whereas in the empirical model the gestation period is naturally longer and has economic underpinnings. Second, the toy model ignores the role of the government in the market for housing, whereas the empirical model does not. Third, the empirical model comprises nine regions whereas the toy model comprises only two. Nevertheless, the theoretical underpinnings of the empirical model are essentially similar to those in the toy model.

8.3 Hypotheses

Note that Greek parameters in this section are unrelated to those in the previous section.

House Prices

The basic hypothesis to be tested is that panel data for house prices vary directly with demand and inversely with supply:

$$\ln P_{it} = \alpha_i + \beta \ln Y_{it} + \psi \ln POP_{it} + \gamma \ln H_{it} + \lambda \ln \tilde{P}_{it} + \delta \ln \tilde{Y}_{it} + \mu \ln \tilde{POP}_{it} + u_{it} \tag{8.11}$$

where P_{it} denotes house prices in region i in period t, Y denotes personal disposable income, POP denotes population, H denotes the housing stock at the beginning of period t, and tildes denote spatial variables. Equation (8.11) is the counterpart to Eq. (8.5) in the toy model. The signs of all parameters are expected to be positive because they are related to demand, however, γ is expected to be negative because it relates to supply. Regional specific effects are specified to pick up unobserved regional factors, such as fixed amenities, that affect housing demand. Time specific effects may also be specified to pick up macroeconomic variables such as interest rates that affect housing demand. The basic specification in Eq. (8.11), which is derived from an inverted demand schedule for housing, dates back at least to Smith (1969) and has been used in several studies including Bar-Nathan et al. (1998).

As we have seen in Table 7.1, the data used to estimate Eq. (8.11) are nonstationary. The variables in Eq. (8.11) are spatially panel cointegrated when the error terms (u) are stationary. Had the data used to estimate Eq. (8.11) been stationary, OLS estimates of λ and perhaps other parameters would not have been consistent. It would have been necessary to estimate these parameters by ML or IV/GMM as explained in Chap. 3. However, if the data are nonstationary, OLS estimates of these parameters are consistent. Indeed, they are super-consistent as explained in Chap. 7.

Housing Starts and Completions

Housing starts are hypothesized to vary directly with profitability in housing construction as measured by house prices relative to building costs, and inversely with its spatial lag because building contractors engage in spatial substitution (Beenstock and Felsenstein 2015). The Israel Land Authority (ILA) tenders state-owned land for housing construction, which boosts housing construction in the locations concerned. The counterpart to Eq. (8.11) for housing starts is:

$$\ln S_{it} = \alpha_i + \eta \ln (P_{it}/C_{it}) + \phi \ln \left(\tilde{P}_{it}/\tilde{C}_{it}\right) + \gamma \ln (P_t/C_t) + \lambda \ln \tilde{S}_{it} + \mu Z_{it} + \pi \tilde{Z}_{it} + v_{it} \tag{8.12a}$$

where S denotes housing starts measured in square meters, P denotes house prices, C denotes building costs, Z denotes the share of ILA initiated housing construction in the total, and tildes denote spatial lags. Note that Greek parameters in Eq. (8.12a) are unrelated to those in Eq. (8.11). According to Eq. (8.12a) housing construction should vary directly with local profitability though η, and inversely with its spatial counterpart ($\phi < 0$), and directly with national profitability through γ. It should also vary directly with housing policy as measured by Z through μ and π. The variables in Eq. (8.12a) are cointegrated when v is stationary.

The stock of housing measured in square meters at the beginning of period t is defined as:

$$H_{it} = H_{it-1} + F_{it-1} - D_{it-1} \tag{8.12b}$$

where F and D denote housing completions and demolitions measured in square meters. Following Beenstock and Felsenstein (2015), housing completions vary directly with housing under construction (U) and housing starts (S), which implies that the gestation lag in housing construction is endogenous. Building contractors use housing under construction as a buffer between starts and completions; they accelerate completions when the housing market is buoyant and delay them when it is quiet:

$$F_{it} = bU_{it-1} + gS_{it} + f\tilde{F}_{it} + d\tilde{U}_{it} + s\tilde{S}_{it} + w_{it} \tag{8.12c}$$

The absence of an intercept in Eq. (8.12c) guarantees that all starts are eventually completed. This is also the reason why Eq. (8.12c) is not expressed in logarithms. Equation (8.12c) hypothesizes that there may be spatial spillovers in completions as well as in housing starts.

Finally, the dynamics of housing under construction are defined by:

$$U_{it} = U_{it-1} - F_{it-1} + S_{it-1} \tag{8.12d}$$

If S and F are difference stationary, H must be difference stationary according to Eq. (8.12b), and U must be difference stationary according to Eq. (8.12d). Consequently, Eqs. (8.12a–8.12d) are multicointegrated in the sense of Granger and Lee (1989) provided v and w are stationary. See Bar-Nathan et al. (1998) for an application to the national housing market in Israel.

Since $S = S_p + S_g$ where S_p denotes private construction unrelated to ILA, and S_g refers to ILA related construction, and $Z = S_g/S$ denotes the share of ILA related construction, it may be shown that Eq. (8.12a) implies:

$$\frac{dS_p}{dS_g} = \frac{\mu(1 - Z) - 1}{1 + \mu Z} \tag{8.12e}$$

If the numerator is negative, ILA starts crowd-out other starts. If it is positive ILA starts crowd-in other starts.

8.4 Data

The market for land and housing in Israel has some unique characteristics. First, 94% of land is publicly owned and administered under the stewardship of a public agency, the Israel Land Authority (ILA). This government body auctions land to private builders who sell houses to the public under long-term, automatically-renewable 49 year leases. Second, while house building is undertaken by the private sector, this arrangement gives the government long term control over land supply. The government uses housing construction as an instrument of regional policy. It initiates construction in specific regions by auctioning land, and subsidizing development costs in an effort to direct building in accordance with regional development priorities. Such housing construction is referred to as ILA initiated housing.

For our empirical application we use annual panel data for nine regions in Israel for the period 1987–2015. These are the regions featured in the map (Fig. 4.1) in Chap. 4. Although Israel is a small country (population in 2018 is 8.9 m) the regional population sizes are comparable to the yardstick used for defining NUTS3 regions, i.e. 150,000–800,000 population per region. Table 8.1 gives averages for key regional variables in 2000. The vector comprises four variables: real earnings, population, real house prices and the stock of housing (measured in 1000s of square meters). Descriptive statistics for these variables can be found in Table 8.1.

Figure 8.1 plots the regional panel data for population, housing starts, house prices, housing stocks, wages and ILA housing starts. Notice that the latter are unevenly distributed, and are concentrated in the periphery. This pattern results from the fact that ILA's land reserves have already been depleted in the center. Not surprisingly, all variables have grown over time, hence they cannot be stationary. It should be noted that the 1990s witnessed mass immigration from the former USSR, which had major macroeconomic implications, especially for labor and housing markets (Beenstock and Fisher 1997). The population grew in all regions, but particularly in the South where housing was cheaper. In Table 7.2 we reported three types of panel unit root tests (IPS, CIPS, SpIPS) for these and other variables, which suggest that the data plotted in Fig. 8.1 are nonstationary but are difference stationary.

Table 8.1 Descriptive statistics–regional averages, 2000

	Pop (1000s)	Monthly earnings (Shekels)	House prices (1991 prices)	Housing stock (square meters, millions)
Center	847.70	3658.25	250.23	20,206.5
Dan	676.30	3045.94	285.15	20,720.9
Haifa	351.70	3355.99	237.54	11,109.3
Jerusalem	823.50	3134.52	307.41	17,385.1
Krayot	162.20	2587.46	211.19	4828.3
North	1147.10	2915.78	167.87	21,747.1
Sharon	563.40	2639.25	291.24	14,379.3
South	761.10	2743.49	168.57	15,917.0
Tel Aviv	356.20	4088.24	358.11	14,529.8

8.5 Results

The equations to be estimated comprise Eqs. (8.11, 8.12a and 8.12c). We report here results from Beenstock and Felsenstein (2010, 2015) and from Beenstock et al (2018). We continue to define the spatial connectivity matrix W as in Chap. 7 in terms of relative built-up land in 1990 and distance so that W is asymmetric; bigger regions carry a larger weight than their smaller counterparts.

House Prices

In Chap. 7 we noted that cointegration may be local, spatial or global. Model A in Table 8.2 tests for local cointegration. Since parameter estimates from nonstationary data typically have nonstandard distributions, statistical significance cannot be measured by t-tests, which is measured instead by cointegration tests. The critical value for the group-t cointegration test statistic according to Pedroni (1999) is −2.02. The calculated value is just equal to the critical value so that house prices,

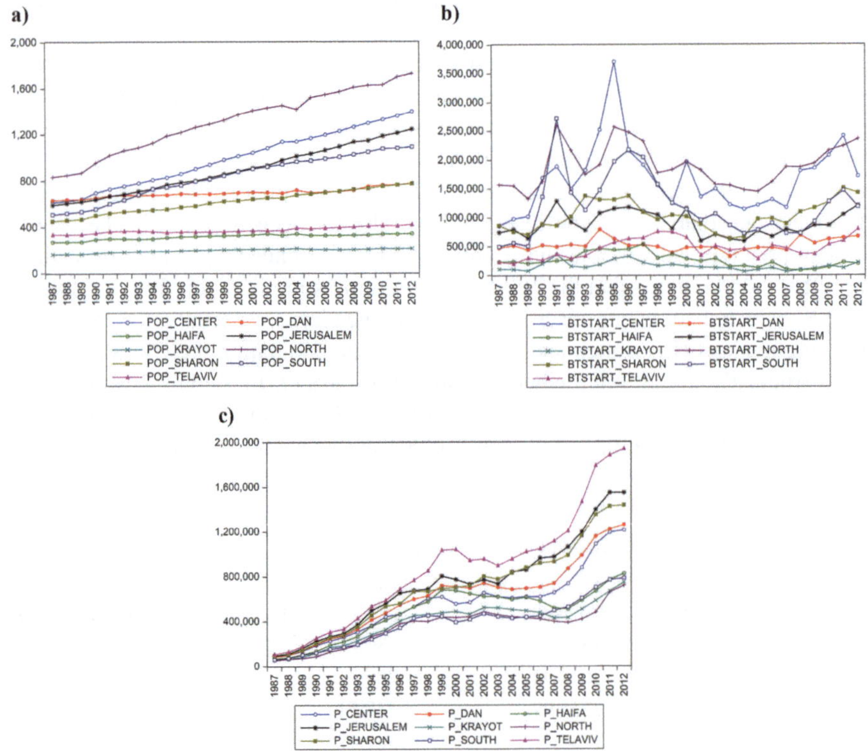

Fig. 8.1 Regional panel data: 1987–2012. (**a**) Population (1000s). (**b**) Housing starts (1000s of square meters). (**c**) House prices (Shekels at 1991 prices), (**d**) Housing stocks (1000s of square meters). (**e**) Real wages (monthly at 1991 prices). (**f**) Housing starts initiated by ILA (1000s of square meters)

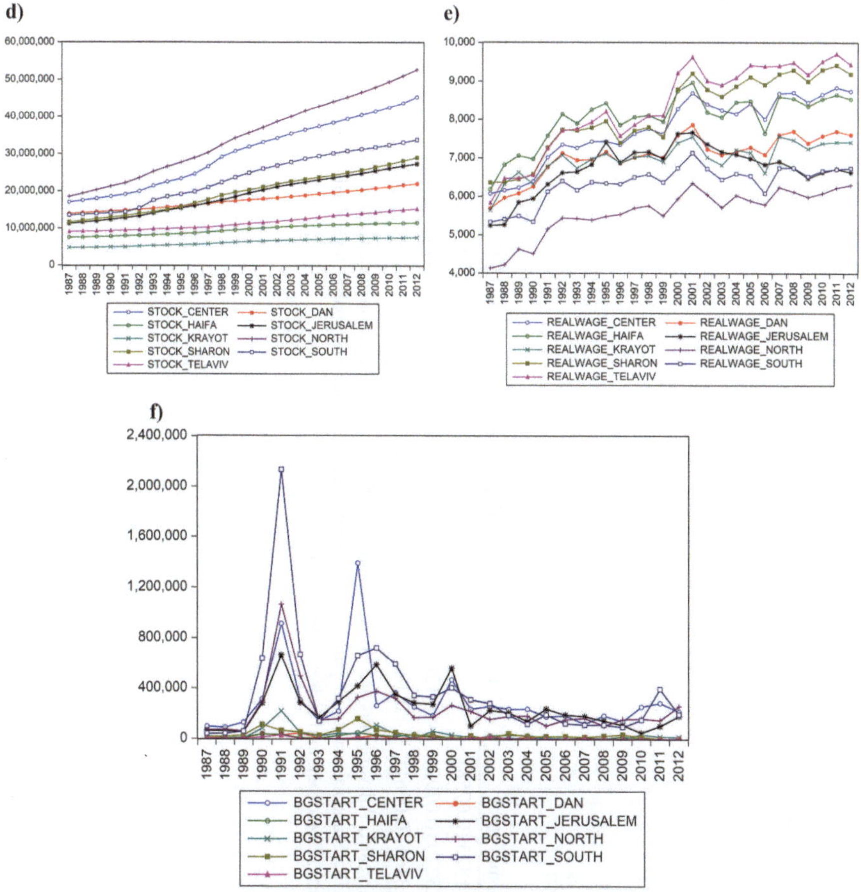

Fig. 8.1 (continued)

population, income and the housing stock appear to be marginally panel cointegrated. Note, however, that Pedroni's test statistic is asymptotic with respect to T but refers to fixed N = 9. The finite sample properties with respect to T of the group-t cointegration test statistic and other test statistics are oversized when T < 120 and underpowered when T < 50 for H_0: $\tau = 1$ (Pedroni 2004). (Recall that τ denotes AR coefficients for residuals.) When T = N = 20 and $\tau = 0.9$ its power is about 65% at p = 0.05. When τ is smaller the power is naturally greater. Fortunately, in our case τ turns out to be small.

In our case T = 18 years. The critical value of the group-t cointegration test statistic for T = 18 is unknown, but it is has to be smaller (more negative) than −2.02. This means that model A is most probably not cointegrated. Also, we note that the error terms of the regional DF cointegration test statistics are spatially correlated, which suggests that the specification of spatial lags might be appropriate.

Table 8.2 House prices: panel cointegration tests

Model	Population	Income	Housing stock	House prices*	Population*	GADF	SpGrho
A	0.9140 (0.0926)	0.1163 (0.0485)	0.1325 (0.0758)			−2.02 *−2.02*	
B	1.4661 (0.0793)	0.0181 (0.0386)	−0.5220 (0.0793)	0.1204 (0.0027)		−2.47 *−2.47*	
C	1.1370 (0.0712)	0.0363 (0.0326)	−0.3165 (0.0661)	0.1841 (0.0061)	−0.0727 (0.0074)	−3.11 *−2.82*	0.17 *0.79*

Dependent variable is the ln real house prices in region i in year t. All variables are expressed in logarithms. Annual data for nine regions during 1987–2004 (NT = 162). Estimated with fixed regional effects and SUR. Standard errors in parentheses. Asterisked variables are spatial lags. Critical value of panel cointegration test statistics in italics (GADF, SpGrho). Source: Beenstock and Felsenstein (2010)

We use a spatial weighting matrix that takes account of both relative size and distance. Hence:

$$w_{ij} = \frac{POP_j}{POP_i + POP_j} \times \frac{1}{d_{ij}}$$

where POP denotes the sample-mean population in the data, and d_{ij} is the Euclidean distance between i and j. The spatial weights are asymmetric ($w_{ij} \neq w_{ji}$) according to relative population sizes, so that a big region affects its small neighbor by more than does a small region affect its big neighbor. Apart from this, the effect of more distant neighbors is smaller. We follow the convention of normalizing the row sum of weights to one by dividing w_{ij} by its mean for i.

In model B we add a spatial lag in house prices. The group-t statistic improves (becomes more negative), but the critical value becomes more negative too so that the cointegration test statistic continues to be border-line. However, the coefficient on the housing stock is negative in model B instead of positive in model A. According to economic theory this coefficient should be negative, because house prices should vary inversely with the supply of the housing. The estimated long run spatial lag coefficient on house prices is positive in model B. The spatial lag coefficient is 0.12, which implies that if house prices in neighboring regions increase by 1% the spillover effect onto the region is 0.12%.

In model C we extend model B by adding a spatial lag in population, which induces a discrete fall in the cointegration test statistic. As a result, the cointegration test statistic ceases to be border-line; the group ADF Statistic (GADF) is smaller than its critical value, suggesting that model C is panel cointegrated. So does the SpGrho (spatial group-rho) statistic introduced in Chap. 7, which allows for spatial dependence between the error terms, indicate that the residuals are stationary. Group rho is only 0.17, when its critical value is 0.79. According to model C the direct elasticity of house prices with respect to the local population is 1.14 and with respect to the neighboring population it is −0.07. The direct elasticity with respect to the housing stock is negative (−0.32) and the spatial lag increases to 0.18. The income elasticity, which was 0.12 in model A is only 0.04 in model C.

Since Eq. (8.11) is an inverted demand schedule for housing, model C implies that the demand for housing in region i in year t is:

$$\begin{aligned} \ln H_{it} = {} & \frac{\alpha_i}{0.32} - 3.16 \ln P_{it} + 0.56 \ln \tilde{P}_{it} + 3.59 \ln POP_{it} \\ & -0.23 \ln P\tilde{O}P_{it} + 0.11 \ln Y_{it} \end{aligned} \tag{8.13}$$

The demand for housing varies inversely with respect to local house prices with a large absolute elasticity (−3.16), and it varies directly with house prices in neighboring regions with an elasticity of 0.59. Housing demand is elastic with respect to local population, but varies inversely with population in neighboring regions. Finally, the local income elasticity of demand for housing is modest (0.11).

The fixed regional effects are quite diverse. In the case of model C, for example, the log difference between the largest fixed effect (Tel Aviv) and the smallest (Krayot) is 0.803, which implies that controlling for covariates housing in Tel Aviv is more than twice as expensive (120%) as in Krayot. The estimated fixed effects polarize into expensive regions (Tel Aviv, Dan, Jerusalem, Center and Sharon) and cheap regions (Krayot, South, and North) with Haifa in the middle.

Housing Starts

Unfortunately data on building costs (C) are only available nationally. This may not matter for materials whose prices are likely to be similar across the country (especially a small country), but it may matter for labor costs. Gyourko and Saiz (2006) report that construction costs vary widely in the United States. However, in a small country, such as Israel, this issue is likely to be less important. We assume, *force majeure*, that regional building costs have a national component, a fixed region specific component (c_i) and a random component (s_{it}), i.e. $C_{it} = C_i + C_t + s_{it}$ in which case C_i is absorbed into the specific effect in Eq. (8.12a), s_{it} is absorbed into the residual, and C_t replaces C_{it} in Eq. (8.12a). If the data were stationary, the latter would induce attenuation bias in the parameter estimates of Eq. (8.12a). However, this problem is mitigated if the data are nonstationary due to super-consistency.

The price of land should also be a component of C. In common with most countries there are no systematic data on land prices in Israel. If relative land prices remained unchanged the unobserved effect of land prices would be picked-up by the fixed effect in Eq. (8.12a), and estimates of the supply elasticities in Eq. (8.12a) would be consistent. If relative land prices varied directly with house prices these elasticities would be under-estimated. However, if relative land prices happened to be stationary these estimates would be consistent since an omitted variable that is stationary is asymptotically independent of house prices, which are nonstationary.

Although there are no data on land prices for the nine regions in the study, the auction prices of the winning tenders for ILA residential building rights are published. We have used these data to construct regional land price indices for six regions during 1996–2012, which are plotted in Fig. 8.2. These data suggest that relative regional land prices have remained reasonably stable over time. The Dickey Fuller statistic for the regression residuals of the logarithms of land prices between each other is −4.14, suggesting that these data are cointegrated. Therefore, the absence of systematic data on land prices might not, in practice, be serious since changes in relative land prices are stationary. Panel unit root tests for logarithms of these variables have already been reported on Table 7.2 from which we conclude that the data are nonstationary but are difference stationary.

We begin by estimating Eq. (8.12a) under the assumption that each region is an island unto itself. Hence, in Eq. (8.12a) we impose the restrictions $\phi = \lambda = \pi = \gamma = 0$. This specification (standard model) assumes that each region in the panel behaves as it might have done had spatial dependence been ignored. The first three restrictions assume that spatial spillovers don't matter, while the latter assumes that local construction is independent of national construction. Subsequently, we relax the latter restriction and estimate γ. We refer to this as the "national spillover model".

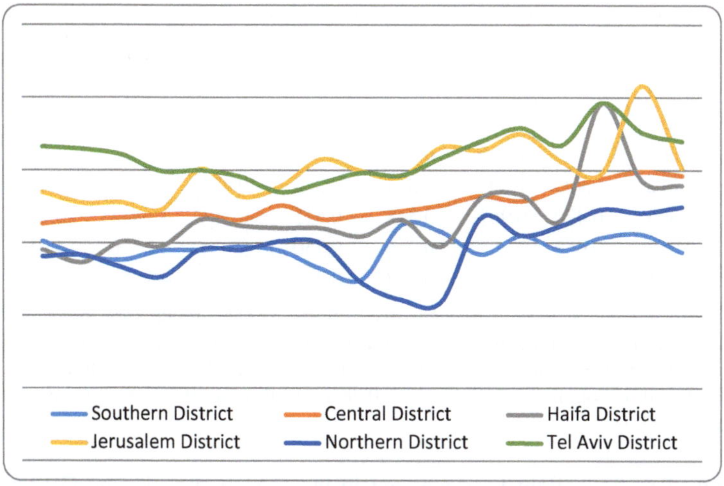

Fig. 8.2 Land prices

Thereafter, we relax the spatial restrictions, but retain the restriction $\gamma = 0$ (the spatial spillover model). Finally, all restrictions are relaxed (the general spillover model).

There are several possible outcomes. First, the standard model is supported by the data, and spatial and national spillovers are empirically unimportant. Second, the standard model is supported by the data but spillover models (national and/or spatial) are empirically superior. Third, the standard model is not supported by the data but the models with spillover are supported by the data. Finally, none of the models are supported by the data. We show that the general spillover model is supported by the data, whereas the standard model and the national spillover model are not supported by the data.

We estimate Eq. (8.12a) with regional fixed effects by SUR. The latter allows the residuals (v_{it}) to be correlated, but not necessarily spatially correlated. Since the data are nonstationary the parameter estimates have non-standard distributions, in which case t-statistics do not indicate statistical significance unless the covariates happen to be strictly exogenous, which is not the case here. We therefore test for statistical significance by dropping variables from the model. If this induces cointegration failure we conclude that the variable or variables concerned are statistically significant.

Results for housing starts are reported in Table 8.3. Model 1 refers to the standard model with no spatial or national spillovers. The estimated price elasticity of supply is 0.247 and the estimate of μ implies that ILA initiated construction increases total construction, and that according to Eq. (8.12e) crowding-in occurs when the share of ILA starts is less than 33%. Model 1 is cointegrated according to all three panel cointegration test statistics. Recall that t-statistics are not reported because, as explained, the parameter estimates have non-standard distributions.

Model 2 refers to the national spillover model. The local price elasticity increases from 0.247 in model 1 to 0.428 and the national price elasticity is slightly negative.

Table 8.3 Estimates of Eq. (8.12c): housing starts (logarithms)

Model	P_i/C	P/C	Z	$\tilde{P}_i/C$	$\tilde{S}$	$\tilde{Z}$	GADF	GPP	PEC
1	0.247		1.488				−3.00	−3.61	−5.65
2	0.428	−0.031	1.321				−3.14	−3.56	−3.06
3	0.355		1.245	−0.257	0.651	−0.391	−3.45	−3.94	−4.52
4	0.312	0.495	1.098	−0.594	0.584	−0.433	−3.46	−3.87	−3.94
5	0.305	0.470	0.967	−0.548	0.515		−3.43	−3.82	−3.83
6	0.258	0.668		−0.716	0.730		−3.576	−4.010	−5.37
7	0.315			0.877	−0.265		−3.45	−4.03	

Notes: Estimation by SUR with regional fixed effects. GADF: group (first order) ADF panel cointegration z-statistic. GPP: group (first order) Phillips–Perron panel cointegration z-statistic. Their one-sided critical value is −1.65 at $p = 0.05$. PEC: Panel error correction statistic (P_τ in Westerlund 2007). For model 4 SpGrho = 0.78 (critical value 0.78). Source: Beenstock and Felsenstein (2015)

Although there is a slight improvement in the GADF statistic, the GPP and PEC cointegration test statistics deteriorate, suggesting that model 1 is preferable to model 2. Model 3 refers to the spatial spillover model. The local price elasticity is 0.355 and the spatial price elasticity is −0.257. This spatial elasticity implies that housing construction in neighboring regions and local construction are close but imperfect substitutes. Indeed, what matters is largely the relative price between local house prices and house prices in neighboring regions. The same phenomenon applies to ILA related housing construction; the local effect is positive (1.245) but the spatial effect is negative (−0.391). Therefore, ILA related construction in neighboring regions induces contractors to transfer their business from the locality to its neighbors. Model 3 includes a spatial lagged dependent variable (0.651) implying positive spillover from neighboring construction to local construction. It also implies that the unconditional elasticities are 2.86 times larger than their conditional counterparts. The GADF and GPP statistics of model 3 improve on their counterparts in model 1. Recall that marginal improvements in $z = N(0,1)$ become progressively harder as z becomes more negative. However, the PEC statistic is weaker.

Model 4 specifies all the variables in Eq. (8.2) and serves as an unrestricted specification of the general spillover model. The local price elasticity of supply in model 1 is 0.312, the national price elasticity is 0.495, and the spatial price elasticity is −0.594. The latter shows that spatial substitution in construction is strong, while the former shows that national and local construction are complements. The sum[1] of these elasticities (0.213) is similar to the local elasticity in model 1. The estimate of μ (1.098) means that ILA construction crowds-in private construction provided the ILA share in starts is less than 9%. The spatial lag coefficient (λ) is slightly larger than a half, so that the unconditional elasticities are slightly less than twice as large as

[1]The total elasticities are larger than this sum because of the spatial lagged dependent variable. The total elasticity is calculated below.

their conditional counterparts. Finally because π is negative, ILA starts have a negative spatial spillover effect. The cointegration test statistics (GADF and GPP) greatly exceed their critical values, but are similar to their counterparts in model 3. Since the only difference between models 3 and 4 relates to national profitability (γ), this suggests that γ is not statistically significant. The spatial group rho statistic (0.78) equals its critical value, suggesting that GADF, GPP and PEC cointegration test statistics, which ignore spatial dependence between the panel residuals have p-values that are too small.

Table 8.3 reports a number of restricted models, which indicate that the group panel cointegration test statistics are insensitive to the various restrictions tested. Model 6 omits ILA related building incentives; the cointegration test statistics hardly change, suggesting that these incentives do not significantly affect construction. Finally, Model 7 differs from other spatial models in that ϕ is positive and λ is negative; local construction varies directly with prices nearby, but there is negative spillover between local and nearby construction.

Since all the models in Table 8.3 are panel cointegrated, we are somewhat spoiled for choice. But some are more cointegrated than others in the sense that their p-values are smaller, especially models 3–7, which are spatial. Although we cannot rule out the standard model in favor of models with spatial spillover, the latter models are more statistically significant because they have smaller p-values.

Figure 8.3 plots the estimated residuals of model 4 in Table 8.3.This spaghetti graph indicates that the residuals, on the whole, mean-revert to zero. However, the residuals for Haifa are an exception, as indicated by the (first order) ADF and PP statistics reported in Table 8.4. Table 8.4 also shows that there is widespread regional heterogeneity in these mean-reverting tendencies; it is strongest in Sharon and the South and it is weakest in Haifa and the North. Table 8.4 further shows widespread heterogeneity in regional fixed effects. The largest fixed effect is, not

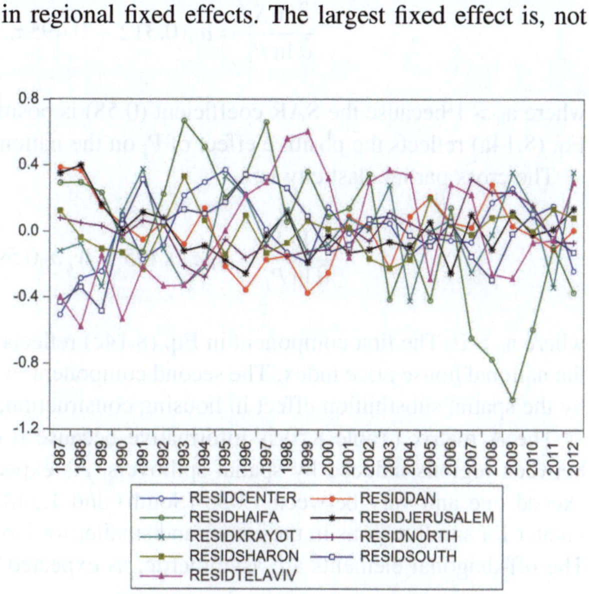

Fig. 8.3 Residuals from model 4 in Table 8.3

Table 8.4 Regional heterogeneity (Table 8.3, model 4)

	Fixed effect	ADF	PP
Jerusalem	0.027	−2.95	−3.234
Haifa	−0.728	−1.061	−1.700
Tel Aviv	−0.648	−2.007	−2.560
Dan	−0.262	−2.561	−2.840
Center	0.972	−1.524	−2.553
South	0.369	−3.081	−2.615
Sharon	0.329	−3.171	−2.673
North	1.349	−1.112	−1.799
Krayot	−1.410	−1.961	−3.100

surprisingly, in the North where the population is largest, and it is smallest in Krayot where the population is smallest.

Using Model 4 in Table 8.3, the solution for the N vector of housing starts (S) in year t is:

$$\begin{aligned} \ln S_t &= A\left[fe + (0.312\mathrm{I}_N + 0.495\pi - 0.594W)\ln\left(\frac{P}{C}\right)_t + (1.1\mathrm{I}_N - 0.43W)Z_t\right] \\ A &= (\mathrm{I}_N - 0.58W)^{-1} \end{aligned} \tag{8.14a}$$

where fe is an N-vector of fixed effects, π is the transpose of an N-vector of fixed regional weights in the national house price index, and A is an N × N matrix with elements a_{ij}. The own partial price elasticity is:

$$\frac{\partial \ln S_i}{\partial \ln P_i} = a_{ii}(0.312 + 0.495\pi_i) \tag{8.14b}$$

where $a_{ii} > 1$ because the SAR coefficient (0.58) is positive. The second element in Eq. (8.14a) reflects the positive effect of P_i on the national house price index.

The cross partial elasticity is:

$$\frac{\partial \ln S_i}{\partial \ln P_j} = a_{ii}\pi_j 0.495 - w_{ij}a_{ij}0.594 \tag{8.14c}$$

where $a_{ij} > 0$. The first component in Eq. (8.14c) reflects the positive effect of P_j on the national house price index. The second component, which is negative, is induced by the spatial substitution effect in housing construction.

The A matrix (Table 8.5) is informative because it quantifies the connectivity between regions induced by spatial spillovers. As expected the diagonal elements exceed one and vary between 1.036 (South) and 1.248 (Dan). They are naturally greater for small regions in the center and smaller for large regions in the periphery. The off-diagonal elements are asymmetric, as expected because W is asymmetric.

Table 8.5 The A matrix for housing starts

	Krayot	Jerusalem	TA	Haifa	Dan	Center	South	Sharon	North
Krayot	1.084	0.071	0.143	0.340	0.193	0.189	0.057	0.110	0.178
Jerusalem	0.050	1.048	0.207	0.075	0.308	0.315	0.099	0.098	0.165
Tel Aviv	0.037	0.077	1.132	0.056	0.414	0.357	0.055	0.099	0.139
Haifa	0.241	0.077	0.154	1.098	0.208	0.205	0.060	0.117	0.203
Dan	0.030	0.070	0.254	0.046	1.248	0.475	0.050	0.075	0.115
Center	0.031	0.075	0.023	0.048	0.500	1.234	0.055	0.075	0.121
South	0.053	0.132	0.198	0.079	0.294	0.309	1.036	0.096	0.166
Sharon	0.060	0.077	0.209	0.090	0.261	0.247	0.056	1.075	0.288
North	0.065	0.088	0.199	0.106	0.268	0.270	0.066	0.195	1.105

For example, the spillover from Tel Aviv to Jerusalem (0.207) is larger than the spillover from Jerusalem to Tel Aviv (0.077). Not surprisingly, spillover effects are larger in small regions. The largest spillover effects are between Center and Dan (0.5 and 0.475). The smallest (0.03) are for Krayot, which is the smallest region.

The diagonal of Table 8.6 reports calculations for own price elasticities using Eq. (8.14b) and the off-diagonal elements report calculations for cross price elasticities using Eq. (8.14c). The own-price elasticities range between 0.36 (Krayot) and 0.487 (Center). These elasticities vary with their elements in matrix A and because the weights (π) of regional house prices in national house prices vary by region. The average direct elasticity obtained by averaging the trace of Table 8.6 is 0.416. The cross price elasticities are negative as expected because of spatial substitution in construction, but some of them are positive. For example, the elasticity of starts in Dan with respect to house prices in South is 0.017. This effect comprises a negative substitution effect and a positive national house price effect in which the latter dominates the former. The cross-price elasticities are asymmetric and range between −0.43 (Center–Dan) and 0.017. The largest (most negative) elasticities are with respect to Dan and Center. The average cross elasticity obtained by averaging the off-diagonal elements in Table 8.6 is −0.107.

Z, the share of ILA related starts in housing starts, proxies ILA incentives to engage in housing construction. ILA starts crowd-out private starts if contractors cut back private construction to build ILA related housing projects. Alternatively, ILA starts crowd-in private starts if contractors engage in more private starts. Since ILA related contracts are subsidized, they might ease the cash-flow of credit-constrained contractors, who respond by engaging in more private starts rather than less. Equation (8.12e) implies that crowding-out occurs if the share of ILA related starts exceeds 14.2%, and crowding-in occurs otherwise.

Model 4 in Table 8.3 is panel cointegrated according to the z statistic for GADF (−3.46), which is clearly smaller than its one-tailed critical value (−1.64). This test statistic assumes that the panel units are independent. The SpGrho statistics have larger p-values than GADF, but all p-values are less than 0.05. Therefore model 4 is spatially panel cointegrated.

Table 8.6 Price elasticities of housing starts

	Krayot	Jerusalem	TA	Haifa	Dan	Center	South	Sharon	North
Krayot	0.36	0.01	−0.11	−0.31	−0.12	−0.09	0.01	−0.06	−0.07
Jerusalem	−0.04	0.405	−0.17	−0.04	−0.24	−0.22	−0.03	−0.05	−0.05
Tel Aviv	−0.02	−0.005	0.393	−0.02	−0.35	−0.26	0.01	−0.05	−0.03
Haifa	−0.23	−0.004	−0.12	0.380	−0.14	−0.11	0.007	−0.07	−0.09
Dan	−0.017	0.002	−0.22	−0.01	0.466	−0.38	0.017	−0.023	−0.002
Center	−0.018	−0.003	−0.20	−0.02	−0.43	0.487	0.012	−0.023	−0.008
South	−0.039	−0.061	−0.17	−0.05	−0.23	−0.21	0.397	−0.045	−0.053
Sharon	−0.047	−0.005	−0.18	−0.06	−0.19	−0.153	0.011	0.393	−0.17
North	−0.053	−0.016	−0.17	−0.08	−0.20	−0.176	0.011	−0.143	0.464

Housing Completions

Estimates of Eq. (8.12c) for housing completions are reported in Table 8.7. Model 1 is an unrestricted model with spatial spillovers. It states that contractors complete annually 43% of outstanding housing under construction, and that current completions vary directly with starts. For every 10 m^2 of starts there is an additional 1.7 m^2 of completions. The spatial lag coefficient is 0.504, implying that completions increase with completions in neighboring regions. There are negative spatial spillovers from buildings under construction and starts, implying that contractors substitute completions between regions. The cointegration test statistics are highly significant. Indeed, their p-values are even smaller than their counterparts in Table 8.3.

Model 2 shows that dropping the spatial variables makes no difference to the cointegration test statistics. Therefore, these spatial variables are not statistically significant. By contrast, in Table 8.2 dropping spatial variables raised the p-values of the cointegration tests. We also carried out some further tests. For example, in model 2 completions vary directly with local house prices, suggesting that contractors accelerate completions when building is more profitable. However, the cointegration test statistics do not change. The spatial group rho statistic is 0.56 which is well below its critical value of 0.79. As in Table 8.3 the p-value of the SpGrho spatial panel cointegration test statistic is larger than its counterparts, which ignore spatial dependence. Model 3 is identical to model 2 except it uses private housing starts rather than total housing starts. The effect of private housing starts on completions is greater than total starts, however, there is a slight deterioration in the panel cointegration test statistics.

The completion lag implied by model 2 is represented in Table 8.8. It follows a cohort of 100 additional starts occurring in year 0. What matters is not the completion of these particular houses, but the completion of housing as a whole when contractors use housing under construction as a buffer. It is for this reason that there is an immediate effect on completions in year 0; these starts induce contractors to complete housing already under construction more rapidly. Completions peak in year1 by which the completions rate is 52.7%. Subsequently, the completion rate increases towards 100%. The mean lag is 2.7 years.

Table 8.7 The housing completions model

Model	U	S	$\tilde{C}$	$\tilde{U}$	$\tilde{S}$	GADF	GPP	PEC	SpGrho
1	0.432	0.169	0.504	−0.074	−0.226	−4.79	−5.16	−9.28	
2	0.432	0.168				−4.73	−5.12	−10.9	0.56
3	0.401	0.276[a]				−4.59	−4.99		

Notes: See notes to Table 8.2
[a]Private housing starts

Table 8.8 The distribution of completions

Year	0	1	2	3	4	5
Completions	16.8	35.9	20.4	11.6	6.6	4.0
Completion rate	16.8	52.7	73.1	84.7	91.3	95.3

8.6 Spatial General Equilibrium

We now turn to the relation between housing, labor and capital markets in spatial general equilibrium. In this section the equations for housing starts, housing completions and house prices are embedded in an SGE model for Israel in which regional employment, population, wages and capital are endogenous. Therefore, population and wages that were assumed to be exogenous in the previous section are endogenous. Because of super-consistency the status of these variables does not matter for inference. For example, in Eq. (8.11) it does not matter that internal migration motivated by regional wage and house price differentials imply that regional house prices and populations are not independent.

The SGE model provides further opportunity to illustrate the spatial panel cointegration methods proposed in Chap. 7. It also includes some extensions presented in Chap. 7 that were not featured in the previous section. These include bootstrapped confidence intervals for the parameter estimates in cointegrating vectors, and tests for weak exogeneity. However, it is first necessary to provide the theoretical context in which housing markets are embedded in SGE models.

This section draws on Beenstock et al. (2018) where we note that two theoretical paradigms have dominated SGE theory. The first, based on Roback (1982), assumes that product markets are perfectly competitive and trade is frictionless. The second, based on Krugman (1991), assumes that product markets are imperfectly competitive and transport costs are salient. This model is known as the New Economic Geography Model, or NEG for short. Both paradigms assume that capital and labor are perfectly mobile, except unskilled labor is assumed to be immobile in NEG. In NEG transport costs and pecuniary scale economies drive the spatial distribution of economic activity and population. In Roback, the spatial distribution of economic activity and population are driven by amenities and the zoning of land. Our SGE model is inspired by Roback rather than NEG.

Theory

We summarize the SGE model's main theoretical features by assuming that a region is "small and open" so that what happens in the region depends on what happens outside it, but not the opposite way around. The region is open to trade, internal labor migration, and internal capital mobility. Land is zoned for residential or commercial purposes, and because housing density is endogenous, the supply of housing space varies directly with residential land and house prices, and inversely with building costs. Although housing is immobile, regional housing markets are related on the supply side because building contractors operate in different regional housing markets, and on the demand side through internal migration. If it becomes more profitable to build elsewhere, building contractors will reduce their activity in the region. The demand for housing space varies directly with population and income in the region and inversely with house prices. House prices in the region are determined by market clearing where the demand for housing space equals the stock of housing space.

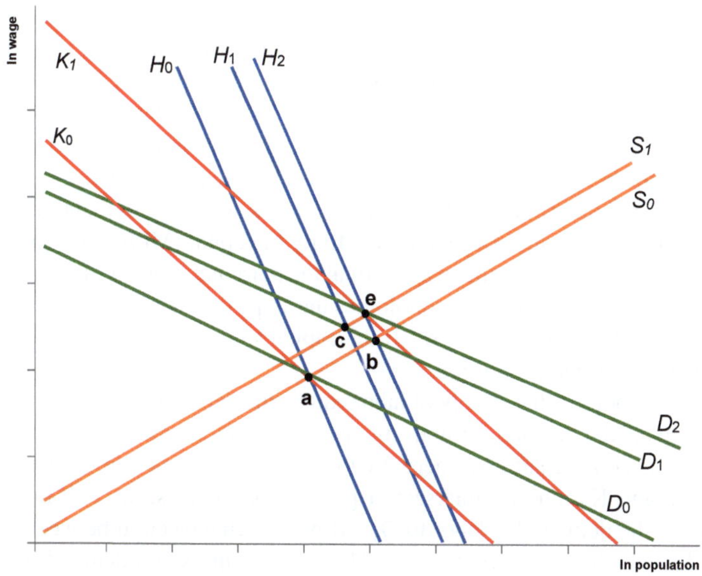

Fig. 8.4 Spatial general equilibrium

Labor demand in the region varies directly with the capital stock and land zoned for commerce, and it varies inversely with real wages. The supply of labor in the region varies directly with relative wages, and inversely with relative house prices due to internal migration. Workers are assumed to supply one unit of labor, hence the participation ratio is determined outside the model.

In Fig. 8.4 the logarithms of wages and the population of working age (POP) are measured on the vertical and horizontal axes. Since the participation ratio is exogenous, the horizontal axis measures the logarithm of employment. Schedule D_0 denotes the regional demand schedule for labor.[2] It slopes downwards, and its location varies directly with land zoned for commercial purposes, the capital stock and total factor productivity (TFP). Schedule S_0 denotes the regional supply schedule of labor; it slopes upwards because internal migration varies directly with wages, and its location contracts if wages increase elsewhere, or if house prices become relatively expensive. The region's share of the national population varies directly with real wages (wages adjusted for local house prices) in the region relative to real wages elsewhere.

Schedule H_0 plots the combinations of wages and population that support regional house prices at their equilibrium level (P_o). It slopes downwards because the demand for housing space varies directly with wages and population, and is flatter the greater the income elasticity of demand for housing space. Above schedule

[2]Because the participation ratio is exogenous employment is proportionate to the population of working age.

H there is an excess demand for housing, which raises house prices and causes schedule H to shift upwards by an extent which varies inversely with the price elasticity of demand for housing. Schedule H shifts upwards if land zoned for housing increases, because P_o is supported by larger combinations of wages and population. Schedule H shifts downwards if house prices and land zoned for housing increases elsewhere because builders prefer to construct elsewhere.

Schedule K_0 plots the combinations of wages and employment (population), which support a constant marginal productivity of capital (MPK) for a given capital stock. It is drawn assuming that wages equal the marginal product of labor. It may be shown that for Cobb–Douglas technologies the slope of schedule K is -1 (as drawn) and the slope of schedule D is $-\alpha$.[3] If the capital stock increases, schedule K shifts outwards by the same proportion.

Initially, at point a, the supply of labor equals the demand for labor, the supply of housing equals the demand for housing, and the marginal product of capital (MPK) is equal to its counterpart elsewhere if capital is perfectly mobile. Hence schedules D_0, S_0, H_0 and K_0 initially intersect at point a. An increase in TFP in the region would raise the demand for labor to D_1. At point b (intersection between schedules D_1 and S_o, which lies above schedule H_0) there is an excess demand for housing because both wages and population have increased. The increase in house prices shifts schedule H_o to H_1 and schedule S contracts to S_1. The new partial equilibrium is at point c (intersection of schedules D_1, H_1 and S_1) at which population, wages and house prices are larger than at point a. This qualitative result does not depend on the relative slopes of schedules D, H and K.

At point c, which lies above schedule K_0, MPK must be larger than at point a because employment and TFP have increased. Subsequently, capital will flow into the region until MPK has returned to what it was at point a. The increase in the capital stock shifts the demand schedule for labor to D_2 so that the new spatial general equilibrium will be point e, where schedules K_1, D_2, H_2 and S_2 (not shown) intersect. At point e wages and population are higher than at point c, as are house prices and the capital stock. However, at point e MPK is what it was at point a. Capital mobility has the effect of accentuating the comparative statics of spatial general equilibrium.

The subsidization of investment in the region would increase the capital stock, which would induce the demand for labor to shift to the right, e.g. to schedule D_1. Consequently, the new SGE will be qualitatively similar (but quantitatively different) to the effects of an increase in TFP. An increase in land zoned for housing would raise schedule H thereby disturbing SGE at point a. Consequently, house prices would decrease in the region, which would shift schedule S to the right. If the capital stock remains unchanged, the new SGE would be on schedule D_0 (to the south–east of point a) because its location is not directly affected by shocks to the housing

[3]The production function is $Q = AK^{\alpha}L^{1-\alpha}$, $MPL = (1-\alpha)A(K/L)^{\alpha} = w$, which implies that the slope of schedule D is $-\alpha$. $MPK = \alpha A(K/L)^{\alpha-1} = \alpha wL/(1-\alpha)K$, which implies that the slope of schedule K_0 is -1. Hence, for Cobb–Douglas technologies schedule D is steeper than schedule K.

market (provided land zoned for commerce does not change). Since employment increases, so must MPK have increased, which induces inward investment into the region.

The Econometric SGE Model

The model presented in Table 8.7 was estimated using data during 1987–2015. Equation I refers to housing starts, and is an updated version of results reported in Table 8.3. Equation II is an updated version of results reported in Table 8.5, and Eq. III is an updated version of results reported in Table 8.2. Equations V and VI are identical to Eqs. (8.12b and 8.12d). In contrast to these tables, Table 8.7 reports confidence intervals for the parameter estimates using the bootstrap method described in Chap. 7. Apart from GADF statistics reported in Tables 8.2, 8.3 and 8.5, Table 8.7 reports SpGho statistics, which test for spatial cointegration. We continue to define the spatial connectivity matrix W as in Chap. 7 in terms of relative built-up land in 1990 and distance, so that W is asymmetric because larger regions carry a larger weight on their smaller counterparts.

Housing starts (S) are determined by Eq. I, in which they vary directly with local house prices (P) relative to construction costs (C) with an elasticity of 0.428, they vary directly with national house prices relative to construction costs with an elasticity of 0.415, and they vary inversely with the spatial Durbin lag of local house prices relative to construction costs with an elasticity of −0.486. The latter implies that building contractors regard construction elsewhere as a substitute for local construction. Housing starts vary directly with construction incentives provided by the Ministry of Housing (Z), and inversely with its spatial Durbin lag, which further suggests spatial substitution in housing construction. Finally, the spatial lagged dependent variable is positive, indicating positive spatial spillover in housing construction (Beenstock and Felsenstein 2015).

Pedroni's GADF statistic (reported in Table 8.7) is negative and statistically significant, suggesting that the variables in Eq. I are panel cointegrated. The SpGrho statistic is the SpIPS statistic for the residuals of Eq. I. However, its critical value differs from that for spatiotemporal unit roots tests. The critical values for SpGrho are reported in parentheses. These critical values are naturally stricter than their counterparts in Table 7.2 because degrees of freedom have been used to estimate β, γ and λ. Since SpGrho equals its critical value (0.78) the p-value for spatial panel cointegration between the variables in Eq. I is 0.05. A comparison of the p-values for GADF and SpIPS suggests that ignoring weak cross-section dependence tends to under-reject the null hypothesis of no cointegration. In terms of the taxonomy mentioned in Chap. 7, Eq. I is *globally cointegrated* because it includes spatial as well as local covariates. Z is assumed to be a weakly exogenous variable in Eq. I. The t statistic of the EC coefficient for $\Delta \ln S_g$ is 0.36 (Table 8.8), hence we cannot reject the hypothesis that Z and its spatial lag are weakly exogenous.

The 95% bootstrapped confidence limits of the parameters are reported in Table 8.9 below their respective parameter estimates. Since the confidence limits are narrow, and their bootstrapped p-values are zero (not shown) these parameter estimates are precisely estimated. The EGLS confidence limits (not shown) in Eq. I

Table 8.9 The model

I.	$\ln S_{it} = fe_i + \underset{0.39\ 0.47}{0.428} \ln\left(\frac{P_{it}}{C_t}\right) + \underset{0.33\ 0.50}{0.415} \ln\left(\frac{P_t}{C_t}\right) - \underset{-0.54-0.43}{0.486} \ln\left(\frac{\tilde{P}_{it}}{C_t}\right) + \underset{1.00\ 1.18}{1.098} Z_t - \underset{0.78\ -0.54}{0.66} \tilde{Z}_t + \underset{0.76\ 0.82}{0.79} \ln \tilde{S}_t$
II.	$F_{it} = \underset{0.32\ 0.39}{0.354} U_{it} + \underset{0.35\ 0.42}{0.389} S_{it}$
III.	$\ln P_{it} = fe_i + \underset{0.87\ 1.18}{1.027} \ln N_{it} - \underset{-1.13-0.83}{0.982} \ln H_{it} + \underset{0.27\ 0.48}{0.375} \ln w_{it} + \underset{1.07\ 1.37}{1.221} \ln \tilde{N}_{it} + \underset{0.38\ 0.49}{0.439} \ln \tilde{P}_{it}$
IV.	$Z_{it} = \frac{S_{Git}}{S_{it}}$
V.	$U_{it} = U_{it-1} + S_{it-1} - F_{it-1}$
VI.	$H_{it} = H_{it-1} + F_{it-1} - D_{it-1}$
VII.	$\ln w_{it} = fe_i + \underset{0.11\ 0.12}{0.114} \ln k_{it} + \underset{0.098\ 0.106}{0.102} E_{it} + \underset{0.14\ 0.19}{0.167} Jews_{it} + \underset{0.49\ 0.54}{0.512} \mathrm{Im}\, mig_{it} + \underset{0.21\ 0.22}{0.215} Age_{it} - \underset{-0.0026-0.0028}{0.0027} Age_{it}^2$
VIII.	$\ln k_{it} = fe_i + \underset{0.082\ 0.094}{0.0881} E_{it} - \underset{-0.044-0.042}{0.4273} \ln L_{it} + \underset{1.093\ 1.121}{1.107} \ln k_{it}^* + \underset{0.091\ 0.096}{0.0936} \ln IS_{it} - \underset{-0.165-0.199}{0.1821} \mathrm{Im}\, mig_{it}$

Legend: EGLS (SUR) with fixed regional effects except for Eq. III, which is estimated by ML. Ninety-five percent bootstrapped confidence intervals reported below their respective parameter estimates, except for Eq. III. S: housing starts (square meters 1000s), S_G: starts initiated by ILA (exogenous), F: completions, D: demolitions (exogenous), P: house price index, C: construction cost index (exogenous), N: population, w: wages, U: housing under construction, k: capital–labor ratio, E: average years of schooling, Jews: percentage of Jews in population, Age: average age of population of working age. Immig: share of new immigrants in the population
Spatial lagged variables are over-scripted with ~
The z ~ N(0,1) statistic for Pedroni's GADF are I −3, II −2.3, III −2.13, VII −5.67, VIII −4.28
SpGrho critical values for T = 25, N = 9 and W as specified in Eq. (8.2) at p = 0.05 in parentheses: I 0.78 (0.78), II 0.56 (0.79), III 0.17 (0.79), VII −0.28 (0.78), VIII 0.20 (0.79)
Source: Beenstock et al. (2018)

are mostly similar to their bootstrapped counterparts except in the case of the coefficient on Z where the confidence interval is wider (0.91–1.27). However, in Eqs. II and VIII the bootstrapped confidence intervals are generally narrower than their EGLS counterparts. They are also not symmetric. In Eq. I the means of the bootstrapped parameter estimates are almost identical to their EGLS estimates. Therefore, there is no finite sample bias in the estimates of Eq. I.

Equation II relates completions to starts and is multicointegrated (Granger and Lee 1989) with Eqs. I and V. It ensures that all starts are eventually completed, which is why there is no intercept, and the variables are not logarithms. Completion rates vary directly with starts because contractors use housing under construction as a buffer between supply and demand (Beenstock and Felsenstein 2015). There are no spatial dynamics in Eq. II because in contrast to Eq. I these spatial effects were not statistically significant. Hence, the variables in Eq. II are *locally cointegrated.* The GADF statistic is negative and significant, and the SpGrho statistic is 0.56, which is less than its critical value. Both tests reject the null hypothesis of no cointegration. In

Eq. II the EGLS confidence intervals are substantially wider than their bootstrapped counterparts and there is no evidence of finite sample bias.

Equation III is an inverted demand schedule for housing, and is estimated by ML because the EGLS estimate of the spatial lagged dependent variable was unreasonably large (0.91). The local price elasticity of demand for housing space is −1.018 (−1/0.982), the spatial price elasticity of demand is 0.447 (0.439/0.982), the local price elasticities of demand with respect to population and income are 1.049 and 0.382 respectively, and the spatial elasticity of demand with respect to population is 1.243 (1.221/0.982). The variables in Eq. III are *globally cointegrated* because spatial and ordinary variables are included in the cointegrating vector. Both GADF and SpGrho reject the null hypothesis of no cointegration.

Bootstrapping Eq. III indicates substantial finite sample bias. The ML estimates reported in Table 8.9 are attenuated with respect to their bias-corrected counterparts for all parameters except lnw. We think that because bias does not arise among the EGLS parameter estimates, it may be that ML estimators are more sensitive to finite sample bias.

Equations IV–VI are identities. Equation VII is a regional "Mincer Model" or inverted demand schedule for labor (Beenstock et al. 2011) in which wages vary directly with capital–labor ratios with an elasticity of 0.135, and the implicit return to human capital is 10%. Wages vary directly with the share of Jews and new immigrants in the population, and have, as expected, an inverted U-shaped relation with the average age of the population of working age. Since there are no spatial variables in Eq. VII, the variables concerned are *locally cointegrated.* The GADF and SpGrho statistics clearly indicated that these variables are panel cointegrated. Several variables in Eq. VII are assumed to be weakly exogenous. The t statistics of the EC coefficients for schooling, immigrants and age are reported in Table 8.10.

Schedule S in Fig. 8.4 is estimated by regressing population shares on relative real wages (RRW) for five regions. Unlike the equations in Table 8.4, the data are not pooled, and separate regressions are carried out to estimate:

$$\frac{POP_{it}}{POP_t} = \pi_i + \theta_i RRW_{it} + p_{it} \tag{8.15a}$$

Table 8.10 Tests for weak exogeneity

Equation variable	I Housing starts	VII Wages	VIII Capital–labor ratio
Public sector starts	0.365		
Schooling		2.25	1.3
Immigrants		−0.897	0.206
Investment grants			−0.779
Age		−0.801	
Jews		−0.395	

Notes: The table reports t statistics for the error correction coefficients

$$RRW_{it} = \frac{W_{it}}{\bar{W}_t}\left(\frac{\bar{P}_t}{P_{it}}\right)^{\phi} \tag{8.15b}$$

Where p is a residual, RRW is calculated assuming $\phi = 0.22$, i.e. housing accounts for 22% of consumption according to CBS estimates and over-barred variables refer to national averages. The five regions are Haifa, Krayot, North, Center and Dan, where the relation between population shares and RRW is positive. The estimates of the slope coefficients (θ) on RRW are 0.832, 0.074, 0.592, 2.072 and 5.07 respectively, implying that internal migration is most sensitive to relative real wages in Dan and least sensitive in Krayot. The residuals (p) for these four regions are stationary with GADF $= -2.3$ and SpGrho $= 0.4$.

By contrast, in the other regions such as Tel Aviv and Jerusalem the relations between population shares and RRW slope the "wrong" way in the data; population shares vary inversely with relative real wages. For these four regions we do not estimate θ. Instead, θ is calibrated under the assumption that the relation between population shares and RRW is positive. It appears to be negative because of unobserved relative amenities (a), which increase population shares through inward migration, which in turn depresses RRW because labor supply has increased. In the absence of time series data on regional amenities, we hypothesize that amenities are nonstationary random variables, which are unobservable and are embodied in p in Eq. (8.14a), i.e. $p = a + m$ where m denotes stationary model error. Since a is expected to be nonstationary, so must p be nonstationary.

θ is calibrated at 0.09 in Tel Aviv, 0.1 in Jerusalem, 0.22 in Sharon, and 0.17 in South. For these regions $\pi_i + p_{it}$ is solved by reverse engineering from Eq. (8.14a) using data for population shares and RRW. The choices of θ are made to minimize the variance of the implicit amenities that are embodied in p. The residuals for these regions are plotted in Fig. 8.5. The level of these estimates capture regional fixed effects (π) which are largest in Jerusalem and South and smallest in Tel Aviv. More important are the estimated trends in relative amenities, which by assumption are reflected in the trend in p. According to this interpretation a is increasing in South and Jerusalem and decreasing in Tel Aviv. Indeed, these estimated amenities are nonstationary.

In summary, although the model is estimated econometrically, the theory of compensating wage differentials is used to calibrate the labor supply schedule for four regions. This implicitly assumes that in Haifa, Krayot, North, Center and Dan relative amenities happened to be stationary. This partial recourse to calibration would not have been necessary had time series data been available for regional amenities.

Equation VIII in Table 8.9 determines capital–labor ratios (k). Regional production technologies are assumed to be Cobb–Douglas:

$$Q_{it} = A_{it}K_{it}^{\alpha_i}L_{it}^{1-\alpha_i} \tag{8.16a}$$

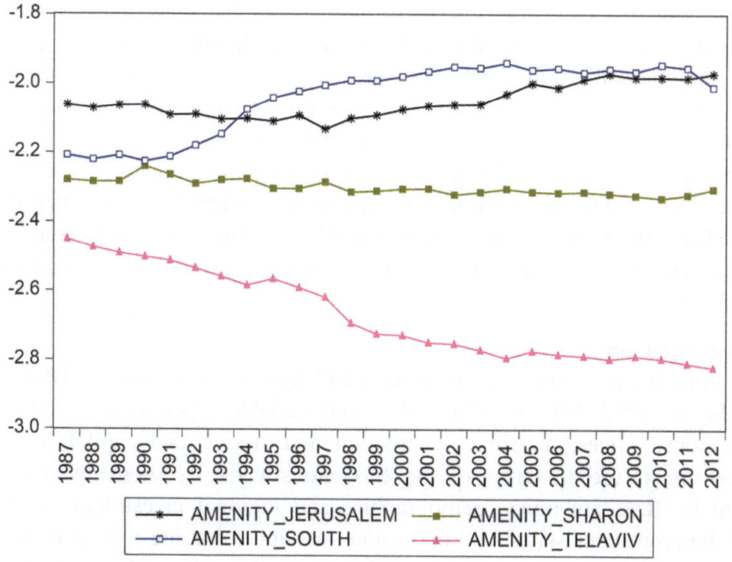

Fig. 8.5 Implicit amenities

where A denotes TFP. The cost of capital is $(r_t + d)(1 - s_{it})$ where r denotes the rate of interest, d denotes the rate of depreciation, and s denotes the rate of investment subsidy. If s was zero, the user cost of capital would be the same in all regions. If r + d is the same for all regions, profit maximization implies the following relationship between the capital–labor ratio in region i and the capital–labor ratio outside region i denoted by k^*:

$$k_{it} = \left[\frac{\alpha^* A_t^* (1 - s_t^*)}{\alpha_i A_{it}(1 - s_{it})}\right]^{\frac{1}{\alpha_i - 1}} k_t^{*\frac{\alpha - 1}{\alpha_i - 1}} \tag{8.16b}$$

Notice that the elasticity of k with respect to k^* is unity when $\alpha_i = \alpha$. Apart from this, k varies directly with relative TFP and the subsidization of capital.

In Eq. (8.16b) it is assumed that the rate of interest is the same for all regions. If the regional cost of capital varies directly with regional risk exposure, it may be shown that the linear homogeneity between capital and labor implied by Eq. (8.16b) is violated. For example, an increase in population in a region, which increases employment would induce a proportionate increase in capital when $r_i = r$. If, however, r_i increases as a result of greater regional borrowing, the increase in capital will be less than proportionate. To test for this, k should vary inversely with L in Eq. (8.16b). This is the theory underpinning Eq. VIII in Table 8.9 where the fixed effects reflect α_i/α and average TFP differentials. Since TFP is expected to depend on human capital, Eq. VIII includes schooling, and age of the population of working age, which suggests the physical and human capital are complements. Apart from this, the elasticity of k with respect to k^* (k elsewhere) is slightly larger than

1, suggesting that capital is internally mobile. On the other hand, the negative coefficient on lnL is consistent with the hypothesis that the regional cost of capital varies directly with capital risk exposure, suggesting that capital is imperfectly mobile (Beenstock 2017). Finally, k varies directly with capital subsidies. The elasticity of *k* with respect to regional investment grants is about 0.1.

The variables in Eq. VIII are *globally cointegrated* because k^* is a spatial variable. The GADF and SpGrho statistics for the residuals indicate that the variables in Eq. VIII are panel cointegrated. Equation VIII includes three variables (E, IS and immigrant), which are assumed to be weakly exogenous, as confirmed in Table 8.10.

Model Properties

To illustrate the properties of the model a full dynamic simulation (FDS) is calculated during 1987–2015 in which the state variables (population, employment, wages, house prices, housing construction and stocks, and capital in the nine regions) are solved in terms of the exogenous variables (housing construction initiated by ILA, amenities, demographics and regional investment grants). The model therefore consists of 72 endogenous variables that are solved in each time period. The FDS serves as a base run for counterfactual simulation in which the exogenous variables are perturbed in 1994. The model is state-dependent temporally and spatially. It is temporally state-dependent because it is slightly nonlinear since variables are specified in levels and logarithms. For example, Table 8.9 includes housing starts (S) in Eqs. II, V and VI and its logarithm in Eq. I. Equations II, V and VI gives rise to temporal dynamics in the model despite the fact that Eq. I is static; the dynamics are entirely induced by the relations between housing stocks and flows. This means that the same shock in e.g. 2000 would produce slightly different effects than its counterpart in 1994. The model is spatially state dependent because the spatial weights matrix (W) is asymmetric and because the regions vary in size. Therefore, a given shock will have a bigger effect on a smaller regions and it will have a bigger effect if it occurs in regions that are more spatially connected. This means that the spatial diffusion of shocks depends on where they occur, as well as when they occur.

In linear models with spatial lagged dependent variables, the partial derivatives of dependent variables with respect to independent variables may be obtained analytically by matrix inversion as described in Table 8.5. In dynamic nonlinear models, matrix inversion is not feasible. We therefore resort to numerical methods by including the construction of spatial variables in the model coding. This simulation methodology takes into account for nonlinear models the issues raised by Debarsy et al. (2012) for linear models in the calculation of spatio-temporal impulse response functions. Consequently, the spatio-temporal impulse responses embody the direct and indirect spatial relations between the variables, as well as their direct and indirect temporal dynamics.

We exaggerate the shocks so that their spatio-temporal impulses should be graphically visible. Figure 8.6 plots the spatio-temporal diffusion on housing starts, house prices, wages and population of a permanent 64% increase in public sector

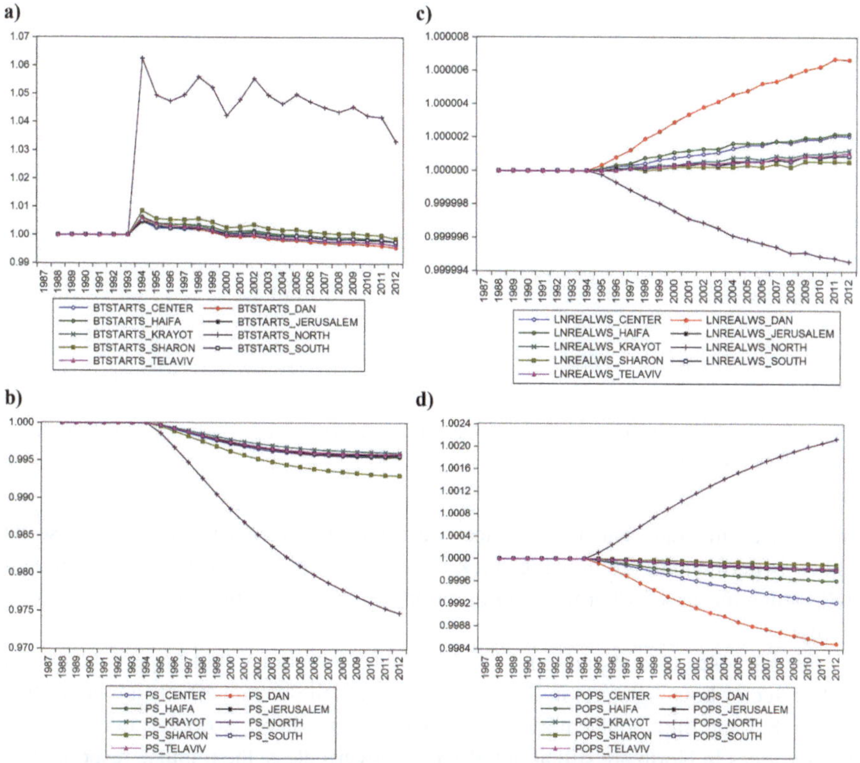

Fig. 8.6 Simulation: permanent 64% increase in public sector starts in north. Panel (**a**) Housing starts. Panel (**b**) House prices. Panel (**c**) Real wages. Panel (**d**) Population

housing starts in North starting in 1994. Initially housing starts increase by about 6%, which is more than the direct effect of the increase in public sector starts because public sector starts crowd-in private sector starts (Z increases in Eq. I). The housing stock in North increases, inducing a decrease in house prices, which has two effects. First, housing construction subsequently decreases in North because building is less profitable. Second, housing construction increases elsewhere because of spatial substitution in construction. In addition, there is positive spatial spillover between construction in North and elsewhere. This spillover is strongest in Sharon and weakest in Dan and Tel Aviv. The decrease in relative house prices in North induces inward migration especially from Dan and least of all from Sharon. Inward migration to North equals the sum of outward migration from elsewhere. The increase in labor supply in North decreases wages and increases wages elsewhere, especially in Dan. Capital stocks change less than proportionately (not shown) with employment because according to Eq. VIII the elasticity of capital with respect to employment is 0.57. The implicit cost of capital increases in North relative to elsewhere. Finally, although housing construction stabilizes over time, population in North increases but

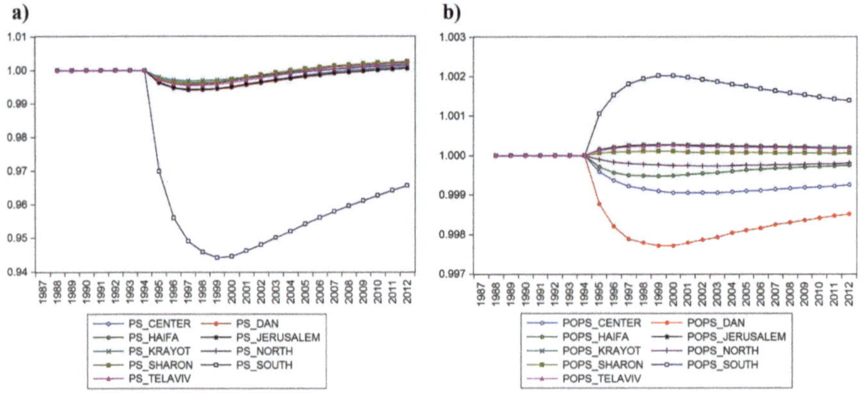

Fig. 8.7 Simulation: temporary 90% increase in public sector starts in south. Panel (**a**) House prices. Panel (**b**) Population

at a decreasing rate, and house prices decrease at a decreasing rate. Because the shock is permanent, the housing stock continues to grow, house prices continue to fall, which induces further inward migration. By 2012 this convergent process is not complete.

For purposes of comparison, Fig. 8.7 plots a temporary (but larger) increase in public sector housing starts in South. As expected, the impact effects are larger than in Fig. 8.5 and the impulse responses weaken 6 years later. However, even by 2012 house prices in North are still about 3% less. Nevertheless, the impulse responses are tending towards zero, as expected. Convergence is slow because of the natural longevity in housing stocks.

Figure 8.8 plots the spatio-temporal diffusion of an increase in human capital in Jerusalem on capital–labor ratios, real wages, populations and housing starts. Because human and physical capital are complements the capital–labor ratio increases in Jerusalem, which raises capital–labor ratios elsewhere (Dan especially) though internal capital mobility. Real wages in Jerusalem increase directly though the Mincer effect as well as indirectly because the capital–labor ratio has increased. The increase in real wages in Jerusalem induces inward migration, especially from Dan. In some regions such as Tel Aviv the population increases, while in others such as Center it decreases. This outcome depends on the relative increase in capital–labor ratios.

Housing demand in Jerusalem increases for two reasons. First, the increase in wages raises the demand for housing space. Second, the increase in population raises the demand for housing. Consequently, house prices (not shown) in Jerusalem increase and decrease elsewhere. The latter happens because although population increases in some regions, real wages are lower. This is why housing construction increases in Jerusalem but decreases elsewhere.

Figure 8.9 plots the spatio-temporal impulse responses resulting from a permanent increase in amenities in Tel Aviv, which makes Tel Aviv more attractive to live

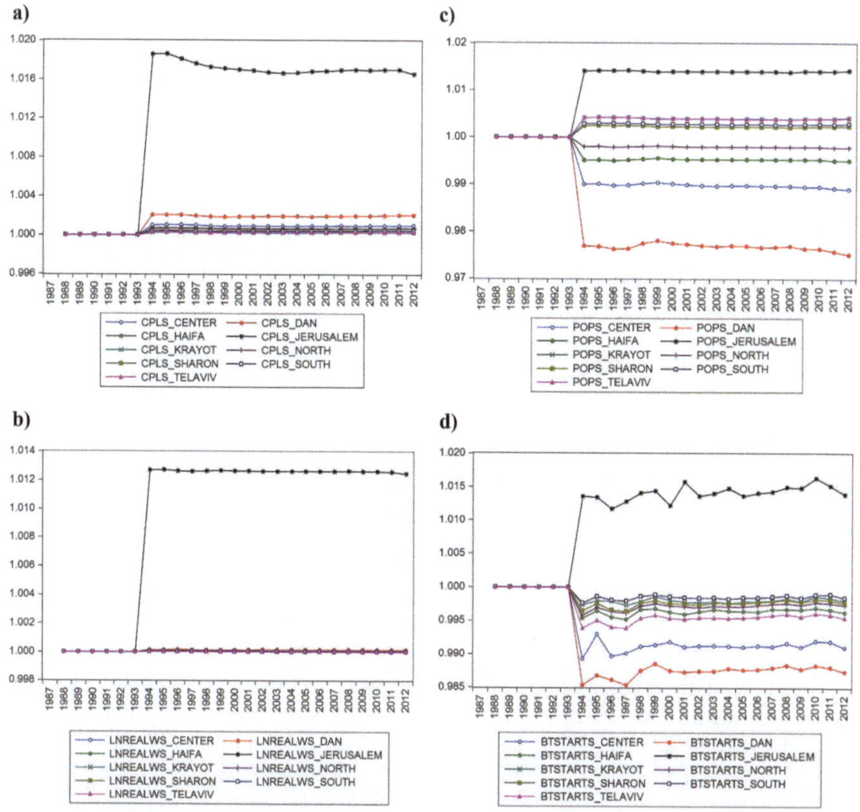

Fig. 8.8 Simulation: 8% increase in schooling in Jerusalem. Panel (**a**): Capital–labor ratio. Panel (**b**): Real wages. Panel (**c**): Population. Panel (**d**): Housing starts

in. Internal migration into Tel Aviv is equally spread across other regions. Internal migration increases the supply of labor in Tel Aviv, which reduces real wages. Notice, however, that real wages fall elsewhere too despite outward migration. This happens because capital–labor ratios (not shown) decrease in all regions. The capital–labor ratio decreases in Tel Aviv because employment increases (Eq. VIII), which in turn depresses capital–labor ratios elsewhere through internal capital mobility. Despite the decrease in wages in Tel Aviv the demand for housing increases because of internal migration, which increases house prices. The latter raises housing construction in Tel Aviv. In the absence of spatial effects in Eq. III houses prices elsewhere would have decreased because wages and population are lower. In some regions such as Haifa house prices are lower because the spatial spillovers that raise house prices are insufficiently strong to counteract the forces that lower them. In other regions, such as Dan and Center, these spatial spillovers are sufficiently strong to raise house prices. Whereas houses prices may increase or

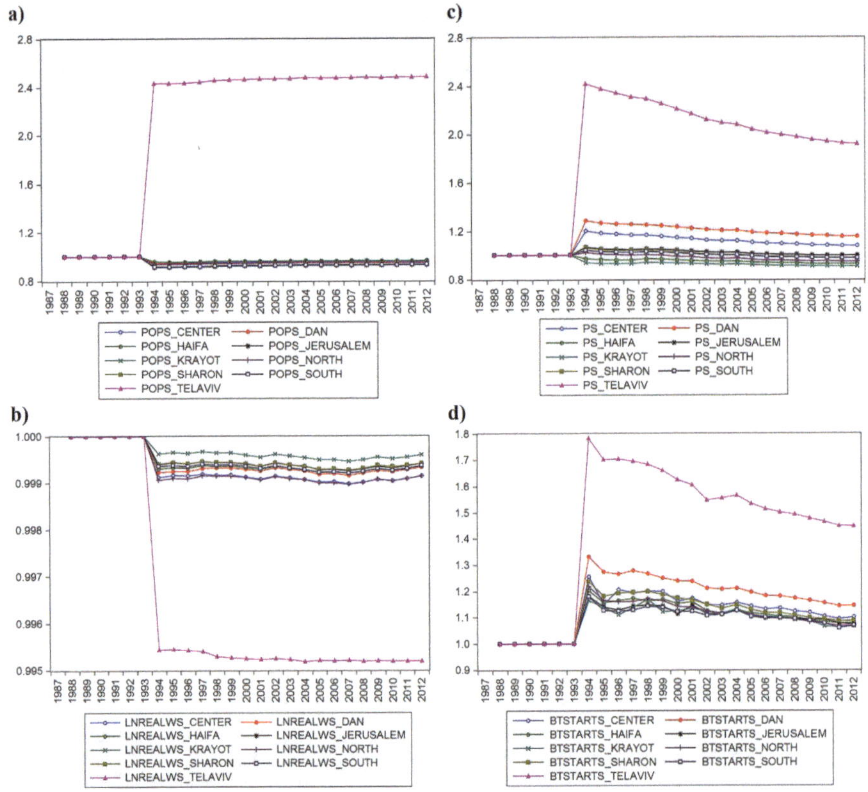

Fig. 8.9 Simulation: 40% increase in amenities in Tel Aviv. Panel (**a**): Population. Panel (**b**): Real wages. Panel (**c**): House Prices. Panel (**d**): Housing starts

decrease, housing construction increases everywhere as a result of the spatial spillover in housing construction.

Figure 8.10 plots the spatio-temporal impulse responses following a prolonged increase in investment subsidies in South, which directly increases the capital–labor ratio in South, and indirectly increases capital–ratios elsewhere through internal capital mobility. These higher capital–labor ratios raise wages especially in South, thereby inducing internal migration into South from elsewhere e.g. Dan and Center. However, the population also increases in some regions such as Tel Aviv as a result of increases in relative real wages. The increase in wages and population in South exerts upward pressure on house prices in South. The decrease in population in regions such as Dan and Center depress house prices in these regions. However, house prices also decrease in regions such as Tel Aviv where population increases because of negative spatial spillover in house prices.

In this chapter, we provide empirical illustrations of the spatial panel cointegration theory developed in Chap. 7. The first illustration refers to a partial

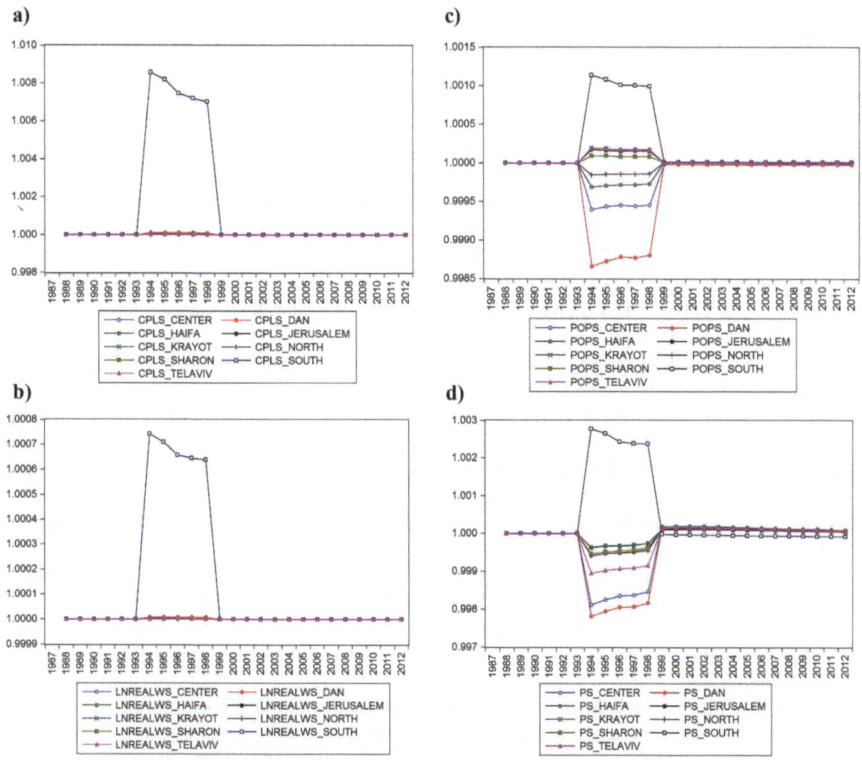

Fig. 8.10 Simulation: A 60% increase in investment grants in south 1994–. Panel (**a**): Capital–labor ratios. Panel (**b**): Real wages. Panel (**c**): Population. Panel (**d**): House prices

equilibrium model of the housing market in Israel. The second refers to a spatial general equilibrium model in which labor, capital and product markets are specified, as well as housing markets. We illustrate the application of the spatial group rho (SpGrho) cointegration test, the bootstrapping of confidence intervals for estimates of cointegrating vectors, the identification of cointegrating vectors, and error correction tests for weak exogeneity. The next chapter is devoted to empirical illustrations of error correction.

References

Bailey N, Holly S, Pesaran MH (2016) A two stage approach to spatiotemporal analysis with strong and weak cross-section dependence. J Appl Economet 31(1):249–280

Ball M, Meen G, Nygaard C (2010) Housing supply elasticities revisited: evidence from international, national, local and company data. J Hous Econ 19:255–268

Bar-Nathan M, Beenstock M, Haitovsky Y (1998) The market for housing in Israel. Reg Sci Urban Econ 28:21–50

Beenstock M (2017) How internally mobile is capital? Lett Spat Resour Sci 10(3):361–374
Beenstock M, Felsenstein D (2010) Spatial error correction and cointegration in nonstationary spatial panel data: regional house prices in Israel. J Geogr Syst 12:189–206
Beenstock M, Felsenstein D (2015) Spatial spillover in housing construction. J Hous Econ 28:42–58
Beenstock M, Fisher J (1997) The macroeconomic effects of immigration: Israel in the 1990s. Rev World Econ 133:330–358
Beenstock M, Ben Zeev N, Felsenstein D (2011) Capital deepening and regional inequality: an empirical analysis. Ann Reg Sci 47:599–617
Beenstock M, Felsenstein D, Xieer D (2018) Spatial econometric analysis of spatial general equilibrium. Spat Econ Anal 13(3):356–378
Cameron G, Muellbauer J, Murphy A (2006) Was there a British house price bubble? Evidence from regional panel data. Mimeo, University of Oxford
Capozza DR, Hendershott PH, Mack C, Mayer CJ (2004) Determinants of real house price dynamics. Real Estate Econ 32:1–32
Debarsy N, Ertur C, LeSage JP (2012) Interpreting space-time panel data models. Stat Methodol 9:158–171
DiPasquale D (1999) Why don't we know more about housing supply? J Real Estate Financ Econ 18:9–33
DiPasquale D, Wheaton WC (1994) Housing market dynamics and the future of house prices. J Urban Econ 35:1–27
Fernandez-Kranz D, Hon MT (2006) A cross-section analysis of the income elasticity of housing demand in Spain: is there a real estate bubble? J Real Estate Financ Econ 32(4):449–444
Gallin J (2003) The long-run relationship between house prices and income: evidence from local housing markets. Finance and Economics Discussion Series, Federal Reserve Board, Washington, DC
Granger CWJ, Lee T (1989) Investigation of production, sales and inventory relations using multi-cointegration and non-symmetric error correction models. J Appl Economet 4:S145–S159
Gyourko J, Saiz A (2006) Construction costs and the supply of housing structure. J Reg Sci 46:661–680
Holly S, Pesaran MH, Yamagata T (2010) A spatio-temporal model of house prices in the US. J Econ 158:160–173
Krugman P (1991) Increasing returns and economic geography. J Polit Econ 99(3):483–499
Malpezzi S (1999) A simple error correction model of house prices. J Hous Econ 8:27–62
Meen G, Nygaard C (2011) Local housing supply and the impact of history and geography. Urban Stud 48(14):3107–3124
Paciorek A (2011) Supply constraints and housing market dynamics. http://www.federalreserve.gov/pubs/feds/2012/201201/201201pap.pdf
Pedroni P (1999) Critical values for cointegration tests in heterogeneous panels with multiple regressors. Oxf Bull Econ Stat 61:653–670
Pedroni P (2004) Panel cointegration: asymptotic and finite sample properties of pooled time series tests with an application to the PPP hypothesis. Economet Theor 20:597–625
Roback J (1982) Wages, rents, and the quality of life. J Polit Econ 90(6):1257–1278
Saiz A (2010) The geographic determinants of housing supply. Q J Econ 125:1253–1296
Smith LB (1969) A model of the Canadian housing and mortgage market. J Polit Econ 77:795–816
Westerlund J (2007) Testing for error correction in panel based data. Oxf Bull Econ Stat 69 (6):709–748

Chapter 9
Spatial Vector Error Correction

9.1 Introduction

In Chap. 8 we focused on the estimation of cointegrating vectors using nonstationary spatial panel data. In this chapter we show how these cointegrating vectors may be used to estimate spatial vector error correction models (SpVECM) as defined in Chap. 7. Whereas cointegrating vectors are concerned with long-run equilibrium relations between spatial panel data, SpVECMs are concerned with their spatiotemporal convergence to these long-term relations. In non-spatial VECMs involving difference stationary variables (Chap. 2), error correction models for individual variables such as y depend on the lagged disequilibria for y as well as the lagged disequilibria for other variables, such as x. In SpVECMs the error correction model for y depends on these lagged disequilibria, as well as their spatial lags.

The cointegrating vectors for y and x are represented by Eqs. (9.1a and 9.1b):

$$y_{it} = \alpha_{1i} + \beta_1 x_{it} + \gamma_1 z_{it} + \lambda_1 \tilde{y}_{it} + \delta_1 \tilde{x}_{it} + u_{it} \quad (9.1a)$$

$$x_{it} = \alpha_{2i} + \beta_2 y_{it} + \gamma_2 w_{it} + \delta_2 \tilde{y}_{it} + \lambda_2 \tilde{x}_{it} + v_{it} \quad (9.1b)$$

where the α's denote spatial fixed effects, spatial lag coefficients are denoted by λ's, spatial Durbin lags are denoted by δ's, and the disequilibrium error components are denoted by u and v, which are stationary by definition of cointegration. Notice that Eqs. (9.1a and 9.1b) are identified because z is specified in the former but not the latter, and w is specified in the latter but not the former.

In Chap. 7 we introduced the concept of spatial error correction, and spatial vector error correction. For convenience, we recall the latter here. The first-order SpVECM associated with Eqs. (9.1a and 9.1b) is:

M. Beenstock, D. Felsenstein, *The Econometric Analysis of Non-Stationary Spatial Panel Data*, Advances in Spatial Science,
https://doi.org/10.1007/978-3-030-03614-0_9

$$\Delta y_{it} = \mu_{1i} + \pi_{11}\Delta y_{it-1} + \pi_{12}\Delta x_{it-1} + \lambda_3 \Delta\tilde{y}_{it} + \delta_3 \Delta\tilde{x}_{it} - \xi_{11}\hat{u}_{it-1} + \xi_{12}\hat{v}_{it-1} + \zeta_{11}\hat{\tilde{u}}_{it-1} + \zeta_{12}\hat{\tilde{v}}_{it-1} + \varepsilon_{1it} \tag{9.2a}$$

$$\Delta x_{it} = \mu_{2i} + \pi_{22}\Delta y_{it-1} + \pi_{21}\Delta x_{it-1} + \delta_4 \Delta\tilde{y}_{it} + \lambda_4 \Delta\tilde{x}_{it} - \xi_{22}\hat{u}_{it-1} + \xi_{21}\hat{v}_{it-1} + \zeta_{22}\hat{\tilde{u}}_{it-1} + \zeta_{21}\hat{\tilde{v}}_{it-1} + \varepsilon_{2it} \tag{9.2b}$$

Where the μ's are spatial fixed effects, the π's are VAR coefficients, the λ's are spatial lag coefficients, the δ's are spatial Durbin lag coefficients, the ξ's are the error correction coefficients, the ζ's are spatial error correction coefficients, and the ε's are iid random variables. In non-spatial panel data the λ's, δ's, and ζ's are zero in Eqs. (9.1a, 9.1b, 9.2a and 9.2b). Hence, in bivariate SpVECMs there are 12 spatial effects. For simplicity, terms in Δz, Δw and their spatial lags have been omitted from Eqs. (9.2a and 9.2b) as have terms in $\Delta\tilde{y}_{it-1}$ *and* $\Delta\tilde{x}_{it-1}$. The expected signs of the error correction coefficients are positive for ξ_{11} and ξ_{12}, and positive for ξ_{22} and ξ_{21}. The expected signs of the spatial error correction coefficients are positive for ζ_{11} and ζ_{21} and positive for ζ_{12} and ζ_{22}.

All the variables in Eqs. (9.2a and 9.2b) must be stationary if the variables used to estimate Eqs. (9.1a and 9.1b) are difference stationary. Therefore, the principles of unit root econometrics, which apply to Eqs. (9.1a and 9.1b) do not apply to Eqs. (9.2a and 9.2b). Instead, standard econometric principles apply to Eqs. (9.2a and 9.2b), e.g. the parameter estimates have standard distributions so that t-tests etc. may be used, and the parameter estimates are consistent but no longer super-consistent. The main econometric concern with respect to Eqs. (9.2a and 9.2b) is that the error terms (ε) should be serially uncorrelated, otherwise lagged dependent variables will not be weakly exogenous for the πs. Another econometric concern is that contemporaneous SAR coefficients (λ_3, λ_4, δ_3 and δ_4) are not identified by OLS.

In SpVECMs as in VECMs error correction is interdependent. Hence, the disequilibrium in x_{it-1}, measured by v_{it-1}, is specified in the error correction model for y_{it} in Eq. (9.2a) alongside the disequilibrium in y_{it-1}, measured by u_{it-1}. In Eq. (9.2b) error correction in x_{it} depends on both v_{it-1} and u_{it-1}. Whereas error correction is implied by cointegration theory, matters are different for vector error correction. If y and x are completely independent vector error correction would not make sense. For example, in the SGE model for Israel reported in Table 8.9, it might be reasonable to expect that vector error correction applies within markets, such as housing, rather than between markets, such as housing and labor markets. In the empirical application below, we test for vector error correction between house prices and housing starts because these variables belong to the same market. It would have been less sensible to test for vector error correction between housing starts and wages. In the final analysis, vector error correction is an empirical matter, except for variables that are completely independent a priori.

9.2 Stability of Error Correction Models

If the variables in Eqs. (9.1a and 9.1b) are cointegrated, by definition it must be the case that the SpVECM in Eqs. (9.2a and 9.2b) implies that y and x eventually converge on their long-run equilibria determined by Eqs. (9.1a and 9.1b). This means that the roots or eigenvalues of SpVECMs must be less than 1. The number of roots in SpVECMs tends to be large since there are MNP roots, where M is the number of state variables, N is the number of spatial units, and P is the lag order of the SpVECM. In Eqs. (9.2a and 9.2b) P = 2 because they are first order difference equations in changes in y_{it} and x_{it} and consequently second order difference equations in y_{it} and x_{it}. Therefore, in Eqs. (9.1a, 9.1b, 9.2a and 9.2b) where M = 2 and P = 2 there are 4N roots. In data sets where N exceeds 100, the number of roots may run into thousands. In what follows we try to expose the basic issues involved by focusing on simple but nonetheless illuminating cases. We begin with time series data before turning to spatial panel data.

Bivariate Time Series: Vector Error Correction

To fix ideas suppose y and x are time series data rather than panel data, to which we shall return. Suppose for simplicity that the VECM is symmetric and does not involve VAR components involving lags of Δy and Δx:

$$\Delta u_t = -\xi_1 u_{t-1} + \xi_2 v_{t-1} + \varepsilon_{1t} \tag{9.3a}$$

$$\Delta v_t = \xi_2 u_{t-1} - \xi_1 v_{t-1} + \varepsilon_{2t} \tag{9.3b}$$

where u and v are determined in the time series counterparts to Eqs. (9.1a and 9.1b):

$$y_t = \beta_1 x_t + \gamma_1 z_t + u_t \tag{9.3c}$$

$$x_t = \beta_2 y_t + \gamma_2 w_t + v_t \tag{9.3d}$$

Equations (9.3a and 9.3b) may be rewritten as:

$$\begin{bmatrix} 1+(\xi_1-1)L & -\xi_2 L \\ -\xi_2 L & 1+(\xi_1-1)L \end{bmatrix}\begin{bmatrix} u_t \\ v_t \end{bmatrix} = \begin{bmatrix} \varepsilon_{1t} \\ \varepsilon_{2t} \end{bmatrix} \tag{9.3e}$$

for which the characteristic equation is quadratic:

$$\omega^2 - 2(1-\xi)\omega + (1-\xi_1)^2 - \xi_2^2 = 0 \tag{9.3f}$$

The roots are:

$$\omega_1 = 1 - \xi_1 + \xi_2 \tag{9.3g}$$

$$\omega_2 = 1 - \xi_1 - \xi_2 \tag{9.3h}$$

Since the ξs are fractions the roots are less than 1 in absolute value. The general solutions for u is:

$$u_t = \frac{1}{\omega_1 - \omega_2} \sum\nolimits_{\tau=0}^{\infty} \left(\omega_1^{1+\tau} - \omega_2^{1+\tau}\right)\left[\varepsilon_{1t-\tau} - (1-\xi_1)\varepsilon_{1t-\tau-1} + \xi_2\varepsilon_{2t-\tau-1}\right] + A_1\omega_1^t + A_2\omega_2^t \tag{9.3i}$$

where the As are arbitrary constants determined by initial conditions. Since the ωs are fractions their effect on u vanish over time. The conditional expected value of u from Eq. (9.3i) differs from zero. However its unconditional expected value is zero because the εs have zero expected value. A similar result applies to the solution for v. Therefore, the parameters of the VECM are expected to induce y and x to converge on their equilibrium values determined in Eqs. (9.3c and 9.3d).

Panel Data: Spatial Error Correction with 2 Spatial Units and 1 Variable

Equations (9.3a–9.3i) may also be used to illustrate the properties of spatial error correction. Suppose there are two spatial units and y_t denotes the time series of a variable of interest in unit 1 while x_t denotes the time series of the same variable in unit 2. Therefore, β_1 in Eq. (9.3c) and β_2 in Eq. (9.3d) constitute spatial lags in global cointegrated vectors, ξ_1 in Eqs. (9.3a and 9.3b) are homogeneous error correction coefficients, and ξ_2 in Eq. (9.3a) is the spatial error correction coefficient for unit 1, and ξ_2 in Eq. (9.3b) is the spatial error correction coefficient for unit 2.

In general the number of roots or eigenvalues (ω) equals NMP where M is the number of variables in the SpVECM, N is the number of spatial units, and P is the temporal lag order. In the 1 × 2 case (when M = 1 and N = 2) the characteristic Eq. (9.3g) is quadratic and has an analytical solution. Therefore, even in the 2 × 2 case, the condition for convergent roots cannot be derived analytically because there are at least four eigenvalues. Equations (9.2a and 9.2b) refer to an SpVECM in which M = 2, there are N spatial units and P = 1, hence there are 2N eigenvalues. In the SGE model (Table 8.9) M = 7 and N = 9 in which case there would be 63 eigenvalues in its first order SpVECM.

Spatial Error Correction: N Spatial Units and M = 2 Variables

In what follows we restrict M = 2 and P = 1 but N is not restricted. Let u_t and v_t now denote N-vectors of error terms generated by cointegrating vectors for the two variables, such as y and x. The SpECMs for these variables are:

$$u_t = (1-\xi_u)u_{t-1} + \zeta_u W u_{t-1} + \varepsilon_{ut} \tag{9.4a}$$

$$v_t = (1-\xi_v)v_{t-1} + \zeta_v W v_{t-1} + \varepsilon_{vt} \tag{9.4b}$$

where, as before, ξ denotes error correction coefficients, ζ denotes spatial error correction coefficients, and ε denotes iid ECM error terms. The solution to Eq. (9.4a) is:

$$u_t = A\varepsilon_{ut} \tag{9.4c}$$

$$\begin{aligned} A &= [\mathrm{I}_N - [(1-\xi_u)I_N + \zeta_u W]L]^{-1} \\ &= \mathrm{I}_N + \sum\nolimits_{\tau=1}^{\infty} [(1-\xi_u)I_N - \zeta_u W)]^{\tau} L^{\tau} \end{aligned} \tag{9.4d}$$

The N eigenvalues will be less than 1 if $1 - \xi_u + \zeta_u < 1$. The solution to Eq. (9.4b) is similar. Because the eigenvalues are less than 1 the unconditional expected values for u and v are zero because A is convergent.

The SpVECM for these variables is:

$$u_t = (1-\xi_{uu})u_{t-1} + \zeta_{uu}Wu_{t-1} + \xi_{uv}v_{t-1} + \zeta_{uv}Wv_{t-1} + \varepsilon_{ut} \tag{9.4e}$$

$$v_t = (1-\xi_{vv})v_{t-1} + \zeta_{vv}Wv_{t-1} + \xi_{vu}u_{t-1} + \zeta_{vu}Wu_{t-1} + \varepsilon_{vt} \tag{9.4f}$$

where ξ_{uu} and ξ_{vv} denote own or within error correction coefficients, ξ_{uv} and ξ_{vu} denote cross or between error correction coefficients, ζ_{uu} and ζ_{vv} denote own or within spatial error correction coefficients, and ζ_{uv} and ζ_{vu} denote cross or between spatial error correction coefficients. Whereas in SpECMs u and v may be solved separately because they are independent, in SpVECMs u and v are dependent and must be solved jointly. For example, the solution for u_t is:

$$u_t = A\{\varepsilon_{ut} - [(1-\xi_{vv})\mathrm{I}_N + \zeta_{vu}W]\varepsilon_{ut-1} + [\xi_{uv}\mathrm{I}_N + \zeta_{uv}W]\varepsilon_{vt-1}\} \tag{9.4g}$$

$$A = \left[\mathrm{I}_N - \left(A_1L - A_2L^2\right)\right]^{-1} = \mathrm{I}_N + \sum\nolimits_{\tau=1}^{\infty}\left[A_1L - A_2L^2\right]^{\tau} \tag{9.4h}$$

$$A_1 = (\xi_{vv} + \xi_{uu})I_N + (\zeta_{vu} + \zeta_{uu})W$$

$$A_2 = -(\xi_{vu}\xi_{uv} - \xi_{vv})\mathrm{I}_N + (\zeta_{vu} - \xi_{uv}\zeta_{vu} - \zeta_{uv}\xi_{vu})W - \zeta_{uv}\zeta_{vu}W^2$$

where A is an $N \times N$ matrix. Notice that u_t depends on temporal and spatial lags of ε_v as well as ε_u. If W is row summed to 1, sufficient conditions for convergence are $A_1 – A_2 = \xi_{uu} + \zeta_{uu} + \xi_{vu}\xi_{uv} + \xi_{uv}\zeta_{vu} + \zeta_{uv}\zeta_{vu} < 1$.

Final Forms of ARSAR Models

In the empirical illustrations below we estimate various error correction models, such as Eqs. (9.4a and 9.4b) for SpECMs, or Eqs. (9.4e and 9.4f) for SpVECMs. Since u and v are generated by cointegrating vectors for $y = Z_y + u$ and $x = Z_x + v$, where the Zs are exogenous variables and include iid innovations, we are naturally interested in the spatial and temporal dynamic solutions for y and x in terms of Z_y and Z_x. These solutions inherit the characteristics of the SpECM or SpVECM from which they are derived. In Eqs. (9.4a–9.4h) the error correction models are AR(1) SAR(1) because they embody first order temporal and spatial dynamics. Hence, the first order ARSAR models for y and x are assumed to be:

$$y_t = \pi y_{t-1} + (1-\pi)Wy_{t-1} + \beta x_{t-1} + \gamma Wx_{t-1} + Z_{yt} \tag{9.5a}$$

$$x_t = \delta x_{t-1} + \varphi Wx_{t-1} + \theta y_{t-1} + \eta Wy_{t-1} + Z_{xt} \tag{9.5b}$$

to ensure that feedbacks between y and x are not explosive $\beta + \gamma$ and $\theta + \eta$ are less than 1 in absolute value. In Eq. (9.5a) the AR(1) and SAR(1) coefficients (π and $1 - \pi$) sum to 1 inducing spatio-temporal nonstationarity in y. Nevertheless, if x is stationary, y might be stationary because it depends on temporal and spatial lags of x, which is stationary provided $\delta + \varphi < 1$. To show this we derive the final forms for y and x.

The final forms for y and x generated by Eqs. (9.5a and 9.5b) are:

$$\begin{aligned} y_t = {} & (\pi + \delta)y_{t-1} + (\theta\beta - \pi\delta)y_{t-2} + (\varphi + 1 - \pi)\tilde{y}_{t-1} \\ & + [-\pi\varphi - \delta(1 - \pi) + \gamma\theta + \beta\eta]\tilde{y}_{t-2} \\ & + [-\varphi(1 - \pi) + \gamma\eta]\tilde{\tilde{y}}_{t-2} + Z_{xt-1} + \gamma Z_{xt-1} + Z_{yt} - \delta Z_{yt-1} - \varphi\tilde{Z}_{yt-1} \end{aligned} \tag{9.5c}$$

$$\begin{aligned} x_t = {} & (\pi + \delta)x_{t-1} + (\theta\beta - \pi\delta)x_{t-2} + (\varphi + 1 - \pi)\tilde{x}_{t-1} \\ & + [-\pi\varphi - \delta(1 - \pi) + \gamma\theta + \beta\eta]\tilde{x}_{t-2} + [-\varphi(1 - \pi) + \gamma\eta]\tilde{\tilde{x}}_{t-2} + Z_{xt} \\ & - \pi Z_{xt-1} - (1 - \pi)\tilde{Z}_{xt-1} + \theta Z_{yt-1} + \eta\tilde{Z}_{yt-1} \end{aligned} \tag{9.5d}$$

As expected, the final forms are second order ARSAR models. The final form ARSAR coefficients sum to $(\beta + \gamma)(\theta + \eta) < 1$. Therefore, despite the presence of a spatio-temporal unit root in Eq. (9.6a), both y and x are stationary. Matters would be different if $(\beta + \gamma)(\theta + \eta) \geq 1$, or if $\delta + \varphi = 1$. In summary, a variable such as y that has a spatiotemporal unit root in isolation, may nevertheless be stationary if it depends on a variable such as x, which in isolation is stationary. If despite this y is nonstationary, so must x be nonstationary if it depends on y.

Spatial Error Correction and Spatial Cointegration

As mentioned in Chap. 7, Yu et al. (2012) compared alternative estimators of spatial error correction models where it is known that the nonstationary variables in the model are panel cointegrated. They did not provide critical values for statistical tests of the null hypothesis that these variables are not panel cointegrated. Nor was this their intention. Nevertheless, Elhorst et al. (2013) and Ciccarelli and Elhorst (2018) use the QMLE estimator suggested by Yu et al. to test hypotheses about financial liberalization and cigarette consumption under the assumption that the spatial panel data concerned are in fact cointegrated. However, it is first necessary to establish that the variables are indeed spatially panel cointegrated e.g. along the lines proposed in Chap. 7. Only then would there be justification in using QMLE to estimate the spatial error correction model.

This two-step process dates back to Engle and Granger (1987) who suggested that in the first stage it is necessary to test whether the nonstationary variables in the model are cointegrated. If they are, they must be related through error correction in the second stage.

9.3 Empirical Illustration of Spatial Error Correction

To set the scene, we begin by illustrating the estimation of a spatial error correction model (SpECM) for annual house prices in Israel in which the cointegrating vector is represented by Eq. (9.6a) taken from Beenstock and Felsenstein (2010) in which N = 9 and T = 17:

$$\ln P_{it} = \alpha_1 + 1.137lnPOP_{it} + 0.036lnY_{it} - 0.317lnH_{it} - 0.073ln\widetilde{PO}P_{it} + 0.184ln\tilde{P}_{it} + v_{it} \qquad (9.6a)$$

$$\text{GADF} = -3.11 \ \text{SpGrho} = 0.17$$

where P denotes house prices, POP denotes population, Y denotes income and H denotes housing stock (square meters). Equation (9.6a) includes a spatial lagged dependent variable and a spatial Durbin lag in population. Since the group ADF statistic is less than its critical values of −2.82 (Pedroni 1999) and SpGrho is less than its critical value of 0.79, u is stationary. According to Eq. (9.6a) regional house prices vary directly in the long run with demand (population and income), vary inversely with supply (housing stock), vary directly with house prices nearby and vary inversely with population nearby.

The estimated residuals (v) from Eq. (9.6a) are used to estimate the SpECM for regional house prices (Table 9.1). The SpECM includes the lagged first difference of the variables in Eq. (9.6a). These include lags of the spatially lagged variables as well as spatial lags of the estimated residuals.

In Table 9.1 both error correction terms are negative and statistically significant, indicating that house prices are both spatially and locally cointegrated. Indeed, the sizes of their coefficients indicate that about 70% of the local error is corrected within a year and 63% of the neighboring error spills over onto the local region. The

Table 9.1 Spatial error correction model for regional house prices (dependent variable: $\Delta \ln P_{it}$)

	Coefficient	t-statistic
Intercept	−0.0005	−0.05
$\Delta \ln P_{it-1}$	0.1732	3.1
$\Delta \ln \widetilde{P}_{it-1}$	0.1006	4.567
$\Delta \ln H_{it-1}$	0.6759	4.521
$\Delta \ln POP_{it-1}$	−0.3926	−3.591
$\Delta \ln \widetilde{Y}_{it}$	0.0762	1.882
$\hat{u}_{it-1}$	−0.7047	−8.622
$\widetilde{\hat{u}}_{it-1}$	−0.6348	−4.63
R^2 adj	0.511	
Standard error	1.035	
DW	2.021	

Method of estimation: Panel SUR with common effects. Source: Beenstock and Felsenstein (2010)

latter also means that if house prices were too high in neighboring regions this exerts downward pressure on local house prices, i.e. there is spatial spillover in error correction, just as there might be with any other variable.

Table 9.1 also incorporates temporally-lagged spatial lags for the first differences in house prices in the autoregressive component of the model. Had this difference been contemporaneous rather than lagged one period, the estimated parameters of the SpECM would not have been consistent, in which case estimation by ML or IV would have been necessary. The same would have applied had the SpECM residuals been autocorrelated, in which event they would have been correlated with the lagged difference in the spatial lag of house prices. However, the panel Durbin Watson statistic indicates that the SpECM residuals are not autocorrelated. Therefore, the estimate of the SAR coefficient (0.1006) is consistent. This means that the current rate of change in local house prices depends on the lagged rate of change in house prices in neighboring regions, as well as the rate of change of lagged house prices in the locality. The spatial lag coefficient is 0.1 in Table 9.1, whereas the coefficient on the lagged dependent variable is 0.1732.

Substituting Eq. (9.6a) into Table 9.1 for $\hat{u}_{it-1}$ and $\widetilde{\hat{u}}_{it-1}$ produces the following ARSAR (autoregressive and spatial autoregressive) model in the logarithm of house prices:

$$lnP_t = \left(0.4685I_N - 0.4045W + 0.1169W^2\right)lnP_{t-1}$$
$$-(0.1732I_N + 0.1006W)lnP_{t-2} + X_t \tag{9.6b}$$

where P is an N-vector of house prices, and X_t is an N-vector of all the other variables in Eq. (9.6a), such as POP_{t-1} and in the SpECM such as ΔPOP_{t-1}. The temporal and spatial dynamics are second order because Table 9.1 is a second order difference equation, which involves W and W^2. There are 2N = 18 roots to Eq. (9.6b), which is too many to consider analytically. However, we may gain some insight by obtaining the conditional roots for unit i and by setting N = 2.

The solution in Eq. (9.6b) for house prices in unit i is:

$$lnP_{it} = 0.4685lnP_{it-1} - 0.1732lnP_{it-2} - 0.4045ln\tilde{P}_{it-1} - 0.1006ln\tilde{P}_{it-2}$$
$$+0.1169ln\tilde{\tilde{P}}_{it-1} + X_{it} \tag{9.6c}$$

House prices in unit i are a second order AR and SAR process and depend on house prices in second order neighbors. Conditional on spatial lagged house prices the two roots of Eq. (9.6c) are less than 1 but complex:

$$\omega = 0.4162(0.5629 \pm i0.8265) \tag{9.6d}$$

The roots are not real because, as mentioned, the ECM model contains a lagged endogenous variable (ΔlnP_{it-1}). However, they are less than 1 because the modulus is a fraction (0.4162).

Setting $N = 2$ in Eq. (9.6b) would generate the following fourth order characteristic equation:

$$\omega^4 - 0.937\omega^3 + 0.4023\omega^2 - 0.1623\omega + 0.03 = 0 \tag{9.6e}$$

for which the roots are: $\omega_1 = 0.5681$, ω_2 and $\omega_3 = 0.032 \pm i0.415$, and $\omega_4 = 0.3049$. The complex roots arise for the same reason as in Eq. (9.6d). Equation (9.6e) implies that the AR coefficients weaken in absolute size with their lag order. The AR (1) coefficient is 0.937, the AR(2) coefficient is −0.4023, the AR(3) coefficient is 0.1623 and the AR(4) coefficient is 0.03. This is why the roots are than 1.

Since $N = 9$ there are 36 roots, which are too many to consider here. Nevertheless, they share the features of Eq. (9.6e). The general solution to Eq. (9.6b) is:

$$lnP_t = \left[I_N + \sum\nolimits_{\tau=1}^{\infty} \left(\Omega_1 L - \Omega_2 L^2\right)^{\tau}\right] X_t + \sum\nolimits_{i}^{18} A_i \omega_i^t \tag{9.6f}$$

where

$$\Omega_1 = 0.4685 I_N - 0.4045 W + 0.1169 W^2$$
$$\Omega_2 = 0.1732 I_N + 0.1006 W$$

and the As are arbitrary constants determined by initial conditions. Since the roots (ω) are (positive) fractions the final term in Eq. (9.6f) tends to zero with time. Equation (9.6f) generates spatio-temporal impulse responses. For example, the response of P_{it} to an impulse in X_i after two periods is:

$$\frac{\partial lnP_{it}}{\partial X_{it-2}} = 1 + \psi_{ii} \tag{9.6g}$$

where $\Psi = \Omega_1^2 - \Omega_2$ embodies a quartic in W. The direct effect is 1 and the indirect effect is ψ_{ii}. Note that ψ_{ii} incorporates up to fourth order spatial effects. The impulse response between spatial units is ψ_{ij} since there is no direct effect. Table 9.1 implies that the direct elasticity of house prices with respect to population is 0.1732 after 1 year. The indirect effect will increase this because the SAR coefficient 0.1006. According to Eq. (9.6a) the long term elasticity is 1.137. The intermediate impulse elasticities are generated by Eq. (9.6f) since population is a component of X.

Spatial lags for other variables such as income also feature in Table 9.1. Indeed, whereas there is no local income effect in Table 9.1 there is a small but statistically significant spatially lagged effect of 0.076. The short run effects of the housing stock and population on house prices in the ECM have opposite signs to their long-run counterparts in the cointegrating vector. The long run effect of housing stock on house prices is negative, but the short term effect is positive. This means that shocks to the housing stock initially increase house prices, but eventually lower them, and because the roots are complex, house prices overshoot their long run value before settling down. The same applies to the dynamic effect of population shocks on house prices, except in the opposite direction.

Finally, we note that because according to the panel DW statistic the SpECM residuals are serially uncorrelated, $\Delta ln\tilde{P}_{it-1}$ is weakly exogenous for its SAR coefficient (0.1006). This means that since this variable has been lagged one period its SAR coefficient is estimated consistently without recourse to ML or IV. Matters would have been different if the SpECM residuals were serially correlated.

9.4 Empirical Example of Spatial Vector Error Correction

There is a natural hierarchy to error correction models, which has four tiers:

1. In the basic error correction model (ECM) the dynamics of y in Eq. (9.2a) depends on u_{t-1} and the dynamic of x in Eq. (9.2b) depends on v_{t-1}.
2. In spatial error correction models (SpECM) the dynamics of y depends on u_{t-1} and its spatial lag $\tilde{u}_{t-1}$, and the dynamics of x depends on v_{t-1} and its spatial lag $\tilde{v}_{t-1}$. In SpECMs there is spatial spillover in error correction.
3. In vector error correction models (VECM) the dynamics of y and x depend on both u_{t-1} and v_{t-1}. In VECMs there is mutual dependence in error correction.
4. In spatial vector error correction models (SpVECM) the dynamics of y and x depend on u_{t-1}, v_{t-1}, $\tilde{u}_{t-1}$ and $\tilde{v}_{t-1}$.

In spatial error correction models the ζ coefficients in Eqs. (9.2a and 9.2b) are assumed to be zero. This means that error correction is induced by "own" or within residuals generated by cointegrating vectors as measures of disequilibrium, and does not depend on measures of disequilibrium regarding other variables. Thus, in Eq. (9.2a) Δy_t depends on u_{t-1} and $\tilde{u}_{t-1}$ and in Eq. (9.2b) Δx_t depends on v_{t-1} and $\tilde{v}_{t-1}$. By contrast, in spatial vector error correction models, the ζ coefficients are not zero so that error correction occurs within and between variables. Hence, Δy_t and Δx_t depend on u_{t-1} and $\tilde{u}_{t-1}$ and v_{t-1} and $\tilde{v}_{t-1}$.

By way of illustration we take two cointegrating vectors from Table 8.9. The first is represented by Eq. I for housing starts (measured in square meters), and the second is represented by Eq. III for house prices (at constant prices). Recall, that Eq. I represents the supply of housing, and Eq. III is in inverted demand schedule for housing. These cointegrating vectors refer to the long run relationships between the nonstationary panel data in these models, which include spatial lagged dependent variables as well as spatial Durbin lagged variables. The panel residuals for housing starts (u) and house prices (v) are plotted in Figs. 9.1 and 9.2.

The residuals are mean-zero, autocorrelated and mean reverting as expected. In Fig. 9.2 the residuals (v) are more correlated than in Fig. 9.1 for u. In Fig. 9.1 the residuals for Haifa are more volatile than the rest.

We use the general-to-specific (GTS) methodology (Hendry 1995) to estimate the error correction model. GTS starts with an unrestricted error correction model in which first differences of all the variables in the cointegrating vector are specified, as

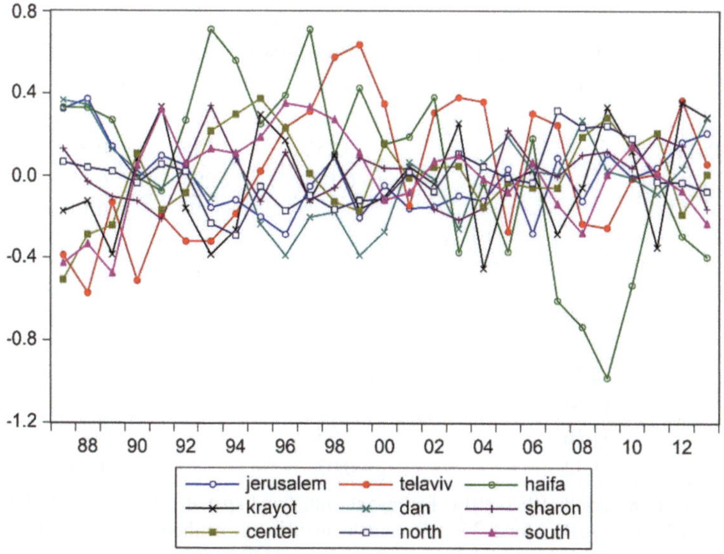

Fig. 9.1 Cointegrating residuals: housing starts (u)

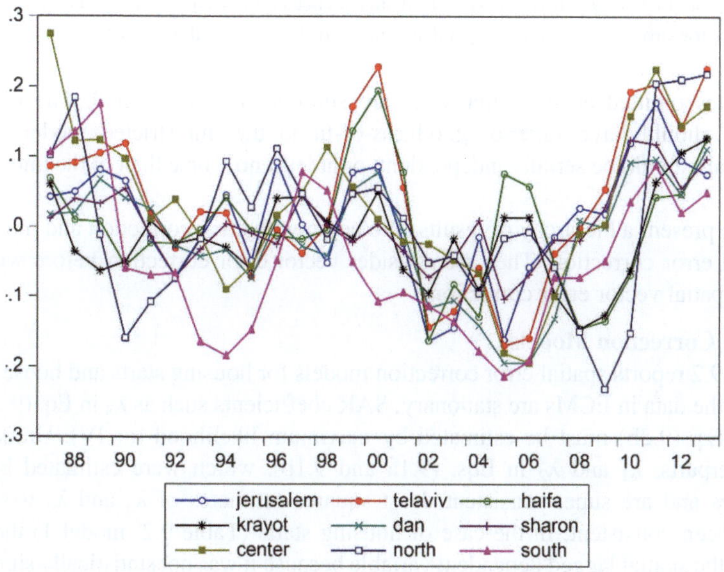

Fig. 9.2 Cointegrating residuals: house prices (v)

well as the lagged cointegrating residuals u_{it-1} and v_{it-1}. GTS is a backward stepwise procedure in which variables are omitted provided their omission does not induce autocorrelation and a deterioration of goodness-of fit in terms of equation standard error or other criteria such as AIC and BIC. To check for path dependence

Table 9.2 Error correction models

	1 Housing starts		2 House prices		3 House prices	
Model	Coeff	t-stat	Coeff	t-stat	Coeff	t-stat
ΔlnP_{it-1}	1.879	3.871	0.320	5.00	−0.441	6.939
$\Delta lnPOPi_{t-1}$			0.252	1.125	0.077	0.407
$\Delta lnYi_{t-1}$			−0.186	−2.29	0.116	0.349
$\Delta ln\tilde{P}_{it}$					−0.155	1.544
u_{it-1}	−0.474	−6.617				
v_{it-1}			−0.286	−6.318	−0.426	−0.69
R^2	0.061		0.044		0.136	
se	0.258		0.057			
DW	2.23		1.93			
LM	13.64		9.92		30.72	
BP	31.16		42.96		108.49	
CD	−1.72		−0.07		−1.70	

Notes: Estimation period: 1988–2014. Estimated with fixed spatial effects. Models 1 and 2 are estimated by EGLS (SUR). Model 3 is estimated by maximum likelihood. The dependent variables are ΔlnS_{it} for housing starts and ΔlnP_{it} for house prices. POP denotes population, Y denotes real wages, u denotes the residuals in Fig. 9.1 and v the residuals in Fig. 9.2. LM is the Lagrange multiplier panel test statistic for second order autocorrelation in the residuals (distributed χ^2_2), BP is the Breusch–Pagan statistic for cross-section dependence in the residuals (distributed $\chi^2_{½N(N-1)}$) and CD tests for strong cross-section dependence in the residuals (distributed N(0,1))

variables omitted at an earlier stage are subsequently respecified. The restricted model should have superior goodness-of-fit to the unrestricted model, and its residuals should be serially independent, or at least no worse than in the unrestricted model.

We present a hierarchy of results. We begin with error correction and move onto spatial error correction. Then we consider vector error correction before we move onto spatial vector error correction.

Error Correction Models

Table 9.2 reports spatial error correction models for housing starts and house prices. Since the data in ECMs are stationary, SAR coefficients such as λ_3 in Eq. (9.2a) and λ_4 in Eq. (9.2b) must be estimated by maximum likelihood (or IV). Unlike their counterparts, λ_1 and λ_2 in Eqs. (9.1a and 9.1b), which were estimated by least squares and are super-consistent, least squares estimates of λ_3 and λ_4 would not have been consistent. In the case of housing starts (Table 9.2, model 1) the ECM omits the spatial lagged dependent variable because it was not statistically significant (SAR $=$ 0.024 with t-statistic 0.25). The error correction coefficient is −0.474 (t statistic $=$ −6.617), implying that almost half of the error correction for housing starts occurs within a year. Apart from this, the only other variable in model 1 is the lagged change in house prices, suggesting that the short term price elasticity of supply in terms of housing starts is almost two, which is much greater than the long term elasticity reported in the cointegrating vector for housing starts (Table 8.9, Eq. I).

The panel Durbin–Watson statistic indicated that the residuals of model 1 are not serially autocorrelated, in which case the lagged change in log house prices are weakly exogenous. This means that the lagged change in log house prices have a causal effect on subsequent housing starts. By contrast, the LM statistic indicates that the residuals are serially correlated. The DW statistic is biased towards 2 when the covariates include lagged endogenous variables. However, there are no lagged endogenous variables in model 1. Table 9.2 and subsequent tables omit contemporaneous first differences because variables such ΔlnP_{it} are jointly determined with ΔlnS_{it}. Therefore, to test whether current house price changes causally affect changes in housing starts would require estimation by IV.

The error correction coefficient in model 2 for house prices (−0.286) is smaller than its counterpart for housing starts. Hence house prices adjust considerably more slowly than housing starts. Although according to model 1 there is no inertia in housing starts, the autoregressive coefficient in model 2 indicates first order inertia in house prices. Apart from this the ECM for house prices suggests that population growth raises house prices, but the opposite applies to income growth. This means that whereas income raises house prices in the long run, the opposite applies in the short run.

Model 3, estimated by ML includes a contemporaneous term in the spatial lagged endogenous variable. Since the SAR coefficient is negative, it implies negative spatial spillover in house prices. In contrast, the spatial spillover in the cointegrating vector for house prices was positive (Table 8.9, Eq. III). The error correction coefficient increases to −0.426 (becomes more negative) from −0.236, but surprisingly it is not statistically significant. Since cointegration and error correction are mirror images of each other, it is not clear why error correction is statistically significant in model 2, but not in model 3.

Finally, the BP and CD statistics test for cross-section dependence in the residuals of the error correction models. Since cross-section dependence and its econometric implications are the focus of Chap. 10, we defer detailed discussion to the next chapter. However, these statistics are reported her for reference. In the meanwhile, we note that since the critical value of chi square for BP is about 50 and the critical value for CD is −1.96 the BP statistic is not significant in models 1 and 2, and the CD statistic is not significant at conventional levels in all models.

In Table 9.6 we report the counterparts to Eq. (9.5b) for the ARSAR coefficients of the error correction models reported in Tables 9.2, 9.3, 9.4 and 9.5 and the cointegrating vectors reported in Table 8.9. The first column refers to lnP_t which is AR(2) and SAR(1) and does not directly depend on S since this variable does not feature in the ECM for house prices or the cointegrating vector for house prices. Since housing stocks feature in the cointegrating vector, housing starts affect house prices indirectly, but we ignore this for our present illustrative purposes. The second column refers to lnS_t, which is AR(1) and SAR(1), and depends on lags and spatial lags of lnP. Since the ARSAR coefficients sum to fractions, 0.84 in the case of lnP and 0.901 in the case of lnS, the $4N = 36$ roots are fractions but some will be complex especially since the AR2 coefficient for lnP is negative.

Table 9.3 Spatial error correction models

	1 Housing starts		2 House prices		3 House prices	
Model	Coeff	t-stat	Coeff	t-stat	Coeff	t-stat
ΔlnP_{it-1}	1.780	3.539	0.295	4.687	−0.380	6.039
$\Delta lnPOPi_{t-1}$			0.292	1.325	0.015	0.083
$\Delta lnYi_{t-1}$			−0.132	−1.551	0.136	0.426
$\Delta ln\tilde{P}_{it}$					−0.169	1.712
u_{it-1}	−0.470	−6.548				
$\tilde{u}_{it-1}$	−0.233	0.753				
v_{it-1}			−0.223	−4.621	−0.032	−0.054
$\tilde{v}_{it-1}$			0.371	3.229	6.090	4.044
R^2	0.062		0.066		0.109	
se	0.258		0.056			
DW	2.23		1.99			
LM	13.91		14.91		24.53	
BP	31.63		47.60		95.47	
CD	−1.18		−1.41		−1.70	

See notes to Table 9.2

Table 9.4 Vector error correction models

	1 Housing starts		2 House prices		3 House prices	
Model	Coeff	t-stat	Coeff	t-stat	Coeff	t-stat
ΔlnP_{it-1}	2.009	4.053	0.317	4.952	−0.440	6.914
$\Delta lnPOPi_{t-1}$			0.235	1.045	0.077	0.405
$\Delta lnYi_{t-1}$			−0.185	−2.184	0.116	0.351
$\Delta ln\tilde{P}_{it}$					−0.159	−1.580
u_{it-1}	−0.474	−6.630	−0.285	−6.307	0.005	0.020
v_{it-1}	−0.245	−1.253	0.019	1.188	−0.426	−0.688
R^2	0.062		0.037			
se	0.258		0.057			
DW	2.23		1.92			
LM	14.02		8.32			
BP	32.23		42.58		108.54	
CD	−1.43		−0.049		−1.685	

See notes to Table 9.2

Spatial Error Correction

As in Table 9.1, Table 9.3 reports spatial error correction models (SpECM). Model 1 in Table 9.3 is the same as model 1 in Table 9.2 except it includes a spatial Durbin lag for u_{it-1}. The coefficient on the spatial error correction coefficient is −0.233, but it is not statistically significant. In model 2 both error correction coefficients are statistically significant. The spatial error correction coefficient is 0.371 and positive. The own error correction coefficient (ξ) implies that if house prices were too high in

Table 9.5 Spatial vector error correction models

	1 Housing starts		2 House prices		3 House prices	
Model	Coeff	t-stat	Coeff	t-stat	Coeff	t-stat
$\Delta \ln P_{it-1}$	1.601	3.047	0.274	4.362	−0.386	6.114
$\Delta \ln POPi_{t-1}$			0.481	2.046	0.016	0.089
$\Delta \ln Yi_{t-1}$			−0.066	−0.753	0.130	0.409
$\Delta ln\tilde{P}_{it}$					−0.174	1.763
u_{it-1}	−0.488	−6.830	0.019	1.196	0.098	0.409
$\tilde{u}_{it-1}$	−0.197	−0.640	−0.172	−2.33	0.552	1.00
v_{it-1}	−0.026	−0.120	−0.236	−4.911	0.060	0.098
$\tilde{v}_{it-1}$	1.185	2.239	0.352	3.081	6.219	4.122
R^2	0.058		0.0511		0.109	
se	0.255		0.055			
DW	2.20		1.99			
LM	13.08		11.50		24.46	
BP	35.56		44.15		92.77	
CD	−1.23		−1.23		−1.76	

See notes to Table 9.2

Table 9.6 ARSAR coefficients

	ECM		SpECM		VECM		SpVECM	
	$\ln P_t$	$\ln S_t$	$\ln P_t$	$\ln S_t$	$\ln P_t$	$\ln S_t$	$\ln P_t$	$\ln S_t$
P_{t-1}	1.034	2.082	1.072	1.981	1.495	1.967	1.023	1.784
P_{t-2}	−0.320	−1.879	−0.295	−1.780	−0.317	−2.009	−0.274	−1.601
$\tilde{P}_{t-1}$	0.126	−0.230	0.469	−0.129	−0.163	−0.123	0.538	−1.326
$\tilde{\tilde{P}}_{t-1}$	0	0	−0.163	−0.113	0	0	−0.238	−0.616
$\bar{P}_{t-1}$	0	0.197	0	0.292	0	0	0.064	0.284
S_{t-1}	0	0.526	0	0.530	−0.285	0.374	0.019	0.512
$\tilde{S}_{t-1}$	0	0.375	0	0.183	0.225	0	0	0.189
$\tilde{\tilde{S}}_{t-1}$	0	0	0	0.184	0	0	0	0.157
Sum	0.84	0.901	1.083	0.897	1.015	0.374	1.04	0.858
Final Form	0.984		1.410		1.011		0.967	

Notes: "Sum" refers to sums of ARSAR coefficients. "Final form" refers to the sums of ARSAR coefficients using Eq. (9.5c)

the previous period, they decrease subsequently. The spatial error correction coefficient implies that if house prices were too high elsewhere in the previous period, this disequilibrium spills-over onto house prices. As in Table 9.2 the panel DW statistic suggests that the residuals are not serially correlated, however, the LM statistic continues to contradict this.

Columns 3 and 4 of Table 9.6 report the ARSAR coefficients generated by models 2 and 1 in Table 9.3. In the case of house prices these coefficients are

AR(2) and SAR(2) while for housing starts they are AR(1) and SAR(2). The sum of the ARSAR coefficients for lnP is close to 1 (1.083) and the sum for lnS is 0.897. The former implies that the SpECM is not convergent and is inconsistent with the result that variables in Eq. III in Table 8.9 are cointegrated. Matters would have been different had the relation between housing starts and housing stocks been fully articulated (as in Table 8.9) since house prices vary inversely with housing stocks. Because this indirect effect has been omitted for present illustrative purposes, the ARSAR coefficients for lnP sum to slightly above 1 in Tables 9.3, 9.4 and 9.5. The final form ARSAR coefficients sum to slightly less than 1. Our purpose here is simply to illustrate spatial error correction when there are only two state variables, housing starts (S) and house prices (P). Had we included the nexus between starts, completions and housing stocks, transparency would have suffered.

Vector Error Correction

In Tables 9.1, 9.2 and 9.3 error correction applies within equations but not between them. In VECM models error correction applies within and between equations. Hence, house price dynamics depend on the disequilibrium in housing starts, and the dynamics of housing starts depend on the disequilibrium in house prices. In VECMs there is no spatial error correction. Results are reported in Table 9.4.

In model 1 there is negative error correction from u and v for housing starts. The former means that housing starts decrease if in the previous period they were too high ($u > 0$), which makes economic sense. The latter means that housing starts decrease if in the previous period house prices were too high ($v > 0$), which makes economic sense if building contractors expect house prices to fall. The former effect is clearly statistically significant, but the latter effect is not significant at conventional levels. In model 2 there is negative error correction from u and positive error correction from v. The former means that house prices decrease if starts were too high in the previous period, which makes economic sense. The latter means that if house prices were too high in the previous period, they grow even higher, which does not make economic sense. Moreover, the former effect is statistically significant, and the latter effect is not.

The ARSAR coefficients sum to 1.015 for house prices and to 0.734 for housing starts (Table 9.6). The final form ARSAR coefficients sum to 1.41. The VECM for lnP is AR(2) and SAR(1) and for lnS it is AR(1) and SAR(0). Whereas the ECMs in Table 9.2 and the SpECMs in Table 9.3 have recursive structures because starts depend on house prices, but house prices do not depend directly on starts, matters are different in the VECMs. Table 9.6 shows that the VECMs are not recursive because house prices depend on lagged starts with a coefficient of −0.285 as well as their spatial lag with a coefficient of 0.225. Since these coefficients roughly offset each other the sum of the final form ARSAR coefficients sum to 1.011.

Model 3 in Table 9.4 is estimated by ML because it includes a contemporaneous spatial lagged dependent variable. The spatial lag coefficient remains similar to what it was in Tables 9.2 and 9.3, and the error correction coefficients cease to be statistically significant. However, the spatial lag coefficient continues to be not statistically significant at conventional levels.

Spatial Vector Error Correction

Table 9.5 presents illustrative results for spatial vector error correction models in which error correction is both spatial and interdependent. For example, in model 1 housing starts decrease if they were too high in the previous year; the error correction coefficient is −0. 488 and is statistically significant. There is a negative spatial lag (−0.197) suggesting that housing starts decrease if they were too high elsewhere, however, this effect is not statistically significant. Nor is the error correction effect of excess house prices (−0.026). On the other hand, there is strong and significant spatial error correction, implying that housing starts increase if house prices were too high elsewhere.

In the SpVECM for house prices three of the four error correction coefficients are statistically significant (model 2). House prices decrease when house prices were too high locally, and they increase if they were too high elsewhere. They decrease if housing starts were too high elsewhere. Surprisingly, house prices depend on local error correction. The ARSAR coefficients in Table 9.6 sum to 1.049 for lnP and to −0.858 for ln S. Their final form counterparts sum to 0.967. The SpVECM in Table 9.6 incorporates six spatial effects; two for house prices (first and second order spatial lags for house prices) and four for housing starts (first and second order spatial lags for house prices and starts).

Our purpose here is not to choose the best, or indeed any, of the error correction models. Rather, our intension is simply to illustrate the hierarchy of error correction models. There is no reason why the best model should not be hybrid. For example, the error correction for one variable might be SpECM while for another variable it might be VECM. Nevertheless, error correction models with final form ARSAR coefficients summing to 1 and more are less admissible because they do not converge to equilibrium. In Table 9.6 this rules out SpECM, VECM and SpVECM.

We have already noted that this artefact happens because for illustrative purposes we chose to focus on only two variables, house prices and housing starts. A complete analysis would have involved specifying the relationship between housing starts and housing stocks, which would have involved error correction models for housing completions. In this case the ARSAR coefficients would have summed to less than 1 because housing starts, housing completions, house prices and housing stocks are spatially coinregrated.

Chapter 7 includes the first episode of a plot that has four parts. The first episode involves spatiotemporal unit root tests for spatial panel data in Israel. The second episode in Chap. 8 involves spatial panel cointegration tests among these variables. The third episode, presented in this chapter, involves spatial error correction between these variables. The final episode is in the next chapter, where we ask whether the spatial panel data in the series are related through common factors rather just spatial dependence alone.

References

Beenstock M, Felsenstein D (2010) Spatial error correction and cointegration in nonstationary spatial panel data: regional house prices in Israel. J Geogr Syst 12:189–206

Ciccarelli C, Elhorst JP (2018) A dynamic spatial econometric diffusion model with common factors: the rise and spread of cigarette consumption in Italy. Reg Sci Urban Econ 72:131–142
Elhorst JP, Zandberg E, De Haan J (2013) The impact of interaction effects among neighboring countries on financial liberalization and reform: a dynamic spatial panel data approach. Spat Econ Anal 8:293–313
Engle R, Granger CWJ (1987) Co-integration and error correction: representation, estimation and testing. Econometrica 35:251–276
Hendry DF (1995) Dynamic econometrics. Oxford University Press, Oxford
Pedroni P (1999) Critical values for cointegration tests in heterogeneous panels with multiple regressors. Oxf Bull Econ Stat 61:653–670
Yu J, de Jong R, Lee JF (2012) Estimation for spatial dynamic panel data with fixed effects: the case of spatial cointegration. J Econ 167(1):16–37

Chapter 10
Strong and Weak Cross-Section Dependence in Non-Stationary Spatial Panel Data

10.1 Introduction

Throughout this volume, we have taken it for granted that cross-section dependence in spatial panel data is induced by spatial econometric phenomena discussed in Chap. 3. In Chap. 1 we observed that cross-section dependence in spatial panel data may assume two forms, weak or strong. According to the latter, cross-section dependence results from common factors, which induce correlation between spatial panel units. According the former, cross-section dependence is induced by spatial interactions between panel units. In terms of Manski's (1993) classification of reflection phenomena, strong cross-section dependence is "contextual" and non-causal, while spatial cross-section dependence is "endogenous" and causal. When cross-section dependence is spatial, distance between panel units matters. When cross-section dependence is strong, distance does not matter. A third possibility (Anselin 1988, Chap. 10) is that cross-section dependence has no structure; it is neither spatial nor induced by common factors. It is induced by seemingly unrelatedness (SUR).

In this final chapter we ask the existential question: should cross-section dependence in spatial panel data be treated as spatial, as we have taken for granted, or should it be treated as strong or induced by SUR? If it is strong, the contents of this volume would no longer be relevant. Instead, the common correlated effects (CCE) estimator proposed by Kapitanios et al. (2011) for nonstationary panel data would be relevant. If it is induced by SUR, estimation should be by EGLS. Bailey et al. (2016) recognize that weak and strong cross-section dependence are not mutually exclusive; both types of dependence might coexist. In their study of changes in log house prices, they propose a two-stage strategy in which they filter house prices changes for common factors in the first stage, and then use these filtered data to take account of spatial (weak) cross-section dependence in the second stage. This approach assumes that estimates of weak and strong cross-section dependence are mutually

M. Beenstock, D. Felsenstein, *The Econometric Analysis of Non-Stationary Spatial Panel Data*, Advances in Spatial Science,
https://doi.org/10.1007/978-3-030-03614-0_10

independent. Would the results have been the same if weak dependence had been filtered out of the data in the first stage, and strong dependence estimated in the second? We suggest below that both types of dependence should be estimated jointly rather than sequentially. A similar point has been made by Halleck Vega and Elhorst (2016), who claim that the two-stage method induces bias in the parameter estimates. We also suggest that instead of using differenced data as do Bailey, Holly and Pesaran, hypotheses should be tested using levels of house prices, even if such data happen to be nonstationary.[1]

The chapter is organized as follows. We begin by discussing statistical tests for weak and strong cross section dependence, and recall the CCE estimator as applied to nonstationary panel data. This is followed by an empirical illustration, which compares weak and strong cross-section dependence. Finally, we return to the empirical case study of spatial panel data for Israel, which began in Table 7.2 with spatiotemporal unit root tests, continued in Table 8.9 with spatiotemporal panel cointegration tests and in Tables 9.2–9.5 with spatial VECMs. Specifically, we check the residuals of the SGE model in Table 8.9 and the residuals of its SpVECM in Tables 9.2–9.5 for cross-section dependence. If there is evidence of strong cross-section dependence, we re-estimate these models using the CCE estimator. Finally, we ask whether the CCE estimator indeed eliminates strong cross-section dependence as expected.

10.2 Methodology

Consider the basic panel data model:

$$y_{it} = \alpha_i + X_{it}\beta + u_{it} \tag{10.1}$$

in which there is cross-section dependence in the error terms (u). To test for cross-section dependence, we may use the Breusch and Pagan (1979) statistic:

$$BP = T\sum_{i=1}^{N}\sum_{j\neq i+1}^{N} r_{ij}^2 \sim \chi^2_{½N(N-1)} \tag{10.2}$$

where r_{ij} denotes the pairwise correlation between u_i and u_j, T denotes the number of time-series observations, and N denotes the number of cross-section units for which there are ½N(N − 1) pairwise correlations r_{ij}. If BP exceeds its critical value, the null hypothesis of cross-section independence may be rejected.

Suppose this to be the case. Pesaran (2015) has proposed the following test to determine whether this cross-section dependence is weak or strong:

[1]In Halleck Vega and Elhorst (2016) the sum of the estimated autoregressive (AR) and spatial autoregressive (SAR) coefficients are either close to 1 and even exceed 1. Note that the presence of spatio-temporal unit roots may induce spurious regression phenomena.

$$CD = \sqrt{½TN(N-1)}\bar{r} \sim N(0,1) \tag{10.3}$$

where $\bar{r}$ is the average of the ½N(N − 1) pairwise cross-section correlations of the residuals, which may be positive or negative. If, for example, N = 3, T = 30, $r_{12} = r_{13} = 0.3$, and $r_{23} = -0.6$, CD = 0 and BP = 16.2, which exceeds its critical value of chi-square. Unlike CD, what matters for BP is the absolute correlation irrespective of sign. If CD is less than its critical value, the null hypothesis of weak cross-section dependence cannot be rejected. If it exceeds its critical value, the null hypothesis of weak cross-section dependence is rejected; cross-section dependence may be strong as well as weak. Notice that cross-section dependence is weak if the average absolute correlation is not statistically significantly different from zero, and BP exceeds its critical value. Note that whereas BP does not depend on the signs of the cross-section correlations, but CD does, BP may be statistically significant even if the opposite applies to CD. On the other hand, if CD is statistically significant, the same must apply to BP.

The intuition behind the CD test is straightforward. If distance between spatial units does not matter for cross-section dependence, increasing N adds more remote spatial units to the sample. Since cross-section dependence does not weaken with distance when it is strong, the average correlation should not tend to zero with N. By contrast, if distance matters because cross-section dependence is weak, average correlations should tend to zero as increasingly remote spatial units are included in the sample. Epidemics eventually run their course so that cross-section correlations tend to zero. However, these correlations do not tend to zero if they are induced by common factors. In this case, Pesaran (2006) proposed the common correlated effects estimator (CCE):

$$y_{it} = \alpha_i + X_{it}\beta + \eta_i\bar{y}_t + \bar{X}_t\eta_{xi} + v_{it} \tag{10.4}$$

where the cross-section mean of y at time t serves as a common factor with spatially heterogeneous loadings denoted by η. Further common factors may be specified in terms of the cross-section averages of the covariates (X), or other variables according to theory. Setting $\eta_x = 0$ for simplicity in Eq. (10.4), the correlation between u_i and u_j is:

$$r_{ij} = \frac{\eta_i\eta_j\sigma_{\bar{y}}^2}{\sqrt{\eta_i^2\sigma_{\bar{y}}^2 + \sigma_v^2}\sqrt{\eta_j^2\sigma_{\bar{y}}^2 + \sigma_v^2}} \tag{10.5}$$

in which distance plays no role because η_i and η_j are unrelated to distance. By contrast, when u is spatially autocorrelated with SAC coefficient ρ ($u_t = Av_t$ where $A = (I - \rho W)^{-1}$) the pairwise correlation between u_i and u_j is:

$$r_{ij} = \frac{\sum_{k=1}^{N} a_{ik}a_{jk}\sigma_v^2}{\sqrt{\sum_{k=1}^{N} a_{ik}^2\sigma_v^2}\sqrt{\sum_{k=1}^{N} a_{jk}^2\sigma_v^2}} = \frac{\sum_{k=1}^{N} a_{ik}a_{jk}}{\sqrt{\sum_{k=1}^{N} a_{ik}^2}\sqrt{\sum_{k=1}^{N} a_{jk}^2}} \quad (10.6)$$

in which distance plays a role because a_{ik} varies inversely with the distance between i and k. Since on average spatial units are not close to each other, the mean of r tends to zero as N tends to infinity when cross-section correlation happens to be weak.

Under strong cross-section dependence $\sum_{i=1}^{N} |\eta_i| = O_p(N)$ i.e. the sum of the absolute loadings is expected to increase with N because each spatial unit is affected by the common factor. By contrast, under weak cross-section dependence the sum of absolute loadings is $O_p(1)$ because as N increases the additional units are more distant from the existing ones. Semi-strong cross-section dependence arises when the sum of absolute loadings increases less than proportionately with N because cross-section dependence does not diminish rapidly enough with distance.

Suppose, for simplicity, that there is a single common factor with factor loadings η_i of which $\eta \neq 0$ in M out of N cases. Bailey et al. (2016) have suggested that $\alpha = \ln(M)/\ln(N)$ may be used as a measure of distance decay, which is bounded between 0 and 1. Since $\bar{r} = O\left(N^{2(\alpha-1)}\right)$ and α is a positive fraction, $\bar{r}$ varies inversely with N; the average cross-section correlation tends to zero unless M = N and $\alpha = 1$, in which event $\bar{r} = O(1)$ and cross-section dependence is strong. If $\alpha < ½$ cross-section dependence is weak because $\bar{r}$ decreases rapidly with N. If $½ < \alpha < ¾$ cross-section dependence is moderate because $\bar{r}$ decreases more slowly with N. If $¾ < \alpha < 1$ cross-section dependence ceases to be moderate and is strong when $\alpha = 1$. When there are K common factors α is the maximum of α_k where k labels common factors. This means that if there is only one common factor for which $\alpha_k = 1$ cross-section dependence is strong.

If the data in Eq. (10.4) are nonstationary, they are cointegrated when the residuals (v) are panel stationary. Critical values for panel cointegration with CCE have been calculated by Banerjee and Carrion-I-Silvestre (2017). These critical values are naturally stricter than their counterparts for independent panel data (Pedroni 1999), but their dependence on the number of variables in the model is surprisingly small. For example, when there are two or three variables the critical values for panel cointegration (GADF) due to Pedroni are −2.124 and −2.453 respectively. When there is one common factor these critical values are respectively −3.23 and −3.24.

An alternative to CCE is to carry out a principal components analysis of the residuals generated by Eq. (10.1) as in Bai and Ng (2004). The principal components constitute common factors, which may be used instead of $\bar{y}$ in Eq. (10.4). The two approaches are not identical. However, CCE has the practical advantage of being easier to implement, and in many instances is justified by economic theory, as discussed below. See Pesaran (2015, Chap. 28) on CCE, principal components and factor models for stationary panel data. Pesaran does not consider the case of nonstationary spatial panel data.

Finally, we note that if cross-section dependence is weak, this does not necessarily mean that it must be spatial. It may simply mean that the error terms are unrelated to distance and are seemingly unrelated. In this case, estimation should be by SUR (seemingly unrelated regression). In Eq. (10.7a) y_i and u_i are $T \times 1$ vectors of y and error terms, x_i are $T \times K_i$ matrices of covariates and β_i are $K_i \times 1$ vectors of parameters to be estimated:

$$Y = \begin{bmatrix} y_1 \\ \vdots \\ y_N \end{bmatrix} = \begin{bmatrix} x_1 & \cdots & 0 \\ \vdots & \ddots & \vdots \\ 0 & \cdots & x_N \end{bmatrix} \begin{bmatrix} \beta_1 \\ \vdots \\ \beta_N \end{bmatrix} + \begin{bmatrix} u_1 \\ \vdots \\ u_N \end{bmatrix} = X\beta + u \tag{10.7a}$$

Hence, Y and u are $NT \times 1$ vectors, X is an $NT \times K$ matrix and β is a $K \times 1$ vector. The covariance matrix for the disturbance terms is:

$$\Sigma = \begin{bmatrix} \sigma_{11} & \cdots & \sigma_{1N} \\ \vdots & \ddots & \vdots \\ \sigma_{N1} & \cdots & \sigma_{NN} \end{bmatrix}$$

where σ_{ij} are cross-sectional. The SUR and covariance estimators for β are:

$$\hat{\beta} = \left(X'\Omega^{-1}X\right)^{-1}X'\Omega^{-1}Y \tag{10.7b}$$

$$var(\hat{\beta}) = \left(X'\Omega^{-1}X\right)^{-1} \tag{10.7c}$$

where $\Omega = \Sigma^{-1} \otimes I_T$

Just as spatial and strong cross-section dependence are not mutually exclusive, so are SUR and spatial cross-section dependence not mutually exclusive. In summary, all three types of cross-section dependence may coexist. It was for this reason that in Chaps. 6, 8 and 9 the spatial models were estimated by EGLS-SUR. We continue this practice in the present chapter.

Note that the application of SUR here should not be confused with the spatial SUR estimator, which involves the estimation of separate cross-section models in each time period, and where $N > T$ (Anselin 1988, Chap. 10; Elhorst 2014, Chap. 3).

Our purpose in the present chapter is to illustrate the tensions between CCE and the spatial econometric analysis of panel data. Although the difference between CCE and spatial econometrics ostensibly only arises in panel data, it arises in cross-section data too. The difference is that whereas in panel data it is possible to distinguish between weak and strong cross-section dependence, in cross-section data the two types of dependence are indistinguishable from one another. Spatial econometricians assume by default that cross-section dependence must be weak. If, however, it turns out to be strong, spatial econometric models will be misspecified. Of course, in cross-section data the researcher has no way of checking. Panel data have numerous advantages over cross-section data. Perhaps a less well-known advantage is that if the panel units are spatial it is possible to distinguish between weak and strong cross-section dependence. As usual, the spatial panel data that we use in this chapter are nonstationary. Therefore, our empirical illustration has to take account of the spatiotemporal properties of the data.

10.3 Regional Investment Policy and Foreign Direct Investment

Our first empirical illustration draws on Beenstock et al. (2017). We begin by providing some background to the empirical illustration, which focuses on the effects of regional investment policy on regional capital investment. It also focuses on the effect of foreign direct investment on regional capital investment. Study of the effects of regional investment policy on capital investment and employment has a long history (Armstrong and Taylor 2000). European evidence regarding its effectiveness is mixed (Dall'Erba and de Gallo 2007; Midelfart-Knarvik and Overman 2002; Pellegrini et al. 2013). The balance of opinion is that regional investment policy has only had a small effect on closing regional gaps through generating capital deepening and jobs in regional development areas. For example, Wren (2005) finds that investment grants administered to assisted areas in the UK are cost effective in creating jobs, but too small scale to deal with the problems of regional unemployment. Also, regional investment policy has a short-run stabilization role in assisted regions but lacks the magnitude to generate economic growth. Recent work examining the influence of regional incentives on the location of foreign investment reiterates this message (Wren and Jones 2011). While foreign investment projects account for as much as about half of the regional investment grant budget in the UK, these projects account for less than 20% of total foreign investment.

Empirical evaluation of regional investment policy in Israel also suggests that its impact has been limited at best, and counterproductive at worst. Using plant level data for 1990–1999, Navon and Frisch (2009) show that regional investment grants had only minor effects on investment and employment. Schwartz and Keren (2006) show that regional investment policy generated employment instability through encouraging 'rotating' enterprises that establish and close down with the cycle of public funding.

Since foreign companies are eligible for regional investment grants, there is a synergism between the study of regional investment policy and the effect of FDI on regional capital investment. There is a large theoretical literature on the effect of FDI on national and regional outcomes. Theoretical models of FDI are ambiguous in their predictions of regional effects. General equilibrium models of trade and FDI are very sensitive to starting conditions and as such, can produce both negative and positive effects associated with FDI (Markusen and Venables 1998). Endogenous growth models generally show more positive long run effects. They predict that new technologies and knowledge embodied in FDI increase TFP in general, and labor productivity in particular labor (Blomstrom and Kokko 1998). Theory is also enigmatic regarding the relation between FDI and regional inequality. On the one hand, the dependency school of FDI sees foreign ownership as exacerbating regional differences in destination countries (Bornschier and Chase-Dunn 1985). It raises capital intensity, generating unemployment in non-competitive sectors. As skill premia grow, inequality increases (Feenstra and Hanson 1997). On the other hand, the modernist school stresses the diffusion of knowledge and technology associated with FDI, which in the long-run leads to a more equitable distribution of income and a rise in TFP (Figinia and Gorg 2011).

Empirical studies have shown that FDI has a polarizing effect on the regional distribution of economic activity if foreign investors prefer the center over the periphery. This is particularly the case for regional capital deepening in developing countries such as Brazil, India, Indonesia and China (Fu 2004; Sjöholm 1999; Zhang and Zhang 2003). China in particular exhibits large regional concentrations of FDI and inequality, although identification issues cloud causality in this relationship (Wei et al. 2009).

Lack of data on regional FDI stocks has impeded the empirical analysis of regional polarization due to FDI. Indeed, we are aware of only three studies, all of which proxy FDI stocks in various ways. Haskell et al. (2007) proxy it with data relating to the share in regional employment of foreign-owned plants in the UK. This implicitly assumes that FDI stocks are proportionate to employment. They show that productivity is higher in foreign-owned firms, suggesting a positive effect of FDI on labor productivity. Ascani and Gagliardi (2015) used regional FDI (not FDI stocks) provided by the Bank of Italy for 103 provinces, to show that regional R&D varies directly with the regional distribution of FDI. Finally, Casi and Resmini (2010, 2014) constructed a dedicated regional FDI database for all EU NUTS2 regions (FDIregio) from micro (establishment-based) data obtained from a proprietary source. These data, however, only count the number of foreign firms in a region regardless of their size, are discontinuous (1997–1999, 2001–2003 and 2005–2007), and make no distinction between plants and firms.

Since FDI is a component of the balance of payments, its provenance by origin is recorded, but its location within the destination country is not recorded. It is for this reason that data on the regional distribution of FDI are not available. The statistical authorities do not obtain data on where FDI was disbursed after being recorded in the balance of payments. Investment undertaken by foreign-owned businesses is part of FDI, but sources on foreign-ownership do not reveal how much investment was undertaken. If foreign-owned firms operate more than one plant, it is impossible to detect from its balance sheet data how much FDI was invested in each plant. In short, the problem of generating data on regional FDI stocks seems to be insurmountable. Furthermore, the regional distribution of capital is unknown in all countries including the US, the UK, Japan and leading industrialized countries (Beenstock et al. 2011; EU 2011). Therefore, it is hardly surprising that the regional distribution of FDI is unknown.

We study the effects of regional investment grants and FDI on regional capital deepening in Israel measured by regional capital–labor ratios. We use data for regional capital stocks, constructed for Israel using the method described by Beenstock et al. (2011). For these purposes, we constructed panel data on investment grants in these regions from administrative sources. However, we were unable to obtain data on regional FDI stocks. To estimate the effects of FDI stocks on regional capital deepening, we use the common correlated effects estimator (CCE) in which the national stock of FDI, for which data are available, is hypothesized to be a common factor, and the estimated factor loadings measure the effects of FDI on regional capital deepening. These loadings are expected to be larger in regional development zones where FDI is subsidized by regional investment grants.

Our unit of observation is the region rather than the firm, which has advantages and disadvantages. An advantage is that spillover effects between firms within regions are more difficult to detect with firm level data than regional data. Spillover effects between regions may be estimated using spatial econometric methods. A disadvantage is that these spillover effects may be concealed in regional data. However, we propose a simple test to determine whether regional investment grants crowd-in or crowd-out investment within regions.

Also, we investigate relations between stocks rather than flows. We investigate the relation between regional capital stocks on the one hand, and stocks of regional investment grants and national FDI stocks on the other. By contrast, previous research has focused on the relation between investment, a flow on the one hand, and investment grants and FDI on the other, both of which are flows. New regional investment grants might not affect current regional investment, but they might affect investment subsequently, as expressed in regional capital stocks. The absence of an empirical relationship between flows does not preclude the presence of an empirical relation between stocks.

Investors regard different locations as substitutes, and perhaps as complements. If firms in region A receive investment grants but firms in region B do not, investors face an incentive to switch their investment from B to A. Similar considerations apply to FDI where the decision to invest in destination A may not be independent of the decision to invest in destination B (Regelink and Elhorst 2015). Indeed, it turns out empirically that cross-section dependence is strong.

The Model

Let $k_{it} = \log(K_{it}/L_{it})$ denote the log capital–labor ratio in region i in period t, let Z_{it} denote the log stock of investment grants, and $KFDI_t$ denote the log stock of FDI capital. Note, that whereas Z is observed by region over time, KFDI is a national time series observed by t but not by i. Finally, let X_{it} denote a vector of covariates hypothesized to affect capital-deepening (k). For example, k might be expected to vary directly with wages due to capital–labor substitution, and if human and physical capital are complements, k would vary directly with schooling, or the experience of workers.

The basic model[2] is:

[2]See Beenstock (2017) for related pairwise tests of perfect internal capital mobility.

$$k_{it} = \alpha_i + \beta Z_{it} + \gamma X_{it} + \eta_i KFDI_t + u_{it} \tag{10.8}$$

where α_i denotes cross-section fixed effects, and γ is a vector of parameters. The parameters of interest are β and η, where the former is the elasticity of the capital-labor ratio with respect to the stock of outstanding investment grants, and the latter is the elasticity of the capital-labor ratio with respect to the stock of national FDI. Notice that η is assumed to be heterogeneous because KFDI is a time series variable, so the latter elasticity varies by region. Parameters β and γ are assumed to be homogeneous, but this is not essential.

A decomposition is suggested to interpret β in which we distinguish between projects eligible for investment grants labelled by G and those that are not, labelled by NG. As explained below, eligibility for investment grants depends on two hierarchical criteria. First, applicants must be located in development zones. Within these zones investment projects must be in specific economic branches (especially industry). Multi-plant firms may have plants in zones that are eligible for investment grants, while other plants are not. Also, single-plant firms in development zones may have investments in eligible economic branches as well as investments in economic branches (such as services and agriculture) which are ineligible.

Let K_Z denote capital directly funded by investment grants, and let K_O denote other capital. K_O includes capital in ineligible economic branches as well as capital in eligible economic branches not funded by investment grants. Within a development zone some firms might have both types of capital, while others only have K_O. Hence, the capital stock in development zones is $K_G = K_Z + K_O$. The capital stock of all firms is $K = K_G + K_{NG}$, where K_{NG} is capital invested by businesses that are not in development zones. Since money is fungible, it is not clear what the effects of project funding are at the margin. For example, it has been claimed (Beenstock 1986) that projects funded by the World Bank are positively-selected. Client countries game the World Bank's selection criteria. They propose their best projects for funding, which they would have undertaken in any case, and use the funds to invest in projects which the World Bank would not have funded. On the other hand, if projects are negatively-selected fungibility is less likely, because the funded projects are less likely to have been undertaken in any case.

It may be shown that β has the following decomposition:

$$\beta = \left[1 + \frac{\partial K_O}{\partial K_Z} + \frac{\partial K_{NG}}{\partial K_Z}\right]\frac{K_Z}{K} \tag{10.9}$$

where the first partial derivative refers to the effect of investment grants on other capital within the same development zone, and the second refers to the effect of investment grants on capital in other regions, i.e. outside the development zone. The former effect will be positive if, for example, recipients of investment grants increase their investment in ineligible economic branches, or they increase investment in eligible economic branches, which did not receive funding. It will also be positive if there are spillovers from investment financed by investment grants onto businesses in ineligible economic branches within the same development zones. If investment grants crowd-out other investments, the first partial derivative will be negative. If crowding-out is complete, the partial derivative is −1 and β tends to zero.

The second partial derivative will be positive if there are spillovers from investment grant projects to investment in other regions. One possibility is that multi-plant firms expand investment in their plants outside development zones when their plants in development zones receive investment grants. If both partial derivatives are zero, Eq. (10.9) states that β equals the share of cumulative investment grants (K_Z) in the capital stock. This elasticity will be greater if there is crowding-in. However, if crowding-out is sufficiently strong β may be negative. Finally, the estimate of β may be used to evaluate the term in brackets in Eq. (10.9) using data for K_Z/K. If this term exceeds 1 regional investment grants induce net crowding-in. If it is less than 1 regional investment grants induce net crowding-out. If it is less than −1 regional investment grants are counter-productive. Of course, if β is not statistically significant, regional investment policy makes no difference.

In Eq. (10.8) KFDI is a common factor in the sense of Pesaran (2006) because it explains strong cross-section correlation between the panel units, and η is the vector of factor loadings. Strong cross-section correlation arises when all panel units are affected by a common factor such as KFDI. By contrast, weak cross-section dependence arises when there is spatial autocorrelation (SAC). In this case, cross-section dependence is localized and dissipates across space. We use the BP statistic defined in Eq. (10.2) to test for cross-section dependence in the residuals, and we use the CD statistic defined in Eq. (10.3) to test for weak cross-section dependence. If BP exceeds its critical value, the null hypothesis of cross-section independence is rejected. If CD exceeds its critical the null hypothesis if weak cross-section dependence is rejected.

We also consider two variants of Eq. (10.8). The spatial variant is:

$$\begin{aligned} &\ln k_{it} = \alpha_i + \beta \ln Z_{it} + X_{it}\gamma + \eta_i \ln KFDI_t + \lambda \ln \tilde{k}_{it} + \delta \ln \tilde{Z}_{it} + u_{it} \\ &\tilde{k}_{it} = \sum_{j \neq i}^{N} w_{ij} k_{jt} \quad \tilde{Z}_{it} = \sum_{j \neq i}^{N} w_{ij} Z_{jt} \end{aligned} \tag{10.10}$$

where the spatial weights (w) row-sum to one, λ is the coefficient of the spatial lagged dependent variable, and δ is the coefficient of the spatial Durbin lag. If δ is negative, investment grants in neighboring regions induce less investment in region i. If λ is positive, there is positive spatial spillover from capital-deepening in neighboring regions. Equation (10.10) should eliminate (or at least reduce) spatial autocorrelation in Eq. (10.8). Equation (10.10) is similar to Eq. VIII in Table 8.9 except for absence of KFDI.

The second variant follows Pesaran's (2006) suggestion to specify $\ln k_t$ in Eq. (10.8) as a common factor, where k_t is the cross-section average of k_{it}:

$$\ln k_{it} = \alpha_i + \beta \ln Z_{it} + X_{it}\gamma + \eta_i \ln KFDI_t + \eta_{ki} \ln k_t + u_{it} \qquad (10.11)$$

Therefore, there are two common factors, $\ln KFDI_t$ and $\ln k_t$. Apart from its econometric motivation, the specification of lnk in Eq. (10.11) has an economic justification. If capital is internally mobile, capital should flow from regions in which the marginal productivity of capital (MPK) is low to regions in which MPK is high (Beenstock 2017). Since MPK varies inversely with k, Eq. (10.11) states that MPK in region i varies directly with national MPK if η_k is positive. Therefore, η_{ki} is likely to vary directly with capital mobility.

If the data are nonstationary, Eqs. (10.8, 10.10 and 10.11) may be estimated by LSDV, and the parameter estimates are super-consistent as explained in Chap. 7. Since the parameter estimates of cointegrating vectors generally have non-standard distributions, we do not report their standard errors or t-statistics, which may be misleading. To test the restriction, for example, that $\beta = 0$ the model is estimated with and without Z and the cointegration test statistics of the restricted and unrestricted models are compared. Several possibilities arise:

1. If the unrestricted model is cointegrated, but the restricted model is not cointegrated, Z belongs to the cointegrating vector.
2. If the unrestricted model is not cointegrated, but the restricted model is cointegrated, Z does not belong to the cointegrating vector.
3. If the restricted and unrestricted models are cointegrated, Z does not belong to the cointegrating vector.
4. If the restricted and unrestricted models are not cointegrated, but the p-value of the latter is smaller than the p-value of the former, Z might belong to some cointegrating vector.

Indeed, on several occasions t-statistics happen to be large (greater than 3) but dropping these variables makes almost no difference to cointegration tests, i.e. these are spurious regression parameters.

Data

Annual capital stock data for nine regions of Israel (see Map 4.1) were calculated during 1987–2010 using the method proposed by Beenstock et al. (2011). The capital stock comprises plant and machinery. This method calculates plant directly from regional data on building completions (square meters) in the business sector published by the Central Bureau of Statistics (CBS). It allocates machinery at the national level to the nine regions according to the ratio of machinery to plant across the economy. For example, if the value of plant in a region is \$100, and the ratio of machinery to plant across the economy is 1.3, the value of machinery in the region is imputed to be \$130 so that K = \$230. Data on employment for these nine regions were constructed by us from Labor Force Surveys (CBS), and data for earnings (deflated by the national CPI) were constructed by us from Household Income Surveys (CBS). Since geographic disaggregation in these surveys is not continuously available prior to 1987, this determines the starting point for our investigation.

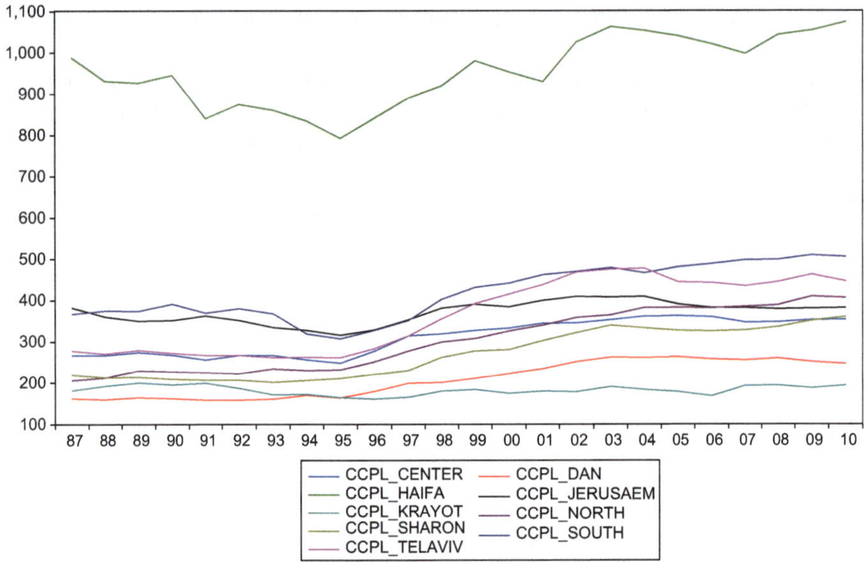

Fig. 10.1 Capital–labor ratios. Thousands of Shekels at 2005 prices

Capital–labor ratios (k) are plotted in Fig. 10.1 in 1000s of Shekels at 2005 prices. The Haifa region stands out as the most capital-intensive part of Israel because heavy industry has been concentrated in Haifa since Ottoman times. There are persistent and substantial differences between capital–labor ratios in the rest of the country. In 1987 the Dan region was the least capital intensive, but by 1996 it exchanged positions at the bottom of the distribution with Krayot. The Tel Aviv region, which in 1987 was in fourth position, temporarily moved up to second position in 2003. On the whole, positions in the distribution appear to be quite stable. Following the wave of mass migration from the former USSR (1989–1995) capital labor ratios naturally decreased especially in Haifa, which absorbed many immigrants. Subsequently, capital labor ratios recovered, eventually surpassing what they were in the late 1980s.

Since 1967 the Ministry of Trade (now the Ministry of the Economy) has operated an Investment Center, which provides investment grants as part of its regional development policy. Businesses in designated regional development zones (A, B and C) are eligible to apply to the Investment Center for investment grants, which are awarded as percentages of the total investment. These percentages are highest in zone A and lowest in zone C. Currently, they are 20% in zone A and 0 elsewhere. Priority is given to export businesses, and to industry rather than to services and agriculture. The criteria have varied over time as have the zones eligible for regional development support. Figure 10.2 plots the allocation of investment grants at constant 2005 prices by the Investment Center in each of the nine regions. The main beneficiaries have been the North and South, and since 2007 the budget of the Investment Center has been cut-back considerably. By contrast, the central

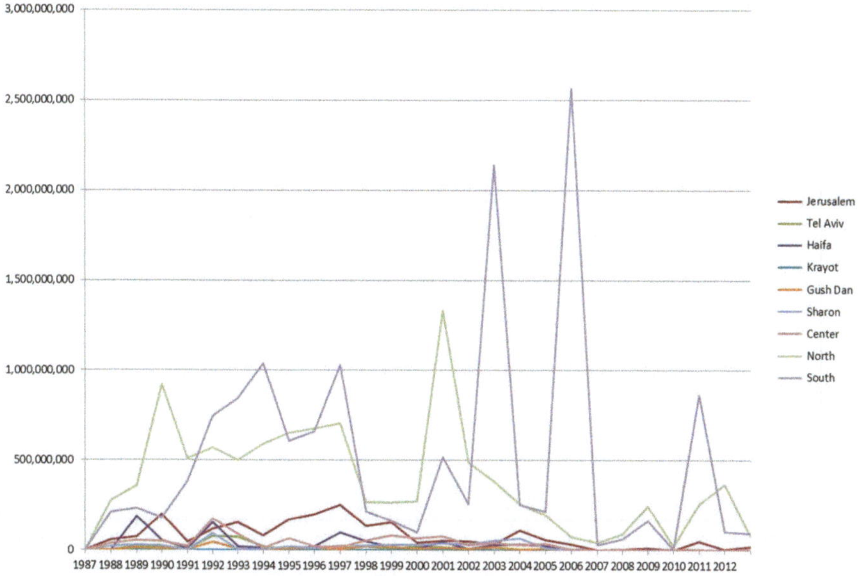

Fig. 10.2 Investment grants (Shekels at 2005 prices)

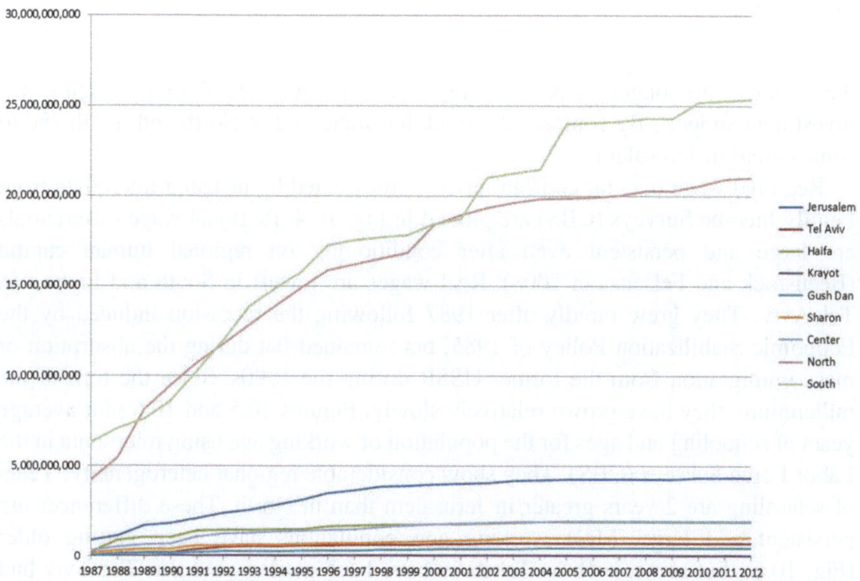

Fig. 10.3 Cumulative capital investment by the Investment Center (Shekels at 2005 prices)

regions (excluding Jerusalem) have received almost nothing, especially since 2000. Figure 10.3 plots the cumulative (since 1967) development grants received by the nine regions. Since these are stocks, the data can only increase over time. However,

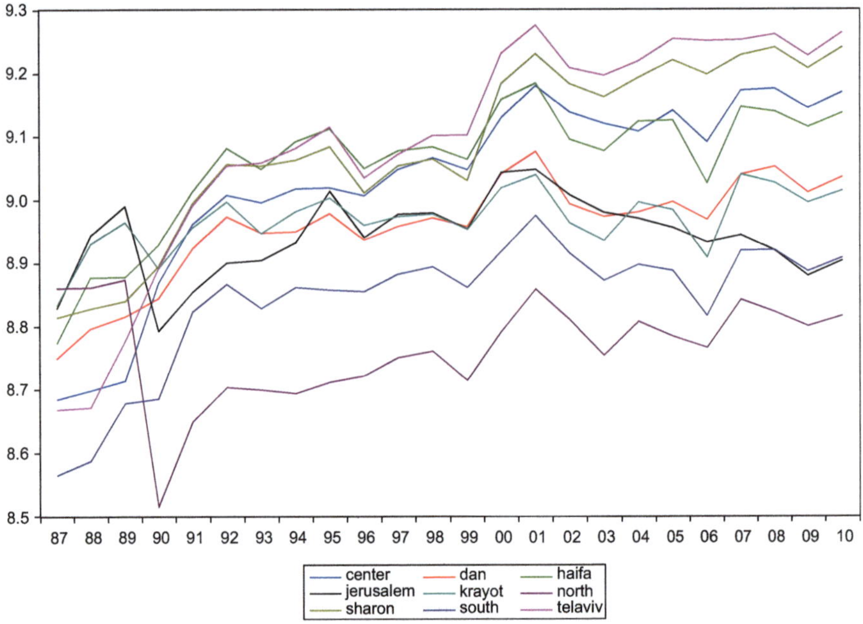

Fig. 10.4 Log real wages

these stocks no longer increase in regions that have ceased to be eligible for investment support. By contrast, the stock has increased in North and South and to some extent in Jerusalem.

Regional wage data (at constant prices) constructed by us using microdata from Family Income Surveys (CBS) are plotted in Fig. 10.4. Regional wage differentials are large and persistent even after conditioning on regional human capital (Beenstock and Felsenstein 2008). Real wages are lowest in South and highest in Tel Aviv. They grew rapidly after 1987 following the recession induced by the Economic Stabilization Policy of 1985, but remained flat during the absorption of mass immigration from the former USSR during the 1990s. Since the turn of the millennium, they have grown relatively slowly. Figures 10.5 and 10.6 plot average years of schooling and ages for the population of working age using microdata in the Labor Force Surveys (CBS). They show considerable regional heterogeneity. Years of schooling are 2 years greater in Jerusalem than in North. These differences are persistent and large. Most working age populations have been getting older (Fig. 10.6), but some, such as Tel Aviv have been getting younger. Tel Aviv had the oldest population in 1987 but has been superseded by Haifa. The youngest population lives in North; there is a 5 year age gap between these working age populations.

Panel unit root tests are reported in Table 10.1 for the data in Figs. 10.1, 10.3, 10.4, 10.5 and 10.6. The IPS statistics assumes that there is no cross-section dependence between the panel units. The CIPS statistics assume that there is strong

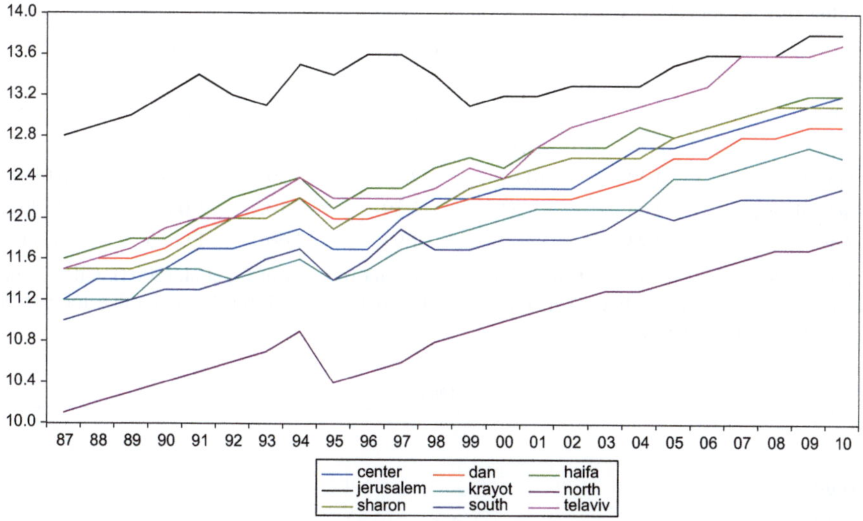

Fig. 10.5 Years of schooling of working age population

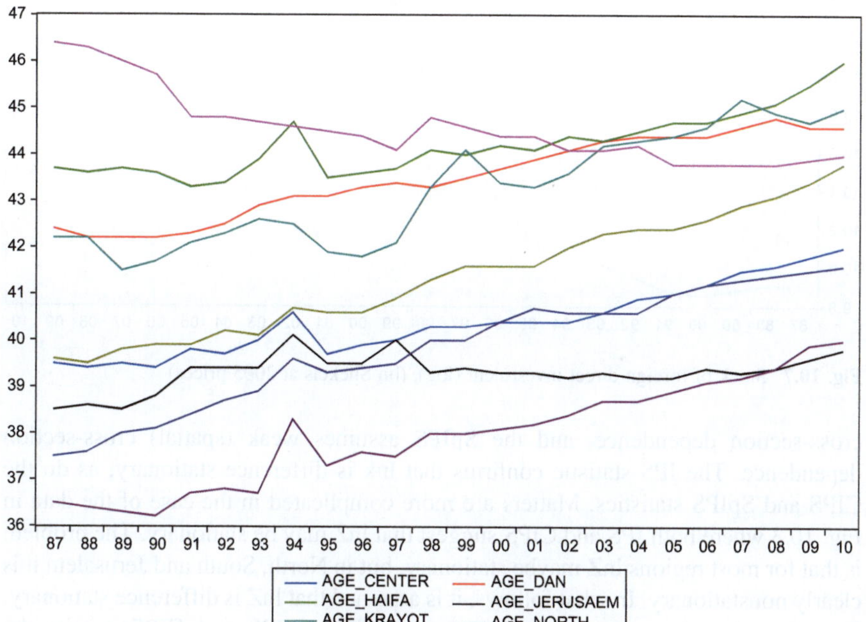

Fig. 10.6 Age of working age population

Table 10.1 Panel unit root tests

	IPS		CIPS		SpIPS	
D	0	1	0	1	0	1
lnk	1.07	−3.92	−1.51	−3.75	1.0019	0.559
lnZ	−8.89	−8.15	−2.28	−3.64		
lnwage	−4.42	−10.64	−2.37	−3.39	0.9998	0.0841
School years	2.85	−9.34	−2.59	−4.10	1.0077	0.1493
Age	2.23	−8.42	−1.93	−3.66	1.0056	−0.0114

Notes: IPS is z-statistic for the heterogeneous panel unit root test of Im et al. (2003). CIPS is the z-statistic for correlated effects version of IPS due to Pesaran (2007). Critical value for SpIPS ($p = 0.05$) = 0.69. See also Table 7.2

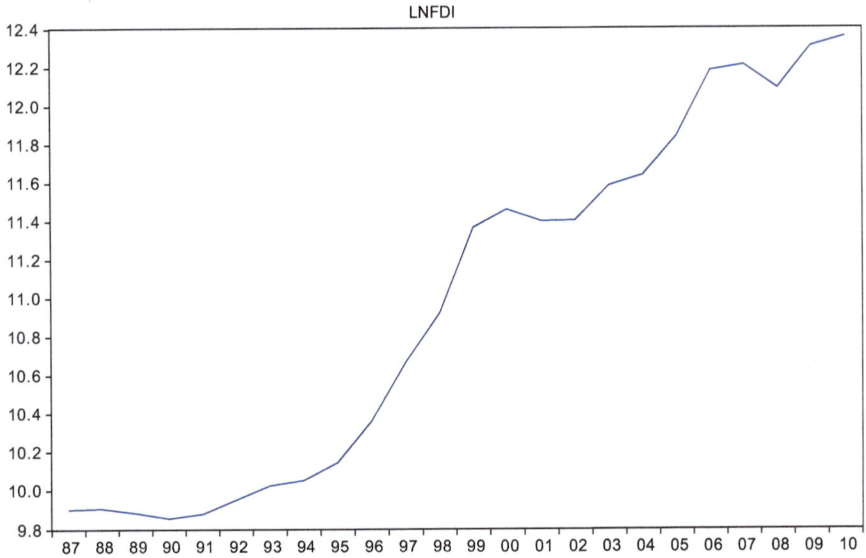

Fig. 10.7 Stock of foreign direct investment (log), (bn Shekels at 2005 prices)

cross-section dependence, and the SpIPS assumes weak (spatial) cross-section dependence. The IPS statistic confirms that lnk is difference stationary, as do the CIPS and SpIPS statistics. Matters are more complicated in the case of the data in Fig. 10.3 where both IPS and CIPS suggest that lnZ may be stationary. The problem is that for most regions lnZ maybe stationary, but in North, South and Jerusalem it is clearly nonstationary. In what follows, it is assumed that lnZ is difference stationary. Surprisingly, real wages are stationary according to IPS and CIPS despite the positive trend that is visible in Fig. 10.4. However, real wages are difference stationary according to SpIPS. School years and average age are difference stationary according to IPS, CIPS and SpIPS.

The stock of FDI is plotted in Fig. 10.7. Note that this variable is a time series rather than panel data. Its first order ADF statistic for $d = 0$ is 0.3, and for $d = 1$ ADF = −4.2. Therefore, KFDI is difference stationary in logarithms.

Table 10.2 Panel regressions

Model	1	2	3	4	5	6	7	8
Wage	0.091	0.275	−0.094	0.011	0.067	0.003		
Schooling	0.115	0.071	−0.091	−0.053	−0.032	−0.049	−0.035	−0.008
Age	0.061	0.075	−0.488	−0.206	−0.016	−0.237		
Age^2	0.0006	−0.009	0.006	0.003	0.003	0.003		
Jews%	−0.282	0.081	0.496	0.288	0.243	0.249		
Z	0.204	0.019	0.010	0.048		0.016	0.037	
Spatial Z						0.032		
Spatial lnk						0.120		
Fixed effects	None	2 way	1 way	1 way	1 way	1 way	1 way	1 way
Common factors	No	No	KFDI	KFDI, $\bar{k}$	KFDI, $\bar{k}$	KFDI, $\bar{k}$	KFDI, $\bar{k}$	KFDI, $\bar{k}$
GADF	−1.36	−1.67	−2.892	−3.180	−2.87	−3.207	−2.981	−2.646
GADF*	−3.86	−4.13	−3.60	−3.60	−3.58	−3.62	−3.57	−3.56
BP	299	277	276	97	161	140	144	182
CD	7.29	−3.51	15.39	−2.78	−2.62	−2.90	−2.84	−2.08
r-bar	0.248	−0.119	0.522	−0.094	−0.089	−0.098	−0.097	−0.071

Notes: Regressand is $\ln k_{it}$. Estimation by EGLS-SUR. GADF* denotes the critical value for GADF at $p = 0.05$ from Pedroni (1999) Table 2 (models 1–2) and Banerjee and Carrion-I-Silvestre (2017) Table 1 (models 3–8). Banerjee and Carrion-I-Silvestre (2017) report critical values for one common factor with 1 or 2 regressors. We have extrapolated their critical values to several regressors using the differences in GADF* between 1 and 2 regressors. Surprisingly, the difference between 1 and 2 regressors is only 0.01 whereas for Pedroni it is 0.36

Results

We begin by estimating Eq. (10.8) by EGLS-SUR without KFDI as a common factor, and without fixed effects. The X variables include real wages, schooling, age and the share of Jews in the regional working age populations. Model 1 in Table 10.2 suggests that the capital–labor ratio varies directly with wages and human capital, as measured by schooling and experience (proxied by age), but it varies inversely with the relative size of the Jewish population. Finally, the estimate of β is 0.204, i.e. the elasticity of k with respect to cumulative investment grants is about 0.2. Since this greatly exceeds the share of investment grants in the capital stock (K_Z/K in Eq. 10.2) the estimate of β indicates substantial crowding-in. We do not report t-statistics for these parameter estimates because they have non-standard distributions.[3] Indeed, despite the fact that they are large, the GADF statistic (−1.36) shows that model 1 is not panel cointegrated because it greatly exceeds its critical value of −3.86. Therefore, model 1 is a spurious regression. Nevertheless, when Z is dropped from model 1 (not shown) GADF increases to −0.83, suggesting that investment grants might nevertheless have a role in determining capital–labor ratios. The BP statistic for model 1 is clearly statistically significant, so we may confidently reject the hypothesis of cross-section independence between the residuals. Since the CD statistic

[3]Confidence intervals may be calculated as in Table 8.9, but we do not report them in this chapter.

easily exceeds its critical value, we may reject the hypothesis that the cross-section dependence is weak.

Model 2 is the same as model 1, except it specifies two-way fixed effects, which is why GADF* becomes more negative. However, nor is model 2 panel cointegrated. The estimate of β continues to be positive, but when it is dropped from model 2 (not shown) GADF remains almost unchanged. Moreover, if model 2 is estimated with one-way fixed effects the estimate of β is negative (not shown) and GADF = −1.77. In model 2 cross-section dependence continues to be significant and strong. However, the residuals are negatively correlated (r-bar = −0.119) instead of positively correlated.

Model 3 estimates Eq. (10.8) by specifying the log of KFDI as a common factor. It induces a discrete reduction in GADF from −1.67 to −2.89, which suggests that KFDI might have a role in determining capital-deepening. The difference between GADF and its critical value decreases from 2.35 to 0.71. However, model 3 is not panel cointegrated even at p = 0.1. Model 3 does not specify time fixed effects, because the common factor is a time series, which largely substitutes for time fixed effects.[4] Despite the specification of a common factor in model 3, the CD statistic more than doubles because the average correlation increases from 0.248 (model 1) to 0.522. Model 4 estimates Eq. (10.10) where the addition of a second common factor (k) induces further reductions in GADF to −3.18, but it too falls short of its critical value for panel cointegration. CD in model 4 continues to be statistically significant, but it is absolutely smaller, as expected, than in model 2.

Dropping investment grants (Z) from model 4 induces an increase in GADF from −3.18 to −2.87 (model 5) suggesting that investment grants improve GADF. Model 6 spatializes CCE by adding spatial dynamics to model 4.[5] These spatial dynamics are expected to reduce weak cross-section dependence, while the common factors are expected to weaken strong cross-section dependence. Since the absolute sizes of BP and CD are slightly larger in model 6 than in model 4, we do not think that spatializing CCE makes sense here. The estimates of λ and δ are 0.12 and 0.032 respectively, but since these parameters make almost no difference to GADF (−3.21 instead of −3.18) they are not statistically significant.

---

[4]If T = N the replication would be perfect. Here T = 24 and N = 9 in which case it is technically possible to estimate time fixed effects.

[5]We use an asymmetric W matrix defined in terms of relative population size and distance. The weight (w_{ij}) assigned to the connectivity between i and j is equal to the population in region j divided by the combined populations in regions i and j. Consequently,

$$w_{ij} = \frac{POP_j}{POP_i + POP_j} \times \frac{1}{d_{ij}}$$

where POP denotes the sample-mean population in the data and captures scale effects and d_{ij} is the Euclidean distance between i and j. The spatial weights are asymmetric ($w_{ij} \neq w_{ji}$) according to relative population sizes, so that a large region has a greater effect on its small neighbor than vice versa. Additionally, the effect of more distant neighbors is smaller. Row sums are normalized to 1 by dividing w_{ij} by its mean for i. Note that W is fixed and does not depend on time.

Model 7 omits four regressors that were specified in model 4, as a result of which GADF increases to −2.98 from −3.18. However, the absolute difference between GADF and its critical value (GADF*) increases. This absolute difference increases further if the stock of investment grants (Z) is omitted as in Model 8. Since Models 4 and 6 have the smallest absolute differences between GADF and GADF*, they have the smallest p-values (approximately 0.1), and are therefore selected as the main models for consideration.

Cross-section dependence is present in all the models in Table 10.2 since BP easily exceeds 55, which is the critical value of chi square with ½N(N − 1) = 36 degrees of freedom at p = 0.05. Cross-section dependence is less pronounced in models 4–7, in which lnk is specified as a common factor. This happens because lnk is correlated with the business cycle, and it accounts for most of the cyclicality in regional capital–labor ratio. The CD statistics reject the hypothesis that this cross-section dependence is weak or spatial, which is why model 6 has no added value. CD is smallest, as expected in models 3–7, but the specification of common factors does not explain away cross-section dependence. The average cross-section correlation is about −0.1, which is statistically significantly different from zero.

A narrow interpretation of Table 10.2 would reject all models as spurious regressions because GADF always exceeds its critical value at p = 0.05. However, models 4 and 6 are panel cointegrated at p = 0.1. Figure 10.8 plots the residuals generated by model 4 in Table 10.2, close inspection of which shows that the residuals fluctuate around zero, as expected in panel cointegrated models. Using these residuals to estimate the panel cointegration test suggested by Westerlund (2007) suggests that they are jointly stationary. Therefore, we do not interpret Table 10.2 narrowly and conclude that models 4 and 6 constitute cointegrating vectors. In model 4 the estimate of the elasticity of capital–labor ratios with respect to the stock of investment grants is 0.048. Matters are more complicated in model 6 because of the specification of spatial lags. Using Eq. (10.2) we compare these estimates to the share of investment grants in regional capital stocks (Z/K), which during the sample period varied between 0.000135 and 0.00092, i.e. investment grants account for tiny fractions of regional capital stocks. Therefore, the estimates of β suggest that regional investment grants crowded-in regional capital.

Estimates of factor loadings are reported in Table 10.3 where we do not report standard errors and t-statistics because these loadings have non-standard distributions. In the case of model 3 the loadings for ln KFDI range between 0.03 and 0.359. North continues to have the largest loading for lnKFDI and Krayot the smallest in model 7. Tel Aviv and South have the largest loadings for $\bar{k}$, and North has the smallest. These loadings largely capture the business cycle, which is most prominent in the former and least prominent in the latter. Neither loadings have center–periphery interpretations. Nor is it the case that the loadings for lnKFDI are larger for regions such as North, South and Jerusalem, which have been the main recipients of regional investment grants. Therefore, it does not seem to be the case that foreign investors have been attracted by regional investment grants.

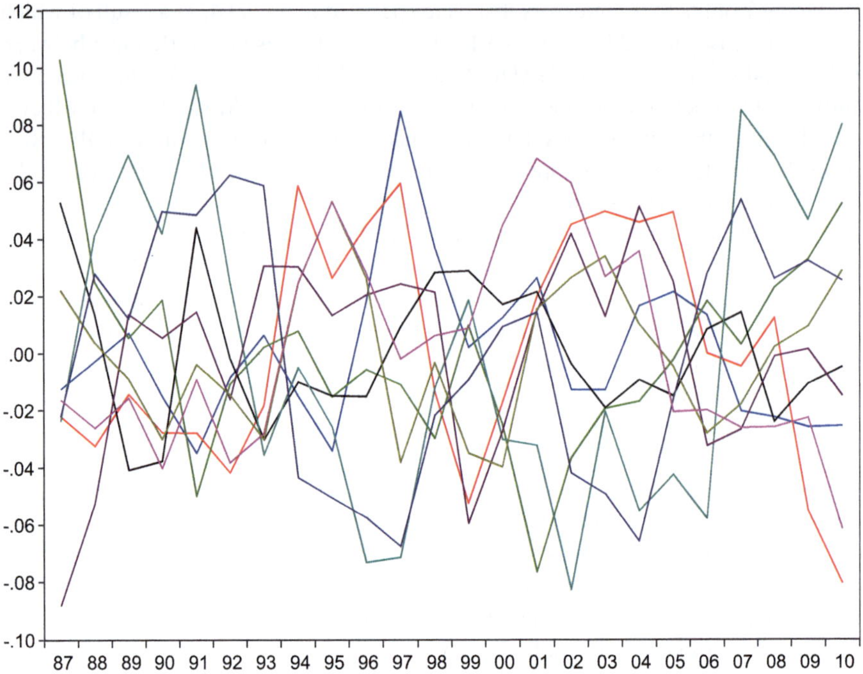

Fig. 10.8 Residuals of model 7 in Table 10.2

Table 10.3 Factor loadings

Model	3	7	7
Common factor	ln KFDI	ln KFDI	$\bar{k}$
Center	0.213	0.040	0.775
Dan	0.238	0.108	0.777
Haifa	0.107	−0.070	1.085
Jerusalem	0.068	−0.093	1.006
Krayot	0.030	−0.099	0.785
North	0.359	0.190	0.534
Sharon	0.285	0.095	0.981
South	0.231	−0.031	1.304
Tel Aviv	0.355	0.049	1.517

10.4 Strong and Weak Cross-Section Dependence in the SGE Residuals

In Table 10.4 we report the BP and CD statistics for the residuals of key variables from a second empirical example. This relates to the SGE (spatial general equilibrium) model for Israel reported in Table 8.9. BP has a chi square distribution with df = ½N(N − 1) = 36 the critical value for BP is 50.1, which is easily exceeded for all variables in Table 10.4. Therefore, we may reject the null hypotheses that the SGE residuals are cross-section independent. Since CD has a standard normal distribution, we may also reject the null hypothesis that the cross-section dependence is weak. For all variables except housing starts the average cross-section correlation is positive.

In Table 10.5 we summarize the BP and CD statistics for the residuals of the error correction models reported in Tables 9.2–9.5, which tell a very different story. There is no evidence of cross-section dependence in the ECM residuals. All BP and CD statistics are smaller than their critical values. In what follows, therefore, we need solely concern ourselves with strong cross-section dependence in the residuals generated by the cointegrating vectors. However, as in Chap. 9, we do not do so for all the variables featured in Table 10.4. For illustrative purposes, we focus on housing starts and house prices.

In Table 10.6 we re-estimate the models for housing starts and house prices that were reported in Table 8.9 using the common correlated effects estimator (CCE) with single factors represented by the cross-section means of lnS for housing starts and lnP for house prices. For convenience we report in parentheses the parameter estimates in Table 8.9. In most cases the signs of the parameters do not change, however, the point estimates are quite different. For example the original elasticity of house prices with respect to housing stocks was −0.982, whereas the CCE estimate is −0.512, implying that housing demand is more price elastic. The most notable

Table 10.4 Test for cross-section dependence in SGE residuals

	BP	CD
Housing starts	128	−3.23
Housing completions	237	14.87
House prices	192	4.98
Wages	339	17.3
Capital–labor ratio	355	2.01

Table 10.5 Tests for cross-section dependence in ECM residuals

	ECM		SpECM		VECM		SpVECM	
	$\ln P_t$	$\ln S_t$	$\ln P_t$	$\ln S_t$	$\ln P_t$	$\ln S_t$	$\ln P_t$	$\ln S_t$
BP	42.96	31.16	47.60	31.63	42.58	32.23	44.15	35.56
CD	−0.07	−1.72	−1.41	−1.18	−0.05	−1.43	−1.23	−1.23

Table 10.6 CCE estimates

Housing starts		House prices	
lnP	0.547 (0.426)	lnPOP	0.309 (1.027)
$\ln\tilde{P}$	−0.300 (−0.486)	lnY	0.139 (0.375)
$\ln\bar{P}$	−0.308 (0.415)	lnH	−0.512 (−0.982)
$\ln\tilde{S}$	−0.518 (0.790)	$\ln\tilde{P}$	0.824 (0.439)
Z	0.481 (1.098)	$\ln P\tilde{O}P$	0.652 (1.221)
$\tilde{Z}$	−0.56 (−0.660)		
BP	122		157
CD	−2.84		−2.18
GADF	−2.38		−3.14
SpGrho	0.266		0.512

Note: Parameter estimates in Table 8.9 reported in parentheses. GADF and SpGrho are first order augmented

Table 10.7 Factor loadings for Table 10.6

	Housing starts	House prices
Center	1.476	0.248
Dan	1.048	−0.237
Haifa	1.972	−0.452
Jerusalem	1.299	0.334
Krayot	2.017	−0.131
North	1.042	−0.141
Sharon	1.223	0.491
South	1.931	−0.043
Tel Aviv	1.450	0.591

sign change concerns the SAR coefficient for housing starts, which is negative (−0.518) according to CCE but positive (0.79) in Table 8.9.

The GADF statistics reported in Table 10.6 are substantially larger than their critical values provided by Banerjee and Carrion-I-Silvestre (2017) and reported in Table 10.2, suggesting that the residuals from the CCE models are not stationary. Therefore, the variables in Table 10.6 are ostensibly not panel cointegrated. On the other hand the SpGrho statistics are less than their critical values (reported in Table 8.9), suggesting that the residuals from the CCE models are stationary. However, a word of caution is necessary. The models in Table 10.6 not only include common factors, they also include spatial variables. Consequently, critical values for cointegration tests should take account of the presence of common factors as do Banerjee and Carrion-I-Silvestre, as well as spatial cointegration as in the SpGrho test. Unfortunately, there is no panel cointegration test for models which allow concurrently for weak and strong cross-section dependence. Therefore, the GADF and SpGrho statistics reported in Table 10.6 are indicative at best.

The estimated spatial factor loadings are reported in Table 10.7. In the case of housing starts these loadings are positive. The largest loading (Krayot) is almost twice as large as the smallest (North). These loadings measure the spatial sensitivity of housing starts to the building cycle. By contrast, the loadings for house prices are of mixed sign, and are much smaller than their counterparts for housing starts. The largest loading is for Tel Aviv (0.591) and the smallest for Haifa (−0.452) and are larger in the center than in the periphery. Where loadings are positive house prices are procyclical and anticyclical where negative.

The CCE results are expected to mitigate strong cross-section dependence in the residuals. In the case of housing starts BP decreases from 128 to 122 and CD is −2.84 instead of −3.23. In the case of house prices BP decreases from 192 to 157, and CD is −2.18 instead of 4.98. The BP and CD statistics are improved by CCE, as expected. Surprisingly the sign of the CD statistic is reversed in the case of house prices, indicating that the average correlation between the CCE residuals is negative instead of positive. The specification of a common factor apparently did too much of a good job in mitigating positive cross-section dependence in the house prices residuals.

This chapter completes a saga that began in Chap. 6 in which the relationship between key spatial panel data for Israel were modelled in first differences in terms of a spatial vector autoregression (SpVAR). We argued there that SpVARs cannot be used to test hypotheses for two reasons. First, economic theory is about levels of variables rather than differences. Second, the structural parameters in SpVARs are under-identified. Therefore, even if economic data happened to be stationary, in which event the SpVAR could have been estimated in levels, the structural parameters would have been under-identified.

Hypothesis tests concerning long-run structural parameters in levels may be carried out using cointegration tests regarding the nonstationary variables in the hypothesis. To implement this strategy using nonstationary spatial panel data, we first require spatiotemporal unit root tests to determine whether spatial panel data are stationary or not. In Chap. 7 we develop critical values for spatiotemporal unit roots tests (SpIPS), and calculate SpIPS for the data introduced in Chap. 6, as well as other spatial panel data for Israel. Second, we require panel cointegration tests for spatially dependent panel data. In Chap. 7 we develop critical values for spatial panel cointegration tests, the spatial group rho statistic (SpGrho), and in Chap. 8 we apply these tests to the spatial panel data in Chaps. 6 and 7.

The next episode in the saga, concerns estimation of spatial error correction models in Chap. 9 based on the cointegration results in Chap. 8. The spatial panel vector error correction model (SpVECM) extends panel VECM models to spatial panel data. The final episode in the saga features in the current chapter. We ask whether the spatial models reported in Chaps. 8 and 9 might be mispecified because the cross-section dependence in the data is induced by common factors rather than spatial dependence, or by common factors and spatial dependence.

We think that mixed dependence models (spatial and common factors) should be applied to spatial cointegration and spatial error correction. We hope that this book, which integrates time series econometrics and spatial econometrics, will help spatial economists adopt new approaches to the spatial econometric analysis of nonstationary spatial panel data.

References

Anselin L (1988) Spatial econometrics: methods and models. Kluwer Academic Publishers, Dordrecht

Armstrong H, Taylor J (2000) Regional economics and policy, 3rd edn. Blackwell, Oxford

Ascani A, Gagliardi L (2015) Inward FDI and local innovative performance. An empirical investigation on Italian provinces. Rev Reg Res 35(1):29–47

Bai J, Ng S (2004) A PANIC attack on unit roots and cointegration. Econometrica 72:1127–1177

Bailey N, Holly S, Pesaran MH (2016) A two stage approach to spatiotemporal analysis with strong and weak cross-section dependence. J Appl Economet 31(1):249–280

Banerjee A, Carrion-I-Silvestre JL (2017) Testing for panel cointegration using common correlated effects estimators. J Time Ser Anal 38:610–636

Beenstock M (1986) The World Bank's contribution to economic development. In: Recovery in the developing world. The World Bank, Washington, DC, pp 34–46

Beenstock M (2017) How internally mobile is capital? Lett Spat Resour Sci 10(3):361–374

Beenstock M, Felsenstein D (2008) Regional heterogeneity, conditional convergence and regional inequality. Reg Stud 42(4):475–488

Beenstock M, Ben Zeev N, Felsenstein D (2011) Capital deepening and regional inequality: an empirical analysis. Ann Reg Sci 47:599–617

Beenstock M, Felsenstein D, Rubin Z (2017) Lett Spat Resour Sci 10(3):385–409

Blomstrom M, Kokko A (1998) Multinational corporations and spillovers. J Econ Surv 12:247–277

Bornschier V, Chase-Dunn C (1985) Transnational corporations and underdevelopment. Praeger, New York

Breusch TS, Pagan AR (1979) A simple test for heteroscedasticity and random coefficient variation. Econometrica 47(5):1287–1294

Casi L, Resmini L (2010) Evidence on the determinants of foreign direct investment: the case of EU regions. East J Eur Stud 1(2):93–118

Casi L, Resmini L (2014) Spatial complexity and interactions in the FDI attractiveness of regions. Pap Reg Sci 93:51–78

Dall'Erba S, de Gallo J (2007) The impact of EU regional support on growth and employment. Czech J Econ Financ 57(7–8):325–350

Elhorst JP (2014) From spatial cross-section data to spatial panel data. Springer, Berlin

EU (2011) Estimating the capital stock for the NUTS 2 regions of the EU-27. Working Papers n°01/2011, DG Regional Policy, European Union, Brussels

Feenstra RC, Hanson GH (1997) Foreign direct investment and relative wages: evidence from Mexico's maquiladoras. J Int Econ 42:371–393

Figinia P, Gorg H (2011) Does foreign direct investment affect wage inequality? An empirical investigation. World Econ 34(9):1455–1475

Fu X (2004) Limited linkages from growth engines and regional disparities in China. J Comp Econ 32:148–164

Halleck Vega S, Elhorst JP (2016) A regional employment model simultaneously accounting for serial dynamics, spatial dependence and common factors. Reg Sci Urban Econ 60:85–95

Haskell JE, Pereira SC, Slaughter MJ (2007) Does inward foreign direct investment boost the productivity of domestic firms? Rev Econ Stat 87(3):482–496

Im K, Pesaran MH, Shin Y (2003) Testing for unit roots in heterogeneous panels. J Econ 115:53–74

Kapitanios G, Pesaran MH, Yamagata T (2011) Panels with nonstationary multifactor error structures. J Econ 160:326–348

Manski CF (1993) Identification of endogenous social effects: the reflection problem. Rev Econ Stud 60(3):531–542

Markusen JR, Venables AJ (1998) Multinational firms and the new trade theory. J Int Econ 46:183–203

Midelfart-Knarvik KH, Overman H (2002) Delocation and European integration: is structural spending justified? Econ Policy 17:323–359

Navon G, Frisch R (2009) The effect of Israel's encouragement of capital investments in industry law on product, employment, and investment: an empirical analysis of micro data. Discussion Paper Series, 2009.12, Research Department, Bank of Israel, Jerusalem (Hebrew)
Pedroni P (1999) Critical values for cointegration tests in heterogeneous panels with multiple regressors. Oxf Bull Econ Stat 61:653–670
Pellegrini G, Terribile F, Tarola O, Muccigrsso T, Busillo F (2013) Measuring the effects of European regional policy on economic growth: a discontinuity approach. Pap Reg Sci 92 (1):217–233
Pesaran MH (2006) Estimation and inference in large heterogeneous panels with a multifactor error structure. Econometrica 74:967–1012
Pesaran MH (2007) A simple panel unit root test in the presence of cross section dependence. J Appl Economet 22(2):265–310
Pesaran MH (2015) Time series and panel data econometrics. Oxford University Press, Oxford
Regelink M, Elhorst JP (2015) The spatial econometrics of FDI and third country Effects. Lett Spat Resour Sci 8:1–13
Schwartz D, Keren M (2006) Location incentives and the unintentional generation of employment instability: some evidence from Israel. Ann Reg Sci 40:449–460
Sjöholm F (1999) Productivity in Indonesia: the role of regional characteristics and direct foreign investment. Econ Dev Cult Chang 47:559–584
Wei K, Yao S, Liu A (2009) Foreign direct investment and regional inequality in China. Rev Dev Econ 13(4):778–791
Westerlund J (2007) Testing for error correction in panel based data. Oxf Bull Econ Stat 69 (6):709–748
Wren C (2005) Regional grants: are they worth it? Fisc Stud 26(2):245–275
Wren C, Jones J (2011) Assessing the regional impact of grants on FDI location: evidence from UK regional policy 1985–2005. J Reg Sci 51(3):497–517
Zhang X, Zhang KH (2003) How does globalization affect regional inequality within a developing country? Evidence from China. J Dev Stud 39:47–67

MIX
Papier aus verantwortungsvollen Quellen
Paper from responsible sources
FSC® C105338

If you have any concerns about our products,
you can contact us on
ProductSafety@springernature.com

In case Publisher is established outside the EU,
the EU authorized representative is:
Springer Nature Customer Service Center GmbH
Europaplatz 3, 69115 Heidelberg, Germany

Printed by Libri Plureos GmbH
in Hamburg, Germany